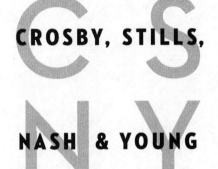

CROSBY, STILLS,

NASH & YOUNG

Also by Peter Doggett

You Never Give Me Your Money

Electric Shock

The Man Who Sold the World

There's a Riot Going On

Are You Ready for the Country

CROSBY, STILLS, NASH & YOUNG

PETER DOGGETT

ATRIA BOOKS

New York   London   Toronto   Sydney   New Delhi

ATRIA
BOOKS

An Imprint of Simon & Schuster, Inc.
1230 Avenue of the Americas
New York, NY 10020

First Atria Books hardcover edition April 2019

ATRIA BOOKS and colophon are registered trademarks of Simon & Schuster, Inc.

For information about special discounts for bulk purchases, please contact Simon & Schuster Special Sales at 1-866-506-1949 or business@simonandschuster.com.

The Simon & Schuster Speakers Bureau can bring authors to your live event. For more information or to book an event, contact the Simon & Schuster Speakers Bureau at 866-248-3049 or visit our website at www.simonspeakers.com.

Interior design by Kyle Kabel

Manufactured in the United States of America

10   9   8   7   6   5   4   3   2   1

Library of Congress Cataloging-in-Publication Data has been applied for.

ISBN 978-1-5011-8302-7
ISBN 978-1-5011-8304-1 (ebook)

For Rachel — and the musicians

INTRODUCTION

Asked, in a 1985 interview, to imagine an alternative lifetime in which he could have joined any musical outfit in the world, Bob Dylan singled out some of the catalysts of American roots music—pivotal bands in the development of jazz, country, and R&B. Then he astounded the journalist by offering a more modern name, one whose critical standing could hardly have been lower in the year of Live Aid: Crosby, Stills & Nash. A decade later, Dylan recorded a rambling folk ballad entitled "Highlands," in which—for the first time in his career—he namechecked one of his contemporaries from the world of rock and pop: Neil Young. It was as close as the notoriously reticent Nobel laureate could have come to acknowledging his admiration for a quartet that had been acclaimed as America's first rock supergroup, and that remains, fifty years later, the most powerful symbol of the so-called Woodstock generation.

David Crosby, Stephen Stills, Graham Nash, and Neil Young—the singer-songwriter collective universally known as CSNY—came together by accident rather than design. Scarred by their unhappy experiences with the bands from which they escaped in 1967 and 1968, they vowed that they would never become a *group*. Instead they set out to prove that it was possible for four irrepressibly creative, willfully egotistical individuals to combine their talents without sacrificing their personal identities. But they hadn't allowed for the impact of artistic and commercial success, which transformed this loose, temporary aggregation of musicians into an institution. Crosby, Stills, Nash & Young have spent approximately two of the past fifty years as a functioning band, and the other forty-eight years fending off questions about why they are no longer together. Almost

1

despite themselves, they created a sound and a myth so powerful that it would hang around their necks as a curse, and remain an enduring source of fascination for the rest of the world.

CSNY was never intended to be a quartet, even a transient one. In 1968, three refugees from successful but confining pop bands stumbled into each other's company and discovered that when they sang together, they made a sound that was unlike anything else. For several weeks that year, ex-Byrd David Crosby, Buffalo Springfield leader Stephen Stills, and Hollies vocalist Graham Nash showed off their party trick for their peers in Laurel Canyon, and watched them gape in astonishment at the harmony blend they had found. All three men had songs to match, intensely personal expressions of romantic, psychological, and political turmoil that chimed with the spirit of their generation. Soon Crosby, Stills & Nash (alias CSN) was an act with a recording contract, and a manifesto that stressed both their brotherhood and their individual independence. They cut a debut album that caught the mood of the times and stoked rampant demand for a concert tour that could transport the Canyon's secret to the rest of America.

Only then did Stills make the fateful decision to invite his sparring partner from Buffalo Springfield, Neil Young, to flesh out the trio's sound onstage. His recruitment brought a fourth maverick voice and mercurial songwriter into the mix. It transformed CSN into CSNY, and irrevocably altered the original trio's delicate balance of power and creativity. The quartet came to national prominence with their performance at the Woodstock festival in August 1969, after which their music and their image became indissolubly linked with the fate of the baby-boomer era.

The road from Laurel Canyon to Woodstock had spanned precisely one year; and over the next twelve months, everything CSNY had built fell to pieces around them. But the resonance of their image, and the power of their music, remained undimmed, even as it haunted the four men's attempts to thrive outside the band. Eventually, and inevitably, the four men came back together, for an epic, groundbreaking 1974 tour that catapulted rock culture into a new era of greed and excess—and also ensured that Crosby, Stills, Nash & Young could never function again as a brotherhood of equals.

How could a union so brief and so troubled have left such a profound impression on American culture? If the initial pull of CSN was their vocal harmonies, what made CSNY so vital, and their legacy so deep, was the impact of their songs—and the personalities that powered them. Indeed, the men and their music became impossible to distinguish: their songwriting expressed exactly who they were, and what was happening around them, and it allowed their listeners to locate their own place in a world beset by conflict and oppression.

Each of the quartet had left a distinct mark on the mid-1960s pop scene, from Crosby's chart-topping singles with the Byrds and Nash's worldwide success with the Hollies to Stills's and Young's tempestuous, inspired work with Buffalo Springfield. With Springfield's 1967 hit "For What It's Worth," Stills had demonstrated that a song could transcend its origins and become an all-purpose rallying cry in an age searching for direction and stability. What marked out CSNY from their peers was that all four members of the band simultaneously discovered the ability to speak *for*, and *to*, their times. They did this in markedly different ways, from Crosby's provocative political rants to Nash's romantic lyricism, Stills's restless self-questioning to Young's ambiguous poetics. But collectively their four discrete voices combined to make up a force unlike any in rock history—a cabal of gifted, driven, arrogant, and fearless lyricists and composers, with the stage presence and raw talent to translate the chaos of a turbulent era into timeless anthems.

It is those tunes—"Carry On" and "Long Time Gone," "Helpless" and "Teach Your Children," "Ohio" and, of course, Joni Mitchell's "Woodstock"—that make up the quartet's most beloved legacy. CSN and CSNY released just twenty-two songs together during their brief flowering in 1969 and 1970, and most of them have become rock standards. They've formed the heart of every concert that the band (in either formation) has performed since then, arousing a collective sigh of joy from audiences, no matter how stale they have become for their composers. But while crowds called out for a reprise of their greatest hits, all four musicians were desperate to forge new ground, documenting the changes in their psyches, their personal relationships, and the society around them. So the story of CSNY is not only a chronicle of artistic triumph and popular acclaim; it's the tale of how four individuals battled to maintain their separate artistic identities when much of their audience simply wanted them to repeat the past.

I'm a fan, and have been unashamed about it, even during those decades when proclaiming your love for CSNY was tantamount to joining a leper colony. For reasons I can't quite explain, but I can always feel, the music made by those four men still touches me more deeply than any other. I can see and describe its faults, but as in any enduring love affair, they are ultimately irrelevant. "Music gets you high," Graham Nash once wrote, and their music always works for me, even without the chemical and herbal aids that used to be synonymous with the band during their most self-indulgent eras.

I've been fortunate to have interviewed, befriended, and worked on projects with many of the members of the band and their circle. What emerged was the story of how four preternaturally talented, and utterly distinct, individuals found their way into each other's company; created music that can still make it feel wonderful to be alive; and then, almost immediately, let the magic slip away. One decade was the key to their collective lives: the period between 1964 and 1974, which carried them from musical apprenticeships to what was then the most lucrative tour in rock history.

Something remarkable happened to bring them together; and something fundamental vanished when their 1974 tour and its aftermath drove them apart. Any sense that CSNY was an active, functioning, *real* band ended that year. Since then, only memories and fragments of the dream have survived: delicious fantasies that have sometimes managed to mask the profound dysfunction of their collective relationship. But there is something so thrilling, so life-affirming, so magical in the sound that those musicians can make and have made together that it is possible to forgive all those decades of missed opportunities; all the "time we have wasted on the way," as Graham Nash once put it.

CHAPTER 1

The lines formed around the corner of Sunset and Clark hours before showtime. Hundreds of fans chose to spend a chilly Valentine's night outside the club that billed itself as "Hollywood's a Go Go." They watched as a procession of celebrities slipped through the Whisky's narrow doorway, their numbers swelled by scene makers and teen columnists. Finally, the less privileged were allowed to squeeze inside and gawp at the elite melee. The go-go dancers strutted in their cage above the dance floor, while the booths hummed with insider know-how and indiscreet gossip. So intense was the crush that stars spilled out of the peacock-fan sofas onto the floor, attempting to maintain their air of distinction beneath the flashing light show while open-mouthed girls nudged each other in disbelief.

Midsong, the DJ faded down his record and the lights flickered into darkness. Then a single spotlight on the stage illuminated the face of one of America's most recognizable pop idols, Micky Dolenz of the Monkees. For a few seconds, he held his practiced smile, before gesturing over his shoulder and uttering the briefest of introductions: "Everybody—here's the Hollies." And after that the collective attention of the Whisky a Go Go—insiders and voyeurs, icons and the idol-struck, Brian Wilson, Sonny and Cher, Marvin Gaye, and sundry Animals, Monkees, and Byrds—was focused on five sharply dressed young Englishmen. For more than ninety minutes, the quintet reeled off an unfeasibly slick set of their own gemlike UK pop hits, separated by impromptu comedy skits, covers of American folk-rock favorites, and break-in fragments of Top 40 standards—"Teddy Bear," "Reach Out I'll Be There," John Sebastian's "Daydream." Steel drums and startling orchestral interventions, taped specially for the show, were skillfully blended into the Englishmen's live instrumentation.

In a booth, Cass Elliot of the Mamas and the Papas, who had taken the Manchester pop band the Hollies under her wing on their first West Coast trip two years earlier, beamed with passionate pride, while alongside her, record producer Lou Adler and ex-Byrd David Crosby exuded a refined blend of hip and exhilarating. Standing a few feet away was another of the same elevated breed, Buffalo Springfield leader Stephen Stills. He recalled that he and Crosby "were there as the kind of unofficial cheerleaders. We got up and yelled and screamed at them because we knew they were so great." After the encores—riotous revivals of Peter, Paul and Mary's "Very Last Day" and Chuck Berry's "Too Much Monkey Business"—the Hollies stumbled offstage to frenzied demands for more, from notables and unknowns alike. Then Stills, Crosby, Elliot, and friends headed for the dressing room, to hurl their congratulations at the band. Four of the English quartet were already clamoring for alcoholic refreshment away from the crowd. But not the fifth: as the Hollies' unofficial leader, Graham Nash, told Dave Zimmer, "I wanted to go hang with David and Stephen and get wasted!" The three musicians, united in their partiality for pleasure and sublime vocal harmonies, headed across the street to Stills's car. Behind in the Whisky they left Mama Cass, who had facilitated the vital introductions that brought the three men together; and Stills's bandmate and sometime sparring partner, Neil Young, who slipped away from the venue with practiced, anonymous ease.

For two hours, those four men—David Crosby, Stephen Stills, Graham Nash, and Neil Young—had shared the same room for the first time. But it was merely a trio who giggled their way back to Stills's house, where they lost themselves in Crosby's famously exquisite and always-at-the-ready joints and added their voices in chorus over some of the era's most creative records. "It sounded nice," Nash remembered vaguely a year later; and so potent was the chemical accompaniment to this encounter, and countless more to follow, that none of the participants was clear exactly what happened next, or where, or with whom; precisely how that ecstatic post-gig celebration triggered personal and musical upheaval, joyous communion, and—once Neil Young had been enticed back into their company—a lifelong cycle of musical fulfilment, frustration, and fragmentation. All that was certain for now was that these three would meet again and create a sound that was both stylistically and geographically far-flung—and yet quintessentially Californian.

California—rich, vibrant, by now almost mythical—is, in the 20th century, more than ever, the promised land.

—*Life* magazine, 1962

Successive waves of mythology—the gold rush, escape from the Dust Bowl, the fantasy factories of Hollywood—had swept millions of Americans west since the mid-nineteenth century, in search of the sun-blessed Shangri-la of California. In 1962, the population of the so-called Golden State surpassed that of the nation's dominant metropolis, New York, for the first time. This milestone prompted *Life* magazine to devote an entire issue to "The Call of California." The photogenic potential of the West Coast made it an ideal subject for a pictorial journal; the male editorial executives could not resist illustrating their assertion that the state boasted "The prettiest, biggest, lithest, tannest, most luscious girls this side of the international date line." Those with more cultural yearnings might be enticed by the ripe jazz scene of San Francisco, where musicians such as Gerry Mulligan, Cal Tjader, and Dave Brubeck were embodying the collision of cool and creativity. The same city was rich in Beat culture, as poets, musicians, and hipsters combined in passionate, transgressive adventures. Also from the coast came an eruption of folk talent, which spanned the harmonies of the Limeliters, the comic routines of the Smothers Brothers, and the crystal purity of Joan Baez. Like a typical new Californian, Baez had been drawn west from Massachusetts, taking up residence amid the consciousness-enhanced hippies of the Esalen campus.

Not that an ear for experimentation or artistic integrity were necessary to inhabit the coastal paradise. The West Coast was easily sold as a beacon of hedonism, from its flawless beaches to the lure of Disneyland. Television and the movies portrayed California as the land of surf, sun, and endless beach parties, peopled by beautiful teenagers bursting with vitality. Not every member of the surf-rock group the Beach Boys could fulfill Hollywood's physical ideals, but their torrent of early-1960s hits offered a vocabulary and a sound for the California teen experience. Their creative fulcrum was Brian Wilson, who channeled his innate genius and fractured psyche into songs that could combine youthful bravado with romantic vulnerability, coated with the exhilarating harmonic blend that was becoming a symbol of the Golden State.

For several years, until his own mental frailty began to contort his songwriting, Wilson's musical landscape was never shadowed by anything darker than romantic disappointment. Yet even the most favored American youth could not avoid intimations of a more abrasive reality: racial discrimination, urban violence, the rumbling uncertainty of nuclear proliferation, and above all, the possibility that they might be removed at random from their homes to serve in Vietnam. Even before US forces were officially posted on active duty in Vietnam, men between the ages of eighteen and twenty-five were subject to being called into the armed forces—"the draft"—under the terms of the Selective Service Act of 1948. Only students, the chronically unhealthy, and the certifiably insane and unstable could avoid their country's command, although legal representation—available only to those of wealthy upbringing, of course—could also help to postpone their call to duty.

Duty was an alien concept to the young David Crosby. "All the schools I went to said I'd never amount to anything and I would end up in prison. They were dead wrong," he boasted in 1975, a decade before their predictions were at least partly fulfilled. "I was thrown out of Santa Barbara City College, four grammar schools, four high schools, and three prep schools. I had an inability to respect authority. They didn't earn it. And they didn't get it."

In June 1955, a couple months shy of Crosby's fourteenth birthday, the LA Times ran a succession of articles recounting the threat that rebellious adolescents posed to decent society and offering warning signs for concerned parents. David Crosby checked every box: chronic indiscipline, resistance to authority, sexual precociousness, petty criminality. "I've always been in trouble," he recalled.

Crosby's parents, Floyd Crosby and Aliph Whitehead, regularly inhabited the New York society pages before their wedding in December 1930. Their younger son's stubborn resistance to any restraints on his behavior heightened the tensions in a marriage that was already beginning to corrode. Floyd Crosby had abandoned a career on Wall Street and become a recognized photographer who won an Academy Award in November 1931 for his cinematography on F. W. Murnau's *Tabu*. Filmed in the South Seas, *Tabu* combined dramatic documentary footage (Crosby's forte) with fictional drama. Immediately after his marriage, Crosby was booked on another lengthy voyage across the Equator. Rather than awaiting his return in Manhattan's polite society, his wife agreed to become "one of the few white women who have accompanied an expedition exploring South American jungles," as the *New York Times* reported when they reached the Uruguayan capital, Montevideo, almost a year later. The paper eagerly noted that Aliph's priority when she reached the city was to catch the latest American movies, taking in three separate performances on her first evening.

Two days before their first wedding anniversary, the Crosbys' party (and their menagerie, stretching from ocelots to anteaters) reached New York, where Aliph was now both a novelty and a celebrity. Journalists quizzed her eagerly about her exploits in the Brazilian jungles, about the tales preceding her from Uruguay that she had shot a tiger—or was it a jaguar?—that had threatened their boat in the Panama River. But the "slender brunette" of twenty-five "showed herself unique among women explorers by refusing to pose for a picture or discuss her experiences."

Within two months, the couple were off to Honduras to pursue the insect and reptile life of Central America. As before, Floyd documented the expedition on film, while Aliph acted as medical officer and pharmacist. Among their essential kit was a phonograph stocked with the latest jazz records, an accordion, a mandolin, and a guitar, although the party's most vital resource was their supply of antivenin for tackling snakebite. Thereafter, Floyd continued to roam the earth in search of dramatic film footage—confronting an aggressive stingray off the Bahamas, for example, underwater photography being his greatest professional joy. Between assignments, he joined the migration to California, where his first son, Floyd Jr. (known as Ethan), was born in 1937.

When the Motion Picture Guild was formed in Hollywood in 1939, promising to produce films on subjects too controversial for the major studios, Crosby was a founding member. But increasingly his talents were directed toward government projects, usually with a progressive political bent—chronicling rural poverty, for example. After the December 1941 attack on Pearl Harbor plunged the United States into war, Crosby joined Air Transport Command, documenting airborne combat with a fearlessness that won him several citations.

He left behind a young family that had expanded that August with the arrival of David Van Cortlandt Crosby. He was gifted by being born in the nation's most alluring state amid material comfort and family prestige. That grew alongside his father's career, which involved groundbreaking cinematography on such memorable movies as *High Noon*. But like most children of his precise age, David had barely seen his father as a small child, and subsequently found him emotionally distant. Instead, the boy's mentor was his elder brother, who mapped out his musical education in cool California jazz. Folk music was a shared family passion, and in their teens Ethan and David learned guitar. David also unlocked his innate sense of vocal harmony, untutored and joyously natural. The teenage boy was a born extrovert who quickly discovered that girls responded to the charisma of an entertainer. After graduating from Santa Barbara High School, he chose to focus on music. He began to try his hand in bohemian coffee bars and clubs—first in his hometown, and then, as he left his teens, as far afield as New York and Florida.

Along the way, he stumbled across others who had abandoned family expectations in favor of the fragile security of life as a hand-to-mouth musician. Guitarist and banjoist Roger [then Jim] McGuinn recalled meeting Crosby at the Ash Grove in Los Angeles around 1960, registering both his talent and his arrogance. Crosby taught him how to drive with a stick shift, and then took him home to his mother—recently divorced from Floyd, who had subsequently remarried. Aliph "made us lamb sandwiches with avocado," McGuinn remembered, before the two teenagers parted company for several years.

While McGuinn was already wedded to the folk tradition that became his vocation, David Crosby's approach was less easy to categorize. His repertoire encompassed folk and blues standards he had gathered from the Weavers and Josh White; but his voice had a hushed delicacy and almost feline grace that often led him to be billed as a jazz vocalist. Around the end of 1961, he was captured by a tape recorder at a café in Colorado, introducing his own song, "It's Been Raining," with a practiced melancholy that served to conquer stray female hearts. "This song came out of a very lonely town, as most big cities are, at about four o'clock in the morning," he whispered into the microphone, "and it came to somebody who had been very lonely for a long time." This calculated self-pity alone would have guaranteed him a partner for the night. But it was followed by a sublimely controlled performance that transcended genre, and presaged more expert compositions ahead. At twenty, David Crosby was already fully formed. All he lacked was experience and an environment in which he could thrive.

> I get high on everything I can, man, and I'm trying to get high on everything. Buddha and Christ and Shiva and Krishna and Mohammad and everybody all seem to say that you should get high on the flowers and on yourself and on making love and you ARE love, and thou art God, and God groks, and the grass is God, and the grass groks, and everything is IT, and if you get into it, the whole universe is yours: playground, playpen, universe!
>
> —David Crosby, 1967

In search of music and love, and a ready supply of dope, David Crosby hitched and rode his way around the United States in the early 1960s, learning how to express himself in song, and seducing women. At least two of them became pregnant, whereupon Crosby promptly left town, only meeting and acknowledging his offspring more than thirty years later. His company of friends and peers grew, from Terry Callier and Bob Dylan in New York to Fred Neil and Vince Martin in Miami. But it was back in California, across the Golden Gate in Sausalito, that he established connections to support him deep into adulthood.

There he fell into a commune, peopled by aspiring musicians such as

Paul Kantner and David Freiberg, and young women who were expected to be servile. "The chicks took care of the house," he explained, "and the guys scored, and scraped up bread here and there, and did gigs and played and sang, and it worked" — at least for the men. In the days before second-wave feminism forced men to confront their oppressive conduct, and brought women together to challenge their patriarchal assumptions, male superiority was entrenched and assumed, even among those who were willing to challenge every other societal norm.

The bible of these communards was *Stranger in a Strange Land*, a Hugo Award–winning 1961 novel by Robert Heinlein. While its landscape of space travel and visitors from Mars situated the book on the science fiction shelves, *Stranger* was more aptly a dystopian satire on human civilization, with a utopian, spiritual twist. At its heart is the strangely innocent "man from Mars," Valentine Michael Smith, who arrives on this planet with telepathic powers and the charisma of an unwilling cult leader. He schools his followers in the unity of all creation, and a notion of transcendent communion among individuals embodied in the word "grok" — a way of knowing and experiencing another person in their entirety. Smith establishes the ceremony of sharing water among the enlightened, creating "water brothers" and "water sisters" who adopt a system of sharing on the basis of need. For young Californians surviving outside orthodox culture, *Stranger* offered both a vision of liberation, and a warning of the hazards of letting the outside world intrude.

The impact of Heinlein's text on David Crosby was so profound that he bought dozens (he claimed hundreds) of copies to give away to friends and strangers in 1963. As he recounted four years later, "I gave them away not because they really say this is where it's at, and here's how to live in the world, and you can keep all your money in the bowl, and everything is cool, and you learn how to grok and we'll all learn Martian and all be telepaths, right? But there's something about sharing water that's [like] getting high, and there's something about how these people lived that's like what happens every time a bunch of nice people start living in the same place." The vocabulary and spirit of *Stranger in a Strange Land* endured in Crosby's conversation and songwriting for the remainder of the decade.

Not that his focus was entirely spiritual. After the commune, Crosby crashed for a while with fellow folksinger Dino Valenti on a former ferryboat turned floating restaurant named the *Charles Van Damme*. Midafternoon, he and Valenti (twenty-one and twenty-five respectively) would cruise past Tamalpais High School, preying on teenage girls and enticing them to onboard parties. "It was like sharks hitting sheep," Crosby told Steve Silberman. "We were merciless. These little girls in crinoline skirts—and we'd be standing there, with a little trail of saliva out of one corner of our mouths. We were terrible, but we had a lot of fun." On his first solo album, a sumptuous, ethereal concoction of vocal harmonies, bursting with unsullied beauty, was titled "Tamalpais High (at About 3)," to commemorate the hour when school was out, and the sharks could begin to circle their prey.

> Cass Elliot is one of the grooviest, happiest, most wonderful things to watch onstage that there is in the whole world. She's a gas, man, just a stone gas!
>
> —David Crosby, 1967

Between busking for dope and dollars, and dallying with schoolgirls, David Crosby moonlighted in the commercial world in summer 1963 with a folk quartet assembled by his brother, Ethan. Folk being the novelty of the year, thanks to Peter, Paul and Mary, the group fell under the patronage of a light-orchestra leader who stamped his brand on them, as Les Baxter's Balladeers. Baxter's name was a commercial beacon, and by October the Balladeers had been recruited for a touring folk package. The ensemble was headed by Jack Linkletter, host of TV's *Hootenanny*—a folk show notorious for blacklisting politically outspoken artists, such as Pete Seeger. Also on the bill was the Big Three, led by a woman only a month younger than Crosby who had recently abandoned her birth name of Ellen Cohen and remade herself as Cass Elliot.

Cass was indeed big by nature and nurture, blessed with a voice that could reach the back of an unamplified vaudeville theater—suggesting that her natural home might be Broadway. The cliché "larger than life" might have been designed for her, as she appeared to laugh off her obesity with savage, satirical humor that tackled the absurdity of everything around her, Cass Elliot included. Like almost everyone who met her, Crosby fell passionately in love (but not lust) with her. They shared a penchant for frequent doses of marijuana (Cass was also gobbling bottles of amphetamines in a vain attempt to shed some pounds) and a sarcastic view of contemporary culture. Their bond went deeper than humor and recreation, however, as she opened her heart to Crosby about her depression, and he offered emotional security rather than the verbal barbs for which he was often notorious. Like most of her subsequent friendships with Californian rock legends, the Crosby-and-Cass rapport endured.

There were scores of these young, fresh harmony groups crisscrossing America during what one wit dubbed "the great folk scare"; a year later, nineteen-year-old Stephen Stills would undergo his own baptism in musical blandness with the Au Go Go Singers. Many of them would be preserved for eternity on tape, among them the "big sound of Les Baxter's Balladeers," as Linkletter promised on an album that chronicled his folk package. For all Crosby's embarrassment, then and since, the Balladeers' four recordings showcased his already remarkable gift for vocal harmony, as he soared above his comrades on the work song, "Linin' Track," and contributed the first of many inventive counterpoints to "Baiion." There was no room in the Balladeers for Crosby to show off his own first adventures in song, however, or to live out the philosophy of Valentine Michael Smith; and after the Linkletter tour, the quartet was soon forgotten. Not so Cass Elliot, who would nourish, amuse, and inspire Crosby in crucial ways throughout the 1960s.

> David Crosby's groove runs from Miles Davis to the Beatles. He's
> kinda hung on the Indian music bit. He likes life, love, freedom,
> awareness, music, sex and sailing.
>
> —*Rave* magazine, 1965

Like his entire generation, Crosby's life changed the first time he heard the Beatles. "I Want to Hold Your Hand" proved that vocal harmonies did not have to be tied to exhausted folk standards and coated in cotton wool. During the early weeks of 1964, Crosby was merely one of many folk musicians struggling to splash some of the Beatles' vitality over his folk club performances. Gradually several of these disparate, Beatle-struck individuals began to cohere into a unit. Meanwhile, he had fallen under the protection of record producer and impresario Jim Dickson, who had distinguished a bluesy edge to Crosby's vocal purr, and was encouraging the young man to sing out. These loose threads were joined when Dickson gave Crosby and his friends Roger/Jim McGuinn and Gene Clark free studio time, lent them the cash to buy electric guitars, and encouraged them to move beyond pastiche. The three soon became five, as they enveloped bluegrass prodigy Chris Hillman to play electric bass, and Brian Jones lookalike Michael Clarke as their drummer. The group had no fixed name: they mutated from the Jet Set to, briefly, the Beefeaters, which as McGuinn conceded "wasn't cool" and "seemed like a throwback to that Hugh Hefner mentality." Finally, they emulated their heroes by distorting a species from the natural world and emerging as the Byrds.

In their fledgling form, the Byrds were blatant Beatles copyists, and both McGuinn and Clark rapidly mastered the art of concocting two-minute pop songs. As Dickson recognized, Crosby's gift for vocal harmony could translate naïveté into sophistication with a single soaring line. But neither his producer nor his bandmates imagined he might occupy a central creative role in the Byrds. His talents—caught for posterity on Dickson's tape recorder—clearly lay elsewhere. As a vocalist, Crosby was encouraged to slur and roar his way through a series of blues songs, which he performed but never convincingly inhabited. Phrasing and control were not an issue; his voice simply lacked the gravitas and weary experience to sell the blues, though his efforts were no less impressive than those of the British R&B fanatics who were beginning to fill the American charts.

The same flaw crippled some of his self-composed material, such as "I'm Just a Young Man." Crosby had indeed been "learning wrong things" since he was a kid, but on record he was no Marlon Brando. Elsewhere on these 1964 recordings, though, the fundamentals of his subsequent career were waiting in chrysalid form: the thrum of a twelve-string guitar in modal tuning, chords plucked from a jazz songbook, the voice rich and melancholy, as if he were already apologizing to a woman he knew he would leave in the morning. All of these elements came to miraculous coalescence on his first recording of "Everybody's Been Burned," a song weighed down by romantic disillusionment but lightened by the determination to persevere at all costs.

There was no obvious room for emotional ambiguity within the Byrds, even when they created a magical synthesis of Bob Dylan's poetry and contemporary pop on "Mr. Tambourine Man," their debut single (aside from an unnoticed tryout as the Beefeaters a few months earlier). "Wow, man, you can dance to that," Dylan told the band when he heard their arrangement. There was a terrifying four-month wait between recording and release, during which Crosby kept both of his uncertain career paths open. Legally, he was now a Columbia recording artist, but his heart remained in folk clubs such as the New Balladeer, where he continued to show off his uncanny synthesis of jazz, blues, and pure creativity, alongside fellow future rock stars such as John Kay and Dino Valenti.

The release of "Mr. Tambourine Man" altered the course of Crosby's life, and the history of American rock and roll. Topping the charts in America and Britain, it catapulted the Byrds to a level of stardom, and attention, for which they were ill prepared. Only Crosby seemed to luxuriate in the spotlight; his colleagues remained taciturn and impassive, earning the band a reputation—often well-deserved—for moodiness. Even the garrulous Crosby overturned media expectations, by refusing to suffer foolish questions or banal photo opportunities. "Dave Crosby calls himself the troublemaker of the group," a 1965 teen magazine reported, before becoming victim to his charms regardless: "Crosby seems to dare you *not* to fall for him."

Audible on their first album merely as a harmonist and driving rhythm guitarist, Crosby was a more dominant presence in public. Beneath one of the band's trademark wraparound fringes, his eyes twinkled with perpetual mischief. His colleagues relied upon Carnaby Street elegance, but Crosby added mystery with a cape, which he retained even at the scorching height of the California summer. The press dubbed him "Batman"; but Crosby shared none of the Caped Crusader's concern for moral decency. He proudly reeled off his list of adolescent misde-meanors for journalists—truancy, refusal to obey orders, petty theft—and laid out a manifesto that must have startled his press agent: "Over half of the people in the country are under twenty-five. The country isn't being run as they know and feel it should be. The discrepancies are too obvious. The wrongness and corruption disturbs and upsets them. And [there's] the uncertainty of the nuclear thing, which is something we've lived with since we were born. They definitely want to change this, and a lot of other things."

Such pronouncements explained why McGuinn, the self-styled "leader" of the Byrds, had to concede that Crosby was their unchallenged "spokesman." For the moment, Crosby refused to involve himself directly in politics, for which he claimed the Byrds had "a universal distaste." His goal was more ambitious, and idealistic: "freedom—personal freedom, freedom of thinking, freedom of being . . . If there's enough of it, it'll take us out of a place where we want to make wars and—probably—off the planet and out. That would be a nice way for us to go." Then, realizing that he was sounding like a cosmic politician himself, he backtracked: "I don't know what's going to happen; I'm not a prophet or a seer, I just live here."

His peers were acutely conscious of that—not least of all Terry Melcher. "I loved working with Terry," Roger McGuinn remembered. "He was probably the best producer the Byrds worked with. But David didn't appreciate him. David was unhappy with Terry because Terry and I had a good rapport, and more of my songs were ending up on our albums, and so David was going, 'We got to get rid of this guy!' He thought that if he could replace him with Jim Dickson, he could get more of his songs out. Instead, we were assigned another Columbia producer, Allen Stanton, who was in his mid-forties. He was an old man to us! We didn't have anything in common. And he couldn't stand Crosby! He would keep me back after the session was over, and say, 'What *is* it with this Crosby? What's wrong with him? Why can't I relate to him?'"

Columbia's microphones captured a typical exchange between Crosby and Melcher, the musician grumbling incessantly, Melcher finally snap-ping: "Why don't you go fuck yourself?" The producer relented a couple of minutes later, insisting "I was only kidding, man," but the tension was unmistakable. It seeped into the band itself, with photo shoots or recording dates often interrupted by ferocious arguments or bear-like scuffles. By late 1965, Crosby was bringing his songs to Byrds sessions, but failing to persuade his colleagues that there was commercial potential in material such as "The Flower Bomb Song" or a musical encapsulation of Heinlein's *Stranger in a Strange Land*, water brothers and all.

A semi-disastrous 1965 UK tour was redeemed when it inspired "Eight Miles High," to which Crosby contributed a verse and the staccato rhythm guitar that jittered and drove through the song. This staggering record owed its spirit to Crosby's musical indoctrination, after he insisted the band listen over and over again to a dub of the first US album by sitar maestro Ravi Shankar, and *Africa/Brass* by jazz saxophonist John Coltrane. "By the time we got home," McGuinn recalled, "subliminally we had been steeped in this music so much that it just came out."

Aside from its modal themes and McGuinn's frenetic guitar work, the title of "Eight Miles High" was sufficient for the media, and those charged with guarding America's radio waves from subversion, to link the song, and the Byrds, with the use of illegal drugs. Crosby scarcely bothered to hide his enthusiasm for herbal and chemical experimentation. Marijuana had been part of his diet since his teens and was sufficiently common among his peers for him to credit the drug for "keeping it loose" in a press interview. "I play high most of the time and I always write high," he explained in 1967. In Greenwich Village, around 1962, he had been introduced to the hallucinogenic mescaline, and in Sausalito he had experimented with lysergic acid (LSD). The effects of his baptism in acid were profound and enduring, though he found them challenging to explain: "Verbalization is a very clumsy tool in all this . . . I have gotten to a place where there was a point of light and it was emanating light, and I hallucinated that it was the life force, and that it was inside of me, and that I was looking inside of me, and that everyone has it, and that it's inside of everyone and that getting in tune with it is what's happening." And indeed "What's Happening?!?!"—the punctuation a hint of his psychological disorientation—was one of the first songs in which he attempted to paint the psychedelic experience in musical colors. As recorded on the Byrds' third album, *Fifth Dimension*, it wallowed in glorious confusion, Crosby almost chortling with glee. The same album held another evocation of an acid trip, "I See You," as Crosby succeeded in wedding his jazz sensibility to cathartic rock and roll. Freed to take on a more prominent role in the band by the departure of Gene Clark—in which Crosby had a steering hand—he was now established as their moving force, his public dominance of the Byrds on the verge of being replicated on record.

In Los Angeles, the creative hub of American rock in 1966, Crosby was greeted by right as an aristocrat. He had turned on the Beatles during an acid trip that sparked John Lennon to write "She Said She Said"; schmoozed as an equal with Bob Dylan when the singer-songwriter was at his most combative; hung with everyone from the Beach Boys to the Rolling Stones; dominated every room he entered with his blend of stoned magnificence and arrogant command. Inevitably he cut a swath through the Byrds' female fans, wherever he traveled—though there were occasional mishaps, as when a missing girl would be located in his room, or a jealous boyfriend in Virginia Beach would recruit a gang of pumped-up jocks to warn Crosby off.

Crosby was self-righteous about his refusal to obey limits and recognize borders—sexual, moral, verbal, or indeed chemical. No foreign substance scared him, and he drifted into sporadic use of drugs that were as yet foreign to the rock generation (although not their jazz elders), such as cocaine and heroin. He did not share these experiences with the Byrds, preferring to investigate these perilous substances with older, trusted friends.

His folk circuit compadre Cass Elliot had followed him into the media spotlight, as the focal point of another harmony band, the Mamas and the Papas. For the rest of her days, she would now be "Mama" Cass, the self-described "richest beatnik in Hollywood," who preempted criticism of her corpulent physique by calling herself "an orange mushroom." "She is a large, very large girl," Lillian Roxon wrote in 1966, "given to Technicolor smocks and high, white boots. Her face is, well, decidedly craggy. Her hair is all over the place. She is unlikely to grace the pages of the glossies with her bikinied presence . . . [but] she is expected to do for excess poundage what Barbra Streisand did for big noses—that is, make it, if not entirely fashionable, then at least the mark of great personal style."

While her personality allowed her to cross between hip Hollywood parties and TV variety shows, enchanting them both, Elliot's continuing battle with depression led her to test out all available distractions and sedatives. Roger McGuinn remembered David Crosby arriving at his house with a pill bottle stuffed with cocaine, a gift from Cass. Her colleague John Phillips, who was already charting his own course for self-destruction, was apparently horrified one day to discover Elliot with a supply of heroin, which she said she had been given by Crosby. (Phillips later blamed Crosby for introducing her to the drug, which Crosby has always vehemently denied.)

The exchange of illegal substances aside, Cass Elliot specialized in a more benign transaction: bringing together friends and acquaintances for their mutual gratification. She loved to share her brood, achieving greater success as an emotional and musical matchmaker than she did in her own romantic life.

In January 1966, Tony Hicks, guitarist with Manchester pop band the Hollies, made his usual round of London's music publishers in search of fresh material. "I came out of Dick James Music with a demo of 'I Can't Let Go,'" he remembered, and the song delivered one of their biggest hits a few months later. "On the same day, I picked up 'California Dreamin''" before anyone in England had heard of the Mamas and Papas." Before the Hollies could add it to their repertoire, the original version entered the UK charts. Three months later, the Hollies made their first trip to Hollywood. At a press reception, they were waylaid by eighteen-year-old DJ and Anglophile Rodney Bingenheimer. "He invited me and Graham Nash to a Mamas and Papas recording session," Hicks said. Nash subsequently admitted that he only agreed in hope of meeting, and seducing, the American group's other female member, Michelle Phillips, who embodied all those alluring qualities promised by *Life* magazine in that 1962 panegyric to California. "Everyone there was having a good time," Hicks continued, "all out of their minds, which was the 'in' thing at the time. After the session, at about two in the morning, we were invited back to one of their pads up in the Hollywood Hills. I was more interested in checking out the 'talent' at the

Whisky, but Graham went—and he's never been the same since! That was the night he realized that he liked the American lifestyle."

Nash's erotic urges were swiftly forgotten once he met Cass Elliot and—like David Crosby before him—fell deeply in platonic love. Several days later, Cass drove to the Hollies' hotel, whisked Nash away, and "asked me if I wanted to meet somebody totally mad, totally bananas." As he recalled nearly forty years later, "I'll never forget it. We arrived at this house with a Porsche convertible outside. Cass strode in without knocking, we went upstairs, and there on a couch was this man in a blue-striped T-shirt, rolling the longest, thickest joint you've ever seen in your life. 'I'd like you to meet David Crosby,' she said to me. She told him I was a friend from England called Graham, didn't say any more than that. I knew who he was, for sure, because I loved the Byrds. But he had no idea about me—though he told me later that he was pissed to discover after we'd gone that I was the guy who sang the high harmonies in the Hollies. Anyway, he passed the joint around, produced another, and that was it—friends for life!"

Graham was a powerful guy, and what he wanted, he got.

—Allan Clarke, the Hollies

If the Byrds were famed for their surly refusal to conform to the demands of the pop media, the Hollies were their polar opposites. "They were like *Vogue* models," said photographer Henry Diltz, another core member of the Cass Elliot cabal. Nobody would have approached the Byrds to advertise shampoo or chocolate, but the Hollies were eager to oblige any request. They were arguably Britain's most reliable hit-makers of the 1960s outside of the Beatles, carefully keeping pace with each trend that the Liverpudlian quartet had pioneered. In this role, they eagerly chirruped their praise of Shell gasoline and Wrigley's Spearmint gum on TV; and posed with models dubbed "the Hollies' Dollies" for a hairspray campaign, with Graham Nash dominating the pictures—the girls' heads tilted against his shoulder or, in one variant, Allan Clarke gazing at Nash in apparent infatuation.

Clarke and Nash—lead and harmony singer respectively, and co-writers since the dawn of the 1960s—certainly shared a unique bond. They were five or perhaps six years old when they first met, as Clarke explained: "When I arrived at my new school, the teacher asked who wanted to sit next to this new boy, and Graham Nash put his hand up. So I sat next to Graham, and we became pals." Though their educational paths parted when they were eleven, the two boys remained close friends who sparked and spurred each other's passion for music. By the mid-1950s, the pair had formed a precocious rock and roll duo. "We couldn't both sing the lead," Clarke said. "I had a stronger voice, so Graham sang harmony." With the arrival in the British charts of the Everly Brothers in 1957, Clarke and Nash found their role models, learning to bond their voices with the same fraternal ease as their American heroes.

Six months younger than Crosby, Nash enjoyed none of the splendor of California in his North of England upbringing. He was born in February 1942 in Blackpool, where his family had been evacuated to avoid the intensive German bombardment of Salford in Greater Manchester. Even without Hitler's assistance, the town was laden with slum housing, and although the Nash family escaped the absolute worst of the town's urban deprivation, their postwar existence was frugal. William Nash (his son was christened Graham William, and later became known to his friends as Willie) was an engineer, who earned enough to keep Graham and his two younger sisters fed and clothed, if never spoiled. But in one of the most significant moments of his life, as Nash has recounted on multiple occasions, his father was imprisoned in 1953 for helping to conceal stolen goods. He returned home, Nash said, a broken man, racked by shame at the ignominy and poverty he had brought his family. He died at the age of forty-six. "I've been living my life for him, ever since," Nash said. "Everything I've done, going to strange places, it's all been for him. I've been conscious of that since the day he died."

Like Clarke, Nash recognized their friendship as the other crucial influence on his childhood: "Allan changed my life completely. Me and Allan were always together, it seemed. We were incredible fans of early American rock and roll. We just ate it up, everything we could find. Our uncles and cousins went with the Merchant Marines and brought back records from the United States, and all the other bands in Manchester and Liverpool were discovering stuff and passing it on. It was a great time." Although Merseyside won international kudos as the birthplace of the Beatles, and hence the home of the British beat boom, Manchester's group scene was equally intense. Nash and Clarke first took the stage as the Two Teens, as early as 1955; or else they were Ricky and Dane Young, mock-brothers in the Everly tradition; or the Guytones; or, expanded into a full-size rock and roll quartet in 1960, the Fourtones, sometimes "Fabulous" in the same way that the Beatles were once "Silver."

Unconsciously, the Fourtones were following a few months behind the Beatles' footsteps, establishing a settled lineup—and a new name—by the end of 1962. In the new year, they began to haunt the Cavern Club in Liverpool, just as the Beatles were starting to outgrow that venue. And it was there that EMI producer Ron Richards, who had handled the Beatles' successful audition the previous year, glimpsed the Hollies for the first time. Decades later, he still recalled watching Graham Nash thrashing his acoustic guitar long after he had broken all the strings, such was the band's frenzied energy onstage. But whereas the Beatles were persuasive—and talented—enough to write all their own singles, the Hollies followed a more conventional beat-group formula: a classic American rock hit as the "plug" side of their single, and maybe one of their own naïve originals tucked away on the flip.

Though there was little difference between their ages, the Beatles, even at their most innocent, sounded like playful young adults on their early records, while the Hollies were excited teenagers. Nothing accentuated that impression more than Graham Nash's agonizingly high harmonies. Like his spiky, Tommy Steele hair, it gave him the air of a precocious kid, to the point where it was startling not to see him in short trousers. His instantly recognizable voice belied his power. Like the Byrds, this was a band in which the frontman was not the most public or forceful voice. The Hollies had multiple virtues: an effortlessly commanding lead singer, in Allan Clarke; an equally admired lead guitarist Tony Hicks; an ebullient, joyous harmony blend; and, in Bobby Elliott, a jazz fan adrift among rockers, arguably the most adventurous and powerful British drummer of his era. Yet it was Nash, like Crosby, who spoke out for the band, and stamped his self-assurance on their image. That was apparent from the cover of their debut album in 1964, on which he was credited as "leader." He dominated the group photograph like a would-be matinee idol, oozing confidence in his own appeal.

That August, he had already earned enough from the Hollies' run of hits to purchase a seventeenth-century cottage outside Manchester, which he intended—so he told the eager teen press—to share with his recently acquired Afghan hound. Within a month, it was reported that "He kept his most important date ever last Friday week in Manchester when he married Rosemary Eccles, a twenty-year-old beautician whom he had known for two years." To keep her entertained while the Hollies were eternally on the road, he and Tony Hicks opened a Manchester boutique, to be co-managed by Rose Nash and Hicks's sister. Not that Rose was entirely happy: "I keep getting into trouble by going to parties without telling my wife," Nash said.

Meanwhile, Nash was imprinting his identity on British pop, always "on the scene," in the parlance of the times, always available for a refreshingly outspoken comment. As the Byrds mounted the charts with their Bob Dylan song, Nash exclaimed: "I don't think Dylan will make it big, pop-wise, in Britain now. He was too rude towards people who were genuinely interested in him." The following year, when Dylan was at his creative peak, Nash admitted: "Nothing he has ever done has ever knocked me out. Perhaps I don't think enough about words." He was equally off-key in his enthusiasm about the prospect of touring South Africa, at a time when the Musicians Union was about to enact a ban on aiding the country's apartheid regime. It was hard to recognize the pacifist of future decades in the youth who claimed that shooting was one of his hobbies, though a childhood interest in oceanography chimed better with the man who would later write a passionate denunciation of the hunting of sea mammals.

His priorities in the mid-1960s were personal, never collective. Quizzed about his political allegiance at the time of the 1966 UK general election, Nash replied: "I never bother . . . no time! I'm too busy looking after myself. It's a selfish attitude, I suppose." He explained his love for America by noting that "Everything seems to be centered around the individual."

That was in July 1966, when his best friend, Allan Clarke, told a reporter: "Graham's a guy that's out to make a lot of money—and he'll get it, too. He gets away with murder—he's that sort of person. He's got an in-built ability to push himself. He'll get what he wants."

Yet both the outside world and the inner chaos of a young man trying to balance marital commitment, public adoration, and deep-seated self-doubt began to leave their mark on the Hollies' growing stash of original material. For all their disavowal of political or social commitment, "Too Many People" on their otherwise orthodox 1965 album *The Hollies* was a bizarre reflection on global overpopulation. The track ended with the menacing roar of a nuclear explosion. On *Would You Believe*, the following summer, "Oriental Sadness" clumsily explored the bones of a disintegrating relationship, while Nash's solo turn on "Fifi the Flea" appeared to be an equally sincere and artless admission of an extramarital affair. By the end of 1966, there was another album, and more Nash self-questioning. "Tell Me to My Face" undercut its frothy samba arrangement with a tale of discord in a seventeenth-century cottage, while "Clown" stripped bare the man who was getting away with murder: "He gives the show of his life," Nash sang, "though he's breaking down."

No wonder that one British pop magazine, more accustomed to chronicling its heroes' plans for Christmas pantomime than conducting psychoanalysis, confessed itself concerned for Graham Nash's mental and physical state. Nervous breakdowns and physical collapse were almost inescapable hazards for the mid-'60s British pop star: tour dates that seemed to have been mapped at random and scheduled by sadists made sure of that. Hollies drummer Bobby Elliott was taken seriously ill but insisted on fulfilling the band's engagements—until he collapsed in Germany and spent a week on the verge of death. Nash's own exhaustion surfaced in early 1966, when he was diagnosed as suffering from a stomach ulcer. He was "put on a strict diet and under orders to get to bed early." But no shows were canceled to make this possible, and for the next decade Nash's body continued to expose any physical frailties or psychological demons, often at crucial career moments.

Almost instinctively, he sought relief outside the Hollies. The band's bassist, Eric Haydock, remembered a June 1966 show in Oxford: "Mama

Cass turned up at our gig, and took him away. He stayed up late with her, had a few drinks, harmonized with her. Then she went back to the States and said to her friends, 'You have to check this guy out, he's a fantastic harmony singer.'" There were rumors that they were writing songs together. That September, Nash and Elliot were reunited in Chicago, where she inducted him into a coterie to which she and David Crosby had belonged for several years. "That was the first acid trip I ever took, with Cass in the Astor Tower hotel," Nash recalled. "I remember specifically that about an hour after we'd dropped, when we were just peaking, I had room service send up some strawberries and cream, and they looked like little beating hearts on a plate." Then reality intervened: "Our road manager, Rod Shields, called my room and said that we were due at a radio station within half an hour, to talk to all the teenyboppers. Great news, when you're on acid!"

The effects were impossible to ignore, as Nash immediately recognized: "When you take a lot of acid, you start to realize just how insignificant you really are. And in fact how insignificant the earth itself is. You get quite humble behind that drug." Reporters found that his pithy comments on contemporary pop trends were now accompanied by lengthy explorations of what he had learned by expanding his consciousness. "Graham talks a lot about the inner mind and psychological things," Allan Clarke complained, "but to tell you the truth, I don't understand half of what he's on about. It's just weird." Nash took one of the Hollies to an artist's studio, but as he explained, he failed to convince his colleague that "there was any beauty in the paintings or in the flat . . . We had a big row about it because he really accused me of being mad. He said I've utterly and completely changed in the last six months—which I'm glad for, because I didn't particularly like myself . . . There's a complete barrier come between us."

As if on cue, David Crosby and the Byrds arrived in London in February 1967, and Nash joined Cass's friend at a press reception. Crosby was clad in the Borsalino hat that he now habitually wore to disguise his thinning hair, and sporting a moustache and luxuriant sideburns; Nash boasted his own facial growth, plus round tinted glasses, like those John Lennon had begun to wear, and one of the Edwardian jackets now mandatory for fashion-conscious English stars. When Nash discovered that Crosby was staying at a bland London hotel called the White House, he invited the Byrd to stay with him and Rose in their Bayswater apartment. In return, Crosby shared what he had with his newfound water brother: marijuana, and the finest concoction of lysergic acid that California (and in particular his friend Augustus Owsley Stanley III) had to offer.

Their trip, Crosby later explained, was "exceptionally beautiful," not least because it was "the basis for the state of a communication with [someone] who is now getting to be probably one of my best friends . . . We wound up driving out to see Windsor Castle in the dawn, which is an incredible experience. We got lost, which was beautiful, and I went walking down beside the Thames along where they have all these beautiful houseboats and barges and boats, and I really love boats, and so it was a beautiful thing." Beyond the hedonism of an experience for which only the word *beautiful* would suffice, Crosby recognized the indelible connection between himself and his English friend: "If you go on the same chemical trip, it attunes you to the other person a great deal . . . We are in the primitive stages of learning how to tune our minds to wherever we want them chemically, and soon electrically." For most of the next fifty years, David Crosby and Graham Nash would now be in tune; not always in harmony, but sharing a psychic connection that would alter the course of their lives.

CHAPTER 2

Buffalo Springfield taught me that frustration, and pressures, was the best way to lose perspective of the music, and what we were supposed to be doing. It gave you the rock and roll crazies.

—Stephen Stills, 1971

In May 1966, Buffalo Springfield opened for Johnny Rivers at the Whisky on Sunset Boulevard. The group "plays with great vitality, but is a bit raucous," pronounced the *LA Times*. The Byrds' bassist, Chris Hillman, introduced himself backstage. "Would you like to manage us?" begged a Springfield guitarist, a snaggle-toothed fireball from the Deep South named Stephen Stills. Hillman murmured something inconclusive but returned with two bandmates. "What do you think of the Springfield?" he asked David Crosby. "I don't like them," Crosby snapped, and the subject was closed.

A year later, both the Byrds and the Springfield were booked for the epochal rock event of 1967, the Monterey Pop Festival. Crosby and Stephen Stills were hanging out at the festival offices with the Byrds' press agent, Derek Taylor, any animosity between the two musicians long forgotten. "The better groups are, everyone knows, bored stiff with their old lineups," Taylor had declared, after a benefit show where the Byrds had been augmented by two musicians from South Africa for what Taylor called "one of the great experiences of contemporary music." In Taylor's office, that spirit continued to excite Stills's imagination: "The whole feeling is one of giving and exchanging, like the jazz scene. We can trade ideas, sit and jam all night. It's a breakdown of competition."

Unbeknownst to Stills, his musical foil in the Springfield, Neil Young, was about to abandon his colleagues on the verge of their most important

TV appearance to date, with Johnny Carson. "That's when Neil had to quit," Stills noted later, "exactly at the time it meant the most." Nobody knew whether it was a temporary mood swing (not his first that year), but the band was forced to bail out of *The Tonight Show*. Young hid in a girlfriend's house in the San Fernando Valley, passively making it clear that he was not about to return, for the TV show or the festival. The Springfield had to confront the Monterey audience, and D. A. Pennebaker's documentary film crew, with a pickup guitarist who barely had time to learn their repertoire.

Pennebaker's subsequent movie, *Monterey Pop*, memorialized and mythologized the festival for posterity. Fifty years on, Stephen Stills's younger sister, Talitha, added the memories of a high school graduate (her brother had caused havoc at Carmel High by bringing the Springfield to her graduation ceremony). "It seemed that all the high school and college kids on the Monterey Peninsula were there," she wrote. "A spontaneous group of people formed, and they went and bought flowers by the bushel loads and handed them out to everyone, and so began a wave of people approaching the law enforcement officers and placing flowers in their pockets, on their ears, on their hats and helmets, in their gun barrels. Most of the young women on these warm June days and evenings were pretty scantily dressed and quite effusively showering love, peace and brotherhood in all directions."

Talitha's brother was one of the few participants in the festival whose experience was less than ecstatic: love, peace, and brotherhood were difficult to sustain in a band subject to the whims of an elusive guitarist. The only semi-prepared Buffalo Springfield were introduced at the Monterey Fairgrounds by Stills's friend Peter Tork, once a Village folkie and now a member of the Monkees, the hottest teen sensation since the Beatles. As they took the stage, many in the crowd noticed that the Springfield boasted not one but two new members. On rhythm guitar and slightly hesitant background vocals was a man in a Borsalino hat, who had dominated the Byrds' set the previous day with a series of wired political pronouncements and a frenetic energy that no natural chemistry could have manufactured. His musical contribution to the Springfield was, in truth, minimal and erratic, but as far as his fellow Byrds were concerned, he might as well have torched their collective future. "It put a lot of people uptight," David Crosby conceded a few weeks later, "but it didn't put *me* uptight, and it didn't put Stephen Stills uptight, because we were two musicians, and we wanted to make *music*."

Two weeks after Monterey, Crosby reinforced his new philosophy at the Hullabaloo Club in Hollywood. "We may be breaking some rules tonight," he announced, "but it's about time someone started experimenting. Besides, music shouldn't have any rules." With that, he and Byrds drummer Michael Clarke lined up alongside drummer Buddy Miles and the still Young-free Buffalo Springfield for a chaotic but thrilling fifty minutes filled, Tom Paegel of the *LA Times* reported, with "driving improvisations and vocal combinations." Paegel imagined that he was witnessing the birth-pangs of a revolution, with "musicians working together for fun and for the betterment of pop music. This theme may be a sign of future pop."

Another observer of these machinations was more cynical, though he had a vested interest: Denny Bruce was a roommate of Neil Young. "David Crosby has only one talent," he reflected many years later, "surrounding himself with talented people. He really wanted to be in the Springfield. Even with the success of the Byrds, he knew that Buffalo Springfield were cooler."

> It's a struggle, isn't it, if you've grown up with one of your parents like ... [*he stops himself and pauses*]. I was watching an interview with Ben Kingsley, who was being asked, what sound do you hate the most? And he said: "The sound of a parent barking at a child, over and over again, about something that they don't understand." *That*'ll create fear and anger in a child later on; *that* will re-emerge.
>
> —Stephen Stills

On the back of the first Buffalo Springfield album, where isolated words were thrown together to create a fragmented account of the five participants, was the ambiguous statement: "Steve is the leader, but we all are." Or, as an early teen-mag profile put it, "Steve Stills is the leader—at least, *he* thinks he is."

"I was trying to be Boss Cat and trying to keep the thing in order," Stills told *Rolling Stone* magazine in 1971. "You gotta dig that part of my upbringing in the South was very militaristic. I was in this military school and was being taught how to be an *officer*. That stuff can't help but stick, way down." So the boy grew up to the sound of "a parent barking," and was taught to place himself in the same position over other men. "My father was a sarcastic son of a bitch," he revealed to Jaan Uhelszki in 2013, and that legacy was passed on. Wounded child and dictator: the inevitable balance of that equation was confusion, resentment, and pain.

While David Crosby grew up in Californian comfort, and Graham Nash in Mancunian poverty, Stephen Arthur Stills could not be sure where he stood. Like Crosby's parents, Stills's mother and father parted company when he was in his teens. By then, he had already called a bewildering variety of locations home: Texas, Kentucky, Louisiana, Florida, and various parts of Central America. Equally unsettling was his father's enigmatic approach to business, with its inevitable effects on the family. He seemed to acquire great riches with ease, and then watch each new empire dissolve, almost as if it didn't matter to him. If Crosby's father was a cinematographer, and Nash's an engineer, Stills's was an enigma, snapped for an instant in myriad guises—promoter of big bands, grain dealer, junior corporate executive, designer of "vital war products," property developer, investment banker, construction boss, marina manager, real estate agent, country club operator. By Stills's own accounts, his father was warm and encouraging, or cold and abusive; or perhaps both, his temperament uncertain until he opened his mouth. Likewise, his parents' lack of sobriety: "They drank," he recalled decades later, "drank a lot."

Even his father's identity was difficult to pin down. It was William Arthur Stills who, in July 1938, married Talitha "Ti" Collard in Hendersonville, Virginia. But in later years, legal documents described his "given name" as Otie Stills, or Otis, or sometimes O. T. Stills. He trained as a teacher in Indiana, and set up home in Carmi, and then Metropolis, Illinois, though when his first child, Hannah, was born there in 1941, he was working in Kansas City. His only son emerged in Dallas in January 1945. Seven months later, William was arrested in Houston after an incident with a seventeen-year-old "hotel information girl," whose father had complained to the police. But Stills insisted the charge was "blackmail," and the case was laid to rest after he had spent several days in jail. A Texas newspaper described him as being "reportedly worth a half-million dollars," the equivalent of $7 million today. His fortune had been lost and regained several times by the time the Stills family established itself in Florida in the 1950s.

By 1958, Talitha Stills was prominent enough in Tampa's polite society to be profiled by the local *Tribune*. In keeping with bourgeois America's strict gender roles, Mrs. Otie Stills was lauded for her skills as a homemaker and hostess, who always "retains her gracious manner." The family were the proud owners of a Riviera-style mansion with swimming pool in Beach Park, which they had purchased in 1956 from a retired general. The article hinted at the flavor of their lives: Talitha was a superb cook, made her children's clothes, and was active in a garden circle. She helped out with the Cub Scouts and the local Red Cross.

Her focus was supporting her husband and nurturing her three children—the brood having expanded to include eight-year-old Talitha (nicknamed "Ti" like her mother, though in later years she preferred to be known as "Tai"). While elder sister, Hannah, was portrayed as an artist, who had "already developed her own style," Stephen (a "thirteen-year-old cottontop") was being supported in his musical ambitions. He was "a budding drummer," the journalist recounted. "Stephen's trap drums are set up in the large paneled family room adjacent to the dining room. All the family loves music and enjoys the collection of jazz records Mr. Stills started in college, the rock and roll recordings from the teenagers, and some of the classical works Mrs. Stills loves." Otherwise, "She is quite proud that Stephen has 'grown to the saddle' so much that he is beginning to look like a Westerner." Missing from this effusive celebration of American success was any sense of tension or fear; the fractures in the Stills marriage, the succession of boarding schools that had ejected their mischievous son, or the depression that would encroach on the youngsters' lives.

A year later, the house in Beach Park was gone, and Stephen's parents were embroiled in a series of court cases—accused of failing to keep up payments on mortgages, business loans, and building materials. Otie opened the Tiotie Beach Yacht & Country Club on Lake Wales, but by 1961 it had ceased operations, though the subsequent legal actions shuffled on until 1963. Long before then, Otie had taken the family on their most disorienting journey to date, from gracious upper-middle-class living in the world's leading economy to the political turbulence and cultural dislocation of Central America.

> I went to high school in Spanish. It was the greatest gift my father could have given me. It flipped my mind and opened it.
>
> —Stephen Stills

Most of Stephen Stills's musical identity was in place by the time he reached his teens. "I was influenced by anything with rhythm," he recalled, and his father's collection of jazz records—the Dorsey bands, Kenton, Goodman, and the rest—ensured that syncopation was his second nature. He would pride himself on his "groove," on being "in the pocket," and would bear down on any musical associates who couldn't match up. His education, formal and musical, was erratic, and scattered, and when he was at home, nobody seemed to have minded that he would steal out with a friend in search of rhythmic stimulation. In Florida alone, he claimed to have seen many of the prime movers of rock and roll and rhythm & blues by the time he was thirteen, from Buddy Holly to B.B. King, Muddy Waters, and Howlin' Wolf. "The sheer power," he said in awe at the memory. "To me, that music was as vital as the Impressionist art period, with magnificent things happening wherever you looked."

With his friend Mike Garcia, a crucial couple of years older than Stills and therefore able to drive, he would "chase all over Florida looking for little record stores and old blues records. Then we would drive for days to see some obscure artist play." There were "all these great black showbands playing in fraternity houses" in Gainesville, and he would sit at their feet like a disciple, soaking up experience. "African Americans were my friends," he explained half a century later, "and they taught me everything useful."

The young Stills burned to reproduce those rhythms in his own life. As careless about dates as any rock star, he would later claim to have been drumming when he was eight years old and playing guitar at ten. His grandmother was a church pianist, and Stephen's tuition paid unexpected dividends at Catholic school: "When I finished my lessons, I would pound away at that good old boogie-woogie music at age eleven or twelve. This old priest stuck his head through the door and said, 'Oh, don't you stop, I was just going to remind you not to break the piano.' He used to sit outside reading his prayer book and listen to me play."

The same school added the solemn intensity of Gregorian chants to his imagination, reshaping the memory of the choral music he had heard in church. From the blues he inherited an unearthly, rasping roar; church expanded his vision of what could happen when voices were raised in euphony, polyphony, or counterpoint. With the bluegrass and honky-tonk he'd heard in Kentucky, and the rock and roll pounding out of the family radio when he and his sisters were in control, Stephen Stills had a collision of tempi pounding through his brain.

School supplied a much-needed sense of structure. For a while, he attended a military academy on the waterfront at St. Petersburg, Florida. "I needed the discipline," he admitted. "I loved the drill. It was a relief to have some organization, because my house was always in chaos." For the first time, he could place himself in the middle of a crowd of musicians and create symmetry out of confusion: "I got a sense of construction, of how to put together the different parts of an arrangement, from being in school bands and orchestras."

For a white kid whose brain pulsated to black rhythms, there was only one feasible outlet in late-1950s Florida: joining a rock and roll band. "As soon as I learned a couple of chords from some friends, I took off," Stills remembered. "I started hanging around with a couple of servicemen from MacDill Air Force Base. I played drums in a rock band when I was so young that they had to draw little lines on my face that looked like a moustache, so I could work in a bar. I was about thirteen or fourteen, but I looked like I was eleven." After a few months, he switched from drums to guitar, and joined the Continentals, a schoolboy group put together by an even younger kid, Don Felder. "I moved from acoustic to electric," Stills said, "having borrowed the lead guitar player's instrument so often that I could just start to make a sound. And then, just at the moment when you start to bear down, and get obsessed, and maybe get good, we were off to somewhere they didn't have any electric guitars."

In later years, his time in Central America seemed to congeal in his brain, reflecting a peripatetic lifestyle in which Stills and his family were never quite grounded. "We were primarily in Costa Rica," he said, "but I spent time in Nicaragua, and more time in Panama, with these people who had a finca there. That was when the Pan-American Highway was just a real wide dirt road. It was there that I learned to drive." There he also rode out into the country and met a beautiful young woman on a white horse, a serendipity he romanticized more than thirty years later in song (CSN's "Panama"). Otherwise his adolescent flirtations with romance required strict decorum: "To get a date with a really nice local girl, you had to approach her duenna, her chaperone, after church. It was very formal, very traditional. But at the same time, I had this sense that people were emotional in a way that they hadn't been back home—they'd burst into tears at weddings and funerals, not keep everything tied up inside." And people would dance: across the isthmus of Central America they swayed to rhythms with local names—mambo, pachanga, merengue—which tapped into a sensuality and sly sexuality that even the hottest American jazz bands couldn't touch. The teenage Stills learned enough Spanish to make valiant advances toward young women, and graduate from every class, until his high school life ended in 1963.

Robbed of his apprenticeship in rock and roll, Stills ingested the time signatures of his adopted lands. But, he conceded, "I couldn't play flamenco guitar very well." Instead, from long distance, he immersed himself in the same folk boom to which the young David Crosby had pledged his allegiance. During 1962, his father arranged for him to sit in front of a microphone at the relay station that allowed Costa Ricans to hear state-funded broadcasts from the Voice of America. The first surviving document of "Stephen A. Stills," aspiring musician, was a tape reel that held five songs, four of which—the likes of "Railroad Boy" and "Dark as a Dungeon"—were familiar prey for stars such as Joan Baez and Peter, Paul and Mary. The last was the self-composed "Travelin'." Though it was little more than an amalgam of traditional folk motifs, such as the bear who went over the mountain and the young man who simply had to roam, it was transfigured by its delivery. This was no unskilled child being indulged by an overoptimistic parent, but a fully formed performer. His hands had already mastered the picking style finessed by country star Merle Travis, with the thumb slapping out a rhythm while the fingers sketched out a melody. Equally imposing was his vocal presence: unmistakeably juvenile, yet with a chilling, melancholic authority that dispelled any sense of pastiche. Again there was a distant parallel with the cinematographer's son in California: both Crosby and Stills owned a *voice*, shaped by influences but emblazoned with personalities that they would soon display to the world.

Once Stills had graduated, he left Costa Rica, and his family, behind. He dutifully enrolled at the University of Florida in Gainesville, where he signed up for political science, a passion heightened by his firsthand experience of stumbling across outbursts of civic disorder in Central America. But he was led astray from his studies (after four days, he once boasted) by the lure of music. His old band, the Continentals, was still in town, with two future members of the Eagles (Messrs. Felder and Bernie Leadon) in its ranks. But rather than trying to squeeze out a space alongside them, Stills headed for the city's meager folk clubs, and a one-girl, two-guy combo with the wonderfully prophetic name of the Accidental Trio. Soon he was in New Orleans, which he would later claim as his hometown; and, within months, Greenwich Village, joining the scrum of would-be Huck Finns who imagined that they might follow Bob Dylan from anonymity to stardom.

The kitchen at Gerde's Folk City [was] where Bob Dylan first sang me "Masters of War," and I felt a chill as he sang that was colder than the aluminium sink I was sitting on.

—Judy Collins's liner notes to *Judy Collins #3*, 1964

Folk music might be creeping across the nation like a virus, but unbeknown to its inhabitants, its borders were slowly beginning to close in, like the prison walls in Poe's "The Pit and the Pendulum." "I spent a whole year, shivering in winter, listening to that voice," Stephen Stills recalled of his time in Greenwich Village, and the record that he would hold as a romantic talisman. This woman, with the oval, "cornflower eyes," her eyebrows permanently arched as if betraying her possession of arcane knowledge, entranced him from the start. *Judy Collins #3*, a cult success in the Beatle-infested music scene of 1964, was a tapestry of songs she had borrowed or been taught by her friends, from Dylan to Pete Seeger. Supporting her discreetly was another village folkie called Jim McGuinn, with whom Stills would soon be sharing a barbed acquaintance. The album included two songs, "Turn! Turn! Turn!" and "The Bells of Rhymney," which McGuinn would draw into the repertoire of his electric folk band, the Byrds. As Stills trailed around the dense maze of Village folk dens where Dylan, McGuinn, and Collins had already served their apprenticeships, it must have seemed that the enticing woman with a voice like sparkling ice was almost alongside him but eternally out of reach. He would not meet her for another four years, only then able to admit that he had held her in his mind as a love object since the first time he had stared into those two-dimensional eyes.

Meanwhile, he circled her old haunts. "I spent two years working these funny little basket-houses," Stills recalled in 1971. "There was a stage at one end and all the performers used to sing for each other most of the night. Then, when every once in a while a customer did come in, we would all immediately go quickly through our sets so we all had a chance to pass the hat round. My overnight success was when I got a regular job at the Café Night Owl, at twenty dollars a night, playing behind Freddie Neil or whoever was around." Again, the encroaching circles: Dylan had backed up Fred Neil the same way, and back in Florida, Neil had become a friend-cum-mentor of another young guitarist, David Crosby.

Around the clubs, Stills and a fellow folk immigrant named Peter Thorkelson discovered that they were sometimes mistaken for each other. Inevitably they met, at the Four Winds Café, and as if playing out a scene from a TV sitcom, began to work together, in twos and threes with fellow guitarist John Hopkins.

There followed an entire year, all the longer if you're nineteen or twenty and impatient for success, when Stills subsumed his identity into a showbiz impresario's idea of a folk group. This had its rewards: regular employment, paid at that; a professional recording session; comradeship on the road; lessons in arranging vocal harmonies from Jim Friedman, whom Stills would credit as his mentor; even a network TV cabaret appearance, introduced by Diahann Carroll and Tony Martin, the hosts of *On Broadway Tonight*. "It was hyped up real big," said Richie Furay, another fresh recruit. "This guy who was Stephen's manager put us in this little playhouse and we did a play with some popular folk songs of the day." The Au Go Go Singers sounded like a glee club compared to the barbershop harmonies of Les Baxter's Balladeers. But their solitary album, eagerly titled *They Call Us Au Go-Go Singers*, allowed Stills two minutes in which to masquerade as a lonesome country-blues troubadour, on "High Flyin' Bird." Three thousand miles apart, he and Crosby were following parallel paths, but on timelines that were markedly out of sync.

As Crosby and the Byrds recorded "Mr. Tambourine Man" in Los Angeles, the Au Go Go Singers were resident at the New York coffeehouse from which they took their name. An opening arose for a pared-down version of the group to undertake a brief tour of Canada at the height of winter. To preserve the purity of the mothership, this offshoot was renamed the Company, and as soon as they escaped the watchful eye of their backers, Stills and his fellow runaways jettisoned the tired Au Go Go repertoire and concentrated on playing contemporary hits from the British Invasion. They were booked for three two-week residencies at franchised clubs in different cities, the first of them Fort William in Ontario. There, in one of several encounters that has been recalled so often as to shed all legitimate claim to being remembered, their paths crossed with a local band called the Squires. The latter's repertoire stretched from ragged frat-rock to traditional folk tunes, all played with the same raucous energy and contempt for finesse. The Squires' leader, Neil Young, and Stills recognized kindred spirits, albeit with markedly different aesthetic principles. After two weeks they were separated for almost exactly a year, and Stills returned to Peter Thorkelson in the Village.

It was late-spring 1965, and almost every folkie in town had found himself a band, or at least a bunch of session men prepared to impersonate one in the recording studio. The Byrds broke, Bob Dylan reinvented himself as a pop star, and a *Billboard* reporter announced the arrival of something called "folk-rock." Stephen Stills recognized that this was something he could easily fake himself and scrambled to find some suitable comrades. He briefly thought he had talked his way—as a bass guitarist, despite never having played the instrument—into the Lovin' Spoonful, the group formed by another protégé of Fred Neil, John Sebastian. But the vacancy was closed, and before Stills could map out an alternative route to fame, the Spoonful had joined the Byrds on the national pop charts. Then Thorkelson realized that success could be located on the map of California, and feeling increasingly isolated in the Village, Stills followed suit.

In Los Angeles, Stills hooked up with the remnants of the Shaggy Gorillas Minus One Buffalo Fish, a folk and comedy ensemble reduced to a duo. But the folk scene was now as anachronistic as a hand loom in the era of mechanical reproduction, and Stills yearned to participate in the ecstatic carnival that surrounded the Byrds. He had begun to try his hand as a composer, fixing chords from the Beatles' songbook together and trying to reproduce the slightly cynical romanticism of their latest releases. An encounter with a draft dodger en route to Canada spurred him to write "Four Days Gone," a soulful piano ballad that lamented "government madness" and allowed him to step outside his own post-adolescent melancholy.

Armed with these songs, and the steely self-confidence hidden beneath his overt shyness, Stephen Stills responded to an ad he'd seen in the *Hollywood Reporter*. "Madness!" it promised. "Auditions. Folk & Roll Musicians-Singers for acting roles in new TV series. Running parts for four insane boys, 17–21. Want spirited Ben Frank's types. Have courage to work. Must come down for interview." Stills checked off the requirements: he'd acted at school, hung out at Ben Frank's all-night diner on Sunset among other aspiring stars, could surely outplay and outsing all the competition—and what twenty-year-old kid wasn't acquainted with madness?

So he joined approximately four hundred hopefuls, waiting in line to meet the founders of Raybert Productions, who had conceived a television sitcom about a fictional pop band provisionally entitled *The Monkeys*.

Bob Rafelson, who conducted the auditions, recalled two years later that, "There was one guy, Steve Stills, whom I liked enormously.

Unfortunately, he wasn't quite right, but he had musical intelligence, and I went so far as to ring him up and ask him along again. When he realized he wasn't going to make it, he suggested I get in touch with somebody he knew, a certain Peter Thorkelson." Renamed Peter Tork, Stills's Village buddy adopted the TV role of banjo-playing loon—an extension of the madcap comedy routines that folk audiences had already witnessed.

In retrospect, Stills was adamant that he had never wanted to act in the series; he merely wanted an outlet for his songs, and was disappointed that Raybert had already commissioned material from the likes of Carole King and Gerry Goffin. In 1967, when Stills was still unknown in England and the appetite for Monkees gossip was desperate, there were frequent references in the press to an applicant who "although good, had not been endowed with a very photogenic set of teeth." Stills's heavily recessed front tooth was not the stuff of Hollywood fantasy, although it could surely have been corrected if Raybert had been desperate to recruit him. The most likely story is that Stills would have snapped up the job if it had been offered, especially as another recruit, Michael Nesmith, quickly managed to bypass the prohibition on the Monkees contributing their own songs. But Raybert may well have recognized that loading their "insane" TV pop group with two men born in Texas, both of whom took their musical careers very seriously, might have undercut their series' comic potential. At heart, Tork was an entertainer, but Stills was a craftsman, for whom ridicule triggered uncomfortable memories that stretched back to the cradle.

This fleeting encounter encouraged Stills to cast around for other avenues of escape. He began to envisage himself as the creative hub of a rock and roll band; all he needed was disciples. He wrote to Neil Young in Canada, and received a note back from his mother, explaining that her boy had traveled down to New York to make it as a folk singer, and left no forwarding address. An aspiring music publisher named John A. Daley heard Stills play, and offered him a deal, cash in hand. He eagerly signed contracts promising to deliver songs such as "You Got It Wrong, You Can't Love," "Break Up Easy," and "I See Another Man," five in total, for which he pocketed $125—and then walked away, only being reminded of his legal commitments when Daley sued for $180,000 five years later.

In the fervid, compressed music scene of Hollywood in 1965, Stills could hardly avoid stumbling into interesting company. Late in 1965, he met Frank Zappa, leader of an ensemble named the Mothers of Invention. Zappa read him the lyrics of the Mothers' latest song, "Who Are the Brain Police?," which depicted a psyche, and a society, melting into madness. Stills also encountered Van Dyke Parks during his brief term as a member of the Mothers. Parks had been a child prodigy as a musician and actor, who had lived through the folk craze and was now playing sessions for anyone who asked with sufficient grace. Fiercely intelligent, given to talking in dense, glittering metaphors, Parks would soon make the fateful decision to collaborate with Brian Wilson of the Beach Boys. (He also played keyboards on the Byrds' *Fifth Dimension*, turning down David Crosby's invitation to join the band permanently.) Meanwhile, he was attempting to bring musical imagination and a sense of culture to Los Angeles rock and roll, and had concocted an orchestral folk-rock arrangement of the "Song of Joy" from Beethoven's final symphony, retitled "Number Nine."

To prepare for its release, Parks assembled a band capable of handling "a combination of rhythm and blues, rock and roll, harpsichord, vibraphone and jingle bells." Stills volunteered, alongside another experienced folkie, Steve Young. As the Van Dyke Parks, they supported the Lovin' Spoonful at one uproarious show in the State Fairgrounds in Phoenix, Arizona. "I played one gig, for screaming teenyboppers," Stills recalled, "and there I was, an impressionable twenty-one, and was smitten with the bug." That night he discovered that the more he moved onstage, the more young girls screamed; "they almost went wiggy," wrote an intrepid reporter from the *Arizona Republic*. Besides their revolutionary take on Beethoven, the Van Dyke Parks tackled recent R&B hits such as "Dancing in the Street," as rearranged by Stills. The journalist captured Stephen Stills's earliest philosophizing about the purpose of his musical career: "We write most of our own [songs]. And if it's someone else's, we do our own arrangement of it. But if it's not your own, it can't possibly put your own message across, and if it can't say what you want said, why do it at all?"

I have to write songs. There's something inside me I've got to get out. Music is the best way I know.

—Neil Young

Scott Young was a familiar name in Winnipeg, Canada, his words eagerly awaited by sports fans in the pages of the local newspaper. He was well respected among the community he reported, and several local luminaries from the sporting world attended his stag party in June 1940. His bride was Edna Ragland, daughter of prominent businessman William N. Ragland. She was a student actor, locally ranked tennis player, and denizen of the Winnipeg Canoe Club, who came from sufficient stock to ensure that her family's travels were dutifully chronicled in the society columns of the *Winnipeg Tribune.* The paper noted their regular summer retreat to William's place up on Falcon Lake, which his grandson would later commemorate in song. Edna's marriage was documented with the meticulous eye for detail usually reserved for a baseball game: the guests at her two pre-wedding celebrations, a week apart; the precise makeup of the floral arrangements in Crescent Fort Rouge United Church; every stitch and seam of her bridal dress and trousseau; and finally, the couple's honeymoon at Lake on the Woods, straddling the Canadian-US border.

Four months after the wedding, the family was uprooted to Toronto, where Scott Young had been recruited as sports correspondent for the nation's largest press agency, the Canadian Press. Now his reportage would be read across the country, lending him celebrity status in the era before television relegated the importance of the printed page. He would occasionally stray outside the field of sporting combat; when a bunch of German prisoners of war escaped from a camp in Heron Bay, Young was assigned to follow the story, which ran and ran (as did the POWs). But his byline would usually be found above game reports or insider sports gossip of unimpeachable repute, Young being trusted as much by hockey players, golfers, and football stars as by his loyal readers.

Two events in 1942 interrupted this comfortable schedule. In April, Edna gave birth to a son, Robert Ragland Young. Within six months, Scott Young volunteered for exceptional duty overseas, leaving the rink and the gridiron for the perilous role of wartime correspondent in London. Edna and young Bob returned to her parents in Winnipeg. Meanwhile, Scott endured the privation of bombing raids and rationing, in his pursuit of stories about the heroic exploits of Canadian servicemen in the front line.

His twelve-month tour of duty over, he returned to Toronto, and his family, in October 1943. Any sense of normality was short-lived: the following March he signed up for the public relations arm of the Royal Canadian Navy. By April, he had headed east to a secret location, and Edna and her son made the familiar journey back to the Ragland home. Scott vanished wherever the navy wanted him, which by late summer 1944 meant joining Canadian troops landing in France to consolidate the advances made on D-day. And then, in December, he was home, Edna and Bob rejoined him; and within three months, she was pregnant again. Her second son, Neil Percival Young, was born on November 12, 1945. He would grow up accustomed to his father leaving home on assignment, and occasionally for less professional reasons.

For a man whose artistic manifesto favored spontaneity over planning and embodied a scorched-earth attitude toward the past, Neil Young would become obsessive about preserving, sorting, and chronicling his life — almost as if it was the only way in which he could make sense of it. In addition, something about Young's work and personality has persuaded many outsiders to immerse themselves in the minutiae of his creative life. The result is that almost every step has now been documented in sometimes excruciating detail: concert by concert, note by note, every artistic whim, abrupt shift of direction and fiery illumination of genius traced, reported, and analyzed. It is as if the painstaking archaeology of his disciples has freed Young to conduct himself without fear of the future or conscious burden of the past, secure in the knowledge that someone else will always unearth the hidden meaning of a career that has often seemed willful and disjointed, despite its brilliance.

From his father, young Neil learned the value of discipline and perseverance for a writer, the magical power of celebrity (reinforced when his mother later became a TV star on a weekly quiz show), and the more dubious lesson that a man can always remove himself from a situation that has become unpleasant or humdrum. He was also given an early education in the vagaries of fate, when he was stricken with polio in the epidemic that swept through Canada in 1951. And throughout his childhood, he was well acquainted with change, his parents shifting town every two or three years until the frail bonds of their marriage came untied, and Scott told his sons that he was leaving home. Neil provided a capsule history of his youth in his song "Don't Be Denied," addressed to an anonymous "friend of mine," but more likely aimed at the man he saw in the mirror.

There were other principles to be gathered from his father's career: that a man should always change to avoid becoming typecast; and, therefore, that it did one's audience—readership, in Scott Young's case—no harm to be shocked or surprised. That was how Scott ended up writing controversial articles on subjects such as abortion, years before the practice was legalized in Canada, or outraging royalists in England by daring to portray the reigning monarch, King George VI, in a short story he wrote for the *Saturday Evening Post*. (It was "a cheap and nasty insult," a London paper complained.) One minute he was penning radio plays; the next, dramatic novels set in Canadian cities, or short stories for *Ladies' Home Journal*, or whimsical columns about family life; and, through it all, truest to his heart, the sports journalism that was his trademark, and which came to him more naturally than anything else.

The young Neil inhaled his father's freedom and his mother's sense of yearning and disappointment and refashioned them for his own personal and professional use. But he also echoed Stephen Stills in his passion for music—rock and roll, especially the guitar instrumentals of the Shadows; rhythm & blues, as discovered on late-night radio stations; and the trusty tales of Americana, the folk and country heritage available to anyone in North America at the turn of a radio dial.

Like millions of other kids, he dreamed of being in a band; like thousands, he tried to make it work; and like few others, he persevered for years with an ever-shifting cast of characters and an array of band names, from church dances, high schools, and glee clubs in Winnipeg to occasional forays into the Fourth Dimension club in Fort William, Ontario. His most enduring combo was the Squires, with whom he discovered a guitar sound, heavy on reverb; an ability to craft songs that were almost like those on the radio, except with an individual twist that annoyed most listeners but enthralled a few; and a singing voice that was anything but orthodox yet expressed the way he felt with the same individuality displayed by mavericks such as Bob Dylan.

But small clubs and school halls in Canada could only take Young so far, and as he approached his twentieth birthday, he searched around for a viable route into the future. As with Stephen Stills, the destination was more important than the journey; which is how at one moment Young might be attempting to keep alive the spirit of the Squires; at the next, channeling the spirit of Jimmy Reed on some purposefully banal blues tunes with an old school friend; or sneaking across the US border without a passport, to audition as a soloist at Elektra Records.

On December 15, 1965, he taped a series of one-man demos for the folk label that already boasted Stills's female icon, Judy Collins, and his guitar mentor, Fred Neil, among its roster. The seven songs he unveiled that afternoon included "Sugar Mountain," a boyish lament about old age (written when he passed twenty) that would endure in his concert repertoire for decades, and "Nowadays Clancy Can't Even Sing," the first of a long series of enigmatic lyrics that painted all around a subject without ever quite revealing their focus. But any gleam of promise was disguised by Young's uniformly dull guitar playing—every piece set to the same plodding strum—and the banality of his other material: mock-poetic, undoubtedly Dylanesque, but entirely lacking in insight or cohesion. Elektra let him down gently.

Yet at the moment when he was seeking solo recognition, Young was also signing up for an adventure in which he was guaranteed merely a supporting role. James Johnson Jr. enlisted in the US Navy in his mid-teens but fled to avoid Vietnam. He took the customary draft-dodger road to Canada, where he founded an R&B group with the ironic name of the Sailor Boys. To camouflage his identity and legal status, Johnson disguised himself as Ricky James Matthews—and then effectively subverted his attempts at secrecy by forming another band known as the Mynah Birds (after a Toronto café) in which he was the only black member.

His sidekick in the band was "a superbad bass player named Bruce Palmer," who numbered among his acquaintances Neil Young. Memories of this period were murky and contradictory, but around the end of 1965, the Mynah Birds found themselves a man short, with the prospect of an audition at Motown Records in Detroit on the horizon.

Matthews's stew of contemporary R&B and Rolling Stones–inspired garage rock might have been designed to intrigue at least one of Neil Young's musical personalities. But in keeping with his rebranding as a folkie soloist, Young had just swapped his electric guitar for an acoustic twelve-string. Matthews wasn't daunted; Young might be able to add some folk-rock mystique to the band's style. In mid-January 1966, the Mynah Birds drove to Detroit, where they laid out their repertoire for Motown's staff producers. The professionals helped to tailor Matthews's songs into acceptable shape, and after three days of sessions, a single was created, entitled "It's My Time." Young added only a distant acoustic guitar, and any chance to expand his role was thwarted when Motown discovered that Matthews was a fugitive from military justice. He was persuaded to turn himself in, on the promise of a future Motown deal. While he moldered for a year in a navy brig off Brooklyn, the white Mynah Birds flocked back to Canada.

Their paths would soon collide with another bunch of young hopefuls. Richie Furay, his prospects of folk stardom squashed by the collapse of the Au Go Go Singers and the Company, was now reduced to working in a factory in Massachusetts. Early in 1966, he wrote to his distant friend Stephen Stills. To his surprise, he received a phone call from California. Stills gushed down the wire that he had just formed a folk-rock band and that Furay was the vital missing ingredient. Furay packed up and flew out to California, to be greeted by an exuberant Stills and the news that his combo was now a duo. "We started shooting folk songs we had written at each other," Furay recalled. The pair set themselves up in a one-room apartment on Fountain Avenue, four blocks down from Sunset Boulevard, and waited for fate to intervene.

Meanwhile, Neil Young and Bruce Palmer set out from Toronto on an erratic course southwest, which would lead them across the US border—with the customary Canadian explanation that they were merely taking the long cut to British Columbia on superior American roads (US customs officials always approved). Mishaps and delays perfectly timed their arrival in Hollywood to coincide—in an accident that would surely make the perfect opening for the screenplay of *The Buffalo Springfield Story*—with Stills and Furay heading along Sunset in the opposite direction. Precisely who recognized whom is lost in the endless retelling of this story, although Young made identification easier by driving a hearse. "Neil came over to the apartment that night, and he brought Bruce Palmer with him," Richie Furay recalled.

"Everything happened fast for us," Furay remembered with awe. "One day, Stephen and I are sitting around in a little apartment, writing songs; the next we're playing for fifty people at the Whisky. Three weeks later, we have people lined up around the block to see us, including all these record company presidents." In Young, Stills, Palmer, and Furay, they had the makings of a band, minus a drummer. Barry Friedman, who worked at the Troubadour and was an early booster, put them together with Dewey Martin, an outspoken would-be R&B singer with more professional experience than the other four combined. Martin tipped the balance in favor of Canada, three members to two, and ensured that four of this putative band now believed they could be the front man. Only the enigmatic Bruce Palmer (accurately portrayed on their first album cover as "inscrutable" and "the unknown factor") was content to lurk in the shadows.

Friedman's informal network ensured that the five men rented two adjoining rooms in a beat-up Hollywood motel, which boasted an empty lounge that now doubled as a rehearsal studio. Within a few days, the quintet (still unnamed) was offered an unbilled set at the Troubadour. At which point someone saw a steamroller, somewhere, which carried on its side the brand of the Buffalo-Springfield Roller Company. The sign was discreetly purloined, and Buffalo Springfield were born. Van Dyke Parks always insisted that he had christened the band, while others assumed Friedman was responsible. Assorted variants of the tale appeared in interviews and press releases ever afterward, although two ingredients remained constant: there had been a steamroller, and there was now a band.

Four days after the Troubadour show, and with just a handful of songs to their name, they were on a brief California jaunt, opening for the Byrds; then a run of local high schools, to check their teen appeal;

and finally, just a month into their collective career, they were resident at the Whisky for six weeks, and such a hot folk-rock property that they required careful supervision. Instead, they found a couple of managers.

> I had seen these two way-out record producers riding around in their long limousine, one of them skinny and quiet, the other one with a beard and a carload of enthusiasm. They were just right for us.
>
> —Stephen Stills, 1966

Blame Tom Wolfe, whose 1965 profile of Phil Spector ("The First Tycoon of Teen") in the *New York Herald Tribune* created the myth of the modern pop starmaker. Thereafter every entrepreneur worthy of the name needed a gimmick, a style, a presence that would cast their clients into the shadows. Charlie Greene and Brian Stone did not disappoint. Having set their mark by manufacturing unlikely stars—not to mention proto-hippie icons—out of Sonny and Cher, they were happy to bask in their own self-styled charisma. The details mounted up: matching limos, each equipped with a TV, a desk, and a bar; antelope tuxes; an office on Sunset, peopled by girls in waist-high miniskirts. No wonder that they were being cited as "Hollywood's hit purveyors of the mod mystique and trog cult."

Greene and Stone moved in on Buffalo Springfield like cheetahs. No matter that Stephen Stills and Richie Furay had just signed a management contract with Barry Friedman; the predators nudged him aside and began to talk about sums of money that sounded incredible for an unsigned band. On June 8, 1966, they procured the requisite signatures on a contract that would give them not only the customary 25 percent of the band's earnings, but also 75 percent ownership of the publishing company they intended to form for the band. Later that week, they approached Atlantic Records, to whom they had shopped Sonny and Cher eighteen months earlier. Label boss Ahmet Ertegun flew back from Mexico City to see the Springfield at the Whisky. "I was completely blown away," he recalled. "The talent in that band was obvious, from the first time I saw them. And I couldn't resist Stephen Stills. He reminded me of Bobby

Darin, who I had signed about ten years earlier. The great thing about Bobby was that he probably had a better sense of time than almost anyone I ever worked with. He was always swinging. And Stephen was like that, too. Bobby would not play second fiddle to anybody. He basically had to be in the driver's seat. And I recognized the same thing in Stephen."

Greene and Stone had given the band a $5,000 advance on signing the management deal; now they recouped immediately, as Atlantic not only splashed out on the band, but paid the canny managers $12,000 for half their share of the Springfield's publishing. The two entrepreneurs proceeded to sell themselves with the same vigor that they were applying to their new clients. They even claimed to have been responsible for finding the legendary steamroller sign and then seeking a group to fit the brand. As Charlie Greene noted, "Money is now no problem. We have it. What counts now is achievement."

First came publicity. The hand of a Hollywood agent could be detected when the press were informed that Dean Martin's daughter, Deana, had heard the Springfield on the radio, and phoned their "manager," one Steve Stills, to request that they play her eighteenth-birthday party. "Steve asked her for a date," this unlikely tale continued, "but specified it had to be in the morning because he's busy all the rest of the time. Now he's showing up at the Holmby Hills home of the Martins to pick up Deana and they go for horseback rides." Two objectives achieved: publicity for the Springfield, on the back of the Rat Pack, and a timely boost for a teenage girl who was about to launch her own singing career. Nothing more was heard of the Stills-Martin liaison.

"Everyone in the music industry these days seems to be talking about a new group, Buffalo Springfield," an influential teen magazine claimed four months into their career. Peter Noone, the toothy heartthrob who fronted chart sensations Herman's Hermits, did his best to sell the Springfield to British fans ("They're fantastic . . . going to be really big"). As Richie Furay remembered, "We were told from the very first time we performed that we were going to be the biggest thing that ever happened. And we believed it." Only in retrospect could Furay recognize that "there were so many vultures around us that were trying to lead us this way or that way. It was really difficult for us."

None of that difficulty was apparent when the band performed live. Like the Beatles, who were adamant that they never sounded as good as when they were unknowns in Hamburg, the Springfield launched from a peak. Their sets combined original material, contributed almost entirely by Stills and Young, with raucous covers of R&B hits such as "In the Midnight Hour" and "Keep On Pushing." Their "gimmick," at a time when pop guitarists restricted themselves to an interruption between verses, was the guitar reciprocity between Young (ostensibly the band's lead instrumentalist) and Stills. Their interplay would almost always be described in terms of combat—duels, battles, wars—but the protagonists shrugged off this interpretation, preferring to see it as a conversation. As Stills recalled, "We developed that thing where, after each of us has gone nuts, one of us will pick up a little phrase we learned from Jimmy Reed, or Chuck Berry, or Keith Richards—the masters, in other words—and the other guy plays exactly the same thing. It was never that sense of competition that everybody made it out to be."

Sadly, as with the Beatles, the ecstatic catharsis of the band's live performances was never captured professionally on tape, although early in their career they did briefly explore the outer limits of melodic expression in the recording studio. "Buffalo Stomp (Raga)" pushed the Byrds' post-Coltrane modal explorations into the realm of the avant-garde, over a single unwavering chord. As Stills flirted with the melody of the Beatles' "If I Needed Someone," Young pushed out beyond key signatures with a reckless, joyful lack of concern. It was as if the band had been allowed a preview of the Velvet Underground performing "Run Run Run"—which is possible, as VU acetates had been given to the Springfield's label many months earlier. (Meanwhile, David Crosby and Graham Nash had seen the Velvet Underground perform with their Exploding Plastic Inevitable revue at the Trip on Sunset Strip in May 1966.) Onstage, the Springfield would extend this free-form extravagance, Stills never quite leaving the harmonic terrain of the blues, Young content to offer atonal shards of guitar noise.

Nothing like this ever came close to appearing on Buffalo Springfield's albums. Having imbibed their own publicity too deeply, Greene and Stone now viewed themselves as record producers, with the result that the band's early singles and debut LP were rickety wooden frames, ready to be fleshed out by someone who understood how to build a wall of sound.

The Springfield themselves were too engrossed in internal politics to notice, at least until it was too late. The war that many observers claimed to witness onstage was actually enacted in the studio—quietly, but with demoralizing consequences. When the band's three avowed composers entered Gold Star Studios in Hollywood to show off their wares, Richie Furay had to take a minor role compared to Stills, George against the latter's John-and-Paul. Meanwhile, Young offered up his own composi- tions, with Stills and Furay chiming supportively behind him.

To Stills's fury, Young's "Nowadays Clancy Can't Even Sing" was ear- marked as the band's first single. To Young's horror, his voice was declared uncommercial by Greene and Stone, and Richie Furay was schooled to imitate the composer's phrasing, but not his whine. The same substitution was maintained during the album sessions, although Young was permitted to chant two songs that Furay simply lacked the vocal menace to handle. As a sign that their producer-managers didn't fully understand what they were doing, one of those Young cameos, "Burned," was chosen as their second release. Whether or not he could sing, the Springfield were being presented as Neil Young's band.

In terms of orthodox song construction, of reflecting the scene around him, Stephen Stills was by far the most commercial composer of the three. His songs added the slightest tinge of folk and country to the pop melodicism of Lennon and McCartney, and echoed the romantic irony the Beatles had displayed on their *Rubber Soul* album.

In keeping with his public image, Young's material was more myste- rious and melancholy. The first lengthy press profile of the Springfield painted Stills as loud and extroverted; Young as "Sensitive, poetic and extremely nonviolent, because 'I used to get beat up a lot when I was a kid.'" The first two of those qualities were evident in his songs, couched in a mood of gentle desolation. He might be inaudible on the band's first single, bar the keening voice of his harmonica, but his soulfulness could not be masked. On their second, he cried out incoherent words of despair ("burned . . . flashed") as if he were speaking a secret teen language. Stills, meanwhile, was approaching his lovers with medieval courtesy, as the title of "Sit Down, I Think I Love You" illustrated. Young's songs were urgent, compelling, oppressive; as yet, Stills's work was merely melodic, well-crafted, and eager to impress, shining where Young's clouded any possibility of romantic fulfilment. But, crucially, Young's songs did not sell.

PROTEST! Police mistreatment of youth on Sunset Blvd.

In front of PANDORA's BOX, 8118 Sunset Strip.

Youth will not be pushed off the Sunset Strip!!! Police must stop being the pawns of unscrupulous real estate interests!!

NO MORE shackling of 14 & 15 yr olds; arbitrary arrests of youths; disrespect and abuse of youths by police.

—Leaflet handed out to kids in Hollywood, November 1966

The Sunset Strip in West Hollywood was the playground of movie stars and socialites, a gallery of flashing neon, deluxe convertibles, and celebrities who lived out their hedonistic fantasies in front of photographers and gawking onlookers. Then in 1965 the Byrds took up residence at Ciro's, where the menu's Early Bird Special was rechristened to celebrate the quaintly spelled guests. Other venues shifted their focus teen-ward, and a street once synonymous with adult sophistication was now filled with underage admirers of youthful rebellion.

The city fathers regarded this development with distaste and collaborated with the local police department to banish these low-spending, high-maintenance, provocatively clad kids from the Strip. Several venues had their permits to admit customers under the age of twenty-one withdrawn; others were forced to insist that no one under eighteen could be admitted to dance, let alone drink, unless accompanied by a responsible adult. The final stage in the forced rebranding of this entertainment paradise was the introduction in early November 1966 of a ten o'clock curfew for those unwanted teenagers.

On the eleventh of that month, the first disobedient teens gathered in protest but were quickly dispersed. A more organized rally was planned the next night, outside Pandora's Box, one of the clubs crippled by the curfew. Every weekend into early December, rival lines of riot police and righteous teenagers glared, sparred, and jostled with each other. The youngest of those who had ignored the 10:00 p.m. deadline were carted away in cuffs, while their peers marched with picket signs, blew bubbles in the faces of their enemy, or simply offered them flowers. As the *Los Angeles Free Press* noted, "The enormous crowds that have gathered around Pandora's Box to demonstrate, to agitate and to spectate are a powder keg. If this powder keg is ignored, if its nature is over-simplified, it may well explode." For Hollywood teenagers, either too young or too privileged to be serving in Vietnam, the skirmishes on the Strip provided a gentle introduction to repression and the politics of generational divide.

Not everyone in the wider pop community shared this sense of outrage. A few days after the first of what were soon branded "Riots on Sunset Strip," Frank Zappa composed and recorded a song that simultaneously accused the CIA of infiltrating Hollywood's privileged neighborhoods and dismissed the marchers and their friends as "a vast quantity of plastic people." But the "riots" drew musicians and actors alike to witness, and in some cases join, the protests. David Crosby, Peter Fonda, and Jack Nicholson went down the first weekend with cameras; Crosby watched from an amused distance while Fonda threw himself into the crowd and was promptly arrested.

Crosby now moved easily among Hollywood's young lions, artists, and radical fashion designers, and Fonda shared his lifelong passion for sailing. (Fonda had also just finished making the movie *The Wild Angels* with director Roger Corman—who regularly employed Crosby's father, Floyd, as a cinematographer.) Such elite company was still only visible from a distance by Buffalo Springfield, who were in San Francisco when Fonda was arrested. But two weeks later they were back at their spiritual home, the Whisky. Their Saturday-night show on November 26 featured a reunion between Stills and Peter Tork, who briefly joined the band onstage for an a cappella rendition of a kid's song written by his brothers, "Alvin the Alligator." Then Stills drove a few blocks over to Pandora's Box: "I went down to see what it was about—or drove past it, actually," he explained a few weeks later. With several decades' further hindsight, he recalled: "I'd been working on [a song], a shout-out to the guys on the line in Vietnam. Then I came upon this stupid situation on Sunset Boulevard. I turned the car around and went back to my house and finished the song in the time it took me to write down the lyrics."

As his lifestyle became more erratic in the 1970s, Stills would sometimes claim that this song, given the semi-ironic title "For What It's Worth," had nothing to do with Sunset Strip—that it was solely about Vietnam, or maybe about some revolution that he believed he had seen firsthand, bullets flying around his head, as a kid in Central America. Sometimes he even boasted that he'd written it in 1964. But nobody in Los Angeles at the time believed for an instant that Stills was writing about anything other than their very own riots, which petered out before Christmas 1966.

By then, the Springfield had recorded Stills's song, hooked around a bass line, guitar harmonics from Young that rang like a ship's bell, and a chorus so wonderfully vague in its disgust and unease that it could be transferred from protest to protest down the decades without a word being changed. Yet for all its timeless universality, "For What It's Worth" was less a plea for action than a disconsolate request for a generation to notice what was happening beyond its psychedelic bubble. Stills was a reporter, not a participant, and even those on the barricades were nothing more than "children," crying "hooray for our side." In the end, the fear was not injustice, or violence, or repression, but the very act of being afraid; the paranoia that the man might "come and take you away," rather than the man itself.

Further afield, "For What It's Worth" served as a beacon for those alarmed by the war in Vietnam, protestors and soldiers alike; and its gentle humanity, embodied by Stills's expertly controlled vocal performance, ensured that it fit into all-hit radio alongside the likes of "Penny Lane," "Happy Together," and "Dedicated to the One I Love." It proved to be an unrepeatable achievement for the Springfield, combining utter simplicity with a political resonance that would endure beyond the lifetime of the band.

For three glorious weeks in spring 1967, Stills could bask in the pleasure of seeing two of his compositions in the national Top 40 chart, as the Springfield were joined by Van Dyke Parks's genteel, baroque arrangement of "Sit Down, I Think I Love You" for the Mojo Men. It may be no coincidence that this was exactly when Neil Young's commitment to the Springfield began to waver, leaving Stills's fresh dominance unchallenged.

As his songwriting suggested, Young regarded the pressures of fame with the same ambiguity that a cat greets a plate of vegetables. Success was fine; being constantly under scrutiny and under obligation was much less comfortable. "Neil flipped out in the Whisky, and so did I, and so did Bruce," Stills recalled, "because there were all these chicks hanging out and feeding us more and better dope." Young had begun to suffer from epileptic fits, and soon he would recognize the link between his seizures and psychological pressure. Then another discovery: to prevail in a confrontation, he could suggest to his bandmates that he was about to lose control. And that in turn seemed to enable him to keep the fits at bay.

Meanwhile, even the least acute observer of the backstage relationship between Stills and Young could register the tension. Dewey Martin was both acute and an unwilling referee: "They were both egomaniacs. There was always a fight—over who played what solo and how long it would be. We were playing somewhere down in Orange County, and they came off the stage and started fighting, and it was like two old ladies going at each other. I had to get between the two of them and pull them apart." Stories like this accumulated, with a variety of weapons—chairs, guitars, sometimes simply fists—but always with the same protagonists, and the same inconclusive outcome. (One exception was the Springfield's first night in New York, where Bruce Palmer turned up his bass to the point that it exacerbated Stills's congenital hearing problem. Stills asked him to turn down, and Palmer "slapped me across the face. So I went completely purple with rage and put him through the drums.")

With *Johnny Carson* and Monterey looming, one of the Springfield's two creative linchpins suddenly vanished. There were multiple reasons why Neil Young might have abandoned the band on the verge of recognizable success: fear, boredom, physical and psychological insecurity, resentment at being outflanked by Stills, ultimately a refusal to play the game when the game got serious. For the moment, Buffalo Springfield survived; but, not for the last time, Young's passive withdrawal placed him in a position of power, leaving Stills behind him to pick up the pieces and somehow carry on. Meanwhile, Young watched from a distance, waiting for the right moment to return.

CHAPTER 3

Berkeley political activists are going to join San Francisco's hippies in a love feast that will, hopefully, wipe out the last remnants of mutual scepticism and suspicion. So they're going to stand up together in what both hope to be a new and strong harmony.

—Radical newspaper *Berkeley Barb*, January 1967

It was time to cast off divisions, gather forces, and lay foundations for a new society. The radical lion would embrace the psychedelic dove; street fighters would commune with poets; iconoclasts become seekers of eternal truths. The hordes in San Francisco's Golden Gate Park on January 14, 1967, were a Gathering of the Tribes, a Human Be-In, in which everyone who sought a revolution of the body or mind could recognize and embody their true selves. "Welcome to the first manifestation of the Brave New World," said the master of ceremonies.

Speaker after speaker set out utopian visions. Acid guru Timothy Leary unveiled his manifesto: "Turn onto the scene; tune into what is happening; and drop out." Antiwar activist Jerry Rubin called for rebellion against the conflict in Vietnam. The Grateful Dead and Jefferson Airplane let loose their fantasies in music that knew no boundaries. Psychedelic adventurer Dick Alpert dreamed aloud the turned-on, tuned-in future: "In about seven or eight years, the psychedelic population of the United States will be able to vote anybody into office they want to. Imagine what it would be like to have anybody in high political office with our understanding of the universe."

Beyond the borders of San Francisco, the Mobilization peace activists confronted the draft system that clouded the future of every young

American male. Almost two years shy of the presidential election, leading figures in Lyndon Johnson's own party were clearing open ground to the left of their embattled leader. Senator Eugene McCarthy was the first to speak out unashamedly against the war in February 1967, followed by civil rights activist Martin Luther King Jr. By early March, Robert Kennedy, brother of the late president, was calling for immediate peace talks and a cessation of US bombing raids.

Fantasy was redrawing reality, or so it seemed to the young. True, there were reverses: despite the "riots," and Buffalo Springfield's hit record, the disputed haunts of Sunset Strip were being demolished or closed to teenagers. The Trip, for example, rebranded itself the New Crescendo, substituting a Latin dance group for its hippie rock bands. But who cared about The Trip when the trip was becoming a universal experience? There was a brief moment, in the early months of 1967, when LSD—acid, instant expansion of the mind—was freely available on certain streets in California and New York, and (as yet) perfectly legal. No wonder that the drug's self-styled prophet, Timothy Leary, was the sage of the moment.

Creativity and expansion of the consciousness were synonymous in this new Shangri-la. David Crosby offered his services as a guide: "The inside of your head is a gigantic spaceship, and we are blinded babies walking around pulling switches, trying to find out how to turn on the light. The switch is there, the capability is there. You could be a full telepathic. You could surpass this whole plane and flick to a whole other thing instantly, if you knew how to do it! Anybody could do it if they found the controls, and the controls are in your head. So: get high and look. Play around and find out what you can do, 'cos you can do a lot more than you think you can."

How did this multidimensional understanding manifest itself? "Rock and roll groups have to use telepathic messages or else they can't play really good music," Crosby explained. "You get up to about a seventy percent level with just sheer technique, but to play the really magic stuff you have to be in rapport with the other cats. You've got to know exactly what is happening on levels that are nonverbal. You've got to be linked to the other people." Without that telepathy among the Byrds, "we're shitty," he admitted. "You can fuck us up with a bad sound system, a bad audience, or by putting us through bad scenes before we get there." Or, he warned prophetically, "it can happen by one of us, or two of us, or three of us, or all four of us getting our egos involved and forgetting that we love each other, and that we're all the same person and that it's cool. We love each other. When we remember *that*, we play. When we don't, we make noise."

All too often in 1967, Crosby's message seemed to be ignored. Possibly their most vocal fan, Derek Taylor, reported dejectedly that summer: "The Byrds, one of the best groups in the world, were again terrible in the Whisky here. I cannot work it out. They seem to have a death-wish which is only thwarted by their indomitable heartbeat. I love them and deplore them."

Yet on record, the Byrds' output was virtually flawless. Their February 1967 album *Younger Than Yesterday* demonstrated a power shift within the group, as Crosby and bassist Chris Hillman supplanted Roger McGuinn as the prime creative force. Hillman's songs, like those of Stephen Stills across town, were masterful interpretations of current pop styles; Crosby's, by comparison, hinted at that fifth dimension heralded on the previous Byrds LP. While his portrait of the "Renaissance Fair" floated and soared with psychedelic majesty, "Mind Gardens" cast off orthodox song structure with melodramatic swagger, as Crosby intoned a portentous, slightly clumsy metaphorical poem over a tangle of electric twelve-string guitars, some woven into the mix backward to heighten the sense of stoned surrealism. So fertile was Crosby's imagination at this point that he and the Byrds could afford to discard, and then apparently forget, arguably the most beautiful song he had yet composed, "It Happens Each Day." He recorded a blueprint for the song, multitracking his own harmony vocals for the first time and approaching a wary romantic encounter with imagery that was both eerie and transcendent.

Better still was to come. From spring into early summer, he labored to perfect the song that would become his first Byrds A side, "Lady Friend." His bandmates were unenthusiastic, especially when Crosby stripped out their vocals and substituted several layers of his own voice. At the last moment, he added a chorus of trumpets, soaring over the ecstatic guitar riff like an angel choir. It was a thrilling, remarkable record, a triumph of solitary inspiration, and the pinnacle of his work with the Byrds. But it didn't sell, with the result that Crosby himself came to believe that it was an artistic failure, rather than one of the finest records of this or any other year.

I'm cheesed off with everything at the moment. I find it hard to live my life the way I want to.

—Graham Nash, January 1967

Crosby's collision of creative discovery and commercial disenchantment was suffered by several of his friends that year, as artistic innovation, aided by chemical and herbal stimulation, outpaced the ability of the public to understand exactly what was going on.

The Hollies began the year at a peak of popularity, having established themselves in America with the banal but irresistible "Bus Stop." But his recent immersion in the acid experience had forced Graham Nash to confront their output with a disenchanted eye. "I analyzed a few of the songs we'd written, and they were bullshit," he told Barry Miles. "They were really, really bad songs. I decided then I wouldn't churn out so much rubbish. I would go more on quality than quantity. Now I'm taking my time over songs and really analyzing them as I go along. They're a lot better for it, I think. Because the kids aren't fools, you know that, man!"

He set himself the task of dragging the Hollies, a bunch of happy drinkers who were wary of outthinking their audience, into the psychedelic era. "Graham began to be quite different from us," remembered his childhood friend Allan Clarke. "He wanted to be something other than he was with the Hollies." That was manifested first in his appearance. "Graham was wandering around in a frock, and thanks to him, we all had caftans," Bobby Elliott recalled with an embarrassed grin.

Nash knew no half measures. If acid wasn't available, he found other ways to remake the world: "I had four tape recorders, one in each corner of the room, and I would play the signal from one to the other. The distance between the record head and the reproduction head is about a quarter of an inch, so everything would get staggered slightly. And then

I'd drink amazing quantities of brandy and put one of those strobe lights on, and I was in heaven for a while."

His challenge was to persuade the Hollies, and their fans, to let him lead them astray. Everything about their current situation annoyed or frustrated him, from performing live ("I want to pack up a lot of the touring thing") to churning out three-monthly fodder for teenage kids ("I would like it for once if we did something that really shook people, even if it wasn't commercially acceptable"). He imagined touring with a string quartet, or ballet dancers, or a poet. "I don't want to see a bloody poet!" guitarist Tony Hicks exploded.

In May 1967, the London music scene was ripe with rumors that Nash was about to leave the Hollies for a solo career. For once, he was beyond the reach of the pop press, having taken his wife on the hippie trail through Morocco. His destination was chosen, he explained, "because it's completely different and because no one else goes there." But he had heard the Rolling Stones expounding about the opportunities that North Africa provided for sunshine and herbal invigoration. "I took the train," he explained a couple of years later, "from Casablanca to Marrakesh, and also Tangier and Rabat. It cooled me down a lot, I think." Clutching his acoustic guitar, he began to assemble a song called "Marrakesh Express" that would simply recount what he saw on the trip: "Every line in that song is true," he recalled. "I was open enough to react to the circumstances and lucky enough to be in the right place for this melody to come through."

Nash returned to London less angry about the Hollies, but he was already pushing his colleagues beyond the point of comfort. The B side of "On a Carousel" was a psychedelic anthem entitled "All the World Is Love"—five months before the Beatles declared "All You Need is Love" and recruited Nash to sing with them on TV. June 1967 saw the release not only of the Beatles' *Sgt. Pepper*—acclaimed almost in the moment as an epochal moment in Western civilization—but also the Hollies' *Evolution*, with flower-power artwork prepared by Nash's friends in the art collective, The Fool. The Hollies hadn't traveled as far or as quickly as the Beatles, but this record tackled such incongruous fare as existential despair ("Then the Heartaches Begin"), teenage carnality ("The Games We Play"), and sexual inadequacy ("Rain on the Window"). There was also "Stop Right There," a frank admission of marital disharmony: "I wrote it the morning the Hollies came back from America," Nash recalled.

Stranger times lay ahead. That autumn saw Nash admitting to a teen magazine that he had been so stoned the previous night he had shaved off his beard, though he couldn't remember doing it. The bewildered journalist found him burning joss sticks at his Bayswater home and listening to Frank Zappa. Nash explained that while he had once been "an unenthusiastic atheist," he now believed "there is someone in control of the universe." Earthly racial differences could be explained by extraterrestrial intervention, he added: "It's my belief that other planets each put their own type on Earth, and are watching to see who wins out."

Despite his rapid transformation from pop star to sage, Nash believed that it was "impossible" that the band would ever move too quickly for their admirers. Only a few weeks after the Byrds' "Lady Friend," he masterminded an equally majestic single, "King Midas in Reverse." For all its orchestral pomp and rhapsodic sense of release, the song was a stark admission of misery amid success, with Clarke and Nash harmonizing: "It's plain to see it's hopeless, going on the way we are." As Clarke recalled, the Hollies' producer Ron Richards "said that 'King Midas' was not going to be a hit. He said that, if it was up to him, he wouldn't release it; but if we wanted to, he could. And it turned out he was right."

Although Nash and Clarke still insisted on the value of "King Midas," the rest of the band wanted to pursue a more conservative path. But it was too late to alter *Butterfly*, the Hollies' most overtly psychedelic experiment. Issued just five months after *Evolution*, it baffled the band as much as their public. There was no mistaking the album's dominant force, as Nash's vocals now outnumbered those by the group's ostensible lead singer. He made no attempt to disguise his sources of inspiration on the blatantly trippy "Postcard" and "Wishyouawish," or on the declaration, "Ego is dead," which he contributed to "Elevated Observations," or indeed on "Maker," an overt homage to David Crosby's "Mind Gardens." Perhaps inevitably, Crosby now proved to be Nash's strongest supporter. Without actually naming him, Crosby revealed that he had a friend who was "locked in with a certain set of people at a certain level. All of a sudden you walk over and you give him about five times as much room and respect as anybody else has given him, and bam, he goes, Zap! Change! Grow! Give him room, man."

> They are true musicians. I've seen them get so engrossed in their music, they eventually got in a circle and completely forgot there was an audience.
>
> —*Ottawa Journal* profile of Buffalo Springfield, 1967

The success of "For What It's Worth" didn't just threaten the internal stability of Buffalo Springfield; it also made them query their future. "We didn't want to get pegged as a 'protest' group," Stills recalled. "Nothing would have been more silly than finding a list of things to get upset about, so that I could write some more songs about how outraged I was." Instead, "We were hassling among ourselves as to what to do next, because what to do next had suddenly become very important. We became scared—we didn't want to blow it."

The Byrds and the Hollies had evaded a similar crisis by simply repeating the style of their first hit. Only later did they begin to venture into unfamiliar territory. The Springfield's album had been produced in the same spirit: establish a sound and stick to it. But once Greene and Stone were ousted, and Atlantic boss Ahmet Ertegun let the band themselves (or, more accurately, its individual members) loose in the studio, any effort at maintaining a distinctive Springfield brand was abandoned. "We want to make every song different," Stills insisted in 1967. "The Beatles did the same thing."

The Beatles also relished recording songs with anarchic fade-outs: conversation, orgasmic groans, and raucous jamming all crammed into the mix. But the Springfield did it first—only to hide the evidence for a further six years. "Ballad of the Bluebird," as Stephen Stills originally envisioned the song, was an ode to the imaginary woman in his Judy Collins fantasy. Trimmed in length, to less than two minutes, and title, the June 1967 single of "Bluebird" was an astonishing exhibition of guitar virtuosity and self-confidence. It mixed Stills's unfeasibly dextrous fretwork with Young's more visceral lead, striking a perfect balance between tight control and fearless improvisation. But the single merely hinted at what had happened in the studio. Stills's concept was to dissolve his sophisticated pop song into the kind of extended jam that the Springfield would exhibit onstage. And that was how "Bluebird" survived in their live repertoire, as a vehicle for the band to explore sonic adventures that, as the *LA Times* reported later in the year, "made the psychedelic efforts of the [Blue] Cheer and the [Grateful] Dead sound amateurish." It would continue to grow, often encompassing themes such as Ravel's "Bolero," until by 1968 it might extend for twenty minutes or more.

By then, Stills was already imagining that the band would record "a symphonically formed rock and roll piece that takes up one side of an album." In 1967, he prepared a ten-minute edit of his "Bluebird" jam, feral howls, random dialogue and all, for the band's second LP. Then he thought again, chopped the tape where the jam began, and hired banjo maestro Charlie Chin to add a coda that was the converse of psychedelia: a throwback to the Appalachians before electricity reached the mountains.

Neil Young's aesthetic favored immediacy over the considered rethinking in which Stills indulged. In 1967, he was already beginning to perfect the "Aw, shucks" style of explanation that would become his trademark response to queries about his work: "Just because I wrote a song doesn't mean I know anything. I don't know very much about all the things that are going on around here, all the scenes, all the questions. All I know is just what I'm writing about. And even then, I don't really know." His skill was to channel that uncertainty into songs that were both enigmatic and direct, such as "Mr. Soul," issued alongside "Bluebird" on the Springfield's first post-hit single. Besides introducing a lifelong guiding principle ("Is it strange I should change?"), the song wallowed in his newfound fame even as he despised it. Young was both inspired and repelled by the girls who surrounded the band. As Tai Stills recalled, "The groupies pursued them relentlessly, like at the backstage door, where they let the guys know they would do anything, which ran the full gamut. My brother would call me at two or three in the morning and ask if I would escort his guests out of his hotel suite and down to a car."

Teenage fans attracted to those occupying the Top 40 had no further need to concern themselves with the Springfield. No matter that

"Bluebird" and "Mr. Soul" represented the band's creative forces at their respective peaks: the single failed ignominiously to match their previous success (though not as ignominiously as "Lady Friend" did for the Byrds).

It did not help that Young was unavailable to promote the record. Instead, he had fallen into the eccentric company of arranger-producer Jack Nitzsche, veteran of sessions with Phil Spector and the Rolling Stones. Denny Bruce managed Nitzsche for many years: "Jack was a very bright, articulate guy who always ended up getting in trouble. He was just a natural rebel, who hated anyone to tell him what he should be doing with his career." He was therefore the perfect match for Young. As Bruce recalled, "Neil played me a new song called 'Expecting to Fly' in his one-room log cabin. He told me, 'This is something I'll probably never get to do with Buffalo Springfield,' because at the time there was some criticism of his vocals, both from the group and the record company.

"So, he played it, and afterward he said, 'You know, I can really hear the Everly Brothers doing this song.' Now Jack was my best friend at the time, and he had a meeting a week earlier to produce the next Everlys LP. So it didn't take a rocket scientist to say to Jack, 'I'd like you to meet my good friend Neil Young, who has a great song.' This was before we all had tape recorders, so I had to arrange a meeting up in Neil's cabin.

"Neil played maybe as far as the end of the first verse, and Jack interrupted him and said, 'Fuck the Everlys, you've gotta do this yourself.' Neil got into this whole thing about, 'I don't know if I can bring a song like this into the group.' Jack said, 'I don't give a shit about your group. I know guys who can play this the way it should be played.'" Nitzsche took Neil into the studio, without telling the Springfield, and helped him create a suitable soundscape for an eerie song about the traps and snares that surround romance. "Jack gave Neil his solo career with that song," Denny Bruce said. "And it gave Neil the confidence to leave the group. Jack gave a copy to Mick Jagger, who called him up and said, 'This is the best record I've ever heard.'

"Neil was so impressed by that he persuaded me and Jack we should all move to London. So we all got our passports ready—and then DJs in the States started to flip over the 'Bluebird' single, and play 'Mr. Soul.' When Neil heard himself on the radio, he said, 'Perhaps I'll stay here after all' and suddenly he was back in the band." Young offered a more prosaic explanation for his return: "I was starving to death. I didn't have any money."

Jagger's reaction wasn't unique. When "Expecting to Fly" was released, Graham Nash and Allan Clarke played it endlessly and were inspired to write their own avian ballad, "Wings," complete with two rival sets of lyrics and breathtaking vocal harmonies.

Stephen Stills had one last shot at combining creative advancement with chart recognition. Aside from his ongoing infatuation with the idea of Judy Collins, and the ever-present attention of his more sexually aware fans, Stills harbored an ongoing crush on another female vocalist. Before the Springfield had formed, he had seen "a horrible group with a great singer" at the Matrix in San Francisco: the Great Society, fronted by Grace Slick. In her pre-Airplane incarnation, Slick played guitar, piano, and flute onstage, besides singing like the embodiment of self-assurance. Stills was simultaneously entranced and terrified, desperate to form a group with her, but too scared to ask. "Back then I was really very neurotic and would always think of things to do, then not do them," he admitted later.

In time, he would be introduced to Slick by Crosby, and lose none of his dry-mouthed admiration, even when he could hang out with her at the Jefferson Airplane house on Fulton Street. Jamming at Crosby's house around the time of Monterey, the two men became fixated with a simple chord change in the Springfield's favorite D-modal guitar tuning. Crosby offered a vocal riff, and Stills concocted a song about his imaginary life with Grace Slick. Like the unwitting star of "Bluebird," the "Rock 'n' Roll Woman" of his new song was tinged with sadness but remained, like Slick herself, impossible to pin down (not that Stills had dared to ask). Crosby stood over the Springfield in the studio until the track had been perfected. "Rock 'n' Roll Woman" hit radio hard, climbed valiantly toward the Top 40—and then stalled just outside, ensuring that it would never escape cult status.

All of these songs—"Bluebird," "Mr. Soul," "Expecting to Fly," "Rock 'n' Roll Woman"—were included on the November 1967 release of *Buffalo Springfield Again*, arguably the most eclectic album of the mid-1960s. So too was Richie Furay's first recorded composition, "A Child's Claim to

Fame," which affectionately scolded Young for his semidetached attitude to the band: "Make-believe is all you know, and make-believe is a game." Young clearly wasn't too affronted, as he played on the track. Only close inspection of the album credits revealed exactly how fragmented the Springfield had become, and how many outsiders were required to translate a year of isolated sessions into a group. The *New York Times* reviewer described the record as "one of the most varied and weird and beautiful things I've heard"; too varied, as it transpired, for significant success.

David Crosby, Graham Nash, Stephen Stills, and Neil Young had all pushed themselves to peaks of creativity, imagination, and artistic courage in 1967, and each had failed to gain mass acceptance. They had outgrown their bands and were in danger of isolating themselves from their audience. Something had to change, and inevitably it would be Crosby who signaled the path all four would soon follow.

> I want to retire in five years and sail off in a big schooner.
>
> —David Crosby, May 1966

For all the energy and industry devoted to creating and preserving the image of 1967 as the Summer of Love, the twin Californian capitals of psychedelic pop were displaying extreme symptoms of exhaustion. An alternative society seemed to have been born in San Francisco, around the intersection between Haight and Ashbury streets (where David Crosby could sometimes be found at the collective HQ of the Grateful Dead). Now, as George Harrison discovered when he accompanied Derek Taylor on a post–*Sgt. Pepper* sightseeing tour of this supposed paradise, "It was like the Bowery, with down-and-outs, desperate sick people all thinking that Derek and I were one of them." What had once been a joyous carnival had become a commercial bonanza, as hawkers sold "hippie" trinkets and artifacts to day-trippers who had come to see the long-haired animals in their natural habitat.

In Los Angeles, meanwhile, where nobody would be shocked by commercialism, pressure was coming from within. The Mamas and the Papas were the prime movers, and headlining act, of the Monterey

Pop Festival, but their progress was being checked by marital discord between John and Michelle Phillips and the increasing erraticism of Mama Cass. Her weight seesawed according to her intake of chemicals; she was arrested in London on a theft charge and opened her home to any taker who came to the door.

John Sebastian and the Lovin' Spoonful had migrated from New York to LA, and inevitably fallen into Cass Elliot's social circle. But their perennial air of stoned grooviness was undercut by a drug bust in which two of the band avoided arrest by fingering their pot dealer to San Francisco police. Overnight, they metamorphosed from darlings into pariahs, who were forced to bail out of the Monterey festival to avoid the possibility of a subpoena. Back in Los Angeles, there were calls to blackball and boycott the group. "DEMONSTRATE YOUR DISLIKE," screamed the ads placed by the Freedom League of the Brotherhood of Smoke. "WOULD YOU PAY FOR A FINK'S TRIP? Complain to your DJ about Spoonful on radio. Burn your Spoonful albums, pictures and mementoes," just as evangelical Christians had burned Beatles albums during John Lennon's "more popular than Jesus" controversy the previous year. There was also a message for the Spoonful's female fans: "Don't ball them."

It was ironic, to say the least, that the Spoonful should be busted, while David Crosby openly proselytised the use of a glittering variety of hallucinogens and other illegal stimulants. But Crosby's enemies were closer to home. For all the stoned majesty of his public persona, epitomized by his flamboyant raps about the JFK assassination and the joys of LSD during the Byrds' Monterey show, he was becoming increasingly isolated inside the band he had helped to form. He was omnipresent on the Californian scene, one of the few who could bridge the widening gulf between the (supposed) authenticity of the San Franciscan acid-rock bands and the (equally supposed) plasticity of Hollywood's purveyors of pop. He could jam with Jimi Hendrix, who joined Stephen Stills and their mutual friend, drummer Buddy Miles, for an epic bout of improvised madness after Monterey. (Meanwhile in London, Hendrix was being encouraged to write songs with Graham Nash, who shared a house with Jimi's drummer, Mitch Mitchell.) Crosby was the star most likely to pontificate on Vietnam or LBJ, free love or free dope; a twinkle-eyed presence in every significant room. But, in the eyes of his fellow Byrds, he had also become a monster of egotism and arrogance; "a little Hitler," as Roger McGuinn would dub him.

Crosby told Johnny Rogan in 1981 that the other Byrds "were worried about me hanging round Stills, because they knew he was better than they were."

"He was always eating into somebody," McGuinn complained. "He was starting to lose interest in the group, and his buddies in the Buffalo Springfield and the Jefferson Airplane were saying, 'Come on, David, you can do better than that.' And he was saying, 'Yeah, man, but I've got to be loyal to McGuinn and Hillman, I can't let them down.' Being noble and everything. And all this time we were wishing he'd split, because he was heavy, hard to handle, being a little too outspoken and hip for the wrong reasons, and he started getting very like a tyrant on the material."

Gary Usher, the latest in a line of Byrds producers to meet with Crosby's disapproval, recalled that "David was usually fighting the rest of the group" in 1967. "He was extremely difficult to work with in those days . . . if he didn't have his own way. He knew what he wanted and could be very distasteful to be around." Usher recalled the Byrds attempting to record "Goin' Back," a touching but sentimental Goffin-King song about childhood. Crosby turned it down flat, then "reluctantly agreed to cut the song, but let it be known that he would not participate or help out with any ideas. McGuinn got to a point where he just couldn't take it anymore. Finally, he said, 'Look here, Crosby, I've had enough of your bullshit. If you don't want to be part of this song and the group, just get your ass out of here. We don't want you or even need you.' Crosby turned red, and you could sense him burning. He just picked his guitar up and walked out of the studio and never came back." McGuinn's recollection was that Crosby headed immediately over to a Jefferson Airplane session, taking with him a new song that the Byrds had attempted but never finished. "We all agreed he had to be sacked," McGuinn said.

Around the second week of September 1967, McGuinn and Chris Hillman drove their Porsches over to Crosby's house in Beverly Glen. What happened next has been retold so many times that it is fixed as a fake visual memory in the minds of everyone who wasn't there. McGuinn recalled: "It was terrible, because David was in a really happy mood.

David was like, 'Hi, man, how are you?' We walked up to him like storm troopers and said, 'David, sit down. I got some bad news for you.' He said, 'What, man?' and I said, 'Look, Chris and I have been talking, and we have decided that we don't want to work with you anymore.' 'Oh, man,' he said. 'Wow, man, we could make some good music together, wow,' and I said, 'I know, but we can make some good music without you.' I felt bad. I still do. I'm sorry I did it. Stupid decision."

From the vantage point of 1970, when Crosby could peer down at the Byrds far beneath his lofty perch with CSNY, he could afford to exaggerate the encounter: "They said I was crazy, impossible to work with, an egomaniac—all of which is partly true, I'm sure, sometimes—that I sang shitty, wrote terrible songs, made horrible songs, and that they would do much better without me. I took it rather to heart." Four years later, he was prepared to admit that during his final months with the Byrds, "I was a thorough prick all the time. I don't blame them for not liking me." On occasion, McGuinn would suggest that the decision to leave the Byrds had been made at least in part by Crosby himself: "He just had to get out." Stephen Stills, well acquainted with all three participants in the drama, noted wryly in 1971 that "David likes to say he got thrown out, but I think his leaving was by mutual agreement."

That was certainly the story sold to the press in the days after his departure. Then the first issue of a new underground magazine named *Rolling Stone* offered the first of many subsequent variations: "His patience gone, McGuinn decided it would be better for the group's morale if [Crosby] left. Crosby went willingly, asking only that it be made public that he had been asked to leave."

Before this confrontation, Crosby had been waiting for the Byrds to complete their next album, *The Notorious Byrd Brothers*. Instead, he was gone before he had recorded his lead vocals for three new songs. To his everlasting disgust, the remaining Byrds did not abandon those tracks but added vocals themselves—in some cases rewriting his lyrics, because they did not have Crosby or his original manuscripts at their disposal.

One song they did not retrieve was "Triad." Instead Crosby passed it to Jefferson Airplane, and Grace Slick's interpretation illuminated their 1968 album *Crown of Creation*. The Byrds' unfinished version, faster and sloppier, reflected a vain attempt to turn it into a pop song. It was perhaps better suited to Slick's fearless image than to the Byrds', being nothing less than a defense of multiple sexual partners. Once again Crosby couldn't resist reviving the "water brothers" imagery from *Stranger in a Strange Land*. But the lyrics made clear that this particular threesome would involve the singer and two "sister lovers"; and that the women, or rather girls, had minds that were "still growing," as if he was back outside Tamalpais High with Dino Valenti.

The Byrds certainly performed "Triad" at the Whisky during Crosby's final appearances with the band; the *LA Times* carped that "Crosby's voice slipped into a hackneyed nightclub style." Yet by the time that he chose to revive the song during his CSNY concerts in late 1969, it suited Crosby to boast that his previous outfit had refused to consider playing it, on the grounds of moral outrage. "A certain member," Crosby told an audience in Detroit, "got red in the face, and stormed out of the room saying, 'That's a freak-out orgy song, and I won't sing it.'" McGuinn explained patiently that "David thought I was censoring him, that I was mindless and unhip . . . But 'Triad' was simply a bad song." When Crosby briefly reunited with McGuinn and Hillman in 1991, the latter insisted on setting straight "one common misconception" about Crosby's departure: "Roger and I didn't have any trouble with David over moral grounds." And finally, the guru of sexual experimentation had to come clean: "I spread that one around to make them look bad for throwing me out of the band."

A few weeks before he left the Byrds, when he still imagined that he might fold "Triad" into the band's philosophy and stay, Crosby had been anticipating a trip to Scandinavia: "I'm going to buy a boat. I got the money in the bank. Sailing is the most joyous and consciousness-expanding experience in my life, next to making love and my music." His fantasy, besides accumulating pliant young women, was that other people might join him: "Get a bunch of boats traveling around together, a sea tribe of people that live mostly off of what they get from the seas and a little off what they traded in various places, and some of their royalties from the songs they used to write." That last phrase was telling; Crosby clearly didn't imagine that he would always be making music for a living.

A few weeks later, a Californian magazine declared that "Crosby has acted out his dream and dropped out! David has purchased a 58-foot schooner, and is at this moment sailing serenely somewhere in the blue Caribbean." A more cynical reporter suggested that he had set out on a world cruise but had to cut his journey short in Florida "when he discovered that his ship had a rusty bottom." Crosby had indeed bought a schooner designed by John G. Alden, *Mayan*, and it did require repairs before it could embark on epic voyages beyond civilization's grasp. Until his settlement from the Byrds' partnership came through, he borrowed the $22,500 required from Peter Tork of the Monkees. (Strangely, the official US Coast Guard records show that the *Mayan* was not legally transferred into Crosby's name for another eighteen months, and that the purchase price was just $10; apparently such discrepancies were common in maritime circles, where sales tax was seen as an unnecessary evil.)

Crosby found the *Mayan* in Fort Lauderdale, having decided to revisit the welcoming community he had found in Florida five years earlier. Mama Cass flew down to see him and begged him to take her fifty or sixty miles into the Caribbean, to the shores of Bimini, in the Bahamas. It was there, so she had heard, that "a temple has been spotted, protruding two feet above the surface of the sea in well-sailed waters." She believed this was evidence of the lost city of Atlantis. Crosby and Elliot never solved that mystery, though they did manage to track down Fort Lauderdale's renowned Polynesian restaurant Mai-Kai, where they were spotted together in early November 1967. By then, Crosby had abandoned his immediate plans to set out on a world cruise, but not because of any deficiencies in his boat. Quite simply, he had fallen in love—not with Cass, but with another singer who would affect his life, and those of his closest friends, in surreal and unimagined ways.

> As if they take their cue for their lives from the shifting shale beneath them, the people of Los Angeles are always involved in some rapturous, spectacular earthquake.
>
> —Ellen Sander, *Trips*

In the final weeks of 1966, David Crosby, Peter Fonda, and former child actor Brandon de Wilde were tight companions in Hollywood—photographing the Sunset Strip riots or experimenting with new designs for "electric" clothes fitted with flashing lights. At Christmas, two of the three set off for the island of Cozumel, down the coast of Mexico from Cancun. In his memoir, Fonda recalled that Crosby's stay was brief, as he was "totally paranoid that Gram Parsons was going to run off with his girl in his absence." Crosby was right to worry, as the devilishly charming trust-funded Parsons did steal his girlfriend, Nancy Marthai Ross, away.

Crosby knew Nancy from Santa Barbara, where both were notorious for defying convention. So it was inevitable that they would bond when their paths crossed in 1965, by which time the five-years-older Crosby was a rock star and Ross had already abandoned one marriage to FDR's grandson and was sleeping with movie star Steve McQueen (who was married to actress Neile Adams). Ross seems to have seduced Crosby's imagination by refusing to have sex with him immediately, unlike the groupies who regularly serviced stars on Sunset Strip. "He thought I wouldn't stay unless he bought a house," she told Parsons biographer Ben Fong-Torres, "so he went and bought a beautiful house on Beverly Glen." The purchase was insufficient to ward off the challenge from Gram Parsons, although Ross's betrayal didn't capsize relations between the once and future Byrds. Crosby would join Parsons in the studio in 1969 to sing a soaring harmony part on the Flying Burrito Brothers' "Do Right Woman."

Nancy Ross and Roger McGuinn had one thing in common: they both regarded David Crosby as a tyrant. He was also, Ross remembered, very unwilling to share his money. Despite this, she had apparently promised to marry him in early 1967 (although Crosby never confirmed this story). The imbalance of power between stars and their girlfriends allowed—perhaps even legitimized—such behavior. Another young woman recalled her first encounter with Stephen Stills around the same period: she said he walked up to her at a club, and without an introduction said simply, "I think you and I can make it." She politely turned him down.

Christine Hinton, who celebrated her seventeenth birthday when "Mr. Tambourine Man" hit the Top 10, and two friends became utterly infatuated with the Byrds around 1965–66, and started a fan club for the group, which they figured would ensure regular rendezvous with the musicians. Hinton's passion was focused on Crosby, while the others set their hearts on Chris Hillman and Gene Clark. The three even rented an apartment opposite the Whisky so they could monitor the Byrds' regular visits there. By 1967, Hinton had moved in with Crosby, though onlookers found it difficult to decide if she was his lover or his maid.

The folksinger Roberta Joan Anderson was made of tougher stuff. Under her married name of Joni Mitchell, she had written several songs that were becoming standards. Among them was "The Circle Game," intended to counter the mock-defeatist message of "Sugar Mountain" by her friend, fellow Canadian and fellow childhood polio victim, Neil Young. The two musicians had shared a house briefly after the collapse of her marriage. Joni's song gave its name to an album by Tom Rush, who in turn alerted Judy Collins to Mitchell's songwriting—the result being that Collins cut three of her songs on her *Wildflowers* LP, which was being readied for release as David Crosby left the Byrds.

Mitchell's work ranged from the deeply poetic to the frankly twee, the latter sometimes taking precedence in front of an audience. Though her giggly stage persona suggested she was only in her teens, she had already packed vast experience into her twenty-five years: her illness, her battle to escape her conservative upbringing in Saskatchewan, her pregnancy at age twenty-one after a brief relationship, her marriage to an older singer, and her decision to have her months-old daughter adopted. She had made regular TV appearances in Canada; set up her own publishing company; mastered a slew of alternative guitar tunings, which helped to give her songs an otherworldly air; experimented briefly with an electric rock group, the Siegel-Schwall Band; and performed at the 1967 Newport Folk Festival, where she was stunned to discover that the audience already knew who she was, even if they had never heard her sing. There she connected with another Canadian poet and songwriter, Leonard Cohen, in a passing liaison that would be renewed in time. She painted, which was a vocation, made hippie jewelry and decorations as a hobby, and had a voice that could slip around the octaves with ease, to the point that she would occasionally sacrifice melodic unity to the pleasure of indulging her rich vibrato. She was also shy, apparently, prone to crippling bouts of self-doubt, and, at the same time, supremely self-confident, almost along the lines of a California rock star. She looked frail and defenseless behind her chic makeup but lacked nothing when it came to ego.

Mitchell had freshly returned from her first visit to England when she settled in for a week's residency in late September 1967 at the Gaslight Café in Coconut Grove, twenty-five miles down the Florida coast from Fort Lauderdale. Joni was the headliner, as befitted the woman whose songs had been recorded by nationally known artists. She was preceded every night by Estrella Berosini, seventeen years old, who knew David Crosby from his previous visits to the Grove. "David would sweep into the clubs with his Byrds cape on," she recalled to Sheila Weller, and one night at the Gaslight, he marched in and told Estrella that he planned to become a record producer and wanted to work with her. Perhaps doubting his motives, Estrella told Crosby that he should hear Joni Mitchell. She claimed that Crosby replied, "She's just another blond chick singer," with the same certainty that he'd dismissed Buffalo Springfield. But he stayed and slid immediately into Mitchell's growing band of well-connected acolytes.

Their encounter became an essential part of rock mythology. Cameron Crowe heard Crosby's most succinct version of the tale: "I stopped taking drugs for a while, bought my boat, and started getting healthy out in the sun. I stayed there a few months and felt real good. I walked into a local coffeehouse and there was this girl singing 'I had a king in a tenement castle.' I went, 'What?' Then she sang about two other songs, and after I peeled myself off the back of the room, I realized I had just fallen in love."

He was ripe for reinvention, having shed not only the Byrds but also his home in Beverly Glen (now rented to his friend disc jockey B. Mitchel Reed) and, effectively, his commitment to Christine Hinton. She couldn't match Mitchell's effervescent charisma but maintained her ambiguous place in Crosby's circle.

Crosby would describe himself much later as being "extremely fascinated with the quality of the music and the quality of [Joni Mitchell]. She was such an unusual, passionate, and powerful woman." They passed songs back and forth, Crosby unveiling work in progress such as "Guinnevere" and "Laughing," Mitchell able to trump him at will with half a dozen new masterpieces. "I think she just outgrew me," Crosby would admit with long hindsight, Mitchell's talent and presence forcing him into a rare position of humility.

Despite later differences between them, Crosby never retracted that initial flash of amazement and devotion. Mitchell, by comparison, grew more acerbic about Crosby with age, her original affection for him decaying into little short of contempt: in an interview just before she suffered a debilitating health crisis in 2015, she described her former lover as "a human-hater." In earlier decades, when her life and psyche were perhaps more balanced, she acknowledged his sense of humor, his twinkling eyes, his boundless and (at the time) much appreciated passion for her work, his generosity, his prowess as a sailor. Even at her most positive, however, she remained a keen judge of character. In two lines, she captured the core of the man: "He can make you feel like a million bucks. Or he can bring you down with the same force."

The two songwriters enjoyed the briefest of idylls in Florida, Crosby driving both Mitchell and Berosini at breathtaking speed through the streets of the Grove and around Miami Beach. Three days after Joni finished at the Gaslight, she began a stint at the Second Fret in Philadelphia. There she wrote and performed a song in which she delineated her romantic options, among them a man who is "waiting for a schooner / and he thinks he's met a queen"—confirming that the *Mayan* was not yet seaworthy; and, more pertinently, that Mitchell perhaps doubted that she could live up to Crosby's fantasies. By the end of the year, the song had gained an extra verse which summarized the philosophy she had chosen ("She will love them when she sees them / They will lose her if they follow") and a suitably spiky title "Cactus Tree." By then, she had returned to the Gaslight and camped out on the *Mayan,* so she could sing, "He takes her to his schooner / And he treats her like a queen," the inference being that this was merely what she deserved.

Between her two sojourns in Florida, Mitchell inhabited folk clubs across North America, including a one-night stop at Stephen Stills's old folkie haunt in New York, the Café Au Go Go. There she entranced a young booking agent named Elliot Roberts, who gave up his job at the

William Morris Agency and accompanied her to her next engagement in Detroit. Almost without discussion, he became her manager. He then met David Crosby, assuming the same role for him.

Once Joni Mitchell left the Gaslight at the start of October, Crosby was torn between staying in Florida and becoming her traveling companion. He was there with her at least once in Philadelphia, and in New York, where Crosby and Mitchell taped the briefest of demos at her apartment—a tantalizing blueprint for a vocal partnership that might have been. Just one minute long, it featured their two voices joined in harmony on a song she was writing about him, "The Dawntreader." (True to form, she would eventually come to deny any link between Crosby and that tale of a sailor.) Then, after a lengthy run in Toronto, she joined Crosby in California, where they (and Roberts) crashed at the house he had rented to Mitchel Reed.

While they were there, Crosby introduced Mitchell to Mo Ostin, boss of Hollywood's hippest record label, Warner-Reprise. A man who had already offered recording contracts to Van Dyke Parks and Randy Newman was never going to be wary of a woman so obviously talented. Ostin agreed to sign her, Crosby inserted himself in the deal as her producer, and the pact was made before Christmas 1967. An official photograph documented the signing. It showed Crosby, his hair already draped down over his shoulders but visibly thinning on top, looking distinctly seedy between Roberts, in a mod London jacket, and the conservatively attired Ostin.

The company executive probably imagined that the novice producer would create a typical Warner album of the time: poetic, eclectic, wrapped in lavish orchestrations, most likely arranged by Van Dyke Parks. Mitchell wanted the songs to run as free as her persona in "Cactus Tree," and for nothing to obscure the lyrics. Crosby placed himself defiantly between the singer and corporate expectations. The only outsider allowed to contribute to the sessions was Stephen Stills, who added bass to one song. Mitchell explained during the making of the record that she had initially been excited by the potential of a multitrack recording desk: "I went crazy and thought of all kinds of harmonies. But between David and me, we managed to laugh and sort of realize we were ruining it. Cut back, and take maybe one little three-note passage that really did enhance it, and scrap all that other gunk that we'd put in."

Mitchell was recording at Sunset Sound in Hollywood. At first, she had to wait for gaps in the lengthy sessions Stills was staging for the final Buffalo Springfield album. When Neil Young made one of his rare appearances at the studio, Joni proudly introduced him to Crosby as an old friend. Most often, though, she waited patiently for Stills and Crosby to finish their men's talk. Then Sunset opened a second room, which Mitchell was the first to use. She had already boasted of Crosby's skills as a producer: "He has very good judgment. He also gets very good sound out of me in the studio." But, as her friend Joel Bernstein reflected, "David really didn't know what he was doing. When they handed the record in, the master was rejected for technical reasons. There was distortion on the vocal track in the mix, which hadn't been there on the original tapes; there was really loud hiss; and you could hear Joni's foot tapping on the mike stand." The much more experienced John Haeny was recruited to rescue the tapes. At the time, Joni was happy to blame the original engineer, jazz pianist Art Crist, who died soon after the sessions: "He was very ill, drinking a lot, his wife had just left him." Several decades later, she placed the burden squarely on Crosby's shoulders.

By the time the *Joni Mitchell* album was finished, she was already drifting away from her mentor-disciple. She would later recount happy memories of riding up and down the Hollywood Hills in Crosby's Mercedes, listening over and over to a cassette of the Beatles' *Magical Mystery Tour* album. He remembered that "We went back to LA and tried to live together. It doesn't work." "They were breaking up in the studio," Bernstein recalled, "both crying, with the glass window to the control room between them." Stephen Stills dubbed her a "love gangster" and wrote a song to cement that image. Crosby's most revealing commentary came when he stopped by a Monkees session on February 16, 1968, and recorded a new song called "Games." Ostensibly intended for the Monkees to cover, it was actually an effort at catharsis. Crosby recounted how an affair that had blossomed "in the sunshine" had then decayed "in the rain" and "bad air" of New York and LA. What killed it was competition: the quest to be the better songwriter, the dominant ego, the most successful performer.

Despite that, Crosby could not restrain a final message: "Love you." They would continue to hook up throughout 1968 but were no longer a couple.

Instead, he concentrated on the joy of introducing her talents as a singer and composer to his friends. As he recalled, "My favorite trick at the time was to invite everyone over, get a joint of dope that was stronger than they could possibly smoke, and get her to play, and they would walk out stupefied." Graham Nash would soon fall under the same spell.

It used to break my heart when the group were away for great stretches at a time. That was a long time ago now. I think I've become hardened to the fact that he's not always going to be around.

—Rose Nash, spring 1968

Like many pop wives in the late 1960s, Rose Nash did not accompany her husband on tour. Unlike most, she did not always wait patiently at home for her husband Graham's return. She spent four months in New York during 1967, accompanying the girlfriend of Hollies guitarist Tony Hicks on her assignments as a model. But she had no interest in infiltrating Graham's scene. "It's not my nature to make small talk with people I don't know and have nothing in common with," she explained.

Life as the partner of one of Britain's most visible pop stars did not exactly thrill her. "I wish he'd give it all up," she complained. "I think it's a drag." She was happiest when they were alone in their apartment, and he was playing her songs he'd just written. But those moments were rare. "The flat is so noisy," she said. "Most of our friends are in the pop business, and they just drop in and start strumming on the guitars we have around. Usually it's two chords and the same six words—until I want to run out screaming!"

Rose insisted that Graham "hates clubs." But however impatient her husband had become with the British pop scene, he was still naturally gregarious and eager for fresh experiences. Equally, he loathed the idea of begging shamelessly for public approval. Yet that was what he and the Hollies did when they recorded "Jennifer Eccles," a playful but embarrassingly banal tune which took its title from Rose (Eccles) and Jennifer (Clarke). "Graham and I were very down about our lack of success with 'King Midas,'" Allan Clarke remembered, "so we decided to write something that couldn't fail. And it turned out to be one of our biggest sellers. Graham was appalled, but to me 'Jennifer Eccles' represented stability. I wanted to be in the business for a long time, and I thought we should give the people what they wanted." Nash's distaste hardened when he registered how his new friends in California reacted to the song.

No sooner had the Hollies flown in from London in February 1968 than David Crosby plucked Nash from his hotel room and took him to a party at Peter Tork's house. Earlier that day, Crosby had jammed with Jimi Hendrix and friends before the guitarist's Shrine Auditorium show. Now almost everyone he knew in Los Angeles—apart from Joni Mitchell—was gathered at Tork's new Laurel Canyon home, previously owned by television actor Wally Cox. As Crosby and Nash wandered around, they came into a room where a man was hammering feverishly at a piano. Nash watched openmouthed until the madman paused. "That's the guy I've been telling you about," Crosby said. "That's Stephen Stills." Four nights later, the three men were together in Stills's car after the Hollies' show at the Whisky, sketching out a fantasy future in which they might all share.

Nash resumed life with the Hollies in Florida. One month and a dozen cities later, they arrived in Ottawa, Canada, on the afternoon of March 15. Local journalists were pacified with a brief press conference, during which Nash insisted, "We're a happy group, and all our songs are intended to make people happy." Then they played two sellout shows at the Capitol Theatre. Afterward . . . well, here stories diverge. Nash recalled a press reception at which he was introduced to a stunning young woman with long blond hair, clutching a massive Bible. By contrast, concert promoter Harvey Glatt remembered taking Nash to Le Hibou, a local coffeehouse, where the same meeting took place after Joni Mitchell had finished her late-night set. He said that afterward, he, Nash, and local rock performer Bruce Cockburn went briefly to Mitchell's Château Laurier hotel room. "It was clear something was happening between Graham and Joni," Glatt recalled, "so Bruce and I left."

Nash himself was too dazzled to be concerned about the details. Crosby had already played him some of Mitchell's work, but the experience of hearing her live, singing the best songs he had ever heard in his life, in *that* voice, floored him. So, no doubt, did the night of lovemaking that followed. The Hollies star awoke the next afternoon alongside the still-sleeping Mitchell, suddenly aware that he had to be onstage a thousand miles away in Winnipeg before nightfall. There was a hurried goodbye, but no promises from Mitchell, leaving Nash to stagger back to reality—doubting everything in his life that he had assumed was set in stone.

> Neil Young has again quit the Buffalo Springfield, which might suffer the dwarfism which has afflicted the Byrds.
>
> —*LA Times*, March 4, 1968

The disintegration was slow and all too public. Dates were canceled, touring schedules crumbled away, record sales slowed. By March 19, 1968, it had become impossible to assemble a quorum of Buffalo Springfield members in one studio. Studio engineer–turned-bassist Jim Messina took on the thankless task of trying to persuade his new colleagues to finish another album. Stephen Stills never turned down an opportunity to record but was forced to rely on friends and session men to make up a band. Neil Young offered "I Am a Child," a wry retort to Richie Furay's critique on the previous Springfield LP, but didn't even perform on the other song he contributed, "On the Way Home." Stills interpreted the lyric as Young's farewell message to him and the band: "I won't be back till later on / If I do come back at all." Then Young confirmed what was already obvious: after their next US tour, he would no longer be a member of the Springfield. Their first European visit, planned provisionally for late summer, was left to hang in the wind.

So too were three members of the band, Young, Furay, and Messina, when police raided a house on Topanga Canyon Road. Neighbors had complained that there was a loud party in progress, and when police entered the premises, they found five men and ten young women, several ounces of marijuana, and a quantity of dubious seeds—but not the ostensible resident of the property. That was Stephen Stills, who had bailed out of a window as the cops knocked at the door. Also left behind was English guitarist Eric Clapton, only there because Cream's gig that night in Denver had been canceled on short notice; plus Stills's sisters and his current girlfriend. They were carted away to the Sybil Brand Institute for Women; the men to county jail.

Initially, the entire party was accused of being present in a house where illegal drugs were being consumed. Despite the prima facie evidence against them all, charges against the women were dropped, while prosecutors chose to proceed against all but one of the men on the lesser count of disturbing the peace. They were found guilty by Malibu Justice Court and fined. The exception—the price for being English, perhaps?—was Clapton. His drug case went to trial, but the judge threw it out of court.

The convictions shattered any last sense of unity among the Springfield and did nothing to dissuade Neil Young from leaving the band. The road ended where it had begun, in Southern California on May 5, as Buffalo Springfield headlined a five-act package. "This is it, gang," Stills announced as he took the stage. Two minutes later, the performance was cut short by security demanding that exuberant fans resume their seats. "Sorry for that interruption," Stills drawled sarcastically, before kicking back into "Rock 'n' Roll Woman." The hourlong set ended with a twenty-three-minute extrapolation of "Bluebird," which gave Stills and Young—each of whom had acknowledged how tense they were feeling—a last opportunity to act out their complex relationship through their guitars. "The Long Beach audience left their seats to mass at the edge of the stage during the long last song," reviewer Pete Johnson reported, "applauding and cheering emotionally as the group concluded their set." "We love you," Stills said plaintively, and with that, the Springfield were gone.

What had finally driven Buffalo Springfield apart? The *Chicago Tribune* blamed lack of airplay and managerial problems. *Rolling Stone* pinpointed "a combination of internal hassle, extreme fatigue combined with absence of national success, and run-ins with the fuzz." In time, almost all the protagonists would have their say. Neil Young's account was typically vague: "We all got tired of it, and just couldn't hang in there. And as far as our interrelationships were going, they were being hurt because the group was becoming bigger than us. And it was all hanging us all up, and whatever we had for each other was disappearing, because the group was getting too much." Dewey Martin blamed economics: "The people who handled our business screwed us out of a lot of money." Richie Furay identified "ego clashes . . . It was supposed to have been a group and it wasn't." And Stephen Stills spoke from his heart: what killed the Springfield was "sheer frustration."

It was Stills's friend Ellen Sander who delivered the most convincing and prophetic verdict, in the *New York Times*: "One of the most obvious reasons for the group's demise is that there were too many leaders."

CHAPTER 4

After two years of the dominance of electric pop groups, the singer-songwriter with the pre-Edison guitar is making a comeback.

—Robert Shelton, *New York Times*, July 1968

A s the song declared, it was "Uno Mundo"—one world. But that world was united by the screams of continents racked in anguish. Only one thing could heal the wounds: the groove. It was a Latin stew of salsa, boogaloo, and pachanga, syncopated horns, percussion, and bass, all obeying the rhythms that crackled through the nervous system of Stephen Stills. If ever a 1960s single begged to be placed on a loop and allowed to run until the dance floor was littered with enervated bodies, it was this one.

A year before Santana planted Latin music in the heart of rock culture, "Uno Mundo" testified to the depth of its creator's immersion in the sounds of Central America. But as the last record issued by Buffalo Springfield before their split, it demonstrated that the group was no longer a reality. Neil Young took no part in the recording, leaving Stills to overdub layer after layer of his own design, all serving the song's irresistible call to dance.

Even within the narrow boundaries of white popular music, "one world" was an increasingly distant fantasy. Gulfs were opening between singles and albums, pop and rock, teenagers and the young adults who had been schooled on rock and roll and couldn't follow their parents into a white-bread world of Perry Como and Andy Williams. Most industry strategists continued to sell the music as if its audience were a single, gullible child, but the musicians and their fans knew that their culture was both divided and divisive. The Beatles were able to extend their vision of universality through their 1968 double album into 1969's *Abbey*

Road, but only by making eclecticism their guiding philosophy. Beneath them, the audience was fragmenting into a dozen different genres and subgenres, each of which demanded specialized marketing and music making. Those who listened to hard rock might despise country rock; likewise, British blues and progressive rock, or acid rock and folk rock. While pop remained focused on the instant assessment of the Top 40, rock was becoming a profitable business—profitable enough, indeed, for major record labels to sign such esoteric artists as Joni Mitchell.

Her first album stole quietly onto the market around the time the Springfield capsized, garnering glowing reviews, but barely denting even the most generous sales chart. (Its peak position in the leading US trade mag *Billboard* was number 171.) Compliments continued to flow when Mitchell paraded her talents through the nation's most prestigious folk clubs. She was poetic and inspired, beautiful and important; she was, quite simply, "exceptional." Her songs also led both sides of Judy Collins's *Wildflowers*, a baroque folk album that avoided all the dominant trends of the age but clung defiantly to the upper reaches of the US LP chart.

As a committed folkie, and the man feted for having given the young Bob Dylan his first major press coverage, Robert Shelton had a vested interest in seeing his beloved acoustic troubadours supplanting the boorish, cacophonous idols of the rock age. But his *New York Times* judgment proved to be accurate and presented the victims of recent well-publicized splits among California's rock fraternity with a pressing question. Could they survive on their own?

> If I could just see Stephen . . . I'd really like to see him. Out of all of them, he is the one I like best, but it's the things that he's surrounded himself with that I can't cope with. I'm not in any part of that scene.
>
> —Neil Young, October 1968

When Neil Young met Joni Mitchell's manager, Elliot Roberts, he recognized someone who might be able to steer him into the future. First, he had to maneuver Roberts away from the job that he wanted, as manager of Buffalo Springfield. Then he sprang his surprise and asked Roberts to manage him as a solo artist. As soon as the Springfield collapsed, Roberts began to negotiate a deal with the same label that had signed Mitchell. Warner-Reprise boss Mo Ostin agreed to Roberts's terms, which emphasized royalties over a large advance. But Young still emerged with sufficient cash to buy a small house on Skyline Trail, in Topanga Canyon.

He could not have chosen a more symbolic exit from the Hollywood scene. Skyline Trail was a westernmost outcrop from the boulevard that snaked its way up the mountains from the sea. Young's home enjoyed an uninterrupted view across valleys and peaks. It was half a mile, as the eagle flies, twice that by car, from the dogleg curve around which Topanga Canyon's more secretive inhabitants would gather—the General Store and the Canyon Kitchen.

Young would drive up to the Kitchen most mornings for breakfast and flirt with its owner, Susan Acevedo. Her talents extended beyond cooking: a couple of years earlier, when Buffalo Springfield were camped out in the Canyon at the height of their fraternal camaraderie, she had been a mainstay of the Playhouse company and staged productions at the Topanga Canyon Community House. In 1966 she starred in a Clifford Odets drama that proved so popular that the ensemble was required to revive it on several occasions. Its title? *The Country Girl.* A reporter noted that Susan had "Sweet Judy Collins eyes," making it almost inevitable that Stephen Stills would later jest that he was "deeply in love" with her.

But it was Young who fell in love with Acevedo. He quickly set up house with her and her young daughter, Tia, in Topanga, and in the early afternoon of December 1, 1968, Neil Young and Susan Acevedo were married in their Skyline Trail home.

Young told a visiting journalist that he was thrilled to escape the city and enjoying his distance from stardom and its demands. "Most of all," Pete Johnson wrote, "he likes being out of a group—'I'm ecstatic. It's great!'" Instead of socialites and star-seekers, Young had eased himself into a very different environment. His mentor Jack Nitzsche was never far from hand, and Young had secured another ally in the staff producer of Tetragrammaton, a small label founded by comedian Bill Cosby and his manager. David Briggs came with none of Nitzsche's proven hit credentials, but his acerbic personality and basic philosophy of recording ("Be good or be gone") triggered something in Young that had lain dormant during his years with the Springfield.

Not that Briggs's aesthetic principles were in evidence as Young began to assemble his first solo album. Far from recording and singing live with a band, as would become his lifelong preference, Young laboriously constructed his self-named debut from endless studio sessions. He dubbed, overdubbed, and redubbed multiple guitar parts, tinkered with his vocals, brooded over the precise structure of his songs. "It took me and Jack Nitzsche a month to put down the tracks for 'The Old Laughing Lady,'" he recalled.

Since the birth of his professional career, Young had cannibalized his own material. The same fragments of melody, or lyrical couplets and themes, would recur from song to song as he learned his craft. Now he plundered the scrawled lyrics and half-forgotten chords left over from his time with the Springfield. The instrumental "Falcon Lake" became the foundation for "Here We Are in the Years." Young had once told a teen magazine that Stephen Stills had written the music for a prospective Springfield tune called "The Old Laughing Lady." Now it reemerged, in near identical form, with Stills's name excised from the credits. The most powerful track on the album also had a connection with Stills, who (along with the composer) was one of the subjects of his compelling study of urban alienation, "The Loner."

One song wasn't considered for the album. Young might have felt alienated from Los Angeles, but he was still signed to one of its record companies and would depend on its radio stations and reporters for publicity. It would be another five years before he dared to perform "LA" in public. "I didn't release it at the time because I was paranoid," he explained then, and its apocalyptic vision of an "uptight city in the smog," teetering on the edge of destruction, was not exactly an olive branch toward Hollywood.

The city wasn't the only focus of his paranoia. An *LA Times* reporter was the first outsider to hear *Neil Young*. He recounted that its creator "worries about a single which will be released from the album, about the sequence of songs on the record, and about the mix—the relationship of instruments and voices. He plays it, and is alternately proud and fretful, wanting it to be the best he could possibly do, thinking first that it is, then that it isn't, then that it is, and so on." That lack of conviction would find its way onto the record itself and threaten to smother Young's solo career as it was born.

David Crosby, like most of the successful set in California, keeps himself churning with things to do and deals to make.

—*Fort Lauderdale News*, August 1968

Because he "hangs out" so much, there is a tendency to think he isn't producing much. In a sense, this is true.

—*Rolling Stone*, June 1968

When Jerry Hopkins profiled the "LA Scene" for *Rolling Stone* magazine, he identified David Crosby as "the winner of the Man-You-See-at-Every-Gathering Award." ("Cass Elliot runs a close second," he added.) Despite his apparent inactivity since leaving the Byrds, Crosby was still "an integral part of the LA scene," Hopkins said, "thanks, largely, to his track record as a musician, but also because he is so volatile and opinionated."

Yet in a decade when movements and trends were measured in weeks rather than years, Crosby's disappearance from the marketplace seemed like an act of self-sabotage. He had his boat, his friends, his drugs, his guitars, his girlfriends (although not the woman he thought he loved most), but no recording contract, no schedule, no focus, no path into the future. His friend Ellen Sander remembered Crosby asking Cass Elliot plaintively if she could suggest someone who might be able to produce him.

His faith in his own production skills had been dented by the sonic flaws of the Joni Mitchell tapes from Sunset Sound. Not that Mitchell shared his self-doubt: when her sometime lover Leonard Cohen was in Hollywood in May 1968, she suggested that Crosby should produce him. At least two songs, "Bird on a Wire" and "You Know Who I Am," were attempted, the latter featuring an uncharacteristically hesitant vocal harmony from Crosby. But there was no creative rapport between the two men; perhaps because Crosby realized that Mitchell and Cohen's relationship was far from dormant. Cohen attended Mitchell's opening at the Troubadour in June, and the pair were reported to be "very much in love." "I think he's my strongest influence," she explained the following year. "He's a very romantic man, but I'm more of an optimist, whereas he's more Catholic and into dark misery." She was clearly irresistible to her songwriting peers, as two weeks later, Jimmy Webb bombarded her with red roses when she played the Bitter End in New York. All the while, Crosby and Mitchell were still reported to be "constant companions." Maybe the stress of separating and arranging these rivals was beginning to tell. "I see omens," she admitted in June. "I see lots of them, although I don't know what they mean." Soon afterward, she was admitted to a hospital in Los Angeles, diagnosed as suffering from hepatitis.

Crosby continued to prowl around the city, ever open to experiment as opportunities arrived. Meanwhile, Christine Hinton would continue to keep house for him at Lisbon Lane. Reflecting six years later, Crosby would scold himself for having overlooked her: "You go out looking for princesses, man, and you ignore the little person hanging around that you've known for a long time." His love for "the little person" was undeniable, but so was the gulf between his vision of romantic commitment and hers. Many years later, Hinton's friend Salli Sachse would recall: "Christine was always anxious, always ready to please. David treated women badly, but then, so many guys did."

When he wasn't in Hollywood, or on the *Mayan*, Crosby could sometimes be found up at Paxton Lodge in Plumas County. There the boss of Elektra Records, Jac Holzman, was funding a commune peopled by young male songwriters and even younger female companions. Among them was Jackson Browne, who, when he arrived in Hollywood, had watched starstruck as David Crosby strolled into the Troubadour on Santa Monica Boulevard, "two eighteen-year-old girls under his cape." Once Crosby heard Browne's songs, he elected himself the teenager's mentor. As Browne remembered, "He said, 'Look, I'd love to produce your record.' He had just been working with Joni Mitchell, so I knew he could do it. But it was kind of maddening, because it never quite seemed to happen. I was trying to get his attention for a couple of years, but he couldn't stop long enough to do it." The Crosby that Browne met was the Great Encourager: "There was something conspiratorial about him. He would meet a younger person and would say all kinds of supportive and interesting things, but in a way to suggest, 'How I envy you, you're at the beginning, with everything ahead of you.' He would flatter you and build you up, which was incredible. And then you wouldn't see him for several months."

Jackson Browne joined the select group of musicians who were always welcome aboard the *Mayan*. But he detected a naïve elitism among Crosby and his friends: "The prevailing philosophy in his circle was this. They all had boats, and they all had this really ideal life—they were hippies with dough. And they were always talking about how, if things got tough, politically or whatever, they would just leave. In their minds, they were sailing off into an ethereal future that doesn't really exist without a lot of work, and a lot of support from other people. They would get high, and just rap about this fantasy. It was enticing, but at the same time it was obvious to me that it had no roots in reality."

The ultimate expression of that fantasy took shape on the *Mayan*— the child of collective experimentation, and Crosby's infallibly exquisite selection of dope. His former Sausalito communard, Paul Kantner, was now one of the guiding forces of Jefferson Airplane, San Francisco's most defiantly anarchic acid-rock band. Like Crosby, Kantner prided himself on his refusal to kowtow to power. "Our watchword was, 'Question authority,'" he recalled. "Pull America's dirty baggage out into the light, and let people make their own healthy decisions. You should fuck with people who need to be fucked with. It's a civic obligation." Between the Airplane's professional obligations, Kantner and other members of his clan would visit the *Mayan* wherever it was moored; in Florida, off the Bahamas, or eventually in Richardson Bay, off Sausalito. During their hazy, paradisiacal encounters, drugs would be consumed, orgiastic fantasies fulfilled, and, without any sense of obligation, several era-defining songs would emerge. "We created our own special space," Kantner explained, "and we figured out a way to do things differently from how they were being done everywhere else in America. We figured we didn't have any responsibilities, except maybe to provide a good example on a personal level, and just get along with everyone we met."

It was Crosby who provided the guitar lick beneath two songs that raised the Airplane's revolutionary flag in 1969, "Volunteers" and "We Can Be Together." Crosby also showed Kantner an open-C guitar tuning that would transform the way he approached his instrument. "He might well be responsible for half of my musical career," Kantner conceded many years later.

In return, Kantner listened as Crosby unveiled a series of wordless instrumentals and vocal experiments, many of which he had already performed for producer Paul Rothchild in a March 1968 demo session. One of the pieces, more structured than the rest, sparked Kantner's imagination. He looked across the cabin of the *Mayan*, and began to improvise words about "Wooden Ships," which became the focus of a sci-fi mind-movie in which a bunch of anarchic, utopian hippies wash up on an idyllic island shore after a nuclear apocalypse. Crosby prefaced the scenario with a dialogue between survivors, opening with a line about the communicative power of a smile, which he had borrowed from a sign outside a Florida church.

As the power of Crosby's dope took hold, creativity lapsed, and the song was set aside. Then Stephen Stills—less partial to marijuana than most of his contemporaries were—came aboard and picked up the glazed fragments of the collaboration. "It kept drifting around," Stills told Paul Zollo. "So, I went down belowdeck and finished it off. Everyone else was up watching the stars." Stills added the darkest verse, a glimpse of the horror the survivors had escaped. With the meticulous attention of a craftsman, he also polished "Wooden Ships" into coherent shape. (The Airplane provided a hint of what might have been with their *Volunteers* album. Its draft of the "Wooden Ships" lyrics located the action precisely in July 1975 and added free-form verse about "silver-suited people" in "the pitchblende night," none of which was ever sung.)

Besides drugs, Crosby jolted his musical imagination into fresh ways of thinking by evolving ever-more-abstruse ways of tuning his guitars. These allowed him to create unrecognizable chords that would float and hum across the deck of the *Mayan* and slowly evolve into songs. One such retuning unleashed the glorious melodic flow of what became known as "Song with No Words" and was also the fertile ground for the piece that emerged as his anthem.

The saga of "Guinnevere" was taking shape as he left the Byrds and evolved to reflect his halcyon days on the Florida coast with Joni Mitchell, riding bicycles around the bay. In English legend, Guinevere (note the spelling) was King Arthur's wife who had a tragic love affair with his knight, Lancelot. The mythology has been spun through countless variations down the centuries, but in them all, Guinevere remains an archetypal emblem of romance: a quest worthy of any hero. The tale was reshaped in T. H. White's immensely popular 1958 fantasy novel *The Once and Future King*, which in turn was the basis of the 1960 Broadway hit *Camelot*. Onstage, Guinevere vowed her intention to follow the "Simple Joys of Maidenhood," reinforcing her popular image as a symbol of innocence. She clearly entranced the Scottish folk singer Donovan, who serenaded her on his 1966 LP *Sunshine Superman* (Neil Young later identified "Guinevere" as his favorite Donovan song).

In Crosby's recasting of the myth, "Guinnevere" is identified in three ways, each of which (so Crosby revealed later) could be equated to a particular woman. He consistently identified the last, with "golden hair," as Joni Mitchell; the second, drawing pentagrams, as Christine Hinton (although subsequently his girlfriend from 1966, Nancy Ross, would claim that "I drew pentagrams on the wall" of the house in Lisbon Lane). And the first? Crosby always refused to say. Ultimately, this linking of fact and fiction is reductive and demeaning to a song of entrancing beauty—and it also misses the point. Throughout the lyrics, Guinnevere is compared to the actual subject of the song, an unidentified "you," named only as "my lady." All the "Guinnevere" women have gone, but "you" remains, as an enduring standard of love and perfection, as flawless as Stephen Stills's "Bluebird."

Crosby's melody was equally haunting. It would become the ideal vehicle for his decades of vocal collaboration with Graham Nash. But, as originally recorded in June 1968, it was effectively a duet between Crosby and the exquisite modal voice of the bass guitar played by Jefferson Airplane's Jack Casady. Another friend, Cyrus Faryar, weaved an Indian melody over the opening chords on bouzouki, one of the stringed instruments providing the latticework for the interplay between Crosby and Casady. The finished piece was perfectly of its moment, of an age in which young musicians took on the roles (and robes) of Arthurian legend, and also eternal, undying in its power to stop time and bring the fantastic within reach of the everyday.

In the winter of 1967–68, it was still possible for young American song-writers to imagine that they represented some form of counterculture, without paying the least mind to the nation beyond their privileged surroundings. Slowly the walls of oppression were starting to close in, and even the least political hippie had to concede that (as Crosby would write) "Something's going on here that surely will not stand the light of day." There were multiple triggers for outrage and action: the nationwide protests against the war, which saw draft cards destroyed, draft board offices blockaded, and many activists (including Joan Baez) arrested; the march on the Pentagon chronicled in Norman Mailer's *The Armies of the Night*; the targeting of Black Panther Party leaders by police and the CIA; or the inflamed situation in Vietnam itself. As Lyndon Johnson prepared to concede that he could no longer command the support of the US people and withdrew from the 1968 presidential race, rival candidates emerged who demanded the respect, at least, of the young, militant, and/or black population.

Senator Eugene McCarthy took the lead in disavowing the war. Four months later, another candidate took to the stump: Robert F. Kennedy. The tragic glamor attached to his family heightened his campaign; even such determinedly nonpolitical musicians as Roger McGuinn of the Byrds rallied to the cause. But on June 4, 1968, Kennedy was shot in a Los Angeles hotel after claiming victory in the California Democratic primary. He died the following day.

The assassination of Dr. Martin Luther King Jr. two months earlier had sparked despair and fury across the African American community. The murder of RFK sent much of America into a deep depression. There were no riots; just a vague universal sense that the very foundations of democracy were under attack—and that the younger Kennedy was both a hero and a martyr.

David Crosby was not impelled to write on the day Martin Luther King died. But the RFK assassination crossed a line. "I couldn't go to sleep, and I was mad and a little frightened," he recalled the following year, "same as everybody else was. It's bad enough to lose your first leader [JFK] but when you start to lose the second . . ." He channeled his frustration and grief into a brooding, almost monochordal howl of protest: "Long Time Gone."

Eight days later, Crosby pulled Stephen Stills into United Western Recorders in Hollywood, and the pair began to assemble the song. Crosby was restricted to electric rhythm, while Stills added two layers of lead, bass, and rudimentary drums. The emotion of the moment was captured in Crosby's voice, but the basic structure was awkward and anticlimactic. Only a set of descending vocals from Stills on the final chorus offered some much-needed variation. Unlike his first attempt at "Guinnevere," which had already achieved perfection, "Long Time Gone" was far from immaculate, and Crosby knew it. But who needed a career when there were such tantalizing distractions?

> We used to hang out in the pool at Peter Tork's house, with all these naked girls ready to serve us in any way we wanted.
>
> —Jackson Browne

In little more than a year, a short-order cook at a Village café became one of the most desired pop stars in the world. It was true that Peter Tork's role as the zaniest of TV's Monkees belittled his musical pedigree. But Tork recognized the power of the profile and wealth he had been given. "To me," he reflected in spring 1968, "a cat wearing a bright-flowered shirt is a step further along the evolutionary ladder than his old man in his gray flannel suit. And if he drops acid, too, that's something else. If one person drops acid, two hundred people will feel it. Everyone he comes in contact with will be affected. I've taken acid, and that makes every viewer who watches me on television more aware. I've given him a contact high."

The same response was noted by anyone who dared to inhale within the vicinity of David Crosby. So, it was inevitable that Crosby—and of course Stephen Stills, an old Village compadre—should spend much of

summer 1968 in and around the pool at Tork's lavish home in Laurel
Canyon. The house at 3615 Shady Oak Road had five bedrooms, orange
carpets, white walls, and a blue swimming pool, all set at the end of a
long, narrow driveway that discouraged uninvited guests. Dope, drinks,
and food were on tap; sex was almost compulsory. It was the ultimate
fantasy, and it was available to everyone who fit in. If you grew your hair,
could handle a guitar, distrusted the Amerika of LBJ, and didn't bogart a
joint, then you were probably naked poolside at Tork's house that summer.

Or else you were in Cass Elliot's swimming pool on 7708 Woodrow
Wilson Drive, two miles further down the Canyon. The house was home,
so her sometime bandmate John Phillips recalled, to "Cass's eclectic band
of stoned hippie worshipers—poets, struggling musicians and would-be
actors, sun-fried beach bums, debauched playboys, drug sponges and bikers." Phillips's then-wife Michelle said that "Problems arrived inside the
house wearing pants or shorts or nothing at all. Cass was easy to intrude
upon." Not that Cass cared: she assumed that Crosby would arrive in her
pool by midafternoon, bringing friends, talented and otherwise. Stills was
an equally familiar guest; likewise, any of the Hollies when they were in
town, especially Cass's particular sweetheart, Graham Nash.

A more select crew were free to knock at 8217 Lookout Mountain
Avenue, where Joni Mitchell had bought her first Los Angeles home that
spring. Tiny by comparison with Tork's mansion or Cass's party house,
the Mitchell residence was transformed into a one-woman art colony, all
found objets d'art, stained glass, and bohemian frippery.

The joy of Laurel Canyon was that from its switchback heights, you
could look down on the smog that coated and poisoned the city below,
content that you lived in paradise. (Within a few years, the toxic clouds
were creeping inexorably up the Canyon, proving that you didn't need
to pave paradise to tarnish it.) Whether you were a loner or a sybarite,
you could easily hide yourself away amid the miles of winding streets
concealed behind cypress trees and rocky outcrops. Aside from Tork,
Mitchell, and Elliot, the Canyon was host to Frank Zappa, Micky Dolenz,
Eric Burdon, Jimmy Webb, John Densmore of the Doors, Van Dyke
Parks, Phil Ochs—each adding his own slant to the multidimensional,
multi-angled vision of a utopian society that was the Canyon in 1968.

When Mama Cass's band crumbled into ruins that spring, she set out to tap into Laurel Canyon's multifarious seams of talent and create the ultimate tribute to the scene over which she still presided. She envisaged an album called *In the Words of My Friends*, to which each of her celebrity playmates would contribute a song: Crosby, Stills, Nash, Mitchell, John Sebastian, Tork, the entire hierarchy of Hollywood pop; perhaps even Bob Dylan and the Beatles. In the end, the album took its name from a hit single, *Dream a Little Dream of Me*, and most of those chums were not represented. But Stills did lend some subtle electric guitar, and Nash offered a song that he might never have dared to record himself, an acerbic blast at a lover (or wife) entitled "Burn Your Hatred" ("out on someone else," as the chorus demanded).

At the same time, Cass began to fantasize about combining her dearest friends into a group, something not quite permanent or occasional, but an organic hybrid of the faces she would prefer to meet at her poolside every afternoon. Crosby was first on the list, because barely a day went by when she didn't see him; and Stills, his Canyon sidekick; and Graham Nash, if he could be persuaded to abandon his life in England and become her fantasy roommate; and, stepping dreamily into the realms of the impossible, perhaps Paul McCartney as well? (Even the Lennon-entranced Cass didn't imagine that she would be able to tease her favorite Beatle away from his wife Cynthia, or for that matter, Yoko Ono.)

If there were sympathetic people around her, and heady smoke in the air, Cass would muse aloud about this wild combination of talent and how it might sound—something like the magical chimes that could regularly be heard around her pool, as stalwarts and newcomers raised their voices in impromptu song. Nobody took her too seriously, though; it was only Cass, indulging another vision of paradise.

> It was recorded late at night when everybody was feeling loose, on, and ready. The result is not a hype, not a put-on, but a beautiful jam—a Super Session. It'll mess your mind over!
>
> —Columbia Records ad for *Super Session*, summer 1968

Cass Elliot was not alone in imagining the potential of combining individuals into a sublime whole. In late 1967, a similar fantasy was shared by Elektra Records producer Paul Rothchild. "He had this project called Supergroup," remembered one of the participants, keyboardist Alan Gerber. "It was like a talent contest: about fourteen musicians were brought together, and only about three of us survived that process, rather than being thrown out. Eventually we ended up being called Rhinoceros. When word got out about how we had been put together, the press were ready to tear us apart."

Instead of Supergroup, the plaudits were reserved for *Super Session*. Keyboardist Al Kooper, who had just left Blood, Sweat & Tears, recruited guitarist Michael Bloomfield, drummer Eddie Hoh, and bassist Harvey Brooks to jam and record an album. Two days were set aside in May 1968; but Bloomfield fled town after the first. Kooper made hurried calls around New York in search of a replacement and procured a survivor from one of his favorite bands, Buffalo Springfield. For several hours, Kooper and Stephen Stills kicked around ideas before setting out on a meandering version of Donovan's "Season of the Witch" and a Dylan tune Kooper had helped bring to life three years earlier. Still short of material, they essayed a vocal duet on another Dylan song, "I Shall Be Released," which was ruled out for contractual reasons. They were just about to revive Stills's own biggest hit, "For What It's Worth," when Brooks offered the gorgeous "Harvey's Tune," which required no input from the guitarist whatsoever.

Once it was over, Stills gave the day no further thought; this was just another outing in the studio, like his session work with Jimi Hendrix. To his amazement, Kooper chose to share the limelight on the finished album equally with Bloomfield and Stills, and Columbia Records threw their marketing force into hyping a record that apparently featured "three greats together for the first time, feeding each other's souls." (No matter that Stills and Bloomfield never met during the sessions and were not heard on the same songs.) The album reached the US Top 10, and suddenly Stephen Stills was a name that carried commercial weight as well as cult recognition.

Whereas the death of the Springfield had passed with little comment, Stills's future was now rife with speculation. There was talk that he might join Roger McGuinn in the Byrds, or re-create Al Kooper's central role in Blood, Sweat & Tears. Peter Tork played select journalists an acetate of Stills acting as a one-man band on the Traffic song "Dear Mr. Fantasy," to demonstrate that he didn't need a group. Meanwhile, rumors circulated that the Springfield might reunite without him. "No chance," said Neil Young.

Without ever announcing their intentions, Stills and David Crosby were hedging around the possibility that they might form a band together. They were committed enough to the idea to ask their mutual friend Buzzy Linhart to come on board in a trio. "I knew those guys," Linhart explained, "and they were always starting projects and then just dropping them two days later. I figured that group was just another one of those daydreams." He had another reason to be cautious: "Stephen and David are so opinionated musically, that I wondered if they would always be at each other's throats."

Meanwhile, Stills was vaguely assembling material for a solo album, uncertain whether he was making the record itself or merely a set of demos to attract a producer. In July 1968, he cut two more tracks on which he sang and played every instrument, "Who Ran Away?" and "49 Reasons," mining once again his familiar seam of romantic disillusionment. A few months earlier, Neil Young's friend Ricky James Matthews had arrived in Los Angeles, having served his time for skipping the navy. Matthews subsequently claimed to have stolen Stills's girlfriend, first hooking her up with hairstylist Jay Sebring, then retrieving her for his own use in Toronto. A similar scenario was described in "49 Reasons": the loss of a lover to a "drifter," leaving Stills to lament, "I let that man play his hand / I let them go."

If there was no anguish in Stills's tale, it was because he was taking consolation elsewhere. Judy Collins, the subject of his romantic fantasies in Greenwich Village, arrived in Los Angeles on June 1, 1968. She was grieving for the recent loss of her father, while her current relationship with a journalist was slowly corroding. She had come west to record a new album, after the unexpected success of *Wildflowers*, and engineer John Haeny threw her a welcome party at his house so she could meet the musicians. Among them, she would write, was "possibly the most attractive man I had ever seen . . . His wrists were tanned, as though he'd spent most of his days on a horse in the sun . . . Then his eyes found mine, and we gazed at each other, transfixed. I knew then that he would change my life." Stephen Stills had finally met his Bluebird.

As Collins remembered it, the couple were soon "making music all day and making love all night." She did not realize, yet, exactly how long Stills had admired her, or how difficult it would be for her to match the fantasy he had been embellishing for years. For the moment, the album sessions were productive and thrilling, the romance bloomed . . . and then Collins told her six-years-younger lover that she needed to go home to New York. The idyll was over, to be replaced by months of recriminations and reunions, which would tax both participants to the limit and spur Stills to a lifetime peak of creative catharsis.

I can't say if I'll be leaving the Hollies. I can't answer that.

—Graham Nash, May 1968

A week after the Hollies returned from Canada, they were back on all too familiar ground: Abbey Road in London. Graham Nash was still reeling from his fleeting encounter with Joni Mitchell and found little consolation in the studio. "I wanted to record 'Marrakesh Express,'" he recalled, "but everyone else said it wasn't good enough." "It wasn't us," drummer Bobby Elliott explained, "but it might have been Ron Richards, our producer." "We never refused to do it," keyboardist Bernie Calvert concurred, "but Graham must have felt a little bit disheartened if the band wasn't rushing to do it again." The song progressed no further than a rudimentary backing track, with no vocals. "The arrangement sucked," Nash said. "There was no life to it."

Still he wanted to keep faith with the Hollies, despite admitting that "I believe in a completely different musical direction to that in which the Hollies are going, and right now I feel as if I'm letting myself down, not doing as I want." So, a solution was found, to satisfy both sides: Nash would record a solo album in America. "My output of songs has been much greater than the Hollies have been able to cope with," he explained. "And they are very personal, un-Hollies type of numbers."

Nash was scheduled to fly to the States in June 1968 with his wife; but realizing that this would preclude a reunion with Joni Mitchell, he managed to leave Rose behind. He arrived in New York, where Mitchell was resident at the Bitter End, to discover that she was sharing her apartment in Chelsea with Leonard Cohen. Nash poured his disappointment into a pair of songs he grouped together under the title "Letter to a Cactus Tree" (ironically borrowing the name of the Mitchell lyric that acknowledged her romance with David Crosby). Nakedly, embarrassingly raw, Nash's words recalled their liaison in Ottawa and how he had awoken to discover a note that said, "I will find you once again." Part two of the medley was set in Manhattan where he slept "half a block" down the street from Mitchell and Cohen. Nash lamented that he was "competing with a poet for your favors," his hopes "fading day by day."

Then it was back to work, with the Hollies, in a succession of engagements that might have been designed to demoralize him. There was no hint of psychedelia in the 1968 incarnation of the band: as guitarist Tony Hicks said, "We've moved from having no image at all to going hippie and now being very straight. We're moving in the right direction now."

So it was that Nash and the other Hollies appeared on BBC-TV with country singer Bobbie Gentry, clad in tuxedos, colored shirts, and bow ties. Nash and Gentry shared the vocals on an excruciatingly twee rendition of "Louisiana Man," tailor-made for a middle-aged, middle-of-the-road audience. Black tie and evening dress was obviously their new image. Two weeks later, they were in Split, Yugoslavia, for a live television concert in front of an audience who might just have been certified dead. They played their now-standard mix of hits and folk tunes, augmented by a jazzy version of "A Taste of Honey"—"a good crowd-pleaser," as Nash recalled with a grimace many years later. There was camaraderie, at least, as they faced the most unresponsive crowd of their lives; the Hollies banded together like schoolboys, ridiculing the audience between songs. ("This is for those of you who couldn't care less," was how Nash introduced "On a Carousel.") But after Split, the Hollies had to return to the studio, where Nash unveiled two new songs: "Man with No Expression," written by his friend Terry Reid, with a few lyrical amendments by Nash; and "Survival of the Fittest," a sarcastic account of a female performer who "lies to herself and her public." It is not hard to imagine that the actual focus of the song was closer to home, as Nash winced his way through a cheesy arrangement of Bob Dylan's "Blowin' in the Wind" and prepared for the next ordeal. The group were now booked into one of England's premier cabaret venues, the Batley Variety Club. Here they would perform for an audience who wanted a three-course meal, a drink, and some lighthearted entertainment, and on cue, the Hollies delivered. The tuxedos were returned to the wardrobe, and instead the band took to the stage in white suits and the obligatory bow ties.

For years afterward, Nash would tell audiences that he had only donned his white suit under duress, but the other Hollies remember that it was actually his idea. "Graham kept changing his mind," Allan Clarke recalled. "One day he'd want to do something, the next he wouldn't. Almost everyone was doing the cabaret circuit in those days—and Graham was all for it." The Hollies opened with the mock-Latin Paul Anka hit, "Eso Beso," and then mixed comedy routines with a smattering of their hits. There was even an opportunity for the crowd to sing along with a children's favorite, first recorded by Peter, Paul and Mary. "The audience were delighted and called for more," a reviewer noted. Nash finished the week and pleaded: "I can't take touring anymore. I just want to sit at home and write songs." But the Hollies had already made the corporate decision to record an album of material by Bob Dylan, rearranged for their new cabaret following.

Q: How did you feel standing on the stage of the Batley Variety Club in 1968, dressed in a white suit, singing "Puff the Magic Dragon"?

Graham Nash: I didn't feel good.

David Crosby: *Excuse* me? Wait a minute! Do I smell *blood* in the water?

Nash: Yes, I sang "Puff the Magic Dragon," absolutely.

Crosby [*disgustedly*]: For *what*?

Nash: For money.

Crosby: With whom?

Nash [*defensively*]: The Hollies.

Crosby [*gleefully*]: No, no, no!

Nash: It was right at the time when we were doing "Blowin' in the Wind" also, and I said, "I've *had* this."

Stephen Stills: That was the Dylan album you were doing?

Crosby: Yeah, but you didn't *tell* us about "Puff the Magic Dragon."

Nash: Well, it's not a bad song.

Stills: Actually, David, I used to sing it, too.

Crosby: Well, you're *both* a pair of poofs, what can I tell you?

Nash: It was not a good feeling. I'd come to the end of my lollipop with the Hollies. You've got to understand, I'd been smoking dope with these two maniacs in America for at least a year and a half by that time . . .

Crosby [*singing sarcastically*]: Puff the Magic Dragon . . .

Stills: Shut up!

—1991 interview with the author

In New York and Los Angeles, between her concert engagements, Judy Collins and Stephen Stills tried to build a coherent relationship out of their mutual infatuation. They bickered, made love, argued, sang, and drank: "I was an alcoholic," Collins admitted years later, "but it took me a long time to realize that I was dependent on that drug." Neither could understand how an affair that had begun with such certainty could unravel so quickly.

When she was on tour, Stills stayed home and complained about it with a guitar in hand—emerging with a song for the ages, "You Don't Have to Cry." It painted him as the veteran who had seen through the madness of touring ("it quite nearly killed me"); her as the foolish and errant lover who had chosen to put career before caring. It was about the evils of showbiz, he would explain later, "especially New York–style showbiz." In the same bout of creativity, he wrote an innocent testimony of affection, "My Love Is a Gentle Thing." A week or two later, all the confusion and emotional tumult of his relationship—plus his college

lessons in alliteration—were channeled into a wordy but heartfelt statement of patient love, "Helplessly Hoping."

The same title might have been applied to David Crosby and Graham
Nash, both of whom were clinging to the idea that Joni Mitchell might
settle her restless heart with them. Crosby could console himself on the
Mayan in Florida or in the certainty that Christine Hinton would be there
for him. (As one of his friends recalled, "David's attitude to women back
then was always, 'How well can you serve me?'") But Nash was beset by
"decisions, decisions—what to do with my life?"

During the Hollies' week at Batley, Nash stayed at Oulton Hall in
Leeds, smoking dope and, like Stills, soothing his turmoil with a guitar. The previous year, during one of the stoned interview rambles that
emphasized his distance from his colleagues, Nash had explained that
"I've come to think that you need to live your life by a code—my code
being, at all times, be as good as you possibly can." Now he placed that
thought at the center of a song that would become an anthem for the
remainder of his life: "Teach Your Children." From the personal, and
a hint of the despair that had ruined his father's life, the song quickly
became universal, a simple but profound statement of the dialectical
relationship between parents and their kids.

In the same night, Nash also wrote "Right Between the Eyes," a confession to an unnamed friend that he had slept with his wife, and "Lady
of the Island," which he later admitted was a love ballad for two women—
neither of them Joni Mitchell. (Terry Reid helped him complete the latter,
with the result that each man emerged with his own set of lyrics.) "I felt
isolated," he would remember of this burst of inspiration, "really alone."
Yet he still imagined that he might be able to record these intensely
personal songs with the Hollies.

Within a matter of days, he received an invitation from Lookout
Mountain Avenue. Joni Mitchell had just returned from the Philadelphia
Folk Festival, where she had taken the crowd by storm despite suffering
the aftereffects of her hepatitis. Nash, meanwhile, had a week to spare
between the recording of "Listen to Me," a throwback to the pre-acid
Hollies sound, and a prestigious live performance on the BBC music
show *Colour Me Pop*.

He took the nonstop flight across the Pole to Los Angeles, around August 31, 1968, and rang Mitchell from the airport. She was not alone. "David and Stephen are here," she explained. Nash bit back his disappointment, and told her, "Tell them to wait and have dinner with us." Then he went out to the Canyon.

At which point facts and memories become blurred. The story has been told and retold from multiple perspectives, and situated in several locations and times, each revision subtly different from the rest. Like the myths of creation that claim to underpin the world's religions, every variant has its true believers. Quizzed in the twenty-first century, Crosby and Nash swore that it happened at Joni's house; Stills said that the hostess was Mama Cass, because he would have been too shy to perform in front of Joni Mitchell. Other options are available: John Sebastian's home or swimming pool; Stephen Stills's place; or perhaps Paul Rothchild's sitting room. The *ur*-story, the foundation of the myth, was delivered by Graham Nash when he was with Mitchell in New York for her February 1969 show at Carnegie Hall. "We were sitting in [Joni's] living room in Laurel Canyon one night," he explained, and "they"—David Crosby and Stephen Stills—"did this song in two-part harmony, and I added a third part."

That basic element remains unchanged. Crosby, Stills & Nash was born when the two sang to the one, and the one (after requesting multiple repeats) chimed in with a third harmony part. "This stuff coming out of the three of us was quite something," Nash told me. "I'm a harmony freak, and I'd never heard anything like it. We sang that one verse, and then started laughing hysterically—laughing with joy. We couldn't believe what we'd found. And then once we'd discovered that sound, that unique blend of putting my voice with David and Stephen's, that was it—we just kept singing."

The identity of the song is slightly cloudy: most accounts mention "You Don't Have to Cry," though Crosby originally suggested that they began with "Helplessly Hoping" (which would have compelled Nash to undertake a phenomenal feat of lyrical memory). Nash even once insisted that their debut performance was the Beatles' "Blackbird," which hadn't yet been released. Crosby placed Mama Cass in the room, and she may indeed have brought Nash in from the airport. Other putative witnesses insisted that John Sebastian was there, though he never made that claim himself.

More confusion surrounds the date. Having set the scene at Mitchell's house, Nash immediately complicated the issue when he repeated the story over the following year. Now he remembered that the creation of Crosby, Stills & Nash occurred immediately after the Hollies' February 1968 show at the Whisky. He even moved the venue to Stills's house—which made a strange kind of sense, because in February Mitchell had not yet bought her house in the Canyon. Stills reinforced the post-Whisky tale, although it is hard to see how CSN could have been performing songs he'd written about Judy Collins, when he had yet to meet her.

So, the most likely explanation is this. CSN certainly shared a car after the Whisky show, and were quite possibly together at Cass Elliot's house in the twenty-four hours before the Hollies left town for Florida. Given the personnel and the location, it is unimaginable that they would not have sung together—perhaps as a trio, perhaps as an ensemble; enough, in any case, to register pleasure and anticipation that it might happen again. Six months later, the trio were at Mitchell's house on the day Nash flew in from London, and the legendary performance of a Stephen Stills song took place. Then they repeated the trick, giggling as they went, for Cass, Sebastian, and anyone else who cared to listen.

Ultimately, the fine details are irrelevant. "I knew what it *was*," Nash recalled. "And I knew we would do it again, as soon as we could. Plus, there was the rush of a new 'love affair' with two other singers. Musically, that was thrilling for me, hearing their songs, and being encouraged by them to write, which was something I wasn't used to. 'Boy, I like that "Marrakesh Express,"' they told me. How could I *not* be excited by that?"

Not that there was time to bask in this mutual glow. Within a few days, Nash was on the return flight to London. Meanwhile, his new coterie had driven up the coast to the Esalen Institute, for the 1968 Big Sur Folk Festival. Joan Baez and Judy Collins, the leading sirens of American folk, were the billed headliners, and Stephen Stills naturally tagged along with his lover. The rogue element arrived in David Crosby's VW bus, which opened to reveal Joni Mitchell and Mama Cass Elliot. They were immediately invited to play, and the weekend's schedule relaxed into impromptu magic—Crosby and Stills performing together as a duo for the first time, Stills supporting Collins, and as a finale, Judy, Joni, Cass, and Joan leading the entire gathering in a soaring rendition of Bob Dylan's "I Shall Be Released." Six thousand miles away, Graham Nash was haunted by the same dream.

CHAPTER 5

Everybody knows the revolution's coming. That's all that has to be said. It's not gonna happen easy. It's not gonna go away. It's just inevitable.

—Neil Young, November 1968

The American left staked its unity on a show of strength at the Democratic National Convention in August 1968. It hoped to tip the balance against the leading Democrat contender, Vice President Hubert Humphrey, in favor of Senator Eugene McCarthy, who had pledged to stop the war in Vietnam. Either man would surely start as the favorite in a presidential race against the Republican nominee, three-time loser Richard Nixon.

The anarchic self-publicists of the Youth International Party (the Yippies) had no time for a failed system of electoral democracy. Yippie leaders Jerry Rubin and Abbie Hoffman demanded "the Politics of Ecstasy," with "five hundred thousand of us dancing in the streets, throbbing with amplifiers and harmony." As August grew closer, they began to toss around a fantasy list of those who would participate in Chicago, from the Beatles and Bob Dylan to Frank Zappa and Jefferson Airplane.

Judy Collins sang at the press conference that launched the campaign. "My father had a radio show in which he castigated the McCarthy witch hunts in the 1950s," she remembered. "We were raised to speak our minds. So, it was natural for me to sing about peace, war, and injustice, as well as love." When the Yippies' plans were exposed as confrontational, Collins began to back away. "I was not interested in putting myself in a situation that was going to be chaotic and possibly dangerous," she explained. Others among her peers were equally reluctant to be used as cannon fodder for Rubin and Hoffman's brand of political theater. Al Kooper jumped ship after his Fender Telecaster was stolen by a fan at a Yippie fund-raiser. Paul Kantner, who boasted later that Jefferson Airplane "should have been arrested as traitors a dozen times," thought that "the idea was fucked up from the start. I appreciate the fact that some people did bother to go there and get their heads kicked in on our behalf, but I couldn't see any reason for us to go and get beaten up."

At no point did Hoffman and Rubin approach the composer of "For What It's Worth" or the man who had told the Monterey crowd that JFK was the victim of a treasonous conspiracy. When Chicago's Festival of Life disintegrated into street battles and police brutality, and demonstrators chanted "The whole world is watching" as news cameras rolled, Stephen Stills and David Crosby were in California, bent on hedonism, and grappling with the uncertainties of romance. Nor did either man react as the New Left coalition unwound in the aftermath of Chicago and Richard Nixon was duly elected as the thirty-seventh president of the United States. Their focus, and that of their friends, was more insular — not collective political action, but a community of song.

"There's a tremendous number of groups who have broken up," John Sebastian said that September, "and what's happened is, seeing that they were all friends anyway, they're getting together, but not in groups. Everybody's been through an evolution almost simultaneously." Sebastian and Graham Nash had already been approached by Donovan to participate in a festival of pop songwriters. The three men discussed the plan when Nash flew back to California in mid-September 1968. Ostensibly he was trying to recruit American artists to appear at Save Rave, a charity event he was staging in London on December 8. But his aim was to consolidate his new relationships on the West Coast. He slid comfortably back into the Laurel Canyon scene but discovered that Joni Mitchell had flown to New York for a TV show, prior to spending two weeks in London. Any reunion after Nash's return was hampered by the presence of his spouse. Graham and Rose duly attended an official launch party for Save Rave, "putting an end to rumors that the couple were to split," as a gossip columnist noted. Then, the day before Mitchell headlined a festival of contemporary song at London's Royal Festival Hall, Nash flew to Sweden with the Hollies.

While he was away, John Sebastian let slip to an *LA Times* journalist the real purpose of Nash's Californian vacations. "Stills and Crosby have been singing with Graham Nash of the Hollies in informal sessions," Pete Johnson reported. "Nash is still with the British group but is enjoying a busman's holiday." There was talk that the three men might be joining Eric Clapton for a second *Super Session* album. The New York trade magazine *Record World* investigated the rumors and concluded that the impromptu CSN gatherings "will probably not result in a group due to contractual conflicts."

Remarkably, these American stories did not reach London, where Graham Nash maintained public allegiance to the Hollies. His friends in the Canyon were less discreet, however. Stephen Stills confided to Neil Young and his manager, Elliot Roberts, that CSN was no longer a party trick but a functioning group, and Young passed on the news to an underground paper in Michigan. "You can't print that," Roberts interjected, "or it'll get a lot of cats in trouble." "Shit, that is ridiculous," Young countered. "Everybody must know. Print it." And so they did—but not until late January, by which time the scoop was decidedly stale.

Eventually, pretense became impossible to maintain. As Hollies drummer Bobby Elliott recalled, "We had 'Listen to Me' out, and *Top of the Pops* wanted us—and Graham was over in the States and couldn't get back in time. It would have gone Top 3 if we'd done it. He was hanging on and hanging on, trying to hedge his bets." On his return, "there was a meeting at our manager's office," keyboardist Bernie Calvert said. "Graham came in and said, 'I'm leaving.' I was really upset, because I had a lot of respect for him, and I said the wrong thing: 'Do you think you're irreplaceable, Graham?' I didn't want him to go, and it came out all wrong. Graham did a kind of double take, looked at me, and shrugged his shoulders."

In the moment, Nash seemed to realize that he was about to abandon the man who had been his best friend for more than twenty years: "So I asked Allan Clarke to come with me. Did I want him to join CSN? I don't know what I was thinking. Obviously, that wouldn't have worked—well, who knows? But it would have been different, anyway." Clarke was so dazed by Nash's decision that he had no clear memory of being asked to join him in California: "He said later that he would have taken me with him if I'd latched on to the idea. But I had a family, and I couldn't suddenly give everything up to go to the States."

Nash wasn't just leaving the Hollies; he also told his wife that their marriage was over. "I never regretted it for a second," he said later. "People say, 'Didn't it take a lot of balls to leave your group and your family and your country?' No. When I first started singing with David and Stephen, my world changed. I decided to follow my heart, like I've always done, and it's always stood me in good stead."

There remained the formalities: fulfilling the final shows in their schedule, both charity affairs; negotiating a release from the Hollies' writing and management contracts; and scraping together enough cash for the flight and cab fare. Then the split had to be made public. At first, Nash was reluctant to acknowledge his plans. "I shall go to America and sing with some of my friends," he declared, "not for recording, just for pleasure and experimentation. Then I go my way as a solo singer and songwriter. I've made enough bread not to have to earn money for a while." One British magazine insisted that "He may go to America, but it is unlikely that he would settle permanently there."

In the immediate aftermath, Allan Clarke was shattered — and resentful. He told *Melody Maker*, "All of Graham's songs are very slow and very boring. He wants to go all soppy, artistic and beautiful." Bobby Elliott agreed that "Allan took the split the hardest. It really hurt him. In some ways, he had more qualifications for a solo career than Graham. Graham had the best harmony voice around, but Allan was more of a lead singer."

Like a mistress making sure her lover would leave his wife, California then came to London. John Sebastian touched down first, followed by Stills and Crosby. They gathered up Nash and drove out to Donovan's cottage in Hertfordshire, where five stray voices were joined in harmony. "We've just been looking around, taking it all in," Sebastian reported. Were they forming a group? "I doubt it. Well, I definitely won't be — I don't want to be in a group scene anymore. I don't know whether the others are going to form a group—I think it's unlikely they would. Not a regular gigging group."

Sebastian recounted how "Stephen and Dave and I used to get together in California. David has this great voice for harmony. And then suddenly Graham Nash appeared—and it was incredible. Dave has a high voice, but Graham would be about an octave and a half higher. We really get a lot of fun out of just blowing together." There was only one drawback: "The moment it's taken off an informal level, and turned into a business, you get all the hang-ups of contracts and that sort of thing. It's working well at the moment because we're all friends who play together."

Back in the States, Judy Collins said that she and Stephen Stills were planning to record together: "We want to do a single—something Western, perhaps." She expressed her distaste for most contemporary rock ("unbearably loud and redundant") and admitted, "What I've missed recently in rock and roll is music." Then she brightened and explained that her boyfriend was in London with his new band: "It's going to be a very musical and sensational thing."

In retrospect, Collins would concede that this was a period of intense turbulence in her relationship with Stills. She was drinking heavily; he was equally excessive in his habits. She felt pressured by his possessive nature; he felt betrayed by her need for independence. "We spent that winter arguing, via long-distance telephone and sometimes in person," she wrote in her autobiography, "about how we were ever going to make our relationship work if neither of us would give an inch." What Collins did not know was that Stills had begun to channel his increasing sense of frustration, and his mounting despair, into a set of songs that would become the backbone of his new repertoire.

At last, a group with three fine singers, capable of doing the most complicated harmonies, and a group of three well-respected composers. More important than the Cream—this liaison, if it ever gets on record, which it surely will, will be the most significant group of 1969.

—Barry Miles, *International Times*, January 1969

The tale that Graham Nash was embarking on a solo career could not be maintained for long. In late November 1968, he began to invite select friends from the London pop press to visit him in a top-floor apartment on the corner of Moscow Road and Salem Road in Bayswater, a block from the city's oldest department store. The flat contained a two-track recording console, which had been used to tape jingles for pirate radio stations. The press discovered that he was not alone: with him were Stephen Stills and David Crosby. "We're not starting another group," Nash was quick to insist. "For a start, we're all signed to different labels. But we're pioneering. We may come together on a more permanent basis." Nash called it "a musical workshop"; Crosby, "a rock seminar." Stills explained that "Frank Zappa had this idea of getting all the good musicians under one roof and then letting people come and choose who they wanted to put together—like one big orchestra."

Contractual freedom was their anthem: "We're not their private property," Nash said of the record companies to whom they were signed. Crosby added: "We are all in a situation of freedom to look over what's going on. There's a whole new scene around the corner. I don't know what it is yet, but every musician I know is in the same position. We don't want to be pop stars—that's a dull trip."

Yet for all their talk of individuality, the three men acknowledged the power that they could wield together. "The initial feeling is almost sacred," Nash said of their vocal blend. "We're just making a joyful noise," Crosby added, "and it's spreading." "It's a unit with three arms," Nash said, "and we can wander out on any of the arms." Pushed for a definition of their sound, Crosby laughed and said, "It's like trying to describe fucking!"

The three men sketched out a future in which they and their friends might drift in and out of each other's company, picking their companions and their identity on a song-by-song basis. But eventually Nash revealed that they had begun to think beyond an impromptu collision of voices and characters. He stressed that there would be no collective name for this loose ensemble: "That would brand us. What I envisage I'll do in the future is to be part of a mother company with the others, but still with our own individual companies inside it."

Corporate issues aside, the three men also had to confront the knowledge that each of them had an ego to match his talent. Roger McGuinn had already testified to David Crosby's attempts to seize creative control of the Byrds. And in recent months, Crosby's companions had been brazen about their unshakable self-belief in the studio. "I have to clarify the arrangement of the song, mix it and put it all together," Stills had stated. "Essentially, I'm controlling the session." Nash went even further with the Hollies: "I want to write songs and sing them and produce them and mix them and have a say in the cover. This is because I think I'm right."

But there were compensations in sacrificing their independence, even for three self-confessed control freaks. The trio offered them mutual reinforcement, a haven for experiment, and most of all a vehicle for the serendipitous collision of vocal tones that had made them laugh with joy at Joni Mitchell's house a few weeks earlier.

None of them was a stranger to singing in harmony. That was Crosby's major contribution to the original Byrds; Stills's joy since his baptism in the Au Go Go Singers; and Nash's speciality in the Hollies. As Eric Haydock recalled, "The Everly Brothers paid the ultimate compliment by saying that if one of them ever died, Graham was the only one who could replace him." Crosby would often call him "the best harmony singer on the planet." "Nash can fill harmony records by himself faster than the three of us can do them," he insisted once. "He can do all three parts and then three more in the time it takes either of us to do one." ("That may be due to the fact that we're stupid!" Stills interrupted.)

Of the three men, Crosby was the master of vocal arrangement. The standard way of presenting three voices was for one to sing the melody, and the other two to add the third and the fifth notes in the scale, above or below the lead voice. Crosby would always look for an alternate way of voicing the harmonies, shifting the gap between the voices in a single phrase, daring to find an apparent discord that would resolve itself majestically in the following bar. Nash reckoned that "The most natural sound of all for us is Stephen taking the melody, David doing the harmony, underneath or over, and me going over the top of whatever those two are doing."

Beyond that, as Nash reflected many years later, "Anyone can sing the notes that CSN sing. It's just that they don't sound like us. The Hollies and CSN could sing the same notes on a chorus, and it would sound completely different." "It's a particular combination of textures and sounds and inflections," Crosby added. "The peculiarity of three human voices is not something you can duplicate." They would soon evolve unique CSN vowel sounds to overcome the gulf in accents between Nash's nasal Mancunian, Crosby's mellow Californian, and Stills's raw Southern drawl. They would hold notes at the end of lines, daring the others to be first to gasp for breath; soar high in an ecstatic rush of voices; sometimes even sacrifice the meaning of a word to the glorious thrust of harmonies. On a song such as Stills's "You Don't Have to Cry," (probably) the first they ever attempted, their vocal union was so tight that it was impossible to distinguish the melody from the harmonies around it. In whatever order they were stacked, Crosby, Stills, and Nash created a chorale that was utterly distinctive—and quite magical.

"I realized the power of CSN one of the first times we played the 'Suite' for anybody," Nash recalled. "People I respected, who were powerful voices themselves in the music industry, I saw their mouths fall wide open. I saw them look at me and David and Stephen and go, 'What the fuck did I just hear? I've never heard anything like that in my life.' That's when I knew, as a writer and singer, that we were getting through, we were communicating."

The "Suite"—"Suite: Judy Blue Eyes," to reveal its inspiration—was the artistic heart of this new phenomenon. "It's all about this chick," was all Stills would say when it was released, but that disguised the hours of craft and weeks of agony that had created it. Around a guitar tuning he had been taught by Bruce Palmer of Buffalo Springfield, Stills constructed a collage of musical fragments, each of them a snapshot of a relationship in constant flux. Across its seven-minute expanse, it veered from utter despair to ecstatic union, climaxing with a set of three short verses, each of which might have been designed to display the CSN harmonies in their peacock finery. And finally, to relieve the romantic tension, the "Suite" exploded into a thrilling wordless chant, over which Stills waxed lyrical, in his schoolboy Spanish, about his desire to see Cuba. (He traveled there at last in 1979.)

The song had evolved over several painful weeks in the early fall, one of a set that Stills committed to tape, perhaps as late as November 1968.

The sequence was released many decades later as *Just Roll Tape*, with the misleading suggestion that it dated from several weeks before Stills and Collins first met. What was striking in retrospect was the depth and breadth of the material that Stills already had at his command, from the memoir of Southern ballroom etiquette that was "Change Partners" to the raucous Delta blues of "Black Queen." As if anticipating his own future struggles with stardom, Stills delivered a gentle scolding to the publicity-hungry John Lennon on "The Doctor Will See You Now" ("Do you know better than anyone else?"). But his obsession was the uncertainty of romance, and nothing prodded that wound more acutely and precisely than "Suite: Judy Blue Eyes."

Those who mounted the stairs to the top of 16 Moscow Road were treated to an exhibition of these gems and more. Nash had finally found a welcoming home for songs that the Hollies couldn't wrap their heads around, such as "Marrakesh Express," "Man with No Expression," and "Lady of the Island." Crosby unveiled "Guinnevere" and greeted underground journalist Barry Miles with a song that even this bastion of the British counterculture struggled to comprehend: "Now his style is longer," Miles reported, "more drifting, he ties up dozens of open-ended notes just in the nick of time, singing double treble quadruple time to his own accompaniment. Taking exceptional risks, long climactic chord build-ups are capped by a single weird chord as firmly as the pyramids were topped with capstones of gold (like the final mad chord in a Thelonious Monk solo)." There was much more of the same, as Miles experienced "Déjà Vu" for the first time. His stunned, almost incoherent reaction wasn't uncommon. "I thought Crosby was mad," Nash remembered of his exposure to the same song. "It didn't make any sense! Where was the verse? Where was the chorus? I knew I had to work with this guy."

The trio made a demo tape in their Moscow Road flat, which Stills carried to the first-floor office on 3 Savile Row. This was the professional home of Derek Taylor, the publicist who had been one of the masterminds of the Monterey festival the previous year. He was now ensconced as the stoned, borderline insane but always affable PR head of the Beatles' Apple Corps, the recording arm of which had been launched three months earlier. Stills was eager to claim a place on their roster and did his best to enlist Taylor's support, only to discover that the Apple man was overcome by the distractions of a business founded on the dubious principle of "controlled weirdness." Taylor apologized for his lack of attention. "See you when we're famous," Stills said, and walked away.

At Taylor's urging, Apple then came to Moscow Road, in the person of George Harrison, who was still jetlagged after a flight from California. He listened politely to CSN's sales pitch, only for Stills to say exactly the wrong thing to a man who was already feeling overshadowed by his more prolific colleagues in the Beatles. "I wasn't really thinking," Stills admitted. "I turned round and said, 'Hey, would you ask Paul if he'd like to produce us?' I didn't know at the time that Paul was busy working with Mary Hopkin, and didn't have time, and it was George that wanted to produce us. So I stuck my foot well in it. I'm not sure George ever forgave me for what I did, and I don't blame him really." CSN would not become Apple recording artists—a blessed escape, given the company's rapid descent into financial and legal chaos.

Meanwhile, Graham Nash had to tear himself away from Moscow Road for his final engagement with the Hollies on December 8. Earlier in 1968, he had imagined Save Rave as a star-laden charity extravaganza, which would be filmed by Apple, or screened live by the BBC, and would feature the Hollies alongside Jimi Hendrix, the Beatles, and the Rolling Stones. Instead, Nash found himself at the London Palladium on a distinctly more mundane bill. "It was all a bit strained," Tony Hicks remembered, "and then David Crosby came into our dressing room, which made it even more strained." Nash recalled Crosby arriving with "his leather cape, his hat and his cane—you know, he's a bottle of vibes, that guy. It was obviously a tense moment, because it was my last show with the guys, and here was one of the main reasons I was leaving." Onstage, Nash recalled, "There was one point when I remember thinking, 'Shit, is this *it*? What am I *doing*?'" But their spot was so short that Nash barely had time to reflect before it was over. The Hollies performed brief but typically professional extracts from their cabaret set— "Carrie Anne," "Dang Me," "Blowin' in the Wind," and "A Taste of Honey"—to the customary rousing reception. But nobody onstage mentioned that Nash was leaving, and there was no emotional farewell. The next morning, he and Crosby collected their acoustic guitars and headed out to Heathrow Airport for their flight to Los Angeles, leaving behind Nash's personal and professional security—and almost all of his money.

> Maybe some group will come along and be big, you know, but who cares? It's happened so many times now, it's like a 1969 car. Who cares? We all know it's not going to be any better than a '68 car. It may look a little different, but it's the same thing.
>
> —Neil Young, October 1968

The poster outside the Bitter End in New York announced the headline attraction: "Reprise recording artist" Joni Mitchell. In half-size print below was the support: "Neil Young: former Buffalo Springfield star." It was late October 1968, Young's first solo album was being readied for release, and the best advance publicity he could muster was second billing at a venue that held merely 230 people. The trade magazine *Cashbox* reported the opening in ecstatic terms, repeating the word "beautiful" like an incantation. But the praise was reserved entirely for Mitchell: for Young's contribution to the evening, not a word was spared.

A few weeks later, Young was pictured in *Time* magazine—but merely as an unnamed client of a Laurel Canyon astrologer named Kiyo. Almost a year after he had left Buffalo Springfield, Neil Young was anonymous and irrelevant—not a scene maker like David Crosby, or a participant in a Top 10 *Super Session* like Stephen Stills, but merely a "former star." As if to reinforce the point, Young's song "On the Way Home" was released as a Springfield single in late 1968, climbed to number 82 in the *Billboard* charts the week of the Bitter End premiere, and promptly vanished.

That still outshone the performance of "The Loner," Young's first solo single. On the rare occasions when his name was mentioned in the press, nobody seemed sure whether or not his Reprise album had actually been released. When it was, Young's vocal presence was so low-key that it was as if he were trying to hide from the public (technical issues with the final mix were held responsible). Reprise offered to let Young remix the album, at which point somebody thought it might be sensible to include the artist's name on the front cover—the original pressing merely displaying a painting of Young by a Topanga Canyon friend of his wife.

In an attempt to raise Young's profile above the horizontal, Reprise prepared an advertising campaign in the underground press that portrayed him as reclusive and near-sociopathic. The same ad department, famed for its irony, had already promoted Joni Mitchell as being "90% Virgin," on the tenuous basis that she had reached only 10 percent of her potential audience. Young's publicity was equally misguided. Decorated by a picture of the artist bent forward in his kitchen, his hair masking his face, the ad described Young in the aftermath of the Springfield's demise, "where he wanted to be: on his own. Unadvertised, unpromoted, unvictimized, unbugged. Up in Topanga, brewing, brooding, his stiff black hair dangling, making an ungainly Gothic arch across his forehead . . ." and so it went on, as if he were Kaspar Hauser, unaccustomed to human contact, speaking a language only he could understand. The reverse psychology continued as the copywriters promised that Young was "No fun. Challenging, absorbing, frustrating . . . about as much fun as *Peer Gynt*. And not sexy. Not in any sense we're about to explain right here anyhow. No, not Mr. Magnetism." Not surprisingly, album sales were minimal.

A somewhat different face was presented when the "brooding" artist appeared at the folk venue Canterbury House in Ann Arbor, Michigan, in November 1968. He was still self-effacing, as if wary of forcing himself on the audience, but between songs he was droll and even playful. For almost the last time in his life, he was being treated on his immediate merits, not his reputation; there was no applause of recognition as he began songs that would soon become rock standards, no danger of fans drowning out his acoustic guitar with their Pavlovian approval. Joking about his brief employment at a Toronto bookstore, he uttered a prophetic explanation: "I got fired for irregularity, because I couldn't be depended upon . . . to be consistent." In a radio interview a few weeks later, he belied that image, insisting: "I'm convinced that nothing's gonna stop me."

Caught between sets in Ann Arbor, he told the local underground rag how much he preferred life as a solo artist to being in a group: "It's much better. It's less hassle." Would he ever join another band? The answer was definite: "No." Nor was he tempted to abandon the acoustic guitar: "Nobody will ever dance while I play."

When Young returned to the city in early February 1969, nothing seemed to have changed. A week later he was back at the Bitter End, this time as a headliner, and as the show began, Young was still clasping his acoustic, letting his hair trail across his face as he leaned forward into the mike, muttering dry asides between his songs. Then it was intermission— and the crew began to set up for an electric band.

Quizzed about his musical tastes the previous year, Young had criticized the new Beatles album, championed the Stones, described Jimi Hendrix as "really great" and Stephen Stills as his only possible rival. But he reserved his richest praise for "a complete new thing," a band who had recently issued their debut album, to even quieter commercial response than his own record had attracted. "The Rockets are the best new group we've heard in the last two years. I'd rather listen to them than to any other group."

What he didn't mention was that the Rockets were his friends, and that he had plans for them—or, at least, some of them. The heart of the band was the rhythm section of Billy Talbot (bass) and Ralph Molina (drums). "We have our differences, Billy and I, but it's more like a brother thing," Molina explained. "He hates me and I hate him . . ." and Talbot intervened, "But we still love each other." In conversation, the pair could grumble and bicker like an old married couple, but their rudimentary musical skills were transcended by the way they locked together, in the same relentless, almost pedestrian rhythm. In the early 1960s group Danny and the Memories, they joined forces with Danny Whitten. "He was funny and really talented," Talbot said of their troubled companion. "He was alive. He was great." "He was a motivator," Molina cut in. Talbot dug deeper: "Danny had things inside of him. He was a Taurus. He didn't talk about stuff that was inside of him, but every once in a while he would explode. There were some things that happened to him when he was a young kid that were really heavy duty. Today, it's all out there—child abuse, mentally or physically, all that stuff that kids go through. In those days, nobody really talked about it." Whitten would confirm Talbot's judgment in his most enduring song, "I Don't Want to Talk About It."

Young was still fresh to California when a girl called Autumn introduced him to Talbot. "He used to come up to my house in Laurel Canyon," the bassist recalled. "We'd sing—him, Danny, Robin Lane, who was Danny's girlfriend then and later Neil's girlfriend—whoever else was around." By then, Danny and the Memories had metamorphosed into the Rockets. "We were a jamming band," Talbot explained. "We would play these two- or three-chord jams for an hour. That's what we did. Then we went in with Neil, and we naturally elongated his songs just the same way." When the Rockets made their solitary album in 1968, only one track, "Let Me Go," approached that style, with Bobby Notkoff's fiddle keening over the unmoving backdrop of the band. The rest of the album was less distinctive, almost murky, half-written by Whitten, who sang as if he were trying to hide his identity from the FBI. It was an almost perfect counterpoint to Young's own record.

Quizzed about how the Rockets, an independent band, mutated into Crazy Horse, the abbreviated backing crew for Neil Young, Talbot could only say, "It happened in pieces." Molina looked almost distraught for a second and said, "I don't like to think about it. Neil played with us, and the next thing I knew, we were doing the songs with Neil. I didn't think of it as a long-term thing. The Rockets were still there. We were just going to play these songs, then come back."

Young borrowed Molina, Talbot, and Whitten for his sessions at Sunset Sound in March 1969, then called upon Notkoff and Robin Lane to embellish individual songs. Young played Lane "Round and Round," which she remembered from her initial meeting with him two years earlier. "We started to rehearse," she said, "or so I thought. We played it twice, and suddenly he said that was it. I thought it was nuts recording like that." Young conceded that they were all "absolutely stoned out of our minds in the studio," and on headphones you can hear them swaying around the microphones, as if swimming through the air.

That typified the new approach of Young and his producer, David Briggs. The multiple overdubs and endless, insecure prevarication of his debut album were gone. Instead, he set out to capture the moment, rather than a *perfect* moment. "We were really feeling each other out, and we didn't know each other, but we were turned on to what was happening,"

Young explained a year later. "I wanted to record that, because that never gets recorded." Before work began, he had imagined an album that would reflect his revised live show: "On one side I'll be alone, and the other side will feature the group." But once he began to play with Whitten, Talbot, and Molina, he couldn't push them aside.

The unknowing simplicity of the band's playing forced Young to excise frills from the arrangements. Two lengthy songs echoed Talbot's account of the Rockets' unending jam sessions, with the rhythm section cutting back the original double-time tempo of "Down by the River" in the studio and creating an almost featureless landscape for "Cowgirl in the Sand." These two songs dominated the album physically, each stretching for more than nine minutes, and formed the centerpiece of their stage sets. "Down by the River" was the eerier and more mesmerizing of the two, with a chorus that might have been a killer's gallows confession. But as Young explained, "There's no real murder in it. It's about blowing your thing with a chick. It's a plea, a desperation cry."

Having chanced upon the ideal blank canvas for his self-expression, Young wasn't going to let it slip away. Whitten, Talbot, and Molina found that they were now known as Crazy Horse, although they assumed it was only a temporary masquerade. "After the stuff with Neil," Talbot said, "we did a couple more tracks with the Rockets. But Neil wanted to go out on tour, and everybody in the Rockets got frustrated about that." So Crazy Horse stuck around, and their former bandmates were left to puzzle over how they'd been cast aside.

Nobody seemed likely to get rich out of the new deal. Reprise decided that Young was now "unpretentious, honest, direct, sincere, down-to-earth" and tried to capitalize on his authenticity by offering "Free Dirt" from Topanga Canyon to anyone who bought his album by mail order. Few took the bait. By June 1969, when Stephen Stills came to hang out (and jam) with Young and Crazy Horse at the Troubadour in Hollywood, it was already apparent that *Everybody Knows This Is Nowhere* was not going to be a hit. It splashed briefly into the *Billboard* charts well outside the Top 100, and then headed down and out. Two albums into his solo career, Neil Young had found a band of soulmates, but not an audience.

Today's scene is becoming more like the jazz scene, with artists free to jam together as they please, without feeling obligated or restricted by a group's identity.

—Steve Winwood, Traffic, December 1968

To avoid sacrificing their individuality to another band name, refugees from recent group implosions preferred to retain their own identities. And so it was, in December 1968, that a supergroup was born: Mason, Capaldi, Wood, and Frog. The participants had recently escaped their roles in Traffic and Wynder K. Frog, and now promised to exist both as a quartet and four discrete soloists—freed from petty restrictions and ego wars. (The liaison lasted barely more than a month.)

It was as if they'd learned a script written by what the British press insisted on calling "Nash's Supergroup." There had been no announcement of the latter's new identity—they shared the creed of their mutual friend Peter Tork, who insisted that "Boundaries are nowhere: everybody can be in my group, and I can be in everybody's group." But privately they already recognized that what made them special was the combination of the three. Cass Elliot, the first person to envisage this blend of singers, was deflated but understanding: "When we all eventually got together, I discovered that the three of them were so good that they just didn't need me. That was really the bitterest blow—though I'm pleased for them, because the sound is absolutely incredible."

It was also frustratingly on hold. As Crosby and Nash left London for Los Angeles on December 9, Stephen Stills opted for a flight to New York, and Judy Collins. He didn't return to California for several weeks. Meanwhile, his putative partners arrived at Crosby's Beverly Glen home to find Joni Mitchell in residence, immediately throwing their romantic triangle off-kilter. The stress clearly told on Nash, who was taken ill the following day as Crosby hosted a party. Mitchell gathered him into a cab and took him home to Lookout Mountain Avenue. Mitchell and Nash were now, officially, a couple; albeit, at first, nurse and patient.

Meanwhile, Stephen Stills began to assemble a band. He'd already offered a job to bassist Harvey Brooks while he was swimming in Cass

Elliot's pool a couple of months earlier, and also sounded out pianist Paul Harris, whom he had met through Judy Collins. His drummer of choice was Dallas Taylor, whose baptism in the music business had been scalding. In April 1966, Taylor was the eighteen-year-old drummer in an Arizona bar band, with a fake ID that "proved" he was actually twenty-two. When Corky's Tavern closed one night, he and guitarist Walter Moore were attacked in the parking lot by four young workers from a local holiday resort, who objected to the musicians' Beatle haircuts. Both men were treated in the hospital and released, but several hours later Moore died from a brain hemorrhage at a friend's apartment.

Taylor headed out to the more tolerant climate of the West Coast and joined a band named Clear Light. Within weeks, they had landed a cameo role in a James Coburn movie, *The President's Analyst* (although nothing was visible of Taylor but his hands, flailing at a drum kit). More crucial was their Elektra deal and the visibility it provided them. "We had this gig at the Electric Circus," Taylor recalled, "and David Crosby showed up. Afterward, he said, 'Hey, you guys are really great!' That night was the first time Crosby and I went out and got loaded together—but not the last!" Crosby made a point of plugging the band in interviews ("Wow! The Clear Light is a nice group").

Taylor's experience of working with Paul Rothchild was less satisfying. "Our thing was spontaneity, and in the studio, it just got squashed. Paul would make us do the same track fifty times over, and we'd be sick to death of it long before that point." It didn't help that the band was sharing one room at the Hotel Albert in the Village and fighting for rehearsal space with the Lovin' Spoonful in a basement "that was so leaky, it was always full of water. I'm amazed none of us ever got electrocuted." Clear Light broke up in 1968, and Taylor drifted into the Canyon scene, jamming with Stephen Stills whenever the songwriter needed to work off some frustration.

John Sebastian suggested that Stills should invite Crosby and Nash out to New York, where they could crash at the singer's holiday home on Sag Harbor. On December 22, 1968, the trio made their recording debut, with Paul Rothchild at the controls. They faced a fundamental question: should CSN present themselves unadorned, natural, "wooden" (as Crosby would term their acoustic music)? Or should they follow the rules of professional record-making, and sweeten their sound with over-dubs? They had witnessed the impact that their three voices could exert on a room, but would that power transfer to radio and vinyl?

Of the three men, Stills was the sonic perfectionist, and his influence prevailed. Rothchild supervised as the three men cut a basic acoustic track, with Stills on guitar; double- or even triple-tracked the voices; and then let Stills loose with electric bass and one, sometimes two, lead guitar parts. The results, as Joel Bernstein complained, "were so lame that you wonder what was going on." The mixes were professional but bland, the arrangements pretty but cluttered, and Rothchild was unable to meld Stills's lead vocal on "You Don't Have to Cry" and "Helplessly Hoping" into the Crosby-Nash backgrounds. The finished, hurried tapes were still startling for anyone who had not heard CSN sing before, but they didn't capture the trio's almost unearthly vocal blend.

If their initial day in the studio proved unsatisfactory, CSN did fall in love with the quiet beauty of Sag Harbor. While Crosby returned to Los Angeles and Stills stayed in town to guest at Judy Collins's show in Carnegie Hall, Nash drove back to Sebastian's place to arrange a rental for January. Early on Christmas Eve 1968, he flew out of New York, anticipating that he would be with Joni Mitchell by nightfall. Instead, blizzard conditions ensured that he could get no farther than Detroit, where he sat alone in a hotel, watching a late-night Christmas movie and mulling over the abrupt changes in his life.

Finally, on Christmas morning his flight was called, and he arrived in the Canyon in time for dinner at the house of designer Gary Bur-den, which was where Crosby, Mitchell, and Cass Elliot had gathered. Before he could acclimatize to Pacific time, he was on another plane the next morning with Mitchell, heading back east, not to New York but to the more mellow climate of Florida. The pair relaxed on the coast where Mitchell and Crosby had courted a year earlier, before Mitchell appeared at the second Miami Pop Festival in Gulfstream Park. She ended her set with what had become a hippie anthem, Dino Valenti's "Get Together"—flanked by Village folkie Richie Havens and Graham Nash.

What it comes down to is the music. People will have to listen to the music and judge. I think the music's good. We could be three cats out of the Hamburger Hamlet, and it wouldn't matter. Listen to the music.

—Stephen Stills, March 1969

For all the strength of their union, frailty was built into the CSN partnership from the start. It didn't arise from the most palpable source, a battle of wills and egos between Crosby and Nash over the right to share a home with Joni Mitchell. (It was obvious from the start that, for all her apparent delicacy, Mitchell had the will and stubbornness of an ox, and was not anyone's plaything.) "There was no problem, man," Crosby would reflect. "I loved the guy, and he loved her, and I was happy for both of them."

There would be other stimuli for conflict in the months and years ahead, as was inevitable with three (and soon four) men who were each driven, opinionated, arrogant, and usually certain that they were right. They were each fated to live out the behavior patterns that had been drummed into them since childhood and reinforced in their previous bands.

In the same way that Crosby acknowledged Nash's command of vocal harmony, both men admitted that they could never compete with Stephen Stills's multi-instrumental prowess. They dubbed him "Captain Manyhands," for his octopus-like grasp of every musical tool within reach, without yet realizing that this omnivorous talent would be accompanied by an equally dictatorial attitude to the way in which records should be made. There were clear fault lines in a relationship of equals in which one man was contributing more songs than his partners, and also more, in strict musical terms, to almost every song. No wonder that there was a spat when the three men tried to agree on a name for their band-without-ties. As Crosby recalled, "Stephen did everything he could to make sure that his name would come first. He tried pleading and he tried shouting, but it just didn't sound right. Everyone else knew that it would only work one way: Crosby, Stills and Nash. So I left them all to fight about it and came back when Stephen had finally agreed that we were right." Initially the press would switch the names around, or cut one of them out, or misspell them—until a hit record ensured that the tag would slip off the tongue.

Egos were not the trio's only weakness. A team of harmony singers requires immaculate voices, and there was no team doctor to supervise their condition. All three men smoked (though Crosby avoided tobacco). They were each partial to fine wines and spirits; and they were all taking constant advantage of the availability of cocaine from Latin America, imported in rapidly increasingly quantities to take advantage of government crackdowns on the distribution of amphetamines. The session tapes for their first album caught many occasions on which one of them would say, as Crosby did when they were cutting "Blackbird," "Let's go and snort and listen!" Their drug intake would eventually coarsen their vocal cords and distort the texture of their harmonies.

It would also have a devastating effect on their individual psyches. As Crosby admitted in 1970, "There are certain substances which we sometimes ingest through our nose that increase one's irritability factor, and they're bad for you. That particular substance induces irritability and a tendency toward extremes in everybody that I've ever seen take it." But the cocaine was always there, and so he—and his peers—carried on ingesting. His friend Paul Kantner remembered being introduced to coke at the Monterey festival. "It makes you very cold and impersonal," he explained years later, "not really wanting to deal with others as a band. Coke doesn't help people to get along together. Coke is a very individualistic drug." Within CSN, it helped to turn a tight-knit trio into a very individualistic band. Marijuana, Nash would reflect, encouraged a communal experience; cocaine made one suspicious, untrusting, egotistical, ultimately alone. Or, as James Taylor would put it, "Cocaine can turn you into a monster." It was also addictive, something that was not yet widely understood. Heroin was the drug with the bad reputation; but it was cocaine that would make slaves of an entire musical community, until the whole industry ran on cocaine time, cocaine etiquette, and cocaine ethics.

There was another constant threat to CSN's voices: illness. Graham Nash had left England not only for love and adventure, but also in the hope that a more temperate climate might improve his health. "I came here for a lung cure," he admitted later that year. David Crosby had complained as early as 1967 that he was prone to losing his voice when faced with lousy sound systems or punishing work schedules. Doctors advised him to get proper vocal training, but he demurred: "I'm no great singer now, but I think I would be *less* then." As CSN prepared to regroup in Sag Harbor, Stephen Stills added a new strand to their medical history when he was hospitalized in Boulder, Colorado, suffering from exhaustion and anemia. Meanwhile, his lover Judy Collins was confined to bed after a road accident in Denver. Their problems exacerbated the underlying strain in their relationship and cast a shadow over Stills's thrill of artistic discovery.

Nonetheless, that sense of excitement was renewed when CSN embarked on several weeks of rehearsals on Long Island. Nash's friend Terry Reid dropped by: "They were doing 'Blackbird' in the bathroom there, because of the natural echo. It was the first time I'd heard them. They finished, and I said, 'That's it—I'm quitting the business! I can't compete with that!'"

The plan was to work up two distinct sets of material, one acoustic, one electric, and record a full album of each at Wally Heider's studios in Los Angeles. Studio III was booked for several weeks from February 11, 1969, with Bill Halverson acting as engineer and, perhaps, producer, too. Stills had his eye on the same job, and the royalties that would accompany it. What disrupted the plan was not music, but business.

A trio of inspired egomaniacs could never be served, or indeed satisfied, by the traditional showbiz manager with the cigar and the razor-eyed ambition to exploit his clients. Nor would a sensitive, infatuated soul like the Beatles' impresario, Brian Epstein, have stood the course. Stephen Stills had fallen for the men in sharp suits and limousines when he formed the Springfield; David Crosby made the same mistake when he persuaded the Byrds to sign with the ostensibly hip Larry Spector. They were not convinced that Elliot Roberts—who was still handling Crosby and Joni Mitchell—had the professional experience, or industry clout, to handle them. But Roberts introduced them to a man who ticked every box on the sheet: fearless, tireless, ruthless, and utterly devoted to those who placed their trust in him.

Enter David Geffen, whose blend of cunning, intelligence, and naked chutzpah had already been marshaled to secure singer-songwriter Laura Nyro (of "Wedding Bell Blues" fame) a lucrative publishing deal. He had talked and fibbed his way into a job at the William Morris Agency, then justified it with the deals he brought in. Next, he headed up the music department at the Ashley Famous Agency, bringing the Doors and Janis Joplin on board.

From February 1, 1969, he was the supremo of David Geffen Enterprises, a management company that would also handle his clients' music publishing and, in time, perhaps produce and market their records. Meanwhile, he established himself as Nyro's personal manager (and sometime boyfriend). CSN loved Nyro's music and were equally enthralled by Geffen's uncompromising attitude. His company was launched with the promise that he would now be handling all of CSN's business affairs. But he quickly tired of late-night phone calls from needy artists requiring an ego massage and a new set of guitar strings, so he brought Roberts on board to deal with the human stuff. Geffen was free to focus on his great talents: making deals and collecting cash. As David Crosby would always say, "Geffen was a shark, but he was *our* shark."

His first task was to ensure that CSN won a recording contract worthy of their potential. As Stills had earned Columbia a small fortune with *Super Session*, and Nash was already signed to Columbia affiliate Epic, he focused his attention there. (Ironically, Crosby had also been a Columbia artist with the Byrds. But his apparent creative stasis in 1968 had persuaded the company that he was a lost cause, so his contract was torn up.)

All that remained was for Geffen to secure Stephen Stills's release from Atlantic. He scheduled a meeting with producer and co-president Jerry Wexler. "I knew what I wanted and was determined to get it," Geffen recalled. "But Wexler wouldn't even listen to me. He treated me like dirt." The meeting ended with Geffen being physically propelled from Wexler's office. The following day, Geffen was surprised to receive a phone call from Atlantic founder Ahmet Ertegun. "He invited me to his office, where we sat and calmly discussed the matter. Ahmet was the most sophisticated, amusing, and engaging man I had ever met in my life. Rather than me talk him into releasing Stephen, he talked *me* into putting Crosby, Stills and Nash on Atlantic." Talent was then transferred between corporations, like spies at Checkpoint Charlie: Graham Nash was sent from Columbia to Atlantic, and two former members of the Springfield returned to Columbia, so they could form the country-rock band Poco. The deal ensured that for the first time in their lives, Crosby, Stills and Nash were freed from the immediate need to make quick money—not millionaires, as yet, but comfortably well-off, with the promise of much more to come.

As far as Geffen was concerned, CSN was a trio, and nothing more. But Dallas Taylor, Paul Harris, and Harvey Brooks assumed that they had been hired as full members of the band, who would take their percentage from recording and concert receipts. Geffen refused to yield an inch. As far as he was concerned they could stay with CSN as sidemen or leave. Taylor, who already felt a brotherly rapport with Stills, was encouraged to remain, on the promise that he would be looked after, financially and otherwise. But the brief tenure of Harris and Brooks with Crosby, Stills, and Nash had come to an end. They remained behind to work on John Sebastian's first solo album with Paul Rothchild.

What's still uncertain, because everyone's memories are so vague, is whether CSN themselves were party to this fateful decision. In late January 1969, Stills had left Sag Harbor to go on the road with Judy Collins. Crosby and Nash remained to greet Joni Mitchell, who was performing at Carnegie Hall on February 1. (Backstage, Nash sat uneasily with Mitchell's rather disapproving parents; onstage, Mitchell was given a giant cutout heart by a fan, on which was stenciled the message, "Dear Joni, New York Loves You.") When Nash and Mitchell were interviewed at her Chelsea apartment a couple of days later, Nash explained that he was about to fly back to California to begin work on an album with his new band—which, as far as he knew, was not a trio, but a six-piece. But only four of the six musicians would travel to Wally Heider's studio in the heart of Hollywood, where CSN's sessions began on February 11, 1969.

> I liked the way we made the first album. It was, basically, *I* want to do everything!
>
> —Stephen Stills

The four men barely constituted a band. As an electric guitarist, David Crosby had an acute sense of time; on acoustic, he could fingerpick with great dexterity. Graham Nash's guitar skills were functional but not startling, his piano skills rudimentary at best—and, in any case, he was officially barred from playing on the album because he lacked a valid work permit. Dallas Taylor was a solid, explosive drummer, who could intuitively lock himself into Stills's rhythm. The rest—acoustic and electric lead, bass, organ, piano—was left to Stephen Stills. Little wonder that Neil Young, who didn't visit the sessions, would look back on the *Crosby, Stills & Nash* album as "Stephen's labor of love. He's a musical genius."

He was aided by engineer Bill Halverson, who kept pace with Stills's grueling studio hours. Halverson, who had recently worked with another volatile three-piece, Cream, maintained a welcome aura of calm during the inevitable battles between the main protagonists. As Graham Nash explained, "To deal with three people who have egos like David, Stephen, and I have, you've got to be cooled out. Bill saved our lives more times than I'd like to recall." But the ultimate weight of decision making fell on the triumvirate, and in particular on the omnipresent Stephen Stills.

Not that his bandmates had been idle. David Crosby had bonded with journalist and author Paul Williams via their mutual passion for science fiction. Williams had penned a set of lyrics and asked Crosby to add melodies. At least one of them, "The Word Has Need of New Meaning" (the word being "freedom"), was completed; another, "Dancer," would share its title with a wordless piece Crosby wrote around this time. (The entire set of lyrics was published in Williams's anthology *Pushing Upward*.)

Meanwhile, Graham Nash demonstrated ten songs in various states of completion for Bill Halverson. There were several collaborations with Terry Reid, two of which Reid had already recorded himself ("Man with No Expression" and "Rich Old Lady"). "Marrakesh Express" was retrieved from its limbo with the Hollies, and "Right Between the Eyes" from his marathon writing session in Leeds. "You're Wrong Babe" belonged on the stage of a prewar London music hall; while "Russian Lady," inspired by the same affair as "Right Between the Eyes," was equally banal.

The remaining three songs documented the progress of Nash's relationship with Joni Mitchell. "Letter to a Cactus Tree" captured their first encounter, and Nash's bewilderment when he returned to the States to find Mitchell with Leonard Cohen. "Why Baby Why" was an embarrassing portrait of sexual infatuation ("I wriggle with excitement at the thought of coming home"). Most intriguing was "Pre-Road Downs." "You're elated," he sang delightedly, "'cos I waited a year for you," as if Mitchell had set him an endurance test to check the extent of his infatuation. As yet, the song was unfinished, with Nash scat-singing a wordless chorus. In the studio, Stills took command, sketching out a melody for the missing lines.

The band did their best to exclude outsiders from the sessions, Ahmet Ertegun being among those politely ejected from the control room. But there was one visitor to whom they could not say no. As David Crosby recalled, Cass Elliot showed up while they were recording "Pre-Road Downs" and mock-threatened them: "If you guys don't let me sing, you can't come to my house anymore!" Her voice was smuggled into the mix for the chorus, the solitary intruder into the CSN vocal blend.

The trio's harmonies were so fresh, so energized, so joyfully alive, that they disguised the subtle tricks of the studio. What completed "Pre-Road Downs," for instance, were carefully timed bursts of backward guitar from Stills, woven through the song with a maestro's touch. "Marrakesh Express" was embellished with guitar parts that, as Stills said, sounded "like drunken Mexican cornet players" and employed licks he'd first tried on another 1968 demo, "Who Ran Away?"

Although the final mixes were left purposefully spare, so as not to conceal the voices, the effervescent sonic landscape was not as bare as it first seemed. On almost every song, the vocals were doubled or even tripled, albeit with such accuracy that the duplicity could barely be detected. In a couple of instances, though, simplicity took precedence over sophistication. Crosby and Nash attempted to decorate the bones of "Guinnevere" with multiple vocal parts, plus bass and drums, before realizing that all that was needed was Crosby's guitar and his vocal pirouette with Nash. Likewise, "Lady of the Island" was tried early in the sessions with layered Nash vocals, before he and Crosby returned three weeks later and perfected the song in a single, gloriously fragile take.

Neither of those tunes required Dallas Taylor; in fact, of the ten songs on the finished album, Taylor only contributed to five. ("Marrakesh

Express" featured a cameo from session drummer Jim Gordon, who had worked with Stills on Judy Collins's sessions.) But for electric arrangements, Stills recalled that "Dallas and I were used to just starting with the two of us and making a track. We just used to wait for everyone to leave." One night—or rather early one morning, at 7:00 a.m., Crosby and Nash having retired to their beds—Stills and Taylor set out to revive the ailing arrangement of Crosby's song "Long Time Gone." "I rewrote it," Stills explained, "I put in a chorus. And the next day, I said to David, 'Hope you don't mind, but we took a little license.' He really liked it, so I said, 'Okay, go and sing it,' and he was really pretty nervous once he'd heard the track . . . we kept five [of his vocal takes] without him knowing and then we edited it and got a great vocal. Some people say that's cheating, but it's just using the tape recorder *right*." Convinced that his lead vocal on the record was one triumphant take, Crosby would later tell Ellen Sander that CSN had allowed him to find his voice for the first time. The benign deceit freed him from the accusation by his fellow Byrds that he really wasn't a lead vocalist.

Stephen Stills was no stranger to insecurity, courtesy of his father, but it rarely surfaced in the studio. Bill Halverson recalled being stunned by the session that began with Stills ripping through the complex guitar score of "Suite: Judy Blue Eyes" like a skier skipping along mountaintops. That was followed by a second magic act, as CSN gathered around a single microphone, delivering note-perfect harmonies; then they repeated it twice more, each version fitting seamlessly over the last. Stills overdubbed bass and a second rhythm guitar before adding a churning lead guitar and—in an act of saintly self-effacement—letting Halverson bury it low in the mix. They tried the song again with Dallas Taylor dropping percussive depth charges throughout the song, before deciding that they couldn't top the original (although Taylor was eventually let loose on the latter half of the track). The "Suite" was a masterpiece of studio acumen, a feat of careful construction that still sounded utterly spontaneous.

It was always pegged as the first track on the album—a flawless demonstration of CSN's daring, dazzling brilliance. Sequencing a vinyl LP required the creation of two longer suites, twenty-minute processions of music that would capture the listener from the start and leave them exhilarated and begging for more. "Wooden Ships," an epic, intriguing tale from its conversation between Crosby's and Stills's voices to its valedictory coda, was the perfect opener for the second side. The vivacious pop arrangements of "Pre-Road Downs" and "49 Bye-Byes" were earmarked to close the two suites. But what came between was open to debate, and until late in the sessions, only nine of the eventual ten album tracks were confirmed for inclusion. When Stills gave *Rolling Stone* magazine a sneak preview of the album at the beginning of March, his preferred sequence relegated all the Crosby tunes to the second side of the record. What's more, it included what Stills called "a jazz tune" — Crosby's "Déjà Vu." (CSNY archivist Joel Bernstein confirms that there is no spring 1969 recording of this song in the vaults, so it was either lost or perhaps never actually taped.) Within a couple of days, Stills had reshaped "Long Time Gone," and *Crosby, Stills & Nash* had its penultimate statement in place.

There was one other omission from the record — not just a song, but what it epitomized. When CSN tripped their way around Laurel Canyon, showing off their harmony blend like excitable schoolboys, what thrilled their friends was the unadorned sound of their three natural voices. There were no overdubs, no double-tracking, no backward guitars: just the humanity of Crosby, Stills, and Nash in free flow.

Even the songs on which the trio had first identified their sound were enhanced at Wally Heider's. "Helplessly Hoping" had six vocal parts, not three; likewise, "You Don't Have to Cry." Only one performance during the album sessions captured the original, pure, unvarnished Crosby, Stills, and Nash — and it was rejected because spontaneity was trumped by perfectionism.

When Stephen Stills made his abortive attempt to impress the staff at Apple Records with CSN's demos in late November 1968, he did at least walk away with a copy of the Beatles' new double album. One of its highlights was a deceptively simple-sounding ballad by Paul McCartney, "Blackbird." Stephen Stills mastered McCartney's guitar part and subtly embellished it with passing chords, before Crosby and Nash crafted vocal harmonies around him. In a world where the Beatles were kings, the trio's rendition of "Blackbird" was both a touching tribute to their mentors and a stunning exhibition of their own potential.

At Wally Heider's, they devoted one brief session to the song—the tapes of which demonstrated the fragility that every subsequent CSN performance would face. With such a skeletal arrangement, the slightest misplaced note on the neck of Stills's Martin guitar clanged like an alarm bell, while there was nothing to distract from an off-key harmony. Over and over, CSN began the song, before either collapsing into stoned giggles ("David, if you could keep from ruining my takes," Stills scolded him gently) or drifting slowly off course, usually during the guitar solo. The entire song was a tightrope walk over a windy gorge; it was easier to fall than to make it across. So self-critical did Stills become that even when they achieved a perfect take, he was convinced he'd muffed his solo. Subsequent attempts moved further and further away from fulfilment, leaving the exasperated Stills to moan, "I'm tired of it already." It was lost—and so was the dream of replicating the idyll of Laurel Canyon in a Hollywood recording studio.

What began as a moment of improvisational magic in Joni Mitchell's house in the Canyon was about to become a piece of business currency. Henry Diltz and Gary Burden shot and designed the album cover. CSN posed in front of a wooden shack built for workers at the rail yards on Palm Avenue in Hollywood, but the trio famously lined up in reverse order. When they returned, the lot was vacant, the house demolished. The same team then drove east into the mountains by Big Bear Lake, to model like winter honeymooners in their fur coats for the inner gatefold. (Dallas Taylor's name may not have appeared on the cover, but his photo—taken at the back door of Crosby's house—was cut into the Palm Avenue shot, bearing the expression of a man who'd just been locked out of a party.)

After more than two months of almost-constant proximity, the trio now splintered. Stephen Stills remained in LA to supervise the final mixes of the album; Graham Nash joined Joni Mitchell on a nostalgic return to Saskatoon, as she signed albums for fans in the department store where she used to work; and David Crosby flew to New York with Atlantic boss Ahmet Ertegun.

A couple of weeks earlier, Ertegun had spoken at an industry convention, where he teased his audience by telling them that "the 'now sound' may not be the sound of tomorrow. It may not even be an artist you've heard of before." Finally, he was ready to announce what was scarcely a guarded secret among his peers: Crosby, Stills & Nash were Atlantic artists. They were, he said, "the first group in a while to be based strongly on singing." They would have "the vocal impact of the Everly Brothers" but "they will make as strong, perhaps a stronger, contribution as writers." Crosby slipped alongside him just before the gathering ended, expressing his joy at working with guys who "have paid their dues and don't have to be told what it's all about." Ertegun also laid out what he expected from the band: there would be a second album later in the year, and a solo record from each of the trio, all of them to be released before Christmas 1969. And they would be touring as soon as they found a suitable bass player.

"There will probably be a single," Graham Nash confirmed when CSN regrouped in Hollywood at the end of March 1969, to review the acetates of their album at David Geffen's apartment. He added: "Right now we're in the middle of deciding whether to record a second album straightaway, or to wait and see what happens with our first. People have been offering us fantastic amounts of bread to tour, but the money's not reason enough anymore. I would really like to show the public that it can be done—that a group of people can really get along and enjoy themselves playing music. No matter what, it's going to be interesting to see what happens in the next couple of months." Why shouldn't the idyll continue?

WOODSTOCK 1
THE PLAN

Max Yasgur was the biggest dairy farmer in the area. Turned out he was having a bad summer for hay, and he needed money to feed his cows.

—Michael Lang

Kornfeld, Lang, Roberts & Rosenman: their name might lack the rhythmic flow of Crosby, Stills, Nash & Young, but they too left an indelible mark on American culture in 1969. All four of them were younger than David Crosby but older than Neil Young, and, like Stills and Young, two of them had been working together since 1966. There the comparisons ended, but without the daring and drive of KLRR, there would have been no Woodstock festival—and no legend to shadow the legacy of everyone who was there.

The maverick of the group, and the enduring symbol of everything they achieved, was Michael Lang. He had moved out of New York City to Florida in 1966, at the age of twenty-one, to open a head shop. Inspired by what he'd read and heard about the Monterey festival, he had the reckless ambition—or "stupidity," as he joked in later years—to stage a similar gathering in his adopted home state. As co-promoter, he enlisted Ric O'Barry, best known for training the dolphins seen in the TV show *Flipper*.

The result was the May 1968 Pop Festival in Miami, headlined by Jimi Hendrix. "We did it at a race track called Gulfstream Park," Lang recalled. "The Saturday was magical, we had about forty thousand kids. And then on Sunday it rained, and we had to call the whole thing off. But what impressed me was the effect the festival had on the audience. Miami was off the circuit in terms of what was happening in music, but it really transformed the kids who came."

Later that year, Lang was managing a rock band named Train. Looking for a record deal, he arrived in the Capitol Records office of writer-producer Artie Kornfeld. The A&R man had solid pop credentials, as the co-writer of three American Top 10 hits in the 1960s: Jan and Dean's "Dead Man's Curve," Crispian St. Peters's "The Pied Piper," and the Cowsills' "The Rain, the Park and Other Things." He and Lang were from the same neighborhood in Brooklyn and struck up an immediate rapport.

Together they conceived the idea of establishing a festival site and a recording studio in Woodstock, a quiet town in upstate New York that had attracted unwelcome notoriety as the home of musicians such as Bob Dylan and the Band. In early February 1969, they met John Roberts and Joel Rosenman at an apartment on New York's Upper East Side. Roberts and Rosenman were engaged in building Media Sound, a recording studio in central Manhattan, and had a far firmer grasp of financial reality than the idealistic Lang and Kornfeld. They also shared a background in writing TV comedy, which perhaps gave them enough of a sense of anarchy to be able to handle Lang's utopian visions for a festival. The new quartet's multimedia fantasies were focused on a corporation called Woodstock Ventures, Inc.—whose first task was to stage the Woodstock Music and Art Fair, over a weekend in mid-August 1969.

As its name suggested, the festival promised to deliver more than a rock concert. The corporation claimed it would encompass "a mammoth open-air exhibition of contemporary painting, sculpture and photography." But the ethos of the event didn't stop at the creative arts; the festival would also offer a lifestyle. The site would become a hippie holiday camp, filled with food stalls and craft booths, meditation tents and head shops, everything required to transplant the festivalgoer from Nixon's America to the first glorious dawn of a utopian future. But such a lavish venture required a home, and rural New York wasn't keen to open its doors to an invasion from the city. "The festival was planned for Saugerties, which was about twelve miles away from Woodstock," Lang explained. "Then we looked at Wallkill, which was nearby. It was not an ideal site, but it had the essentials—it had water, it had access, it had enough ground, but it also had a very concerned citizens' committee." They began to mobilize local opinion against the very idea of the festival.

While Lang and his partners were struggling to get the necessary permits, they were also assembling a roster of musicians. "There were some artists we wanted to have but couldn't," Lang recalled. "The most notable was John Lennon—because he wasn't allowed in the country. But part of the fun for me was discovering new talent, which we thought would resonate with the audience." In late spring 1969, Lang was hanging out at the office of his friend, booking agent Hector Morales, when a young manager named David Geffen burst into the room and shouted, "Wait till you hear this!" "Then he played us the first Crosby, Stills and Nash album, before it was released," Lang remembered. "I thought it was amazing. To hear those guys playing together knocked me out. By the end of that meeting, Geffen and I had already shaken hands on a deal that CSN would appear at the festival. As far as I knew, it was going to be their first ever gig."

With tickets on sale, and ads in the underground and mainstream press, the Woodstock promoters faced an abrupt change of venue in July 1969. "The town fathers of Wallkill passed a law which basically made it impossible for us to do the festival," Michael Lang recalled. "The miracle was that the next day we found the site on Max Yasgur's dairy farm in Bethel, which was perfect." With less than four weeks until the festival was supposed to open, the entire site had to be uprooted, transported fifty miles, and reconstructed. "Nothing on this scale had ever been done before," Lang said. "The organization was mind-blowing—there were so many different levels to consider, from publicity to transport to security to keeping people alive. We even had to work out how many Port-O-San toilets we would need. I sent people down to public places, like basketball games and train stations, and they timed how long it would take people to go to the bathroom. Then we multiplied that by two hundred thousand!" That figure was guesswork, however, as initial ticket sales were sluggish, and the promoters feared that they might have overestimated the pulling power of the festival. It was only when upstate traffic started to clog the roadways that Lang and his team realized they had created not just a rock festival, but a logistical nightmare.

CHAPTER 6

I remember what a huge impact that album had, not just on me, but on everyone I knew.

—James Taylor

June 13, 1969: David Crosby showed up at the Hollywood Palladium, as the Who offered the West Coast premiere of their rock opera, *Tommy*. But he could barely reach his seat with all the people offering the same ecstatic greeting: "Wow, man! Crosby, Stills and Nash!"

Their album had been out for two weeks, and it was already the hottest item on college radio. Four hundred thousand copies had been presold to stores, leaving Atlantic Records to fret that they might face a barrage of returns. But at the company's sales conferences that month, reps reported that *Crosby, Stills & Nash* was effectively promoting itself: everyone who heard it wanted to buy it.

Almost without exception, the reviews were ecstatic. "It could be the best album to come out this year"; "it borders on total happiness"; it "could put them in the upper crust of rock, reserved only for the masters." Even those who would become CSN's harshest critics—Robert Christgau at the *Village Voice*, Robert Hilburn at the *LA Times*, the entire staff of *Rolling Stone* magazine—were charmed.

Yet there were hints of what would lie ahead. Christgau noted that for all its strengths, the album "demonstrates the dangers of perfection." Crosby's former colleague Roger McGuinn was prepared to concede that CSN's vocals were superb, although he complained that "The tracks are a little dull, there's no great guitar work." (He could be forgiven his lack of enthusiasm; a contemporary review of a New York appearance by the

Byrds said they were "embarrassing to watch," evidence of McGuinn's "senility.") A rave review of *Crosby, Stills & Nash* concluded that it was welcome relief from "the loud, electronic psychedelics that so many of us have become bored with." Ritchie Yorke's syndicated column insisted that the trio lived up to all the implications of the "supergroup" tag but added: "It is the folksiest and unfunkiest rock album in the last 12 months, and completely unrelated to what's selling at present—Led Zeppelin, Iron Butterfly, Creedence Clearwater." Such praise threatened to present CSN as bastions of good taste in the battle against rock's manic hordes—and nothing could be more damaging to their reputation than that.

Very shortly, Top 40 radio would resound to the unashamedly pop sound of "Marrakesh Express." One of the British pop papers complained that the song had "strong drug connections," but it was scarcely a counterculture anthem. "Hats off to [Graham Nash's] commercial genius," another proclaimed proudly, noting that his English talent was "unclouded by his new American colleagues."

Was this the sound of the revolution? Was Nash, as some critics would suggest, dragging Crosby and Stills away from their roots with his instantly accessible pop? His response was drenched in sarcasm: "I don't feel it's such a terrible thing to touch people, personally. Why am I supposed to apologize because people enjoy my songs?" The suggestion that he might have been overawed by the pedigree of his colleagues was dismissed with the same vigor: "I didn't feel inferior. You've got to understand, I'd had many more hits than both those guys put together, by that point. So, I didn't feel that I was less, or the weak link. I felt that I pulled my weight." David Crosby might symbolize nonconformity and Stephen Stills display multi-instrumental brilliance, but Graham Nash contributed the songs that people would walk away humming.

What everyone wanted to know was how CSN would reproduce their sound onstage. "Initially," Stills recalled, "the idea was to go out like Simon and Garfunkel, because they made a lot of money, and there was two of them and only three of us. But then I said, 'Well, no, man, what's going to happen then is that I'm going to get bored, because I like to play rock and roll music.'"

By the time they reached Moscow Road, in December 1968, the trio already had a blueprint, as Barry Miles reported: "Their planned stage act is an opening with just the three of them doing their communal numbers, followed by three solo spots, each doing their own thing, and ending with the addition of drums and keyboard in a hard-driving rock set." But since then they had hired, and dismissed, a trio of backup musicians. Stills insisted "I need another lead instrument to hit off—to get the magic going." David Geffen had already begun to line up dates for the band, kicking off with the Newport Beach Pop Festival in California. At the previous year's event, David Crosby had instigated a cream pie fight during Jefferson Airplane's set, which climaxed with band, crew, and audience covered in cream. Now his new outfit was expected to make its live debut in front of two hundred thousand people, who would be expecting righteous, midsummer rock and roll.

> You can either smoke or breathe in Los Angeles, you can't do both.
>
> —Cass Elliot, 1969

> There's nothing happening in LA. Everyone's like a zombie.
>
> —Paul Kantner, 1969

Their debut album placed Crosby, Stills & Nash firmly on the southern side of a Californian divide, between the commercial slickness of Los Angeles and the ramshackle improvisation of San Francisco. The chasm was both contrived and organic: it existed, even if only in the mind. David Crosby had roots in both music communities, and approval from the Airplane and the Dead meant more to him than the showbiz smiles of Hollywood. "Los Angeles is a terrible place for musicians," he reflected that summer. "It's not conducive to being a human being. The atmosphere is poison, too many people. It's a police state, a disgustingly ugly place." He wasn't the only musician who felt this way: Neil Young would also admit that "I've lived in Los Angeles for three years, and I hate the place."

In search of community, Crosby headed north, for Marin County. The *Mayan* would eventually be moored at his old haunt of Sausalito, but he also spent time up on Point Reyes Peninsula, in Inverness. He ended up in Novato, where Grateful Dead drummer Mickey Hart already had a ranch. Crosby and Stephen Stills were frequent guests there, Stills taking advantage of the freedom to ride stoned through the park by the creek, Crosby jamming so often with Jerry Garcia that the pair began to think alike. The Dead would subsequently credit this idyllic era for sharpening up their vocal sound. "It's not true that Crosby and those guys ever gave us singing lessons," said Dead guitarist Bob Weir. "It's just that we heard them sing together so often, and so pretty, that something rubbed off on us." By the end of summer 1969, Crosby had rented his own ranch property a couple of miles away, on Indian Valley Road. Inevitably, the house became a commune for Marin County hippies, regardless of whether Crosby was in town.

Back in Los Angeles, Crosby held on to his Lisbon Lane house, though the lower-floor room was now occupied by Peter Tork. In a chilling demonstration of how quickly pop careers could deflate, Tork had been transformed in less than a year from global pop icon to virtual nonentity, unable to secure even the least prestigious of recording contracts. He was forced to give up his party house in the Canyon, and Stephen Stills became the new resident of 3615 Shady Oak Road. When Crosby and Tork hitchhiked over, the only car that offered them a ride was being driven by Peter Fonda.

The Byrds-obsessed actor had a new movie that summer, produced by the same company that had hired Peter Tork. In 1967, the year the Monkees became international stars, Fonda and Dennis Hopper had starred in a biker movie called *The Trip*. (It was directed by Roger Corman, with whom Crosby's father Floyd worked for much of the 1960s.) Fonda now envisioned a sequel, in which he and Hopper would portray hippie cowboys atop bikes rather than steeds, and battling rednecks rather than what Hollywood still called Red Indians. Their characters, Captain America (Fonda) and Billy (Hopper), reflected the styles and personalities of none other than Roger McGuinn and David Crosby.

As he talked up *Easy Rider* to Crosby and Stills, Fonda suggested that CSN should compose the soundtrack. It was inevitable that Stephen Stills would pick up the challenge, returning with a brief, elegiac, devastating chorus entitled "Find the Cost of Freedom." Before then, as Fonda explained, "We began by using music from our own record collections. It worked beyond anything we could have imagined." When he invited CSN over to view a rough cut, they agreed that the movie worked perfectly without them. (An eternal egotist, Hopper would subsequently claim that he threw CSN off the project because they turned up for a screening in a limousine.)

If Stills was deflated by missing out on a movie soundtrack, it was nothing compared to the impact of another rejection in late spring 1969. His relationship with Judy Collins had effectively been on ice during the CSN album sessions, and the thaw never arrived. On May 2, Collins was in Los Angeles for a concert at the Santa Monica Civic. That afternoon, Stills brought over a vintage Martin guitar and—for the first time ever, she claims—performed "Suite: Judy Blue Eyes" for her. She then had to endure the song being blasted out of car radios across the nation—especially after it became a hit single (edited down from its seven-minute splendor, as if with a hatchet, by Stills himself).

While the rumors that Stills and Collins would marry proved to be inaccurate, media outlets high and low were united in the belief that Graham Nash and Joni Mitchell were about to become husband and wife. (Some assumed they already had.) The first hints appeared in print, apparently at Mitchell's behest, within six weeks of Nash moving into her Lookout Mountain home. Soon afterward she wrote a song explicitly analyzing their relationship, which she titled "Willy." "I would be his lady all my life," she wrote, but "He cannot hear the chapel's pealing silver bells." The lyrics portrayed Nash as wary and unable to commit to their relationship; Mitchell herself as naïve, besotted, lovestruck.

The reality was more complex and tilted on a different axis. Friends saw Nash as the devotee and Mitchell as the artist spurred by a more urgent god than love. "Joni has this fantastic drive to create all the time," Nash reflected that summer. "If nothing constructive is done during the day, she feels dissatisfied." It was a credo he would adopt as his own. Meanwhile, he watched in awe as songs of remarkable beauty and insight tumbled out of his lover's imagination. Her second album, *Clouds*, was hovering just outside the Top 30. Mitchell was blossoming as a painter, and was embarking on a screenplay, provisionally entitled *Willy and Ramone*. When Mitchell told Nash, in front of a *New York Times* reporter, "Just sit there and look groovy," it was a joke, of course, a clever reversal of the patronizing attitude you'd normally have heard from a man; but it also reflected the self-certainty of someone at the peak of her powers. Nash, the pop star who could pull any woman, knew that his lover wielded an even more hypnotic power. And there were always new contenders for his place: in April 1969, Nash, Mitchell, Elliot Roberts, and Joel Bernstein went to the Bottom Line in New York to see a promising songwriter they'd barely heard of—a young boy called James Taylor.

> Stephen felt that what they needed to perform live was another musician in the group . . . mainly to have someone in the group proficient enough not as a composer or singer, but rather as a lead guitarist for him to hit from.
>
> —Stephen Stills's official PR biography, 1971

If they wanted to avoid the all-acoustic fate of Simon & Garfunkel (and even they were about to go out with a band), CSN needed more than a drummer. As Stephen Stills explained, "I'm totally addicted to having a loud bass hitting me in the back from four feet away. I'm sorry, but it's a sensuous pleasure that I can't deny." His own bass work on *Crosby, Stills & Nash* was competent and sometimes lyrical, but he wanted to be free to roam on guitar as he had with the Springfield. Moreover, Stills continued to hanker after a keyboard player, or a second guitarist—perhaps one of the musicians with whom he'd jammed in recent years, such as Jimi Hendrix or Eric Clapton. But as he conceded decades later, "I'm pretty easily intimidated. Anybody that's as brash as I can be has to be essentially shy." And though he could communicate easily with music, he wasn't always as skilled with conversation.

During a spring 1969 trip to England with Dallas Taylor, he briefly met Clapton at the filming of a concert movie called *Supershow*. (Stills performed a metallic arrangement of "Black Queen" for the cameras.)

But Stills never quite plucked up the courage to ask Clapton out on the road. Something similar happened with Steve Winwood: Stills recalled trekking through the snow of the English countryside to find him, but what Winwood took away from the conversation was the suspicion that Stills didn't really want to play with him at all. In any case, Winwood and Clapton were about to launch their own tragically flawed idea of a supergroup, Blind Faith.

Crosby and Stills had not entirely abandoned the idea of working with Buzzy Linhart, or for that matter, John Sebastian, but neither was available—or capable—of filling the musical voids Stills had perceived. One man who could have covered both keyboards and bass was Mark Naftalin, who first met Stills in summer 1965. "When I met Steve, I had been hustling for gigs on electric bass," Naftalin recalled. "We spent a pleasant afternoon in his Village apartment. He played guitar and sang his songs, and I played bass through a Wollensak tape recorder." Before that collaboration could be renewed, Paul Butterfield snapped up Naftalin as the keyboard player for his Blues Band. A year or so later, when Bruce Palmer was taking one of his frequent leaves of absence from Buffalo Springfield, Stills tried in vain to entice Naftalin away from the Butterfield band. "I was flattered that he remembered me as a bass player," Naftalin said. But although Stills definitely considered approaching the keyboardist again in 1969, Naftalin said he never made contact.

The dilemma eventually reached the wise ears of Atlantic Records president Ahmet Ertegun. He recalled having dinner with David Geffen and Elliot Roberts, while Stills claimed that he and Crosby were there—or maybe there were two separate New York suppers. Ertegun kept putting Neil Young songs on the turntable and then said how much he missed seeing Stills and Young in the same band. By the end of the night, he recalled, Geffen and Roberts were convinced Neil was the solution to the problem, as if it had been their idea in the first place.

The challenge was to persuade any of the protagonists to agree. Stills was the hardest sell of all: despite the emotional and creative bond between them, he had been scarred by Neil Young's ill-timed series of departures from the Springfield. Why would this time be different? Ertegun fluently persuaded him to give the flaky Canadian one more try.

Young himself was the next stumbling block. He'd vowed never to be in a band again, and didn't consider that Crazy Horse broke his promise—he'd *recruited* them, after all, not joined them. So, he was suspicious when Stills approached him. "I just wasn't into it," he recalled. "I was doing my own thing, and [CSN] were doing their thing." As Billy Talbot explained, "Stephen and Dallas Taylor used to follow us round the clubs, and they'd sit in. We knew they wanted Neil." But what did CSN want Neil Young to be? According to the trio, they always imagined him as a creative partner. Young remembered otherwise—that Stills said his name wouldn't be on the marquee, "but everybody will know that you're there." According to Young, it took about a month to extract a firm pledge that CSN would become CSNY.

Young promised Crazy Horse that this decision wouldn't alter his relationship with them. "We just said, 'Go for it,'" Talbot recalled. Ralph Molina agreed: "It was just another step up for him. And we were young then, we didn't worry about what was going to happen in the long run." Plus, he admitted, it wasn't as if Young and Crazy Horse were the hottest combination in town: "*Everybody Knows This Is Nowhere* was out, but it wasn't really taking off. 'Cinnamon Girl' was getting some airplay for us, but we didn't realize that it was going to explode." Indeed, it would be another year before the song was a hit, and even then it was a cover version that charted first. Young wasn't blind to the fact that joining the most celebrated new rock band in the country would hardly harm his profile. As he conceded in 1970, he signed up on the assumption that the publicity would transform Neil Young and Crazy Horse from a cult attraction into a commercial force.

The week before *Crosby, Stills & Nash* was released, the Boston music magazine *Fusion* gave their readers a preview. "Unfortunately," the paper added, "they are already having internal problems." *Fusion* clearly had a mole in Laurel Canyon, as it was the first outside source to pick up on what was supposed to be a private quarrel. Stills was sold on the idea of CSNY, and Young almost persuaded, but Crosby and Nash were vehemently opposed to adding another singer-songwriter. "We knew that we had something that worked well," Crosby said of CSN, "and we didn't want to fuck with it." "I said no," Nash admitted. "I loved the sound of

CSN so much, and the feeling we had between us, so why would I want to change it?" According to *Fusion's* trusty insider, "Steve Stills did some rehearsing with Neil and Bruce Palmer, reportedly for a future LP."

The facts are unshakable: the three former members of Buffalo Springfield did indeed take over Stills's old New York haunt, the Café Au Go Go, for several days in June 1969, for exploratory jam sessions with Dallas Taylor. But there is no firm evidence that Stills ever seriously considered jettisoning his CSN partners in favor of a Springfield reunion. Instead, the four musicians flew west to Los Angeles. Meanwhile, David Crosby and Graham Nash were back at Wally Heider's, laying down an acoustic demo of "Teach Your Children." "I had already cut a version of that song in late 1968, which sounded as if Henry the Eighth wrote it," Graham Nash recalled. "I played it to Stephen and he said, 'Do me a favor. Don't ever play that again. That sucks. You've got to put a lilt to it, come on, put some country swing to it.'" As with Crosby's "Long Time Gone," Stills intervened to reshape the chorus and provide a musical payoff.

With both halves of the prospective band now in the same city, Crosby and Nash were finally converted to the idea of working with Neil Young. The location and circumstances shifted through the years, depending on who was telling the story and when, but the result was always the same: Crosby was swayed by Young's songs, Nash by his humor and soul. Their verdict was near-identical: "After that meeting," Nash declared, "I'd have given him the country." "By the time he finished singing, we were asking him if *we* could join *his* group," Crosby concurred. Neither of them was swayed by Stills's stories of Young's erratic behavior with Buffalo Springfield.

"I suppose now we'll call ourselves Crosby, Stills, Nash and Young," Stills shrugged when the news first broke. But another new recruit didn't survive long enough to argue about his credit. Within two weeks of flying to California, Bruce Palmer was fired. In a resentful interview many years later, Palmer blamed Crosby and Nash for his exit, and especially Nash. He claimed that Stills shouted at Nash: "Unless everyone in this room remains in the band, I'm leaving." But that doesn't explain why Palmer was removed. Neither does Palmer's insistence that "Once we got to

Los Angeles and started rehearsing at Stephen's house with Crosby and Nash, it became real evident that they were nothing more than backup singers. They didn't like it and decided to change it." But how did sacking Palmer help Crosby and Nash? His account reeked of bitterness and self-defense. Crosby told Ellen Sander soon after the incident that "We were trying to tell him he wasn't making it, and he was insisting, 'Yes I am.' It was really hard to do." Elsewhere, Crosby would say that Palmer was "into Indian music, or neo-Indian music," which again was no real explanation, because so was Crosby. The most likely rationale is that, even in an outfit that would become notorious for its excesses, Palmer simply wasn't reliable enough to stay the course. Before he left, he recorded a handful of tracks with the full band, including a runthrough of "Helplessly Hoping," to see if the song could withstand a bigger arrangement, and a frothy version of Terry Reid's "Man with No Expression," now renamed "Horses Through a Rainstorm." Palmer's playing was slightly uncertain, which would have been enough to offend Stephen Stills's regimental sense of timekeeping.

On June 24, Stills had renewed another Buffalo Springfield connection by watching Richie Furay perform at the Troubadour with his country-rock band Poco. Backstage, he ran into Ricky Matthews, whom he had last seen vanishing with his girlfriend the previous year. He made the instinctive decision to forgive him—perhaps because he'd got a song out of the heartache—and invited him and a young friend named Greg Reeves out to Shady Oak Road. There Matthews claimed that he witnessed Bruce Palmer trying to perform in a state of considerable intoxication.

As ever, there are multiple versions of what happened next. Matthews recalled that Stills and Nash came out to his house: sometimes he would claim that they had asked *him* to join CSNY, sometimes that they had come to poach Greg Reeves. Reeves himself remembered that Neil Young made the first approach, jumping out of a black limousine to greet him on the street. Dallas Taylor claimed that Stills wanted Matthews to play bass but accepted Reeves as second-best. Neil Young turned the story upside down, by insisting that Bruce Palmer was "great as usual" but couldn't stay in the US because he got busted, after which Greg Reeves just appeared. Whatever the truth, Reeves was now in the band, and Matthews (aka Rick James) was free to pursue his own destiny—disco-funk stardom at Motown, and chemical extravagance that would outstrip anything attempted by his former friends.

All that CSNY knew about Reeves was that he was young (nineteen, though later he would claim to have been only thirteen); had worked for Motown (supposedly playing on the Temptations' "Cloud Nine," although Motown veterans insist that was James Jamerson); and was a driving, funky, studio-ready bass player. "He's really made the band tighten up," Crosby reported after their first rehearsals. But it had already become obvious to Geffen and Roberts that CSN—or indeed CSNY—were in no shape to make their debut at a major pop festival, so they discreetly withdrew the band from the Newport Beach bill. Instead, their premiere was pushed back to New York's Fillmore East in late July, when CSNY would face an audience of five thousand rather than two hundred thousand. They had five weeks to invent a live show that would match the ever-expanding expectations of a mass audience.

I won't be·singing that much with the new group, mostly just playing a lot.

—Neil Young, July 1969

Crosby, Stills & Nash was easy to explain, and to sell. They were three songwriters who'd grown tired of their previous bands and discovered that when they sang together, they created a unique sound. But Crosby, Stills, Nash & Young—with Taylor and Reeves? That was an unknown quantity to take on the road. When tickets went on sale for their first shows, all the ads listed them as CSN, with a picture to match. (The same photograph would wind up on the front of their *Greatest Hits* CD in 2005.) Name recognition for Neil Young was virtually zero, beyond avid followers of Buffalo Springfield and those few who had witnessed his club shows with and without Crazy Horse.

That suited Young, as he told Cameron Crowe in 1975: "I didn't have to be out front. It didn't have to be me all the time. I was basically just an instrumentalist that sang a couple of songs with them." In a rare display of modesty, he would admit, "The music was so good, I just wanted to join in. I wasn't into thinking I could improve it, or anything."

Although Stephen Stills had fond memories of his epic guitar jams with Young in the Springfield, he seemed convinced that in CSNY, *he* would be unchallenged as lead guitarist. "Only rarely do Neil and Stephen play guitar together," Crosby confirmed during their rehearsals, "and when they do, it's interlocking parts." Young would provide keyboards or free Stills to sit behind the piano.

Yet there is no evidence that Crosby, at least, viewed Young as less than equal with CSN. Instead, he declared triumphantly, "There's now five writers in the group, can you dig it?" Not only Young but also Greg Reeves were being encouraged to contribute material. What's more, Crosby asserted, the expanded group had shattered any creative boundaries established on their debut album: "Our music is going in every direction that I've been able to figure out. One song comes out like Motown, one comes out South African, one comes out folk, and one comes out like a Bulgarian harmony. We're going in so many directions at once." And unlike that first record, "These are tracks played live."

Every song on *Crosby, Stills & Nash* had been at least partially written before they ever entered Wally Heider's studio. In mid-July 1969, the sextet was in the same venue, but with a marked paucity of suitable material. The CSN songs left over from their earlier sessions, "Teach Your Children" and "Déjà Vu," were not ideal vehicles for CSNY. Much of their time was devoted to trying to create songs out of studio jams, such as the unfocused melodies of "Whole People" and "I'll Be There," both led by Stills; or to rehearsing songs that they could perform onstage. One survivor was Young's "Sea of Madness," an unashamed pop song that was both characteristically dark and uncharacteristically cute. With Taylor and Reeves let off the leash, it also sounded undeniably funky and would retain its place in their live set for a month or two. Less effective was "Cinnamon Girl," as CSNY were unable to equal the raucous energy of Crazy Horse. That left "Down by the River" as the only other song from Young's electric repertoire to withstand the transition from solo career to the big band.

For Stephen Stills, access to a studio was irresistible. When the rest of the band had gone home, he recorded two of the most affecting performances of his life, "4+20" and "So Begins the Task" — entirely alone. Stills would explain that "4+20" was "about an eighty-four-year-old poverty-stricken man who started and finished with nothing," but he was clearly dissembling: twenty-four years old himself, he was still reeling from the death of his relationship with Judy Collins, and this song laid bare his agony. "So Begins the Task" dated from a time when there was still hope but seemed to anticipate that loss was inevitable. "I must learn to give only part, somehow," he sang, before admitting that the only way he knew how to love was to risk everything. Some of the song's imagery was transferred into another epitaph for his heart, "Bluebird Revisited." If his original song for the Springfield had been inspired by the fantasy of Judy Collins, its sequel was fueled by grim reality. It conjured up a vision of Stills alone on Shady Oak Road, obsessively replaying the Judy Collins records with which he had first fallen in love.

As a relief from this soul scouring, Stills devoted one late-night session with Dallas Taylor to crafting an arrangement for a David Crosby song, as they had with "Long Time Gone." Crosby's voyages on the *Mayan* had sparked a hedonistic fantasy of a jeweled ocean, studded with islands from the Windwards all the way to South America. (Inevitably there were compliant women on hand, eager to cook his supper.) Stills loved "The Lee Shore" and crafted a suitably Latin groove for the song, layering instrument upon instrument, and then adding as many of the lyrics as he could remember. The next day, CSNY reproduced it, Crosby almost whispering his vocal, while the band translated the song from ethereal folk into electric rock. But onstage Crosby chose to retain his initial vision, as a tale for an acoustic troubadour.

After a week, it became apparent that the band was wasting money by hiring a professional studio when they could rehearse in the basement of Stephen Stills's house. "I'm happier than I've ever been before," Stills confessed in July. "I've got a feeling this is going to be a lasting thing." But the dream quickly became a mirage. The first casualty was physical: as the band rehearsed, Stills and Young, like all guitarists, immediately turned up their amps. This drowned out the vocals, and as there were no monitors, Nash found himself shouting to be heard. Within a couple of days, his voice was gone, and so were all of CSNY's dates for the next month. Doctors diagnosed polyps and told him that if he didn't stop singing—and speaking—for the next two weeks, they would need to operate. Back at Shady Oak, the band's internal clocks refused to synchronize. Crosby and Nash would arrive for rehearsal to find Stills in bed; Stills would want to play through the night, while his bandmates flagged and then fled. Or the tables might turn. A film crew captured Crosby relaxing in a hammock, while Stills berated him: "You fucking hypocrite. You piss me off." It was the first crack in a fissure that would undermine their personal relationship for the next half century; the first clash of two indomitable wills, set at conflicting angles. "The human dynamic is so crazy," Crosby would concede, "and all four of us are so different." But the Crosby-Stills bond from which everything had begun would never regain its innocent enthusiasm: their shared passion for the music could not withstand their utter dissimilarity in temperament and ideals. Stills always wanted to work; Crosby saw pleasure as the goal and music as a conduit to that end. Nash would attempt—silently, at first—to bridge the gap.

And Neil Young? When it became apparent that tension was rife, and relations unstable, he stepped away—literally, in this instance, as he took advantage of the delay in CSNY's live schedule to record a quartet of songs with Crazy Horse at Sunset Sound. They ranged from the sublime (a stunningly sensitive "Birds," which remained unheard for decades) to the ridiculous (Don Gibson's jaunty country song "Oh, Lonesome Me" slowed into a stoner's lament). The sessions confirmed that, whatever joy he took from CSNY (and he conceded "the music is groovy"), it could never equal the sense of belonging that he enjoyed with Crazy Horse. As he admitted later in the year, "You could compare Crosby, Stills, Nash and Young to the Beatles and Crazy Horse to the Stones. That's the only way I can put it. Another thing I'll tell you: the Rolling Stones are my favorite group." And CSNY? "It's going to make me a lot of money, and that definitely plays a part in my being here."

Groups usually break up because they forget what counts after they become successful. Most of the bands get involved in side trips—the star trips, money trips, the chick trips. They get farther and farther away from what made it all happen in the first place—the music.

—David Crosby, August 1969

Buzzing with frustration as he plucked an acoustic guitar in the corner of Stills's rehearsal room, Graham Nash sat silently as his bandmates assembled a repertoire for the stage. Chicago on August 16 was their latest target: two theater shows before a total of eight thousand listeners. Only hours before their flight, Nash dispensed with his doctor's orders and tentatively lent his voice to their harmonies, aware that the schedule would be capsized if he pushed too hard.

Crosby and Stills were also restraining themselves, anxious to present a show of unity. "I've wanted to work with Stills ever since I first heard him," Crosby proclaimed. Stills affirmed that "The thing we do together is much greater than any one of us. We've got to keep the 'we' more important than the 'I.'" "We want to play music together," Crosby agreed. "I believe we can do it."

It was not only physical frailty and internal dynamics that haunted the band as they prepared for their debut. "This supergroup tag has been putting a lot of pressure on us," Stills admitted. "The minute we walk onstage, everyone will expect us to *be* a supergroup. And we've had hang-ups all the way so far. So, the longer it goes on like this, the more nervous we become. All we can do in the end is shrug our shoulders and do what we do."

And so they took the stage at the Chicago Auditorium, after the audience had been warmed and charmed by a brief set from Joni Mitchell. Here they were at last: Crosby, Stills, Nash . . . and no sign of Neil Young. Instead, the trio sat behind microphones while Stephen Stills struck up the opening chords of "Suite: Judy Blue Eyes." There was a roar of recognition, which died away as CSN ventured out onto the tightrope, their mouths dry, their voices cracking with nervous energy and fear. After several minutes like novice acrobats terrified that they would slip from the high wire, they clicked into the confident routine they'd exhibited around the Canyon nine months earlier. By the end of the song, they were soaring—and so was the audience, which greeted the final chord with prolonged applause. "Golly, we needed that," Nash admitted, and the crowd let loose another sympathetic cheer. After that, the songs came tumbling out—"Blackbird," thrilling an audience who feared they would never see the Beatles again; "Helplessly Hoping," "Guinnevere," "Marrakesh Express," Stills growling "Black Queen," all acoustic, with musicians wandering off and on the stage as if they were heading to the refrigerator for another beer. Finally, Nash introduced a friend named Neil Young, and CSNY were complete. Stills pulled at his Martin guitar, struggling to keep it in tune under the lights. "That's pretty good for country music," Young assured him, and Stills picked out the intro to "So Begins the Task" before Young cut him short: "Maybe it *isn't* that good." Then there was another intermission and feverish activity from the road crew.

When the lights came back up, the acoustic troubadours had mutated into a rock and roll band—ragged, raw-edged, chaotic but alive in the moment. "Pre-Road Downs," "Long Time Gone," "Wooden Ships": the measured perfection of the album was swept aside as Dallas Taylor and Greg Reeves propelled the songs forward, and Stephen Stills sent piercing lead lines across the stage. The climax was a song few in the crowd had heard before, a sprawling murder ballad called "Down by the River," which evolved into a fierce exchange of guitar licks between Stills and Young—the pair eventually merging into a priapic, bestial climax and one final, cacophonous chorus, wildly off-key but fearless with energy and joyous communion. Then the mellow afterglow, as Joni Mitchell rejoined the stage for the hippie anthem "Get Together," as if all that noise had been a momentary aberration. The audience screamed their approval. "We were terrified because we had never worked onstage together before, and anything could have happened," Graham Nash reflected. "But it turned out twenty-five times better than we'd even hoped it would." Next stop: Woodstock.

WOODSTOCK 2
THE PERFORMANCE

They were so good, it was amazing… They'd obviously rehearsed their harmonies to perfection.

—Grace Slick on CSNY at Woodstock

It was pretty shitty.

—Graham Nash on CSNY at Woodstock

News bulletins said it was a disaster area. The music wasn't scheduled to begin until Friday afternoon, but twenty-four hours in advance the fields were already under occupation, as if an entire town had suddenly been uprooted and dropped into the New York countryside. Stephen Stills caught the first hyperbolic TV reports and panicked, ready to pull CSNY off the bill. John Morris in the festival production office took the call and held up the receiver. In the distance, Stills could hear CSN's album playing over the PA system, with wild applause greeting each song. Consoled that they would have a receptive audience, Stills relaxed and assured Morris he'd be there.

Nobody was prepared for what they might find. Nothing had gone according to plan at Woodstock, even after Max Yasgur's farm was filled with all the paraphernalia required to power a rock festival. Michael Lang and his team had bargained on attracting two hundred thousand fans, but more than half a million set out toward Bethel, backing up traffic across New York State. Helicopters had to be chartered to bring the artists in, but the trucks that held their equipment were marooned in the snarl-up. At the site, the rotating stage refused to rotate, the power supply kept being interrupted, and the event was twice visited by epic downpours, with gales to match, which caused the rickety lighting towers to sway and creak over the crowd. Meanwhile the stage itself became waterlogged. "That's what really threw our schedule off," Michael Lang explained. "That's why everything ran so late. The rains would get so heavy that you'd have to shut down, so the musicians wouldn't get fried. Then you had to wait for it to stop, and for everything to dry out again. But it's funny—that's what really solidified this community. You'd expect people to take off and head for the hills, but nobody did. Everybody sort of hunkered down together. And once the rain stopped, they made this giant amusement park everywhere, with mud slides all over the place, and people just had a party."

Music was the reason hundreds of thousands of bedraggled, half-starved people were clinging to any refuge from the mud that seeped through their clothes and their sleeping bags. But once they were there, the sights and sounds emanating from the distant stage paled alongside the communion of simply being there. New York's underground paper the *East Village Other* reported from the front line: "The society up at Woodstock lived on drugs, air, water and hope. There wasn't enough food to go around, but everyone was fed, not enough to drink, but no one went thirsty . . . All the space is taken, clotted with bodies, dots of color, people swaying, sleeping, laughing, talking . . . All senses become sharpened in a throwback to the time when people knew it was important to locate friends in the strange alien universe." As the paper concluded, "The music went on almost independently of this, the greater festival of revelation."

Little of this was apparent to the musicians until they reached the festival site. Some, such as John Sebastian, had been there since the beginning and became embedded in the crowd. Others arrived like tourists, and only then became aware of the surreal world they were entering. Crosby, Stills, and Nash flew in by copter, the craft carrying Graham Nash lurching the final fifty feet to the ground as if it had been held aloft and then let go. But John Sebastian was there to greet them and smooth their passage into the Woodstock spirit, with grass and good vibes. As ever, Neil Young followed alone, arriving at the farm on a pickup truck that Jimi Hendrix had commandeered at a nearby airport.

CSNY were supposed to be onstage on early Sunday evening, but the weekend's second deluge held everybody back several hours. Then the band's equipment wasn't ready, so they were pushed back some more. Finally, around four in the morning on Monday, at least two members of Crosby, Stills & Nash toked up with the Colombian Gold that Crosby's friends Rocky and Big John had brought in for the occasion. Then they walked nervously out in front of a crowd that had looked like an ocean from the air but was now effectively invisible. All CSN could see was a semicircle of their peers behind them, waiting to judge whether this was indeed a supergroup or just showbiz hype.

Under this scrutiny, leading off with the "Suite" was a vow of death or glory. Stills's guitar remained stubbornly out of tune throughout the opening salvo, but CSN were salvaged by their harmonies—wayward enough to sound human, tight enough to prove their bond. After Stills's immortal punchline ("we're scared shitless"), "Blackbird" and "Helplessly Hoping" completed a trio of three-part harmonies, and CSN's reputation was intact. Somehow, amid the tension and the tiredness, David Crosby was able to make "Guinnevere" sound like a sailboat floating over a placid sea on a summer's afternoon, effortless and majestic. A few minutes later, Stephen Stills reduced a sprawling farm to a fireside living room with an equally stunning "4+20."

"I'd just like to present the Buffalo Springfield," Nash said excitedly. But the acoustic duet with Stills that introduced Neil Young to the stage was strangely out of keeping with what had gone before. Young transformed "Mr. Soul," his most muscular Springfield tune, into a slow, modal drone, over which Stills vamped blues licks as if he was trying to keep himself awake.

The electric set provided a much-needed jolt of energy, as "Pre-Road Downs," "Long Time Gone," and "Wooden Ships" punched a hole through the careful perfectionism of the album versions. Young briefly fired into life on "Sea of Madness," having spent most of the set in the shadows, trying to avoid the camera crew. Finally, as dawn approached, CSNY returned to their acoustic guise and delivered a lullaby-cum-prayer for their generation, with "Find the Cost of Freedom." "We were good, thank God," Crosby recalled. "It went down very well."

They had taken the stage as, in the words of Greil Marcus of *Rolling Stone*, "the festival's most unknown quantity." They left as conquering heroes, but heroes who seemed to speak for, and from, the crowd. CSNY looked as if they belonged among the half a million Woodstock pilgrims, as if they should be sitting with their ladies in front of a rain-soaked tent, passing round a joint and a guitar. But they also scorched with an intensity that startled the customarily reserved Marcus into one of the most fervent reviews of his career. "I have never seen a musician more involved in his music," he wrote about the creator of "Long Time Gone." "At one point Crosby nearly fell off the stage in his excitement." And that excitement spread out across the fields, ensuring a state of union between this band and this audience that would pass into legend.

Afterward, as the festival grew from a happening into a myth, the band could afford to bask in what they, and the crowd, had achieved. "Woodstock made me realize for the first time that it was possible to get a half million people together in a peaceful way and have just a great time and not get your heads kicked in," Graham Nash declared. Stephen Stills, the CSNY member least likely to find himself in a hippie commune, still reckoned that, "We came out of the sixties with a few really, really wonderful ideas, and one of them was a sense of community." David Crosby agreed: "Up to that point, we had been scattered hippies. And then, all of a sudden, we were this huge bunch of people, all feeling pretty similarly about things." Neil Young wouldn't go any further than to admit that it "was a turning point in rock and roll history." He added: "It was so big, it was scary." It also locked him into the orbit of his three bandmates, in a way that he had never anticipated.

Once they came offstage, Crosby and Stills bummed a ride in the helicopter reserved for Grace Slick, who was due to join the rest of Jefferson Airplane at the ABC-TV studios on West Fifty-Seventh Street. Dick Cavett hosted the hippest of late-1960s talk shows, and he had booked Jimi Hendrix and Joni Mitchell to appear on what should have been the morning after Woodstock. But Hendrix did not go onstage until around nine in the morning, so when the filming began in Manhattan, he was still performing one hundred miles away, escaping a meandering, frustrating jam with a sudden shift into "The Star-Spangled Banner."

Joni Mitchell had been extracted from the festival bill by David Geffen, to ensure that she didn't miss her prime-time TV spot. "I felt left out," she admitted. "I really felt like The Girl. The Girl couldn't go, but the boys could." Her sense of betrayal increased when Cavett's studio filled with those who'd made it back from Woodstock: the Airplane, slipping the word *motherfucker* past network censors on "We Can Be Together"; Crosby and Stills, the latter proudly showing off the authentic Woodstock mud on his jeans; and a gathering of fans who'd hitched their way back to the city. But there was no Graham Nash, who had stayed behind to watch Hendrix, or Neil Young, who had disappeared into the night as soon as CSNY had come offstage.

Crosby and Stills were gate-crashers, but Cavett took them in his stride. Stills had the chance to offer another resonant version of "4+20," his second of the day, while Crosby educated America about the Woodstock spirit. "It was incredible," he purred. "It was probably the strangest thing that's ever happened in the world." Then he painted an enduring image of the Woodstock Nation: "It looked like an encampment of the Macedonian army on a Greek hill—crossed with the biggest bunch of gypsies you ever saw, man." You didn't need to be steeped in the classics to conjure up the scene in your imagination, somehow more vivid even than the helicopter footage of the crowds delivered on TV news. And as the show finally melted into hippie chaos, the Airplane jamming through the time allotted for Cavett to say his farewells, Crosby and Stills were onstage alongside them, Crosby rattling a tambourine with frantic energy, Stills conjuring up a muddy blues vibe with wah-wah guitar. In that moment, they wanted the day to last forever. What they didn't realize was that for them, and everyone who attended Woodstock, it would do exactly that, freezing them forever in the festival mythology.

CHAPTER 7

Their extraordinarily simple way of conducting themselves before an audience seems to be saying, "See, we're just folks; this is what we're like off-stage, too."

—Alice Polesky, *Changes* magazine, October 1969

After Chicago and Woodstock, the Greek Theatre was hometown—four miles east of the Canyon, past the Bowl and the Hollywood sign. It stood alongside Griffith Observatory, where James Dean watched as Sal Mineo was gunned down at the climax of *Rebel Without a Cause*.

By 1969, the James Dean generation were in their thirties, and they'd outgrown adolescent angst. The summer season at "The world's most beautiful outdoor theater" was tailored for them. Between July and October, the Greek offered a succession of musical entertainment that was stylish, modern but—with one exception—not remotely hip. Hundreds bought tickets for the entire program, sampling the weeklong runs by the Fifth Dimension, Johnny Mathis, Engelbert Humperdinck, Harry Belafonte, Jose Feliciano—and, at the end of August, a double bill of Crosby, Stills & Nash and Joni Mitchell.

Advance tickets were snapped up for every presentation—with one exception. "At first I thought we'd made a mistake," admitted the Greek's director, James Doolittle. He envisaged a three-quarters-empty arena, which would wipe out the profits for the summer. But on the early evening of August 25, Griffith Park suddenly began to fill with hippies, clad in tie-dye and denim, clutching tote bags and backpacks, and exuding the collective aroma of something exotic and almost certainly illegal.

"Act 1," as the souvenir brochure explained, was devoted to Joni Mitchell; wardrobe by Ola Hudson, a black designer from the Canyon who had just opened a Sunset store called Skitzo. As Mitchell sang, people in the crowd looked up and saw something yellow flashing across the sky, a star, perhaps, or a satellite. On such a stoned evening, it didn't seem out of place.

Then came intermission, and the darkness that rock stars require. Shadowy figures moved across the stage and were suddenly caught like intruders in the glare of a single beam. "Hey, you with the spotlight," shouted Stephen Stills angrily. "Not yet!" A few seconds later, they were ready, and CSN set out on another spectacular version of the "Suite."

Seven nights in front of a local crowd gave the band the chance to relax into their music, establish a rapport, and construct an image that would serve them for the years ahead. Graham Nash set the tone at the first show when he joked that they were planning to rename themselves Music from Big Ego. As columnist Judith Sims reported, he "kept making tea and bad puns." The quartet were "very human, vulnerable, accessible. They didn't stand up there aloof in their coolness; they made corny jokes, looked awkward and sincere, and were obviously having a wonderful time." As another observer noted, "Watching them is a bit like having them in your living room." That was their shtick: intimacy, or at least the illusion of the same.

This gift imposed a responsibility on its recipients, to act like friends rather than boorish intruders. When CSN were at their quietest and most vulnerable, the slightest display of rudeness could sabotage the show. One night at the Greek, Crosby and Nash delivered the most tender and delicate version of "Guinnevere" imaginable, and the audience barely dared to breathe. But when they tried to replicate the trick on "Lady of the Island," several of the crowd couldn't restrain their excitement and bellowed incoherently between verses. Nash stopped dead and scolded them: "It's not clever, man." He and Crosby rapped for a while about not wanting to "burn" the audience, and Crosby threw in some hippie patter hot from the Woodstock stage: "You can dig it, man?"

Like any performers, the four men established a routine of introductions and semicomic asides. It took Nash a few months to chime with the American sense of humor, and most of his one-liners in 1969 were greeted by painful silence. Likewise, his attempts to slip into the vernacular: one can only imagine the look on Greg Reeves's face when Nash complimented Stills by saying, "Sometimes I think Stephen is really the spade in the group." Crosby preferred to ignore any appearance of political correctness with remarks about girls: "Sweet succulent young fifteen-year-olds," as he drooled at the Greek. (In the next century, he would still be straying into the same territory, with excruciating public comments about Britney Spears's breasts.) But Crosby was also a born raconteur and a natural wit, whose sense of irony was perfectly in tune with his countercultural audience.

Stephen Stills lamented that he could never match Crosby's mental and verbal agility; his persona was that of a tortured bluesman, unable to keep his emotions in check. Critics were eager to jump on what they interpreted as fake humility, especially when accompanied by a Southern drawl that seemed to deepen in front of a microphone. But for all his well-founded belief in his own musical powers, Stills's self-effacement was real, and every night he embarked on the improvised exploration of the Delta blues tradition that was "Black Queen," he opened himself to being misunderstood, ridiculed, or worse. Audiences seemed to respond to his courage and willed him home in one piece.

The mystery was provided by Neil Young. Still the outsider in the band, an unknown legend, he would remain offstage for thirty minutes or more at the start of every show. If he spoke, it was in a laconic mumble that it would take audiences another year to recognize as irony. Mostly he would remain as anonymous as the unspeaking Dallas Taylor and Greg Reeves, until he suddenly seized the show like a gladiator lifting his victim's head, with the epic finale of "Down by the River." By the time it reached the Greek, the song was regularly stretched to twenty minutes of inspirational jamming, as Stills and Young threw lead lines back and forth like musical jugglers.

For the moment, the instrumental byplay between the two Buffalo Springfield guitarists did not trigger a battle of egos, nor did Stills's apparent attempts to channel the spirit of a gospel wailer on the choruses of "Long Time Gone" provoke grimaces from the song's composer. Performance seemed to banish the dissent that had surfaced during rehearsals; there was no better cure than delirious applause and reviews to match.

Three weeks later in New York, the East Coast received its own CSNY debut, at Bill Graham's Fillmore East. Before the show, journalists tracked down Nash, finding him painfully thin, though he denied that he'd lost any weight; Stills, who "did not talk much, or easily"; and Crosby, who "is friendly, warm, positive and probably mad." Young carefully evaded the press and their inquiries.

"Fantastic!" raved June Harris of *NME*. "Rarely have I seen an act with so much magnetism, so much individual strength and talent." This was despite the flaws that crept into every performance—not just occasional confusion about exactly which key they were in, but the vocal harmonies, which were often wayward during their electric sets. The most glaring offender was Graham Nash, because the arrangements pushed him hardest, and he could rarely hear what he was singing, above the relentless howl of overamplified guitars.

Their audience wasn't in a mood to concern itself with the minutiae of tuning and harmony; they were in the presence of prophets. "David Crosby is the figurehead," June Harris concluded, "maybe because he's the most articulate and poetic." The only cynical response came from the underground, in the shape of the *East Village Other*: "This month's new in-pop expression—FAR OUT—used excessively in LA and San Francisco, was given its indelible Eastern stamp by David Crosby saying it at least 48 times during his recent Fillmore gig." It was a cheap shot, but it hinted at a deeper suspicion: were these archetypal hippie freaks actually capitalist pigs in disguise?

> The turned-on person recognizes that continuous change is the nature of the universe.
>
> —Rasa Gustaitis, *Turning On*, 1969

In the wake of Woodstock, pundits began to query what impelled young people to gather en masse in vast fields of mud. A psychologist cited "the tremendous hunger, need and yearning for community on the part of youth." A sociologist saw the festival as a political gesture of independence from adult society. A historian compared rock fans to the early Christians, valiantly defying persecution. Jimi Hendrix explained that "The only way for kids to make the older generation understand is through mass gatherings. And the kids are not going to be in the mud all the time. From here, they will start to build and change things."

If it was idealism that brought the kids, it was more often naked commercialism that provided the sites for their pilgrimages. Through 1969 and 1970, the rock festival was no longer a once-in-a-season celebration of youth, but an almost-weekly obligation. Leading acts could map out their summers around these potentially lucrative bacchanals. Even if admission was free, the publicity value was limitless. London's Hyde Park had already hosted shows that summer by Blind Faith and the Rolling Stones, and promoter Andrew King confidently predicted that a September 6 gig would outdraw them both. "It'll be a complete San Francisco circus," he promised, featuring "the aristocrat groups of the West Coast"—the Airplane, the Dead, Quicksilver, Spirit, and, topping the bill, Crosby, Stills & Nash. There would, inevitably, be a movie and probably a live album as well. Only one thing was uncertain: whether Neil Young would come with them.

With less than a week to go, London's free festival was abruptly canceled. There were "problems in America," it was explained, and it was proving too expensive to ship all the requisite equipment across the Atlantic. The reality was that CSNY's management had still not procured Graham Nash a US work permit. He could continue to perform while the application was being processed, but if he left the States, he would be unable to return for six weeks, which would force the cancellation of CSNY's dates in early October.

No such issues attended their unbilled appearance at the Big Sur Folk Festival the following weekend. The previous year, Crosby and Stills had dropped in unannounced and made their debut as a duo. In 1969, the ostensible headliners were Joan Baez and the Incredible String Band, because the promoters feared mayhem if CSNY were announced in advance. Joni Mitchell accompanied them, of course, and once again, people sat in on other performers' sets as if they were in the Canyon.

(The exception to this rule was Neil Young, who was nowhere to be seen when spontaneous collectivism was on the agenda.)

There had been summer festivals at the Esalen Institute since 1962, and the idyllic setting of this new age retreat—built around the Big Sur Hot Springs, while the Pacific crashed against the cliffs below—was designed to tease out the spiritual essence of everyone who entered the gates. But Esalen had rapidly become a million-dollar industry; and wherever money was rife, it had to be protected. Signs at the entrance warned "By Reservation Only," and guards were positioned to turn back the curious or impecunious. The Folk Festival was a charitable affair, with performers unpaid, and profits intended for the Institute for the Study of Non-Violence. But there were complaints that the Esalen staff were more concerned with preventing gate-crashers than they were in allowing those who had paid admission to enjoy themselves. When confronted with the "bad vibes" they were generating, an Institute spokesman said that "if anyone was critical of them, it was a reflection of his own soul." As the *Berkeley Tribe* noted, "It's always especially disappointing to see the old establishment uptightness cropping up among a bunch of smooth-talking crypto-fascist flower children."

So, the festival was both a celebration of community and music, and a demonstration of how easily those values could be corrupted. A local artist took it upon himself to register a protest against the outsiders who, he felt, had tarnished the spirit of the event. He ritually confronted the star performers as they launched into their sets. Most shrugged off the interruptions, but—as the subsequent movie *Celebration at Big Sur* captured—one man found it impossible not to rise to his bait.

Early in CSN's acoustic set, the protest began—an incoherent rant about musicians being more interested in money than music. "Just for you, man," David Crosby retorted, "you'll be the only guy we'll tell all day that we're doing it for free. Since you didn't pay, shut up, 'cos we're not civilized." More bellowing, and then Stephen Stills set out to prove Crosby right. The movie captured the fracas: Stills and the heckler tussling, as if in fun, before the fake "everything's cool here" grin left Stills's face and he launched himself at his adversary while Crosby provided mock commentary: "Peace and love, peace and love. Kick his ass."

"I wanted to push him in the swimming pool," Stills admitted later, "and I would have done if it hadn't been for David. I did give him a knee in the old solar plexus, but they didn't put that in the movie!" Eventually the two men were restrained, and a young hippie cupped Stills's face to calm him down, before leading him away. As he left, he looked stunned, broken—a victim of his parental legacy.

Later he sat alone at the microphone and mused about what had happened: "When somebody gets up and freaks out like that, it kinda strikes a nerve, and you end up right back in that old trap . . . I had some guys around to love me out of it, I was lucky." Then, his voice shaky and vulnerable, he muttered, "We just gotta let it all be" and delivered a version of "4+20" that left none of his soul untouched. As another observer recalled, "Everyone there seemed to be able to see through each other's games and disguises and seemed to be too tired to keep up the morale of illusion. People actually looked happier going back to their cars, on the way home. Now they could assume their individual identities and be free from the demands of the long-dead love generation." Even the most idealistic of festivals had been tainted and corrupted by reality.

In music, the hard rockers are turning easybeat. Musical excursions into the areas of volume and distortion are now taking a second-row seat behind adventures in entertainment, and the argumentative material and search for meaningful lyrics have fallen off.

—*Cashbox* editorial, November 1969

"We are going to mess with our image as much as we can," Stephen Stills declared in September 1969. "We could change our name. We could have a seventh guy who appears with us once in a while. Or one of us might do a movie, and we'd play with five. Or maybe someone will do a concert with a different band."

There was an alternative strategy: they could muddy the waters so that nobody would be certain exactly who they were. CSN already had one foot in the pop charts, where "Suite: Judy Blue Eyes" was following "Marrakesh Express" into the Top 40, and another in the album listings, alongside the Doors, Jimi Hendrix, and Blind Faith. To the surprise of everyone at Atlantic Records, *Crosby, Stills & Nash* had also shown up in the R&B Album chart, wedged between Dionne Warwick and Booker T. and the MG's—demonstrating that their audience wasn't entirely white. At the other extreme, "Marrakesh Express" had registered on *Billboard* magazine's tally of the most-played songs on Easy Listening stations. CSN could clearly hit market sectors that might have felt out of place at Woodstock.

To widen their appeal further, they ventured onto television. On the day when they should have been in Hyde Park, they visited ABC-TV's Hollywood studio, taping an episode of *This Is Tom Jones*. The Welsh singer was a rock and roller at heart, whose favorite musician was Jerry Lee Lewis; he loved American roots music and had once been asked to join the Motown stable. But in 1969 he seemed irredeemably square, an impression hardened by his TV variety show.

"ABC were booking these safe, middle-of-the-road acts," Jones recalled. "So, I insisted that I had to choose one guest each week. Crosby, Stills and Nash were my choice, but they were a big band at the time, so there was no argument from the TV company. It was a compliment that a band like that would want to come on my show."

CSNY duly showed up at the ABC Television Center on Hollywood Boulevard with British actor-singer Anthony Newley, then attempting his own slide from square to hip, and *Mod Squad* star Peggy Lipton. "The point of the exercise was originally to try to get across to a whole audience that wouldn't otherwise hear us," Graham Nash explained, "but I'm not sure it was worth it. They treated us badly." "There we were in the middle of a set with giant raindrops, of all things," Stephen Stills complained. "We tried to be creative, but it didn't work." The semi-acoustic "You Don't Have to Cry," with Greg Reeves handling an upright bass, survived more or less intact. But it was their second song that passed into infamy, as Tom Jones took over lead vocals on the counterculture anthem "Long Time Gone."

The rehearsals were rough enough, as technicians cut the band off every time they were about to launch into a chorus. But showtime was something else. "I can duet with anybody," Jones insisted, "and it was a thrill for me to work with a band like that. You can see that on the tape." Nash could only describe the performance as "so fucking jive, it's incredible." Tom Jones had the R&B chops for the song but oversang every line to prove just how deeply he was feeling it. That incited Stills's competitive streak, and the two men attempted to out-growl and out-squeal each other for the rest of the song. While Crosby and Nash tried to hold back from dissolving into giggles, Neil Young carried himself like a man who had walked onto a stage in mid-drama while trying to find the men's room. "That was the first TV we did, and we stopped doing television as a direct result," Nash recalled.

But not before they taped the premiere edition of *Music Scene*, another ABC attempt to pin pop to the small screen. The original concept of head writer Carl Gottlieb (who produced *Celebration at Big Sur* and later co-authored David Crosby's autobiographies) was that it would mix cutting-edge rock with biting satire, courtesy of comedy collective, the Committee. But ABC blunted the satire, and the rock was subject to strict network censorship. The first show included a film clip for the Beatles' "Ballad of John and Yoko," but the offensive word *Christ* in the song's chorus was snipped out.

No words were excised from CSNY's performance of "Down by the River," introduced by mock-hip comedian David Steinberg as a preview of their next album. Forced to perform surrounded by generic teenagers on staircases and podiums, they turned in an astonishing performance. For the first time, a mass audience could see the precise difference between CSN and CSNY—with Neil Young front and center, as if CSN were merely his support band.

Stills and Nash, Joni Mitchell, Mama Cass, and dozens more watched the broadcast at the Laurel Canyon house of comedian Tommy Smothers. He was hosting a reception for Donovan, who performed a brief set and then dove into Smothers's pool. There followed a charity raffle, won by folksinger Phil Ochs who—in a gesture with which Neil Young might have identified—collected his gift basket, mumbled about the hypocrisy in Hollywood and the starving millions in Africa, and tossed his prize into the pool. *Music Scene* seemed even more fake after that. "We won't be doing any more television until we can get a special of our own,"

Stills explained a few days later. "We don't want to have to deal with that establishment anymore."

But they could not avoid all the tentacles of the entertainment industry. Early in the year they had promised a second album, plus solo records by Stills, Crosby, and Nash, for the Christmas market. It was now late September, and they had completed precisely nothing. Atlantic Records was growing impatient. There was a run of concerts on both coasts to complete in early October and then a portentous pause in the schedule: three weeks set aside to record, and mix, the first CSNY album.

> Guys come up to me and say, "Hey, man, you cut your hair—you're not supposed to do that!" and I say, "I didn't cut it—it fell out!"
>
> —David Crosby, 1980

When David Crosby and Stephen Stills dropped in on the spring 1969 sessions for Jefferson Airplane's *Volunteers* album, the room had a strangely familiar look. To cater to the shift in power between Los Angeles and San Francisco, studio boss Wally Heider had opened his first recording venue in the north: Studio C, in the Tenderloin district of San Francisco. The design effectively duplicated that of the room in which CSN had taped their own record, but there the similarity ended. Once you stepped outside, there was a gulf between the gaudy, teeming metropolis of Sunset Boulevard and the seedy, crime-ridden vibe of Hyde Street. Instead of movie theaters and glitzy nightclubs, Hyde was peopled by prostitutes and Filipino gang members, with discreet gay bars nestled between burned-out cabarets and the kind of motels that you rented by the hour.

For Crosby, who took a vicarious thrill from hanging out with bikers and drug dealers, Studio C was a welcome respite from the Hollywood freneticism of Heider's Sunset home. It also had the advantage of being less than an hour's drive from his ranch in Novato. While Stills and Nash partied in the Canyon, and Neil Young hid out in Topanga, Crosby spent a September day with engineer Russ Gary—testing out the new facility as a possible venue for CSNY. Alongside him, rolling joints, fetching coffee, and sitting silently during takes, was Christine Hinton—secure at last in the knowledge that she was Crosby's consort, if not necessarily his only sexual partner.

As Crosby would remember this moment, "I was on top of the world." He was the figurehead of a band, a culture, a movement; the heart of a Northern California music scene that might have been assembled to his design; the owner of a magnificent yacht, fulfilling his lifelong passion for sailing; a carefree hedonist, with the tools at hand for fulfilling two further passions, making love and getting high; and, for the first time in his life, a prolific songwriter. True, many of his compositions did not conform to structures that his bandmates would have employed. His increasingly daring guitar tunings inspired chord patterns that defied analysis—floating, majestic, unimaginably beautiful shifts of melody and harmony that reflected the beam in his consistently stoned eyes.

The music that Russ Gary captured on tape was a mixture of songs and sketches; not fragments so much as impressions, diamond flashes of unrestrained creativity. From these chord progressions, wordless vocal chants, and ethereal airs, Crosby would still be plucking new songs years later: "Where Will I Be?," "Dancer," "Time After Time," and more. There were delicious, meditative patterns that would later be christened "Kids and Dogs" and "Song with No Words"—and if they did not prove to be suitable for CSNY, then they could be set aside for the solo record that Crosby had been imagining for two years. Other tunes were pulled from the near or more distant past: "The Lee Shore," reclaimed from Stephen Stills's Latin arrangement; "Triad," rescued from the Byrds; and "Laughing," a message to George Harrison about the Maharishi, which transformed Dylan's mantra "Don't follow leaders" into a hymn of transcendence and universal trust.

Some of these pieces would be offered to the group; others retained for the moment as private pleasures. But there were two songs at this session that Crosby was already determined to record with CSNY: contrasting snapshots of a soul that could encompass the peaks of hope and fear, spiritual bliss and political paranoia.

On the night Robert Kennedy was shot, Crosby sketched the bones of two songs that captured his despair and anger. If "Long Time Gone" addressed those who shared his outrage, "Almost Cut My Hair"—built around three mournful, descending chords—turned politics into a personal cry of anguish. He would come to regret the simplicity of the song, and its enduring popularity, not least because it gave his detractors the easiest of ammunition. After all, who cared whether or not a rock star went to the barbershop?

For a decade, however, between 1964 and 1974, the length of a man's hair was a matter not just of style but of cultural identity. Crosby was already pushing the boundaries in 1967 when a teen magazine wondered, "How long David Crosby is going to let his hair grow?" That year, his friend Cass Elliot declared with what only seemed in retrospect like melodramatic emphasis: "This country is no longer safe for people who are different, or for long hair and beards." Joni Mitchell met Crosby late that year and recalled, "He was paranoid about his hair . . . having long hair in a short-hair society." Though people laughed at his vanity, especially once it became obvious that he was falling prey to male-pattern baldness, Crosby was issuing a symbolic declaration of independence from the straight world. "I feel like I owe it to someone," he sang, remembering the martyred senator on the floor of the Ambassador Hotel, and "I feel like letting my freak flag fly" (an image he borrowed from Jimi Hendrix's "If 6 Was 9").

"Almost Cut My Hair" was the work of a man mired in the real world. "Déjà Vu," mostly written in 1968 but only completed just before the CSNY sessions, evoked escape from mundane physicality and the constraints of space and time. Roger McGuinn scoffed that "these are concepts he and I used to play with, back when we were working together," as if Crosby was incapable of original thought without him. More potently, in the twenty-first century the songwriter Essra Mohawk has claimed that Crosby based his song on a similar composition of hers, "I Have Been Here Before." She recalled playing it for Crosby on several occasions, at his insistence, when she was visiting Stephen Stills's house in the Canyon. The two writers may have met earlier, as Mohawk was a close friend of Crosby's occasional collaborator Paul Williams.

As recorded on her 1970 album *Primordial Lovers*, "I Have Been Here Before" betrayed her musical debt to another of the era's iconic songwriters, Laura Nyro. The piano-vocal demo issued in more recent years illuminated the similarity in rhythm and theme between the opening line of her song, and the repeated final refrain of Crosby's ("we have all been here before"). So where exactly did inspiration, coincidence, and homage collide? "Déjà Vu" and "I Have Been Here Before" were partaking in a musical and philosophical conversation, but who spoke first? Crosby's lyrics seemed to begin as a response to Mohawk's title . . . or she might have been correcting his speculation ("if I had ever been here before") with certainty ("I *have*"). Evidence on either side is only circumstantial.

What is apparent is that Crosby's song—which didn't gain that final refrain until after he cut his demo at Studio C—was founded on his jazz roots, as its abrupt shifts in tempi and scat vocals testified. It was testament to his faith in the breadth of CSNY's vision that he should submit the song for their attention, and to his power that they not only recorded it but named it the title track of their album. But before then, fate would intervene to sharpen Crosby's paranoia, and stop his flow of creativity in its tracks.

It was the worst thing in my whole life. I wanted to die.

—David Crosby

Six weeks into their touring career, CSNY had racked up two festivals and three US cities: Chicago, Los Angeles, and New York. Next on their slow-motion American tour schedule were three consecutive nights at Bill Graham's ballrooms in San Francisco: the Fillmore on October 2, 1969, and then two shows at Winterland.

Forty-eight hours before they were due to take the stage, Stephen Stills was three thousand miles away, at the Record Plant, New York, in the company of Jimi Hendrix. The guitarist was lost on what would prove to be a yearlong quest—ultimately unfulfilled—in search of a coherent successor to his expansive *Electric Ladyland* album. Uncertain which songs he should be recording, and with whom, Hendrix was eager for distraction and creative impetus—both of which Stills could provide. Stills arrived with his own agenda. Having abandoned his own attempts

171

to capture the spirit of Yasgur's farm after hearing Joni Mitchell's epochal ballad, he wanted to translate her work into his own idiom. He ran "Woodstock" down for Hendrix and drummer Buddy Miles. Hendrix picked up a bass and then, with tape rolling, Stills led the trio through a succession of rough takes. Sometimes he played guitar, sometimes organ, vamping around a riff that he would exploit to great commercial reward the following year. After an hour or so of purely instrumental renditions, he felt confident enough in the arrangement to growl his way through Mitchell's lyrics. As ever, Miles overplayed wildly, careering through the breaks, but the feel was there, and Stills gathered up the tape for the rest of CSNY to hear.

Stills also offered up another semi-formed song, on which he'd already jammed with Dallas Taylor. What began life as "$20 Fine" in California inflated into "$30 Fine" in New York, and the initial take was overdubbed with rival guitar lines by Hendrix and Stills before the evening was out. John Sebastian—who was booked as CSNY's support in San Francisco—dropped by, and the session descended into an inevitable blues jam.

While Stills worked, two of his musical compadres were loose and laidback in Northern California. Graham Nash had flown up from Los Angeles a day or two earlier to join David Crosby at his ranch on Indian Valley Road in Novato. Christine Hinton was always there, of course, and their friend Debbie Donovan, plus strays from the San Francisco rock community, such as several of the Grateful Dead's road and sound crew—Ramrod, Kidd, Slade. They brought women—Eileen, Sam, Paula—and depending on the time of day, and the direction of the winds, any of the Dead might be there; or the actor/writer Peter Coyote; musicians, dealers, stray hippies from the local community and, always, young women. One of them was Barbara Langer, who'd met Crosby through Paul Kantner.

As Graham Nash recalled, Christine Hinton had gone riding, before performing one of her solemn duties, rolling Crosby and his chums a fistful of joints. Then she and Langer gathered together the resident animals, three cats and a dog, herded them into Crosby's VW van, and set off two miles to the veterinarian hospital on Railroad Avenue, where the animals were due for their shots.

Hinton drove almost a mile up the Valley Road, left onto Hill, and then immediately right onto Diablo Avenue, with Mount Burdell soaring in the distance. Langer sat alongside her, the cats crammed onto her lap. Then, as they passed the small wood-frame houses on Diablo, one of the cats broke free and leapt at Hinton, who instinctively turned the wheel to shake it off.

On the other side of the road, forty-six-year-old Valerie Hansen was driving Bus One for the Novato Unified School District, as she had done since 1957. On board were seven elementary-school kids. Hansen saw the VW slowly drift across the white line on the center of the road and sounded her horn to warn the oncoming driver. But to her horror, the van kept coming, as if it had been locked onto a collision course. Thinking until the last second that the van would change track, Hansen braked hard and swerved. Flimsy van hit solid bus head-on and then rebounded across the roadway. The van driver was propelled through the windshield and onto the road. At 2:15 p.m. PST, on September 30, 1969, Christine Hinton was killed by the force of the impact.

Barbara Langer fell back into the van, as the front of the vehicle collapsed like a concertina. One of the cats lay motionless beside her, but the other two jumped clear of the wreck, taking refuge beneath a parked car. On the bus, a seven-year-old boy had been thrown against the seat in front, cutting his lip, but there were no other injuries.

There was an awful silence for a moment, then the children began to scream. An ambulance arrived within minutes—Novato General Hospital was only two hundred yards away—and Hinton's lifeless body was lifted aboard. Her companion was extracted from the wreckage and would survive. They were both rushed to the emergency room, although the medics already knew that Hinton was beyond their help. School officials arrived in cars to take the kids home, while the local Humane Society was called to rescue the surviving felines.

At Indian Valley Road, bohemian ecstasy was interrupted by a phone call. There had been an accident, and Crosby should come at once to the hospital. Ray Slade drove him there, and they arrived in time to see the ambulance, its doors thrown back to reveal the floor slick with blood. Crosby clung to the hope that somehow Christine would be okay. The rest was as inescapable as death. A doctor broke the news and asked if Crosby wanted to see Christine's body. He said yes, and would wish afterward that he'd said no. Then there was only shock and disbelief—that deafening clamor of emotions and sensory perceptions that distorts time and leaves the brain struggling to make sense of the unthinkable. And Christine was gone.

WOODSTOCK 3
THE AFTERMATH

Right after Woodstock, of course, we ended the war in Vietnam [and] got rid of Nixon.

—Graham Nash, 1979

The *New York Times* christened Woodstock the "Nightmare in the Catskills." Published on the morning of August 18, 1969, and hitting the streets as CSNY were still onstage at Yasgur's farm, the paper's first editorial on the festival was little less than an arraignment of an entire generation. "The dreams of marijuana and rock music that drew 300,000 fans and hippies to the Catskills had little more sanity than the impulses that drive the lemmings to march to their deaths in the sea," the *Times* pronounced. "They ended in a nightmare of mud and stagnation that paralyzed Sullivan County for a whole weekend. What kind of culture is it that can produce so colossal a mess?"

The self-proclaimed paper of record was wrong about lemmings, which only march into the sea if they're being chased by a Disney film crew, and it quickly backtracked on Woodstock. Within a week, the "mess" and "nightmare" had been translated by the mainstream media into a triumph of youthful exuberance over epic logistical challenges. *Life* magazine decided that the festival was worthy of a special issue, something it had previously reserved for wars, assassinations, and moon landings. *Time* magazine, not usually slow to lambaste feckless youth, proclaimed that "The festival turned out to be history's largest happening," which "may well rank as one of the most significant political and sociological events of the age."

Co-promoter Michael Lang concurred. "Woodstock changed the way you related to people," he explained nearly half a century later. "It changed your perspective on what the world was about and how people could interact with each other. For me, it was a very affirming experience, in terms of the faith you had in the human race and its ability to maybe survive and come together in a compassionate way."

It was that sense of togetherness—and of astonishment that so many had not only survived the experience but cherished it—that songwriters hoped to capture for the ages. "On the plane back," Stephen Stills remembered, "I was trying hard to think of something to write about the festival. Just as I was on the verge of getting it together, Joni came over and played us her song. She got there first. I couldn't top it."

Joni Mitchell was merely a distant spectator of the Woodstock phenomenon, rather than the festival itself. "I watched everything on TV," she said. "It seemed an amazing thing to me that under the circumstances that many people helped each other out. It was symbolic to me of some idealism." She wondered whether she might have been inspired in the same way had she plotted the same mud-strewn path back from Woodstock as the spectators: "I don't know if I would have written the song if I had gone. I was the fan that couldn't go, not the performing animal. So, it afforded me a different perspective." Her lyrics transformed the festival into a spiritual journey, a generation's collective pilgrimage toward the lingering fantasy of an Edenic garden. But her music clouded that dream in uncertainty, as if she'd already peered beyond the Woodstock myth to glimpse the treacherous landscape ahead.

Like almost every aspect of the CSNY story, the emergence of "Woodstock" is remembered in conflicting ways. Joni Mitchell watched TV news coverage of Woodstock in David Geffen's apartment, or else she was in a hotel room; she had finished the song before CSNY returned from the festival, or she wrote it after appearing alongside David Crosby and Stephen Stills on *The Dick Cavett Show*; she was inspired by hearing Crosby and Graham Nash's firsthand account or (as she insisted vehemently in recent years) they had nothing to do with her creation; she handed them a tape of the song at the *Cavett* studio and suggested they record it, or it was Stills who begged her permission after concocting an arrangement in his head. All that's certain is that she performed "Woodstock" in public for the first time at the Big Sur Folk Festival, four weekends after the *Cavett* show. In a moment of optimism as far-fetched as the festival itself, she attempted to teach the audience at Esalen the chorus of this song they had never heard before.

Yet Mitchell's arrangement of "Woodstock" did not lend itself to mass participation, her sudden melodic climbs in the chorus preventing the song from becoming another "Both Sides Now." It took other musicians to translate it into pop—first Stephen Stills, who reinvented Mitchell's strangely melancholy tune into a rock anthem, and then the English band Matthews Southern Comfort, whose gentle folk-rock harmonies echoed the way in which an acoustic CSN might have handled the song. Both arrangements smoothed away the ambiguity of Mitchell's reading: Stills turned it into a cry of elation and hope, Ian Matthews into the melancholy shadow of a lost dream, impossible to recapture. And both became hit singles, reflecting the eternal appeal of Mitchell's beguiling imagery.

The media preferred to build a more stable vision of Woodstock, as a cultural landmark—birthplace of the Woodstock generation or the Woodstock Nation. Many of those who were there continued to celebrate the festival as a moment in time when communion triumphed over conflict and chaos. "There was a feeling there that you just couldn't believe," Graham Nash recalled. "Getting five hundred thousand people together and having no fights and no murders and no craziness was a great feat, something to be proud of. The first CSN album had something of that spirit—that everybody is really not so different, and maybe we can pull together. Just that hope. When people are having a good time and being moved by the music, you can feel them all become unified behind one force, and that unity continues when the music's over. That's what happened at Woodstock."

CHAPTER 8

My father couldn't express emotions at all. My mother used them rather like a wrench. So, I grew up not really having a clue how to deal with my feelings other than to anesthetize myself, which of course doesn't work.

—David Crosby

Indian Valley Road was unbearable without Christine, and so David Crosby fled to the *Mayan*. CSNY's run of shows in San Francisco and beyond was canceled, as Janis Joplin, Richie Havens, and Santana took over their Winterland slots. John Sebastian acted as their onstage spokesman, explaining that "My very dear friends couldn't be here tonight, because David just lost a very, very dear friend, his lady, and had to go and take a little ride on a boat for a while, just stew for a few days. They're gonna be back picking soon."

Graham Nash and Cass Elliot escorted Crosby to London, "to get away from things," as Cass explained. Crosby's recollection exposed the depth of his grief: "I couldn't handle the fact that she was dead, that I didn't have her anymore. I went completely nuts. For a long time, two or three of my friends wouldn't even let me go to the bathroom alone." In an effort to dampen the pain, Crosby became ever-more reliant on drugs. "I had no way to deal with it," he remembered. "I had no emotional equipment that would help. So, I stuffed it all away, I took heroin as a painkiller, and cocaine, and tried to pretend that nothing had happened." Dazed and anesthetized, Crosby and Nash wandered around the city's music scene, trying unsuccessfully to book studios for CSNY, visiting clubs, and dropping in on friends such as Derek Taylor at Apple.

Back in California, their colleagues filled the unexpected pause in their lives with music. Stills prowled around the clubs on Sunset, jamming with anyone who would let him climb onstage. Delaney & Bonnie said yes, allowing Stills a brief sighting of a young singer named Rita Coolidge. Meanwhile, Neil Young reverted to his natural state, as a solo artist. He had completed a partial remix of his debut album, which discreetly replaced the original in the record stores. For the first time, Warner-Reprise traded on his connection with a more successful unit, marketing the relaunch with an ad headed "—,—,— & Young." Young himself was more focused on another collective: Neil Young and Crazy Horse. They took advantage of the hiatus in CSNY's schedule to snatch some recording sessions in Los Angeles. Alongside a haunting Danny Whitten tune, "Look at All the Things," and Young's equally brooding "Winterlong," the ensemble attempted a long, mesmeric version of a relatively new composition, "Helpless." Young added it to his repertoire for an impromptu one-man show in Ann Arbor on October 16, before rejoining Crazy Horse in California the next day.

Far from planning his future around CSNY, Young was surrounding himself with personal projects. He had agreed to provide soundtrack material for two forthcoming movies, *The Strawberry Statement* (about student radicals) and *The Landlord* (race relations in New York). Some of his first earnings from CSNY had been invested in a Beaulieu Super 8 camera and projector. He planned to collaborate with his wife on 16mm avant-garde movies, record the soundtracks in his basement, and then exhibit them at the Topanga Community House. Their home on Skyline Trail was becoming a creative hub, as Young began to install a sixteen-track recording studio and a film-editing suite. Topanga Canyon, and his marriage, still offered him a haven from the outside world.

Two weeks after Christine Hinton's death, CSNY were once again at the mercy of what Stephen Stills called "managers, and where you have to be at noon" ("You Don't Have to Cry"). Even in the wake of tragedy, they were still required to record an album. But CSNY's block-booking of the Heider studio on Hyde Street began with not a single musician in residence. Instead, engineer Stephen Barncard made safety copies of tapes sent from Stephen Stills's house. Among them was a six-minute jam between Stills and Taylor—the same seven-bar musical section (first heard in acoustic form on a 1968 demo called "Know You Got to Run," and now retitled "You Can Dance to It Real Good") repeated over and over, with Stills wailing on lead guitar, Taylor ringing the changes with different fills and accents, before Stills fleshed the track out with bass, organ, and piano. It was transferred in case CSNY might want to use it, alongside a bundle of demos and tryouts from earlier sessions. The raw material for an album might be there. But what nobody knew, even the musicians themselves, was what kind of band would gather to record it—and who would be in charge.

> I think this album is going to be much funkier than the first one, definitely. It's going to have a more down-home feeling.
>
> —Neil Young, November 1969

> Getting that second album was like pulling teeth . . . There was song after song that didn't make it.
>
> —Stephen Stills, May 1970

Crosby, Stills & Nash documented a musical love affair, a unique harmony blend, and a moment in Laurel Canyon history. From the start, its follow-up was less focused, more uncertain, and clouded with sorrow.

Despite the group's claim to be a collection of individuals, CSN's commercial success had spawned an industry, with all the legal ties that entailed. They had joint management and a joint recording contract, although that only stipulated the presence of CSN, not Y. (The Atlantic deal was amended to ensure that records by CSNY counted toward CSN's contractual obligations, with proceeds split equally between the four musicians. But Young retained his independence as a solo artist, remaining on Atlantic's half-sister label, Reprise Records.) Now they had to deliver an album that would capture both the individual talents of CSNY and the mesmeric power that they had already demonstrated onstage. Key to that power was their rhythm section, and for this album,

CSNY wanted Dallas Taylor and Greg Reeves identified as fully fledged members rather than sidemen. Their generosity only went so far: the drummer and bassist wouldn't be given an equal share of the profits. But as Neil Young declared during the recording sessions, "They really hold the whole thing together." Young admitted that he and Taylor had taken time to bond, but now Young realized that "he is just like me."

Consciously or otherwise, the San Francisco sessions were divided along the same lines as CSNY's live shows. Some songs required the full band; others only two or three members. Given the checkered history of Buffalo Springfield, the obvious threat to the project was a clash of egos between Stephen Stills and Neil Young. Graham Nash identified each of them as "a genius," a description he didn't apply to himself or Crosby—thereby creating a creative hierarchy within this partnership of supposed equals. But, as Crosby would write about the band several years later, "Who gets to be the boss of this bunch?"

Commercially, there was only one answer: the man who had dominated a million-selling album easily outweighed the newcomer whose two solo records had barely registered on the public consciousness. Certainly, Stephen Stills approached the sessions as if, once again, everything depended on him. If his schedule on the CSN album had been punishing, it now approached manic proportions—thanks in part to the way it was fueled. "There was so much cocaine around," Dallas Taylor recalled, "and Stephen and I would just eat up anything that was there. It was crazy—I was crazy, and Stephen was definitely crazy." Together, the two musicians put in eighteen-hour working days, with engineers struggling to stay alive in their wake. "I'd get up at five in the afternoon," Stills explained, "have breakfast, go to the studios, and stay there till noon the next day and then go home and collapse. That went on for three weeks." Even then, Stills would not be satisfied. CSN's friend and sometime publicist Allan McDougall remembered Graham Nash asking him to drive Stills home one morning, because he had been in the studio without a break for three days. Stills invited him in for a drink, and they spent another hour talking, before the musician finally agreed to go to bed. Two hours later, McDougall got a call from Wally Heider's. "I thought you were taking him home!" Graham Nash complained. As soon as McDougall had left, Stills called a cab and was back in the saddle. As Neil Young remarked, "Steve's whole thing right now is the group. It'd be impossible to have everybody into it as much as him. It'd be complete bedlam."

Young was quite capable of creating his own mayhem. He rented a room in a seedy motel down the street, and instead of groupies, invited along two not entirely house-trained bush babies (small African monkeys). "Harriet and Speedy," Graham Nash recalled. "I'll never forget them. They would bounce around the room, shitting everywhere. Only Neil would think of keeping them in his bedroom. They were just as insane as we were."

Beyond the rock and roll war stories, however, were four young men trying to wrestle with the competing claims of fame, ego, money, and creativity—and then balance psychological pressures that could not be assuaged by success or cocaine. Stephen Stills still yearned for Judy Collins, pouring out his heart in a bitter song of love and betrayal called "Ivory Tower." Left unfinished during the CSNY sessions, it was subsequently cannibalized for two Stills solo songs, "Sugar Babe" and "The Treasure," by which time his regret and sorrow would be focused elsewhere.

While Stills regarded songwriting as an outlet for pain, Graham Nash preferred, as he recalled, "to leave people with a positive message—give them something to think about, yes, but also some hope. What's the point in bringing other people down with your sadness?" He was still part of one of rock's most celebrated romantic couples, but his relationship with Joni Mitchell was entering treacherous waters. "I could feel her slipping away from me," he remembered of this period, "and it was frustrating, because there didn't seem to be anything I could do about it. We were still together, but there was this feeling that she wasn't really there." For the album, Nash recorded "Our House," a cloudless, cozy portrait of absolute happiness on Lookout Mountain Avenue and a vase purchased on Ventura Boulevard. But he also felt compelled to revive "Sleep Song," which he'd written during the demise of his first marriage. "I looked around, realized you were leaving me," he sang, as if he was staring into the future.

CSN's debut had been created under the shadow of Stills's declining relationship with Judy Collins. CSNY's sessions were crushed by the weight of David Crosby's grief. However friends and observers viewed his relationship with Christine Hinton, none of them could doubt the sincerity of his response to her death. She became his ultimate symbol of love, and loss; their relationship a touchstone for the bond between man and woman. As he told Ben Fong-Torres during the sessions, "Man, you *know* how hard it is to find a good woman, a woman who's just right—who's with you on every single level. Every step of the way it was right. But you know, at least you know that it *can* happen." It was only natural that he should idealize their lives together; inevitable, too, that in cherishing this memory, he would find it impossible to deal with the pain of losing her or to replace her in his heart.

At any moment during the sessions, even during a performance, Crosby might break down in tears, empty and inconsolable. In a gesture of love, empathy, and gentle persuasion, Stephen Stills wrote him a beautiful lament, "Do for the Others," cutting a demo with Graham Nash to show how it might sound in CSN's hands. It portrayed Crosby as he "cries with the misery . . . lies, singing harmony," before coaxing him to "borrow the life of his brothers" and—with an album to complete—"do for the others." Understandably, Crosby chose not to participate in recording the song.

"I don't consider myself to be a background singer," Neil Young remarked to a reporter during the sessions. That could be interpreted in two ways. Either he was admitting that he couldn't contribute to the exhilarating and exacting vocal blend of CSN, which was undoubtedly true, or that he was not prepared to play second fiddle to anyone. Rather than sparring with Stills for leadership of the band, Young drifted in and out of the sessions. He constantly encouraged CSN to record live, vocals and instruments at the same time, and couldn't understand Stills's insistence that being in tune was more important than being spontaneous. To Young's credit, when there was nothing he could add to a song, he didn't insist on imposing himself, with the result that he would appear on only half of the finished album. This suited his semi-attachment to the band. While Crosby, Stills, and Nash brought their strongest material to the sessions (even if, like "Do for the Others" and Crosby's "Laughing," it ultimately wasn't recorded), Young seemed to have culled his catalog before he arrived, omitting anything dark or provocative. What remained was sometimes patently inferior. Like "Sea of Madness," which CSNY had cut back in the summer, "Everybody's Alone" was perky, poppy, and slight—as if that was all that CSNY required or deserved.

"Helpless" was one of the songs with which Young had convinced Nash and Crosby of his creative potential back in the spring. It was an altogether more appropriate offering for CSNY, with space both for the trio's harmonies and for multiple interpretations of the lyric's ambiguous blurring of dread and nostalgia. "It took us a long time to come down from the speed of cocaine to do a song that slow," Nash remembered. Like Young's other contribution, "Country Girl," "Helpless" was recorded at Wally Heider's, before Young stole away with the tapes to a studio in Glendale. "You'll notice that Neil's tracks sound as though they were mixed differently," Stills said afterward, with an air of regret.

"Country Girl" proved to be the most lavish production on the album, undermining the supposition that it was CSN who tended toward over-elaboration. The song was an epic tribute to Susan Acevedo, erstwhile star of *The Country Girl* in Topanga Canyon. That wasn't its only nod to the past: at its core was "Down Down Down," a fragment which Young had demoed for the Springfield in 1966. Despite Stills's misgivings ("I would have liked to have sung better on it"), "Country Girl" represented the pinnacle of CSNY as a vocal unit, at an emotional pitch that they would rarely recapture in the studio.

Yet perhaps Young's most crucial addition to CSN was persuading them to record as a live band, with an intensity that would have been impossible at the sessions for their first album. Although it was presented (and would often be performed again) as an acoustic tune, Crosby's "Almost Cut My Hair" came alive with electricity. Here at last was an indication of how the band sounded onstage, with Stills (in the left speaker) and Young (right) letting off guitar lines that bit like a cobra, one Young lick inspiring the desolate Crosby into an audible yelp of joy. For him, the song now had a new resonance, as a cry of defiance under intolerable stress—no longer dedicated to an assassinated Kennedy, but to a more recent casualty of fate, taken too soon. As ever, the perfectionist Stills wasn't entirely satisfied, claiming, "We could have played better on the track." "He thought that it was a bad vocal," Crosby explained a few

CSNY in a rare concession to Hollywood fashion, as their collective career began, with Greg Reeves (front) and Dallas Taylor (far right) (*Henry Diltz/Corbis*).

Graham Nash (far left) with the original Hollies lineup in early 1963, clad in leather and Cuban-heeled boots, like the early Beatles (*Michael Ochs Archives*);

and at the dawn of his psychedelic explorations in 1966 (*Don Paulsen/Michael Ochs Archives*).

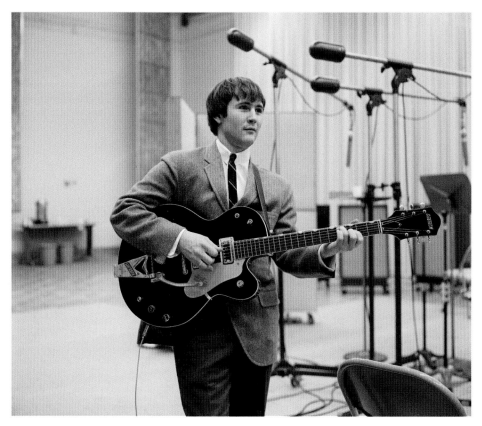

David Crosby at the Byrds' first Columbia session in January 1965 (*CBS*);

and cast adrift from the Byrds in 1967 (*Henry Diltz/Corbis*).

Stephen Stills and Neil Young in a brief moment of Buffalo Springfield harmony, March 1967 (*Henry Diltz/Corbis*).

Neil Young in Malibu seven months later, by now a semidetached observer of the band's decline (*Michael Ochs Archives*).

CSNY was an uneasy blend of two fiery partnerships: the original harmony team, at Balboa Stadium in December 1969 (*Henry Diltz/Corbis*);

and the Stills-Young coalition, at Oakland Coliseum in July 1974 (*Gijsbert Hanekroot/ Redferns*).

Two portraits of fragile optimism at the Big Sur Folk Festival: Stills and Crosby paired in September 1968;

and Crosby with Christine Hinton, two weeks before her death in September 1969 (*Robert Altman/ Michael Ochs Archives*).

Throughout their career, CSNY battled to retain the illusion of intimacy in vast sports arenas such as Balboa Stadium in 1969, where they were drowned out by low-flying aircraft (*Henry Diltz/Corbis*);

and Chicago Stadium in 1974 (*Kirk West*).

CSNY backstage at Oakland Coliseum in July 1974, a study in apparent unity (*Jon Sievert*);

but Neil Young, holding son Zeke, was already primed for departure (*Gijsbert Hanekroot/ Redferns*).

months later. "And it was a bad vocal in the sense that it slid around and it wasn't polished, but it felt like what I meant when I sang it."

Stills would have his way with "Woodstock," another track cut live in the studio, aside from the backing vocals. Young would always insist that Stills had captured the spirit of the song with his original take, whereas all Stills could hear was that he was off-key. "They did a lot of things over again that I thought were more raw and vital sounding," Young complained in 1975. It was a clash of aesthetic philosophies that was won by the man with his hands on the mixing board, and Stills substituted a more accurate vocal after Young had left the studio. Once Crosby and Nash added their exhilarating harmonies, "Woodstock" transformed Joni Mitchell's hesitant, suspicious portrait of a generation in flux into a triumphant rallying cry.

For all their overdubs, those four songs—"Helpless," "Country Girl," "Almost Cut My Hair," and "Woodstock"—were built on the foundations that Young designed: a genuine collective, performing together. Almost everything else was assembled rather than performed. Nothing exemplified that approach better than "Everybody I Love You," for which Stills gave Young a generous co-writing credit. Stills took two minutes of his "Know You Got to Run" instrumental jam with Dallas Taylor from July and added a brief coda. The result was confected, artificial . . . and yet somehow magnificent, thanks to the CSN vocal blend at its most ecstatic.

A similar process of studio construction produced the album's opening cut, "Carry On." "The album was almost finished," Stills explained, "and Graham said, 'We need another "Suite."' I went back to the motel and wrote a song about how the group was then. We stuck the song on the front of a little jam which Dallas Taylor and I had cut three nights before." Taking Nash at his word, Stills built the song around the same guitar tuning as the "Suite"; and if the results were less emotional than that exemplar, they were still anthemic. "Love is coming to us all," CSN insisted from their various states of grief or disillusion. As if to undercut this optimism, Stills followed this aspirational chorus with a reprise of the Buffalo Springfield song "Questions." (Despite his contribution, Taylor did not receive a co-writing credit. Nor did Greg Reeves, although some have insisted, without offering any evidence, that he wrote the song. And neither, for that matter, did the bluesman Doctor Ross, whose riff for "Cat

Squirrel"—later covered by Cream—was the clear inspiration for Stills's guitar intro. The lyrics, at least, were pure Stephen Stills.)

"Carry On," according to Stills, took just eight hours to complete. He claimed that "Déjà Vu," which he later said encapsulated the entire spirit of the album, required more than one hundred takes. Giving with one hand, he took back with the other, blaming Crosby for his intransigence: "It got too important [to him]. He wouldn't give in and let Willie and I help to get it together." When Crosby finally relented, Stills not only straightened out the song's wavering tempo, but also contributed lead guitar, two piano parts, and perhaps the finest bass playing of his life. Like Mama Cass on the first album, John Sebastian was invited to play harmonica on this one track, in recognition of his status as an all-but-full member of the ensemble.

With Young physically absent and (aside from his two leads) missing from the album's vocal stacks, the remaining songs were pure CSN productions. Once again, the trio had to decide how to represent their acoustic sound; once again, they experimented with outside material. The first album's attempts at "Blackbird" were superseded by "Everybody's Talkin'," the Fred Neil tune that Harry Nilsson had sung on the soundtrack to the movie *Midnight Cowboy*. Already a hit single for Nilsson, its inclusion on a CSNY record would have seemed gratuitous, no matter how tenderly they delivered the song. Instead, they turned to a John Sebastian tune, "How Have You Been," which the composer had already earmarked for his long-delayed solo album. At least two takes were recorded: one hesitant, the other (after a bum note from Crosby on the first line) arguably the closest that ordinary mortals would ever come to knowing what it was like to hear CSN for the first time by a Laurel Canyon pool.

In the event, neither song was considered for the album. Instead, the acoustic, unaccompanied sound of the Canyon was heard on only one track—Stills's impossible-to-improve demo of "4+20." He had already set the song aside for his first solo record but was persuaded by Crosby and Nash to donate it to a bigger cause.

"Teach Your Children" might have remained equally bare, once Stills had fine-tuned the arrangement and added the vocal counterpoint to Graham Nash's original lyrics. Instead, Crosby approached Grateful Dead guitarist Jerry Garcia, who was experimenting with a pedal steel guitar in the adjoining Studio D. Despite protesting that he was a mere novice on the instrument, he was persuaded to listen to a playback of Nash's song and add whatever came to mind. After his first run-through, he told the band that he was ready to have a try. To his bemusement, Nash told him that they'd taped his warm-up, and it was perfect.

Garcia's licks gave the song an unmistakeable country feel, much to the amusement of Chris Hillman. "When David Crosby and I were driving round the country with the Byrds," he recalled, "David would go on and on about the sitar, with its sliding scale and no frets. And I'd say, 'Listen to this,' and I'd hit the radio until I found a Nashville station, with steel guitar on it. David would shout, 'I hate that corny, stupid shit,' and turn it off. Four years later, he's got Jerry playing steel for him. But that was David all over." "Teach Your Children" would become the most enduring song in CSNY's repertoire and, as Stills believed, "the best track on the album — head and shoulders above the rest." As Neil Young admitted, "I am proud to have my name on it, although I didn't play or sing a note."

Therein lay a strange truth about the first CSNY album: it was effectively a CSN record. Young only appeared on five of the ten songs and sang on just two; Greg Reeves also performed on just half the record. That was a fair reflection of their early live shows, in which Neil Young was presented as a junior partner. It was also an accurate representation of the hours that each of the quartet put into the project. Stills was there for everything; Nash almost as often, except when he was unable to match Stills's relentless, coke-fueled endurance; Crosby around more often than not, as an escape from the loneliness he felt outside the studio; but Young? Only when necessary. "I have to admit I was totally surprised that Neil wasn't around as much as we were," Nash conceded, but he accepted Young's absence as part of the price they had to pay for his participation. Yet as far as the public was concerned, a record with the working title *Crosby, Stills, Nash & Young* was obviously an equal four-man enterprise. It would take years and, in some cases, decades for the individual credits to be revealed, by which time Neil Young's career would have been transformed by the success of an album in which he was only half-involved.

He remained an outsider for the most painful part of a debilitating process: mixing the multitrack tapes into a form that would be acceptable to everyone. By removing the tapes of his own songs and mixing them by himself, Young ensured that "Helpless" and "Country Girl," at least, would sound the way he wanted, and CSN did not have the nerve to contradict him. He left the rest of the record to them, a distance that would allow him to evade responsibility for their decisions.

When Crosby, Nash, and especially Stills took their turns behind the mixing board, all of the pent-up tensions of the previous few months erupted. The egos had become too big to reach a collective decision, so each of them would sit with the luckless engineer Bill Halverson, and tweak the knobs to their own benefit, before their efforts would be canceled out by the next in line. Nothing dissolved fraternal unity faster than endless bickering, and it was at some point during this enervating game of "turn my voice up" that Graham Nash dissolved into tears at the futility of it all. Almost anything could make David Crosby cry at this point, and so the two harmony partners and best friends howled, while Stephen Stills watched sheepishly alongside them—still convinced that everything would be okay if only *he* was in sole charge.

Eventually, out of this pain and resentment came a record—not the double album that had been promised as late as November 1969, but a collection of ten tracks that were stylistically varied, sonically rich, divided between spontaneity and cool calculation, breathtakingly brilliant, and yet still, somehow, not an adequate portrayal of everything that CSNY could be. To chase down that impossible goal, it was time for the band to get back on the road.

> The young are frustrated, because they're not stupid. They can see the bloodbath coming, and there's nothing in their power to stop it.
>
> —David Crosby, 1970

A year after the protests at the Democratic National Convention in Chicago, eight prominent figures from the antiwar movement went on trial. They were charged with conspiracy to cause a riot, traveling across state lines with the same intention, encouraging demonstrators to use incendiary bombs, and obstructing police officers. The defendants ranged from Yippie provocateurs to academics—the latter apparently chosen to demonstrate the breadth of the plot against America. The proceedings would last for five months, at the end of which Judge Julius Hoffman imposed contempt of court sentences on both the defendants and their attorneys. Two of the eight were found not guilty of the main accusations against them; the remaining six were convicted and given prison terms. On appeal, all those guilty verdicts were overturned. The entire trial was a legal charade, which did more to undermine the establishment than the Yippies' efforts at anarchic insurrection.

Witnesses called to testify included Judy Collins, who was physically restrained when she tried to sing on the stand. Phil Ochs and Arlo Guthrie were also refused permission to enter their songs into evidence. Country Joe McDonald treated the proceedings as a farce, and testified accordingly, in a tone that was part Groucho Marx, part James Dean.

The entire trial merely served to enlarge the gulf between those who believed that the Vietnam War was immoral, illegal, and must be ended by any means necessary and those who saw the young and hirsute as closet revolutionaries. The single incident that aroused the most outrage came on October 29, 1969, when Judge Hoffman ordered one of the defendants, Black Panther Party chairman Bobby Seale, to be bound and gagged in his chair. Seale struggled to breathe while his fellow defendants and attorneys protested against his inhumane treatment. Judge Hoffman eventually intervened to find Seale guilty of sixteen counts of contempt of court. He sentenced the Panther leader to four years' imprisonment, and then ordered him to be retried on conspiracy charges at a later date.

The outrage evoked by Seale's bondage in court made it easier for activist and comedian Hugh Romney (alias Wavy Gravy) to solicit funds for the Chicago 8's soaring legal costs. Graham Nash recalled: "Wavy Gravy, who was a friend of mine, called me and said that the Chicago defendants needed money. He wanted CSNY to play a benefit concert for them. David and I said we'd go immediately, because we thought what had happened to Bobby Seale was disgusting. You cannot tie a man down in court, and gag him, and call it a fair trial. But we couldn't persuade Neil or Stephen to go." Instead, Nash—who was insistent then that "Protest songs don't work, you blow the whole thing"—wrote his first-ever political anthem, "Chicago," with a message to his recalcitrant colleagues: "Won't you please come to Chicago, just to sing . . . We can change the world." Did he really believe that? "There's no doubt about it," he reflected many years later. "But how much? Well, that's another point. We don't have any fucking answers, we just have a lot of questions, the same as anyone else."

Besides the Chicago Conspiracy Trial, America's deepening military involvement in Southeast Asia continued to trouble a large percentage of the population. President Nixon had already authorized secret US bombing raids in Cambodia, about which the public would remain ignorant for many months, and also instituted covert (and illegal) wiretaps of radicals at home. There were regular demonstrations against Nixon, against the war, against oppression, against the entire political hierarchy. But none of these actions seemed to hold back the government or significantly alter popular opinion.

A sense of weariness was entering the antiwar movement. The result was division between those who clung to a belief in the power of non-violent protest and those who believed that only violence could throw the system off course. A splinter group of student activists took the name Weatherman (later the Weather Underground) and launched a series of actions under the title Days of Rage. Though their numbers were tiny, they were able to stage a succession of terrorist bombings across America, one of which resulted in the death of several of their own members. (Paul Kantner and Grace Slick would commemorate one of these "martyrs" on their 1971 album *Sunfighter*, on which both Crosby and Nash performed.)

Their pacifist counterpart, which operated under the name New Mobe (New Mobilization Committee to End the War in Vietnam), was able to outdraw Weatherman on a scale of a thousand to one. Its first demonstrations were the two Moratoriums against the war, in October and November 1969. Nixon's aide H. R. Haldeman recorded in his diary that the president believed that these marches and rallies were "prolonging the war," because America's opponents in North Vietnam would view them as a sign of national weakness.

The first Moratorium attracted crowds of protestors in major cities across the country. On the same day, it was announced that John Lennon was returning his MBE award to Queen Elizabeth II, blaming British support for America's role in Vietnam. The Nixon administration tried to soften the impact of the second Moratorium a month later by creating National Unity Week, designed to prove that support for the war easily outweighed the vocal opposition. But its impact was fatally undermined by the revelations that broke on the Associated Press wire service on November 12. Investigative reporter Seymour Hersh had uncovered a massacre of Vietnamese civilians by American soldiers, which had taken place in March 1968, and then been concealed by military authorities. America was forced to confront the truth of its own national shame—that its young men were just as capable of brutality and criminality as the Communists were.

The next morning, a three-day March Against Death began in Washington, as demonstrators walked in single file to the White House, each carrying the name of a dead US soldier or a site of carnage in Vietnam. On November 15, huge marches were planned in the nation's capital and in San Francisco. The latter coincided with the proposed dates for CSNY's rescheduled run at the Winterland Ballroom, and organizers of the Moratorium hoped to persuade the band, and their friends in the Airplane, to perform at the antiwar event. But first CSNY had to get back onstage—and that could only happen if David Crosby felt capable of facing an audience after the death of Christine Hinton.

> They seem like old friends that you haven't seen for a while, who come back into town and turn you on and tell you stories about the strange people they met on the road. Each of the members write songs that grab you in the gut and don't let you go for days.
>
> —*Berkeley Barb* review of CSNY
> at Winterland, November 1969

Almost imperceptibly, CSNY shifted allegiance from Southern to Northern California during the course of 1969. Crosby led the way, easing his friends into the world of the Grateful Dead. Stephen Stills was stimulated both by his musical conversations with the Dead, whom he announced his intention to produce, and the natural habitat of Marin County. As his relationship with Joni Mitchell declined, Graham Nash began to consider buying a home of his own, rather than relying on the certainty of a bed on Lookout Mountain Avenue. Only Neil Young remained wedded (legally and spiritually) to the Los Angeles area, though tensions were also rising in his Topanga Canyon home, where he yearned for isolation and his wife relished the distracting buzz of outsiders.

Winterland was the clubhouse for the San Francisco rock community. As CSNY began an intensive schedule of recording sessions at Wally Heider's Studio C, their friends in the Dead and the Airplane were staging a three-night run at Bill Graham's ballroom. There was an open invitation for CSNY, individually or together, to come down and hang, maybe jam, whatever felt comfortable. Neil Young wasn't tempted, but the others agreed to attend the October 25 show—and—who knew?—maybe even perform.

David Crosby had not sung in public since Christine's death, only three and a half weeks earlier, and as the studio sessions had already revealed, he was barely in control of his emotions—not to mention his reliance on heroin as an anesthetic. There was no more welcoming venue for his return than Winterland, but ultimately he decided that it was too soon, and he was too vulnerable, to play.

Instead, after Jefferson Airplane finished their second set, and before the Grateful Dead embarked on their own voyage into the mysterious, Bill Graham made an announcement. There were a couple of friends backstage, he told the crowd, and he wanted to ask them out to play a few songs. On walked the instantly recognizable figures of Stephen Stills and Graham Nash. A year after Stills and Crosby had debuted as a duo at Big Sur, and fourteen months before Crosby and Nash would inaugurate their onstage partnership, Stills and Nash performed for more than five thousand people, delivering a cut-down version of the acoustic sets that CSNY had already offered concertgoers at Woodstock and elsewhere. Somewhere in the Dead's vaults is a tape of this unique (for more than a decade) performance, the highlight of which was a typically exuberant rendition of "Black Queen" by Stills. (He craved the chance to perform the song with the Dead and was given the opportunity six weeks later in Los Angeles.) When the Dead finally played, Stills stepped out onstage during Pigpen's perennial showstopper, "Turn On Your Lovelight," trading vocal licks as if he was auditioning for Sam and Dave.

Two weeks later, after intensive studio time had hardened Crosby to the discipline of singing, he was finally ready to resume his performing career. CSNY stood under a drooping tarpaulin on the field of the university campus in Santa Barbara, while security guards wrestled with students attempting to pierce the fences. Five hundred kids eventually broke through, the university authorities banned live shows on the field for the next four years, and the entire ruckus was a welcome distraction from Crosby's emotional ordeal.

On November 13, the day the March Against Death began, CSNY finally made it to Winterland. The knowledgeable San Francisco crowd were acutely aware of Crosby's plight. "His face was so sad you could cry," Robert Greenfield reported. "He sang his songs painfully, his voice ripped out; everybody cheered him. Later they did 'Down by the River' for twenty minutes and Crosby found he could still get it on. A smile returned to his face." "You know something, man," Crosby told the crowd, "you're the reason I moved here." Graham Nash reminded them of their responsibility to speak out at the Moratorium, "then the day after that and the day after that, until we stop the bloody war." And the night ended with a somber rendition of "Find the Cost of Freedom," and Stephen Stills— remembering Christine's fate—begging the audience to "be careful" on their ride home, long before that line became a show business cliché.

The next day, perhaps three hundred thousand people assembled in the Polo Field on a cold, drizzly, mid-November afternoon. The Youngbloods played their rallying cry, "Get Together"; Elaine Brown offered the Black Panthers' national anthem; Phil Ochs delivered a folk song that portrayed Nixon and Agnew as Laurel and Hardy. The cast of the faux-hippie musical *Hair* performed their paean to "The Age of Aquarius." *Star Trek* star Leonard Nimoy also lampooned the president. Representatives of various progressive factions—farmworkers, Chicanos, black Christians, even Rennie Davis from the Chicago 8—addressed the crowd. Each had their own political solution to America's enmeshment in Vietnam. The most radical came from Panthers leader David Hilliard, who threatened to "kill that motherfucker" in the White House.

A couple of hours into the procession of speakers, as the rain began to thicken, Crosby, Stills, and Nash took the stage with their acoustic guitars. The damp air ravaged David Crosby's already wounded tonsils, as the trio performed a handful of songs. The woman who had originally brought them together, Cass Elliot, came out to lend a harmony to "For What It's Worth," Stephen Stills's hymn to political suspicion. Stills read a poem, or so he called it, about the swamp into which "America's children" were being dragged. "Politics is bullshit," Crosby screamed into the microphone, sacrificing the last of his voice. "Nixon is bullshit," Stills qualified, as a registered Democrat. Defiant and hoarse, Crosby warned the demonstrators about the danger of assuming that their new world order would automatically surpass the old one: "If we're not careful, it'll all end up the same way." Then CSN sang the solitary chorus of "Find the Cost of Freedom," Crosby's vocals torn, before heading for the limo that would escort them back to Winterland. That night he stood onstage with his friends, unable to soar to the peaks of the "Suite." He clutched his throat apologetically, and won a cheer when Nash explained how Crosby had lost his voice—like a martyr to the higher calling for which they would all carry the cross.

Fortunately, there was a weeklong pause in CSNY's schedule after Winterland, and they arrived several days early for their next show in Hawaii. By the time they reached the Honolulu International Center Arena, Crosby's voice had been renewed by the tropical heat, and the band were entranced by the Aloha State. They told the crowd that they would be back soon to buy land and build houses, imagining a new, secluded, and sun-drenched version of the Canyon, with their friends—such as John Sebastian, who opened for them, and blew blues harp on Stills's "Black Queen"—in tow.

After this idyll, they flew to Denver, where Stills unveiled his infamous piano medley of "49 Bye-Byes" and "For What It's Worth." "It was really dumb," he would concede a few years later, "but that's what they wanted to hear and, of course, being an entertainer, I was behind it." As it mutated over the months ahead, its melodic content was soon overwhelmed by a free-flowing, foot-in-mouth political rant, built around the poem he had read in the Polo Field. It was excessive, naïve, and patronizing (with its endless references to the "children" he was addressing); but it was uniformly greeted with howls of ecstasy from CSNY's fans. So too was Neil Young, whose appearance sparked lovelorn gasps of "Oh wow" from teenage girls in the audience. (He would soon be described in print as the owner of "the perfect rock star body.") The only way he could follow, and top, Stills's manic rhetoric was to affect a persona of his own — as the wisecracking, too-stoned-for-school hippie who didn't appear to be able to tune his guitar but could be guaranteed to deliver note-perfect renditions of some of his most beautiful songs (on this night, "Expecting to Fly").

Denver was also privileged with electric novelties — an extended arrangement of "Pre-Road Downs," on which CSNY briefly jammed like the Dead; a cacophonous "Woodstock," any subtleties of which were lost in the arena's cavernous echo; and finally almost twenty-five minutes of "Down by the River," which surged and fell in waves like the point breaks craved by Hawaiian surfers. Then it was on to Salt Lake City and Dallas, where Nash debuted "Teach Your Children" and Crosby "Almost Cut My Hair," his voice cracking with grief as memories of Christine came flooding in. The next night in Phoenix, Crosby blamed the airline for their late arrival, and the airline blamed CSNY's crew for turning up with excess equipment. The ninety-minute delay was forgotten when the band began to sing. Then they flew back to California, where their December 6 show at UCLA was promoted with a quote from the *Saturday Review*: CSNY, it promised, were "about the happiest sound since laughter."

I think the major mistakes were taking what was essentially a party and turning it into an ego game and a star trip.

—David Crosby, December 1969

We had to go through an Altamont in order to get the importance of something like Woodstock into perspective. I think we learned far more from Altamont about the new culture.

—Jerry Garcia, April 1972

As Grateful Dead guitarist Jerry Garcia recalled, December 1969 "was a very weird time on the street in San Francisco. There was a lot of divisive hassling among all the various revolutionary scenes." The Dead were booked for a four-night run at Bill Graham's Fillmore West Theater, December 4 through 7, when the Rolling Stones asked them to play at a free concert in Golden Gate Park on the sixth. The Dead could play in the afternoon, before heading a couple of miles back into the city for the night's show. But the Park suddenly wasn't available, and neither was the Sears Point raceway a few miles north of the Dead ranch in Novato. By the time the Stones were offered the Altamont Speedway, it was too late for the show to be organized on any professional level; too late also for the Dead to withdraw from an event that they had effectively agreed to set up on the Stones' behalf. So, the Dead canceled their third night at the Fillmore, instead asking their fans to join them at Altamont.

David Crosby was hanging out with the Dead during their negotiations with the Stones, and he could see a Californian Woodstock on the near horizon. Although CSNY had sold out shows in Sacramento on Friday night and at UCLA's Pauley Pavilion on Saturday, he figured that his band could fly into Altamont by helicopter on Saturday afternoon and then take a jet to Los Angeles for the evening gig. The rest of the band weren't enthusiastic but bowed to Crosby's insistence that Altamont would be too groovy to miss. Santana, the Dead, the Airplane, the Burritos, CSNY, and then the Stones—what could go wrong?

The Stones had arrived in California at the start of November, and Stephen Stills had offered to lend them his house on Shady Oak for the duration of their stay. He anticipated a meeting of rock royalty and was disgusted to find that the Stones' crew wanted him gone from the house before Mick Jagger and Keith Richard arrived. According to roadie Phil Kaufman, Stills claimed to be too sick to leave—until Kaufman evicted him, and Dallas Taylor, bodily from the premises.

A month later, the omens for CSNY were equally inauspicious. Barely rested after their Friday show at the Cal Expo site, they gathered at the Sausalito heliport on late Saturday morning, only to discover that their pilot was refusing to fly. They eventually set off from San Francisco airport in a machine too big to land at Altamont, which dumped them instead at the deserted airport in Tracy. Their roadie Leo Makota hot-wired the only vehicle around, a pickup truck, and drove the band to the Speedway. (Stephen Stills subsequently calmed the owner with a hundred-dollar bill.) The vehicle inched through the crowds, with Stills bellowing out the band's name to clear their path.

Thousands of fans had arrived in the early hours, waiting in subzero temperatures for the gates to open. Inside, they massed toward the stage and awaited what emcee Sam Cutler promised could be "the greatest party of 1969." Cutler's optimism soured almost as he spoke. As Santana played "Soul Sacrifice," Hells Angels from San Jose—recruited by the Dead's entourage as stage security—began to express themselves with pool cues among the hapless crowd. The rest has passed into rock legend: the attack on Jefferson Airplane vocalist Marty Balin, the Grateful Dead's decision to abandon the site rather than risk their lives onstage, the murder of an armed spectator during the Rolling Stones' set. As the first underground press account of the debacle said, "The whole crowd was uptight from the start. They wanted Instant Woodstock." Carlos Santana extended the thought: "They wanted another Woodstock, but they didn't want to make one, they wanted it to just happen to them."

By the end of the day, as a sanguine reporter for the *Berkeley Barb* reflected, "Four babies were born and four people died. An even exchange of souls." Few other accounts were so philosophical. Another witness in the same paper complained that "Love and peace were fucked by hundreds and thousands of people who did nothing. The brothers and sisters had the numbers. They could have cooled the Angels . . . but they let hate happen."

The chaos and angst, the vicious violence and pathetic acceptance of much of the crowd, the collapse of the Stones' quasi-satanic pretensions and rock-star charisma—all that and more was captured in the Maysles Brothers' film about Altamont, *Gimme Shelter*. Cleverly, CSNY managed to ensure that they went completely unrepresented onscreen. As far as posterity was concerned, it was like Woodstock: if you weren't in the movie, you weren't there. They were almost included; the Maysles even persuaded David Crosby to rerecord some of his anguished stage announcements ("Please stop hurting each other, man.") which hadn't been picked up by the film crew. But David Geffen refused to sign a release for any of the CSNY footage to be used.

Even if the recent accounts of Stephen Stills being stabbed repeatedly by an Angel with a sharpened wheel spoke have been ridiculously exaggerated, the performance was hardly one that CSNY would want to remember. Crosby did his best to fool the audience into thinking that the atmosphere reminded him of Woodstock, that they were all brothers, can you dig it? But as the pool cues rose and fell, CSN abandoned their acoustic guise and launched into the shortest electric set they could get away with. Stills transformed "Black Queen" into a grim, metallic dirge, the perfect soundtrack for an event rapidly descending into barbarism. "Pre-Road Downs" illustrated that the band were distracted and shocked by the violence unfolding in front of them; "Long Time Gone" had an air of desperation beyond its usual political paranoia. But during the finale, "Down by the River," people beyond the front of the stage started to relax and clap along. As the *Berkeley Tribe* noted, "It was the first out and out sign that the audience could respond to the music." Before the final chords had even stopped resounding across the barren vista, CSNY were grabbing guitars and hurrying offstage for the safety of another helicopter. As they left, a young woman stood up and screamed, "Christ died on the cross! Mick Jagger is the Devil!" Her madness simply blurred into the scenery.

From the midst of the chaos, rock writer Lester Bangs considered that CSNY's performance had been "ridiculously bad." The radical journalist Sol Stern compared Crosby's demeanor with his rant at the Moratorium, when he had declared music a more powerful force than politics. "At Altamont his music failed him," Stern wrote. "It was unable to affect the violence that was engulfing his band, and he watched dumbfounded as the Angels kicked his fans in front of the stage. At least Crosby could get out. He and his band finished up, and immediately climbed aboard a waiting helicopter, leaving behind their fans." CSNY left so little trace behind them that the Stones didn't even realize they had performed. "I heard they stayed at the airport," Keith Richard said.

When the time came for reckoning, David Crosby blamed the Stones for naïvety (expecting the Angels to be like Hopper and Fonda in *Easy*

Rider), snobbery (the festival was set up to show them off rather than satisfy a crowd), and arrogance. Altamont, he said, was "an ego trip of 'look how many of us there are'. . . I think they have an exaggerated view of their own importance . . . I think they are on negative trips intensely, especially the two leaders." But when it came to the Angels, he said that "I don't dig everybody blaming them," because they were only doing what they were asked to do—protect the stage. It was as if the Hells Angels were wild animals who couldn't be held responsible for their own actions. "Blaming is dumb," Crosby concluded—except when it came to the Stones. "What kind of attitude is that?" the *Berkeley Tribe* responded. "To say 'blaming is dumb' is the same as saying there's no such thing as murder. We're very quick to call cops pigs, but when long-haired dope users slice up a man and stomp on him before our eyes, there's hardly a murmur of protest."

If Crosby was an unreliable commentator on the morality of violence, his opinions carried more weight when it came to the business of rock. Altamont had taught him something, he said: "I don't think gatherings that big are where it's at. I don't think it's conducive to making magic." CSNY, the Airplane, and the Dead agreed that they would never play big outdoor festivals again. Both the Dead and the Airplane soon went back on their vow.

Altamont has passed into history as the anti-Woodstock, the death of the hippie dream, the end of the '60s—"rock's darkest day," in the words of Joel Selvin's book-length history of the event. But for CSNY, it wasn't even the end of the day. By ten that night, they were onstage in front of LA students from the University of California. Stephen Stills read aloud his poem about America's children, and from the crowd someone demanded that he should run for president in 1972. The show was "an unqualified success," according to the *LA Times*; or, in the eyes of teen mag reporter Judith Sims, "boring, annoying, infuriating" because the band talked rather than sang, and when they weren't lecturing the audience about politics, they were endlessly fiddling with their instruments. "They took forever to tune up, take their places, decide which song to sing," she wrote, highlighting the playful spontaneity that many fans found so endearing. "David Crosby changed guitar twice in the middle of 'Guinnevere' . . . They wasted their time and ours. If they would learn to curb their cuteness, their aimless political chatter, they would be the best band on the stage." Of course, it was precisely their cuteness and political chatter, the sense that they were just plain folks like you and me, the sense of being welcomed into the world—in a word, the *intimacy* of it all—that people loved. But there is a psychological and physical price to pay for inviting outsiders into your life, and by the end of the performance, with visions of Angels and pool cues distorting the chemical rush through his membranes, Stephen Stills could take no more. He ended Altamont day semiconscious in the band's dressing room, overstimulated by everything he had taken in.

WOODSTOCK 4
THE BACKLASH

I couldn't believe the things people screamed at us. Such hate, such sickening things, such bad words. Why? We were working harder than anybody—why all that hate, just because we looked different?

—Thelma Schoonmaker, movie editor, and
member of the *Woodstock* film crew

Nobody could accuse Stephen Stills of having hidden his feelings about the so-called Woodstock Nation. "It was lost on me," he said. "They were mostly Grateful Dead people." What's more: "I abhorred hippies. That's fair and accurate."

Neil Young was no more starry-eyed about the festival experience. "I was really uncomfortable because everyone was so jacked," he wrote in his memoir, *Waging Heavy Peace*. A decade after the event, he admitted that "I had a really negative attitude about all those things, about the pop festivals and Woodstock. I went there, but I wasn't really into it . . . I didn't even know what I was doing there. I still don't know."

The fact that two of the key participants—beneficiaries, too, of the ongoing Woodstock myth—should disavow themselves so completely from the festival spirit is merely the continuation of a contrarian argument that was first heard even before the crowds began to gather at Yasgur's farm. It was aired in cavalier fashion by Yippie activist Abbie Hoffman, who harangued Michael Lang in the lead-up to the festival, begging him to use the gathering to promote righteous radical causes. As far as Hoffman was concerned, Lang and his colleagues were "hip profiteers" out to make bucks, and reputations, from the energy of youth culture. In the days immediately after Woodstock, when he was still coming down from the bad trip that had led him to invade the stage while the Who were performing, Hoffman speed-wrote a book to which he gave the sarcastic title *Woodstock Nation*—only to find the phrase borrowed and upturned as a celebration of the entire venture.

The key issue for Hoffman and his ilk was money; or, more accurately, the creation of "hip capitalism," which was designed to use the culture and phraseology of youth for purely commercial ends. It showed its face in early 1968, when Columbia Records began to brand its artists as "The Revolution-aries." They followed through with an insultingly banal advertising campaign around the theme, "But The Man can't bust our music." That emerged after agencies and record companies held a conference to discuss "Selling the American Youth Market," and the FBI began to pressure record companies to withdraw their advertising from underground newspapers that were challenging the US government over human rights and the war in Vietnam.

For Hoffman and his ilk, Michael Lang and his friends were merely busi-nessmen in hippie disguise. The promoters claimed that they faced financial ruin when the festival fences were pulled down and they were forced to announce that it had become "a free festival." But reporters examined the plans for a full-length documentary about Woodstock, with tie-in record albums, and calculated that the promoters would show a healthy profit on the deal. Meanwhile, entrepreneurs large and small began to cash in on the Woodstock myth, selling "Carry It On" T-shirts or "We Proved It at Wood-stock" bumper stickers.

The most eloquent advocate of the anti-Woodstock backlash was Ellen Willis, pioneering feminist and rock critic, who penned a dissection of the festival spirit in a *New Yorker* article entitled "The Cultural Revolution Saved from Drowning." She claimed that the promoters were "motivated less by greed than by their hubris: the ambitiousness of the project was meant to establish them as the pop producers, kingpins of the youth market." She lampooned their "incompetence" and "gross ineptitude," suggesting that disaster was only avoided because "300,000 or more young people were determined to have a good time, no matter what." But her critique went wider than Woodstock itself, toward the rock culture that produced it. Rock, she concluded, "is bourgeois at its core, a mass-produced commodity, dependent on advanced technology and therefore on the money controlled by those in power."

Extending her message, journalist-turned-producer Jon Landau (later Bruce Springsteen's manager) complained that Woodstock marked "the ultimate commercialization" of the underground and its culture. He traced how the festival led inevitably to Altamont, and "an audience once naïvely optimistic [who] turned rancid with cynicism, a cynicism that was but a reflection of the stars whom they admired . . . Altamont showed everyone that something had been lost that could not be regained." And like Woodstock, Altamont was preserved on celluloid, to fix one version of the festival in our collective memory.

CHAPTER 9

This is a science fiction story about a bunch of people who decide they're gonna band together and try to survive together. So, they work out a common language, with music or whatever, and find that they really dig each other, that they're kinda brothers—and they sail off into the sunset. Mind you, it's only a fantasy.

—David Crosby introduces "Wooden Ships,"
Chicago, December 13, 1969

As chaos and stardom impinged on CSNY's world, the "Wooden Ships" fantasy entered a new dimension. Stephen Stills was the first to realize that the song's mysterious narrative might support a motion picture. "David thought I was crazy," he recalled. "It took three days of telling the story for it to sink in, then we all started making up bits." Their scenario involved a nuclear holocaust, from which a handful of Western refugees—rock stars, perhaps, with young, blond, long-haired girlfriends—would seek out the only other survivors, a distant tribe in South America. Together, they would build wooden ships and sail for virgin land where civilization could be reimagined. But however they spun the tale, an ending eluded them.

"All we need is a scriptwriter, and a producer and a director," Stills said in late 1969, and "a budget from someone who doesn't want to take our song publishing in return." He imagined that CSNY would act in the movie—he and Crosby both had experience from school—but that they would also hire Hollywood professionals to keep the project afloat.

The success of *Easy Rider*, and the anticipation aroused by *Woodstock*, convinced Hollywood that rock music might reconnect the teenage audience with the movie business. Warner Brothers, who had *Woodstock* in development and also owned CSNY's record label, agreed to bankroll *Wooden Ships*. But this wasn't the only movie on the band's horizon. Concert promoter Bill Graham had sent them a script called *Please Don't Feed the Guerrillas*. Written by Robert W. Goldman, it told the story of a small American town, taken over by a band of revolutionary outlaws. Graham circulated it around his rock star clients, in the vain hope that someone might bite.

Meanwhile, the rock critic Paul Williams had connected David Crosby with one of his science fiction heroes, the novelist Theodore Sturgeon. As a teenager, Crosby had read and reread Sturgeon's novel *More Than Human*. It highlighted the author's fascination with Gestalt theory, and especially the notion that several individuals might combine to form a single *homo gestalt*, the next step forward in evolution. As he had with Heinlein's *Stranger in a Strange Land*, Crosby inhaled Sturgeon's concepts and vocabulary, employing them in Byrds interviews with teen magazines.

The *Wooden Ships* script promised to advance Sturgeon's screen career, which amounted to a handful of screenplays for *Star Trek*, but no major film credits. By November 1969, he had met the band, digested the rudiments of their story, and set to work. Almost immediately, Stephen Stills's mind jumped ahead to the problem of who might direct the CSNY film. He selected Stanley Kubrick, never imagining for a second that the genius behind *2001: A Space Odyssey* might turn them down. (Kubrick was preoccupied with trying to raise funds for a film about Napoleon, in which he imagined Jack Nicholson taking the central role.) Of course, Stills said, their film "won't have the same cold feeling as *2001*—I hope it will be more like Kubrick's earlier films, with the characters laid out so well. It's got to be done properly."

And characters did indeed prove to be the crux of the matter. Many decades later, David Crosby reflected that CSNY had subjected Sturgeon to "a really unbearable experience . . . We were all such complete egotists by that time." If the ethos of the project was the submission of individual wills to the greater cause, CSNY's behavior totally undermined it. As Crosby recalled, "Each guy would get him alone and tell him how *he* wanted the script to be. And, of course, in each guy's view, *he* was the hero. Mine was populated with young girls—and had all this sex in it.

Stephen's was populated by this lonely military hero out there. Neil took one look at the whole film idea and said, 'No . . . no, man, I don't think so, man . . .' It was hysterical." Sturgeon tried to cram these conflicting visions into a coherent script, but eventually admitted defeat when it became obvious that CSNY's own dramas would make the project untenable. The *Wooden Ships* movie never quite died, however; two years later, David Crosby and Peter Fonda were still kicking it around, although the vision that seemed so real in a cloud of smoke on the deck of their own wooden ship could never be translated onto paper, let alone celluloid.

As CSN discovered (but Neil Young never quite learned), it was easier for musicians to lend their songs to movies, rather than become film composers. It was easier still to offer old songs rather than conjure up a soundtrack from scratch. Neil Young had to abandon his original scores for *The Landlord* and *The Strawberry Statement* (which used previously released songs by Young and CSNY). Graham Nash's "Teach Your Children" was featured in the teen romance *Melody*, while three Stephen Stills songs by the Springfield appeared in *Homer*, a drama about teenage rebellion. "Wooden Ships" itself was heard in the surfing documentary *Pacific Vibrations*, promoted as being "like *Woodstock* on a wave." All of these projects emerged in 1970, exploiting CSNY as a direct route into contemporary youth culture.

The same goal led actor Dean Stockwell to commission a soundtrack for his screenplay *After the Gold Rush* from his next-door neighbor Neil Young. "It was all about the day of the great earthquake in Topanga Canyon," Young told *Mojo* magazine, "when a great wave of water flooded the place. They tried to get some money from Universal Pictures. But that fell through because it was too much of an 'art' project." That was precisely why it inspired Young in a way that *The Landlord* and *The Strawberry Statement* hadn't. He began to accumulate a set of songs that he didn't bring to CSNY sessions.

Although Stephen Stills talked up his movie ambitions throughout the 1970s, dabbling with stories and treatments and volunteering himself as an actor, it was David Crosby who seemed most likely to achieve a career in film. In January 1971, he was in Hawaii with Carl Gottlieb, the head writer for TV's *Music Scene*, working on a script entitled *Family*.

United Artists picked up the rights to both the movie and the soundtrack, which Crosby was expected to compose. This was no fantasy of wooden ships, spaceships, or even rock stars, but "something of a new concept in filming," as co-producer Robert Hammer promised while scouting for locations in Colorado. "The story deals entirely with one day in the life of a nomadic-type family, which sets up camp in the mountains. There will be no nudity, no violence, no obscenity." Perhaps it was the absence of those marketable qualities that led United Artists to withdraw their financing, even before filming had begun.

> As a human, you're always messing up, always hurting people's feelings quite innocently.
>
> —Joni Mitchell, 1970

There was one final sweep of CSNY dates from Pennsylvania to California before Christmas 1969. Gradually, the new material they had recorded (but not yet released) began to infiltrate their live sets—"Woodstock," "Teach Your Children," "Helpless," even "Country Girl," performed by Young alone. In Houston, Stephen Stills tap-danced while Graham Nash slowly worked up the courage to play piano in public. His playing was rudimentary in the extreme (one finger of the left hand, three-finger chords with the right) and his singing painfully off-key, but the audience at the Hofheinz Pavilion were treated to the premiere of a song "about my woman": "Our House." It joined a growing catalog of material that had been committed to tape but would not be released to the public, or heard on radio, for another four months.

When unveiling his hymn to Joni Mitchell and her home, Nash didn't mention that he was also purchasing a house of his own, almost four hundred miles from Lookout Mountain Avenue. His three-story Victorian mansion at 737 Buena Vista Avenue West in San Francisco sat on the edge of Buena Vista Park and looked across Haight-Ashbury, still the city's hippie locale. It required almost total renovation and would eventually incorporate a recording studio (Rudy Records), a photographic dark room, a home cinema, and a spare room that was kept permanently for David Crosby. Its purchase consolidated CSNY's new roots in Northern California and marked a distinct step away from Joni Mitchell. She and her black tomcat, Hunter, remained in the Canyon, where Nash was still officially semi-resident. But in November 1969, she had begun to separate herself from her obligations, professional and personal.

She began by informing her management that she was coming off the road. After completing her existing schedule, she would play nothing but very occasional festival appearances and impromptu guest spots with friends, for the next two years. "She hasn't been able to write since trying to become a superstar," Elliot Roberts explained. She immediately fled to Canada for a month before fulfilling her US commitments, throwing in one last cameo with CSNY in Detroit.

Traveling with them to London in January 1970, she betrayed exactly how alienated she had become from her own existence. "My personal life is a shambles," she admitted, "and it's hard on me knowing I'm not giving anything to people I love. I'm a very solitary person, even in a room full of people." As she reflected later, "I was very frightened." She hated being scrutinized in public or having her lyrics scoured for personal references. Yet at the same time she reserved the right to expose herself utterly in her songs. As David Crosby would recall, "Mitchell can write about people, or your own heart, or your most personal feelings—and she'll drag them right out, just to dangle them in front of you."

As Mitchell finished her third album, *Ladies of the Canyon*, Graham Nash was aware that the world would soon be listening to "Willy," which everyone knew was about him; and "Blue Boy," the protagonist of which "made himself an idol, yes, so he turned to stone." Mitchell's threat was barely veiled: "He will come a few times more / Till he finds a lady statue standing in a door." Perhaps that time had arrived. "I had never been so much in love," Nash recalled, before adding: "I had never been so unsure of myself. I had never been so fragile." Through it all, the two of them were creative to an almost manic degree—painting and drawing, sculpting, writing songs, of course, and taking photographs—as if to stave off a moment of reckoning.

In late 1969, Nash chose to be alone in San Francisco, where he began to experiment with his new Wurlitzer piano. As chords formed into a melody, he found himself examining his life, his romance, his expectations, and his dreams. By the time that "Girl to Be on My Mind" was released in 1972, his partnership with Joni Mitchell had been dead for two years. Long before then, he was already peering beyond Lookout Mountain Avenue for distraction and—who could tell?—resolution, too.

> We get criticized for spending a long time tuning up . . . But when Neil gets nervous, he plays very hard and puts his guitar out of tune, and then has to tune it back down again.
>
> —Stephen Stills, February 1970

The tour schedule inevitably led CSNY back to California. Four days before Christmas 1969, they lined up before thirty-four thousand people in San Diego. Balboa Stadium had been abandoned by the San Diego Chargers because of fears that it might collapse during an earthquake. But its owners were prepared to risk the lives of teenage rock fans. Balboa had one other disadvantage as a concert venue: it was just over half a mile from the city's airport. Sure enough, as the "Suite" approached its climax, an enormous jet passed over the stage, drowning out the music. The sonic problems didn't end there. The onstage monitors issued squeals of feedback, distracting Stephen Stills to the extent that he lurched into the wrong key.

Everything seemed to be out of sync. Bassist Greg Reeves was harangued by members of the Black Panther Party before he took the stage, for the crime of prostituting his talent by playing with honkies. It was no consolation to learn that Jimi Hendrix was enduring similar pressure. "Greg's just been hassled by his own kind," Nash said clumsily, "and it's really far-out, I'm telling you."

The electric set was even more chaotic—tuneless harmonies, cacophonous solos, and such an absence of unity that it became impossible for the group to synchronize their rhythm. The singers were spending as much time off-mike, complaining to the crew, as they were struggling to find a harmony blend. Stills had to take command during "Long Time Gone," counting the time like a drill sergeant. "Wooden Ships" sounded as if they'd never played together before. Even the reliably triumphant "Down by the River" was sabotaged by the wayward tuning of Young's guitar. But still he and Crosby ended the song bouncing up and down in excitement, while the audience danced like the psychedelic freaks at the Monterey Festival. It was as if it didn't matter how or what CSNY played; just seeing them was enough.

Afterward, Stephen Stills was outraged, and adamant that their stadium days were over. "We're not doing any more of those," he insisted. "You get so many people that it's ridiculous. That essential intimate feeling is lost in a football park." Crosby was less concerned: he had met a belly dancer named Annie backstage and briefly set his grief aside. A few days later, CSNY set out on the long-awaited journey back to London, and the Royal Albert Hall.

> There is no limitation in anybody's head as to what we can do or what we are willing to try. I can't see any boundaries in sight.
>
> —David Crosby, London, January 1970

In crossing the Atlantic, CSNY were moving from a continent where they carried huge cultural weight to territories where their status was far more ambiguous. In Britain, they were still "Nash's supergroup," an impression reinforced by the Top 20 success of "Marrakesh Express." The *Crosby, Stills & Nash* album had reached a much smaller audience, barely registering in the sales charts, and "Suite: Judy Blue Eyes" had been ignored by the UK public. Early in 1970, *New Musical Express* held its annual Readers' Poll, which was widely regarded as the most accurate reflection of current pop trends. The Hollies were voted the fourth most popular vocal group in the world; CSNY didn't even feature in the list.

For Graham Nash, of course, the trip was a homecoming, specifically to the venue where he had played his final show with the Hollies. He relished the prospect of an audience who would understand his sense of humor—who might chuckle when he compared David Crosby to the TV puppets Pinky and Perky, for example. Crosby had spent enough time in the UK to understand its cynical view of brash outsiders (especially

Americans). But Stephen Stills and Neil Young had never performed on a British stage, and they craved the respect of their peers and mentors. For Stills in particular, there was the knowledge that CSNY were debuting at the venue where Cream had played their last concert—an event captured in all its excessive glory on celluloid. He dreamed of generating the same reaction from the notoriously hard to please London public, and being treated as an equal by the Beatles, the Stones, Clapton, Winwood, and the rest. CSNY would be facing an audience who scarcely knew about Woodstock, had probably never heard of Altamont, wasn't affected by Vietnam, and hadn't taken to Buffalo Springfield. The nearer the London show came, the greater the psychological burden heaped on Stephen Stills's head.

The band gathered in London a full week before the January 6 show—with the exception of Greg Reeves, who kept missing his plane. In a sign of the times, Crosby, Stills, Nash, and Dallas Taylor shared one flight; Young and Joni Mitchell another. But they gathered happily enough in a rented suite of five apartments over shops in Kensington High Street. The pop press was eager to meet them, even though photographs weren't allowed: "We're a six-man band," Crosby explained, "and Greg ain't here yet." The former Byrd was lauded as the group's official spokesman, and he proceeded to pontificate on politics, civil war, and revolution. He even laid out a plan of action for any activists attempting to overthrow the American government: "I know how it can be done. All you have to do is take the major cities and blow their bridges, cut off their water supply, and shut down their electricity. Inside three days, you'll have millions of starving people in the biggest traffic jam in history. Everything will be crippled."

When Stephen Stills managed to force his way in front of the microphone, he disclaimed any power or responsibility: "Don't build me up into a pop star. I'm no different from you or anybody else. It's just that, because I'm a musician, I can put music to people's thoughts." But his humility ended there. He was soon boasting about his rebel status: "I stood up in front of a lot of people during the Vietnam Moratorium in San Francisco recently and read a poem. So, if there's a list, I'm on it."

Neil Young remained almost unknown in Britain, where his two solo albums had only just been released. "I've reached just about the perfect state," he explained. "I'm part of the group, which I can really dig, and I can also express myself as an individual through my own things. And I need very badly to make my own music, partly because it boosts my ego to the required dimension." Graham Nash restricted himself to platitudes about how wonderful his life was, in every way, and kept a wary eye on Joni Mitchell, in case she revealed any clues about how she viewed their future.

On New Year's Eve, the Californian contingent was invited to a party at Ringo Starr's mansion above Hampstead Heath. This was what Stills had been waiting for: to be in the company of three of the Beatles and their wives (only the Lennons were absent), among dozens of celebrities from the worlds of music and film. Most of those he met assured him that, yes, of course, they were coming to the Albert Hall show, and so the pressure increased. CSNY fell into cabs around dawn, heavily the worse for wear. A couple of days later, Stills bought Ringo a thank-you present (vintage brass candlesticks) at the antiques market in Chelsea; he also picked up a gift for Crosby (a ship's bell for the *Mayan*). Perhaps it was a gesture of peace: pop writer Penny Valentine, who had visited Moscow Road in 1968, pronounced that CSN were just the same as before, "apart from occasional verbal battles between David and Stephen."

The focus returned to the Albert Hall show. "That was the first time we've ever really been affected by nerves," Stills admitted. "We felt some-how as if we were on trial, as if they'd come to judge us rather than to enjoy our music." He had failed to take account of the fact that British audiences had always been notoriously quiet by comparison with their American counterparts—waiting to be impressed and restrained in how they showed their appreciation. It didn't help that as Stills looked out from the stage, he could see familiar (and famous) faces peeking out from the boxes that ringed Albert Hall—or that Paul McCartney left his seat early in the show, apparently never to return. (He had decided to join the masses in the cheap seats at the top of the building.) Stills's ordeal continued: "There was all this bad tension, and we just couldn't make it go away. It was distressing that we let it affect us so much. To be honest, I felt terrible—like an insect being dissected under a microscope."

Little of that sense of scrutiny was apparent to the audience, who heard CSN make their customary tentative start to the "Suite" and then soar.

The crowd's first exposure to "Teach Your Children" was so rapturous that the local reps of Atlantic Records must already have been scheduling it as a single. Neil Young's arrival was greeted with just as much approval, and the acoustic set built until Stills received an ecstatic reception for "Black Queen." Only then, when he embarked on his parochial rant during "For What It's Worth," spouting rhetoric that was foreign to a British audience, did people's attention start to slip.

With the onset of electricity, CSNY began their regular battle with their instruments, which stubbornly refused to stay in tune. Between the interruptions, their first group rendition of Young's "The Loner" was a highlight before "Down by the River" overcame any last British reserve. Still, when they returned for an encore, Graham Nash felt he needed to administer a mild admonishment: "We play better if you clap better."

As the audience filed out, there was no hint of disillusion or letdown. Fans had loved the music, the raps, the humor, the off-the-cuff fragments of songs thrown in along the way (such as Nash and Crosby breaking into a chorus of "Happiness Runs," which Nash had helped Donovan to record two years earlier). Fellow musicians were more critical. Led Zeppelin's Robert Plant complained that "Down by the River" "typified in my eyes just how boring a twelve-bar blues can be if you play it for twenty minutes" and comparing CSNY unfavorably to Crazy Horse, whom he had seen in the States a few months earlier.

It was the infamous British media that delivered the most crushing blows. Most national newspapers were not yet in the habit of wasting their column inches on something as trivial as a pop concert, but the London *Evening Standard* declared that the show had run the gamut "from dullness to dire drabness" and was "extravagantly boring." The following week's music papers carped about the endless tuning and David Crosby's inability to stop talking—one critic calculating that music only constituted about 60 percent of the show. *Melody Maker*'s Chris Welch claimed to have dozed off during the performance; *Disc* said that CSNY pursued "individual ego trips" rather than audience communication. Reviewers from London's two most prestigious Sunday newspapers reflected the polarized response to the show. Derek Jewell (*Sunday Times*) reckoned that CSNY "represent the summit at which the best rock music has arrived"; Tony Palmer (*The Observer*) reported that "They mumbled inaudible jokes to themselves about themselves and fell about the stage in hysterical laughter . . . It was like being at a party where everybody knew everybody except you." Indeed, the show led Palmer to question what rock was for: "Is it just a crashing, witless bore? [CSNY] suggested it might well be just that." This sense of dissatisfaction poisoned the air.

The original proposal for a monthlong European tour had been whittled down until only two other dates remained, in Stockholm and Copenhagen. CSNY were neither the first nor the last American entertainers to discover that if they craved applause and adulation in Europe, England (and especially London) was not the place to look. The Danish show began on a high, and simply built from there, until Stills and Young played out a delicious musical conversation, subtle and acutely interactive, on "Down by the River." CSNY could leave Europe with deafening applause ringing in their ears—except that Stephen Stills chose not to go home.

If anything should ever happen, I reckon Britain would be the only safe, sane place in the world.

—Stephen Stills, February 1970

Proof of CSN's impact on the American music industry was provided in January 1970, when the nominees for the annual Grammy Awards were announced. *Crosby, Stills & Nash* was one of five records proposed as Album of the Year, ranged against the Beatles' *Abbey Road*, *Johnny Cash at San Quentin*, *Blood, Sweat & Tears*, and the Fifth Dimension's *Age of Aquarius*. Most of those contenders also lined up against CSN in the category for Best Contemporary Duo or Vocal Group Performance, while the trio were also nominated for Best New Artist alongside Chicago, Led Zeppelin, long forgotten art-pop group the Neon Philharmonic, and the even more ephemeral singer Oliver. At the gala ceremony in March, CSN lost out to Blood, Sweat & Tears in one category and the Fifth Dimension (of "Up, Up and Away" fame) in another, but were duly anointed the Best New Artist of the year. None of the trio bothered to collect their award.

At London's luxurious Dorchester Hotel, Stephen Stills felt alienated not only from the band he had helped to create, but also from its sense of brotherhood. He was not prone to laying bare his feelings to strangers, but English pop journalist Penny Valentine was charming and empathic enough to loosen his guard. Talking to her in February, he signaled that, for him at least, the dream was over. Whenever he talked about the unit, he always called it Crosby, Stills & Nash, as if that was both the core and the key, and Neil Young an entirely separate issue. And CSN, he confessed, might be all but dead. "It started out as a really beautiful idea," he said wistfully. "We were full of enthusiasm and ideals. Now a lot of that feeling has gone between us." He turned to Valentine: "You know, you even noticed how we'd changed to each other since the last time." That, he explained, was why he was still in England. "The feeling there doesn't escape me—I'm too much of a realist. By the time we'd finished those last concerts, we needed a vacation from each other."

He was not quite prepared to sign a death certificate: "When I go back to America, maybe that feeling of us all liking each other a lot will return, and we'll go on working together." But he began to speak of the band in the past tense, as if writing an obituary: "We did what we set out to do. We said we weren't going to set the world on fire, but we *were* going to make fine music—which is exactly what we did. But things are in a limbo state at the moment."

Trying to explain exactly what had happened, he kept harking back to the Albert Hall show, that sensation of being judged and found wanting. But there was a deeper problem: CSN had been *his* group on the first album, and now it was slipping out of his hands. "I'm so tired," he confessed, "of trying to manipulate all those forces within the band." At no point did he stop to think: perhaps those forces didn't *want* to be manipulated?

Stills already owned a home in Los Angeles and a cabin in the Rocky Mountains. Now he was imagining a house in England as well. "I don't think there's anything more I really need—except maybe someone to share them with," he said poignantly.

For a sense of release, Stills turned back to his salvation: music. He booked a month at Island Studios, which occupied a former church in

West London, and sent out the call for Dallas Taylor and Bill Halverson. The engineer was swift to respond, but the drummer took his time. So, Stills pursued two paths simultaneously—recording as a one-man band and recruiting local musicians. From a club outfit named One, he stole bass player Calvin "Fuzzy" Samuel, who led him to drummer Conrad Isidore, and suddenly he had a functioning band. At another venue, he bumped into a contingent from Apple Records, including Ringo Starr, whom he immediately asked to join the sessions. Starr introduced him to keyboardist Billy Preston, who updated an old Mae West line: "If you can't be with the one you love, honey, love the one you're with." "Do you mind if I steal that?" Stills asked, and then went away to write a song combining the catchphrase with a keyboard riff he'd invented during his "Woodstock" session with Jimi Hendrix.

Ringo invited Stills to Abbey Road, where he was attempting to record his own first solo single. As Stills recalled, "Ringo came in with this little song—that is, he sat down and played eight bars, and said, 'That's it.' So, we all made suggestions"—"all," in this instance, including George Harrison who ultimately composed the bulk of the song. But Stills was there both in February and again in March as "It Don't Come Easy" came together and stayed around to make a more substantial contribution to Doris Troy's Apple album.

When they joined forces at Island Studios, Stills and Starr struck up an immediate musical rapport. The drummer was resolute, reliable, kept impeccable time, and was accustomed from his apprenticeship with the Beatles to absolute efficiency in the studio. In a couple of days, they completed a set of rhythm tracks that Stills would still be utilizing five years later. "I wanted him to play on all the tracks," Stills confessed, "but he thought people would think he had joined my band."

Having visited Starr's London house on New Year's, Stills was now given a guided tour of his Surrey estate by his wife Maureen. The Starr residence in Elstead boasted fourteen rooms, stables, a sauna, a wine cellar, several duck ponds, a river, and almost twenty acres of land. The property had been renovated by actor Peter Sellers, who sold it to the Beatle in 1969. But Starr was now focused on his mansion in the city, and Stills offered to take the country estate off his hands. They came to a deal whereby he would rent the house and grounds until later in the year, by which time another stash of royalties would allow him to complete the £90,000 purchase. "I always wanted to spend some time in England," Stills explained. "Ringo's house is a really good investment." David Geffen advised him against sinking his money into property overseas, but Stills ignored him: "It's so beautiful. I'm going to spend many quiet summers there." To celebrate his arrival, and commemorate its previous owner, he engraved his favorite lyrics from the Beatles' song "Within You Without You" onto a stone wall. "Living in Britain was my salvation," he would reflect later. "That's when my creativity in songwriting exploded."

His solo project expanded at breathtaking speed, as Stills continued to write and record. He was also adapting himself to his adopted home. "I loved getting off the bus and going out," he recalled. "I had to follow fifty cabs to learn the roads, but eventually I learned how to drive around the city." Through jamming and networking, he secured a place at the heart of London's session community and realized that he could construct a fantasy band out of any musicians in town. "The thing I learned about playing with Eric Clapton and all the great British blues guys is that there's a courtliness, a kind of manners involved in jamming," he reflected. "I wouldn't trade that, period, for the world. The issue for me wasn't so much fitting in, or being a chameleon, as simple good manners, which can be a problem when you're going out and getting hammered, and end up looking like a jerk. I realize now that I was simply being shy, and trying to overcome it in a haphazard, clumsy kind of way."

For all his self-deprecation, Stills became the only person ever to recruit Eric Clapton and Jimi Hendrix for the same album. With Clapton, he prepared one of his electric Delta blues tunes, "Go Back Home," left a hole in the arrangement for his guest to fill, and then insisted on using the guitarist's first take, against his protestations. Clapton added an equally fiery solo to "Fishes and Scorpions," before alcohol took control. Stills remembered jamming the '50s rock and roll hit "Tequila" for about an hour, until he slumped into a heap and Clapton vanished. When Stills came round, he cut the definitive take of "Black Queen" and gave credit on the album to his chosen brand of gold-label liquor. "It hurts my throat to sing like that," he confessed.

Jimi Hendrix flew to London in March 1970 and inevitably ended up at Island Studios. There he renewed a relationship that, as Stills recalled, had grown out of mutual affection and understanding: "Jimi gravitated to me and my friend Glenn Campbell, because we were Southern guys who really understood black people. He would come knocking on the door and just sit down to get away from the madness. We'd go out to clubs and say, 'Is the rhythm section any good? Decent? Okay, let's take it.' We did that particularly on the East Coast, down in New Jersey and up in New Hampshire, and then a couple of nights in London, too, at the Speakeasy and Ronnie Scott's. I wish we'd had tape machines at some of our club shows, because they were marvelous." The tapes were rolling at Island, as Hendrix added a solo to "Love the One You're With" (which Stills later wiped). He also helped Stills to arrange two autobiographical tunes, "Old Times Good Times" and "White Nigger," named after "The White Negro," Norman Mailer's essay about hipster rebels who exist outside bourgeois convention. Hendrix clearly didn't find the song or the sentiment offensive, as he overdubbed a series of guitar parts; but when Stills finally issued the track, in 2012, he stripped off the vocal and gave it the euphemistic title "No-Name Jam."

By the time he returned to America in April 1970, Stills had accumulated around a dozen songs in varying stages of completion and anticipated adding a black vocal chorus and a brass section. He imagined that he might be able to release a solo album by midsummer, after which he would return to Britain. "I've considered calling the album *Stephen Stills Retires*," he confessed before he left England. "I might just stop for a while after the tour because I'm really pooped"—a tour that would reassemble the troubled band he had sought to escape three months earlier.

> I chose not to go on the sailing trip that made David and Graham so close, as Captain Crosby would not acknowledge that I actually knew how to sail. Suffice to say, on each of those trips one of the crewmen ended up taking Crosby by the hair and banging him against the mainmast.
>
> —Stephen Stills

"From the moment I climbed into an eight-and-a-half-foot dinghy in 1952," David Crosby explained more than sixty years later, "I knew instinctively what to do and sensed I had done it before. I'm a natural sailor." Behind the wheel of the *Mayan*, he could escape the everyday realities of stardom and bereavement, and the ego sparring of CSNY. The boat was its own self-sufficient world, which demanded the utmost respect from its crew, but repaid the responsibility with an almost spiritual sense of purpose.

Given a space in his working schedule by Stephen Stills's exile in London, David Crosby set out to bring the *Mayan* from its base in Fort Lauderdale through the Panama Canal to California, where he intended to scatter Christine Hinton's ashes in the Pacific Ocean. It was anything but a solitary task. "The cabin below can sleep eight, but six people is more ideal," he explained, "four to keep watch and take turns manning the sails, and two who can alternate cooking and cleaning." His first recruit for a voyage of 4,500 miles was an Englishman who had scarcely ever set foot in a boat: Graham Nash. "Other people would fly out and join us for a few days at a time," Nash said. "I had to learn navigation in a hurry. But that was a lot of fun, steering out there with just you and the stars and a compass to guide you. [It] gives you a whole new perspective on life, when you don't see land for days on end." As Crosby recalled, "By the time we got to San Diego, [Nash] was standing three-hour wheel watches, dependably."

Nash explained, "The atmosphere aboard the *Mayan* is serene. It's not a cocktail party boat. There's no television, and the sea air is not good for electronics, so we don't even have a stereo onboard." Some of that serenity was provided by their sailing mates—old friends of Crosby's from his pre-fame days, roadies from the CSNY crew, even fellow singer-songwriter Ronee Blakley. They phoned her when they reached the Bahamas, because they were short on cash. She collected $5,000 from the CSNY coffers—and then had to play a gig at Carnegie Hall. Unwilling to leave the bills unsupervised backstage, she stuffed them into her under-wear for the evening, before hightailing it to the airport for the flight to Nassau. "We had a ball," she remembered. "I even sang on deck in a satin gown." But David Crosby's most enduring memory of her presence was that she arrived with a typewriter, which mysteriously vanished overboard after the *Mayan*'s captain found her constant clattering too distracting.

That was a petty annoyance compared to the emotional turmoil brought aboard by Joni Mitchell. Being closeted on a boat illuminated all the fractures in her relationship with Graham Nash. He recalled in his autobiography that, almost as soon as she joined the vessel, she denounced her lover as "a woman-hater." (This was only a few weeks after she had written him the most tender of tributes, "My Old Man.") His anecdote prompted some of the most vitriolic passages in Mitchell's interviews with her biographer, David Yaffe. By her account, the voyage (which, for her, lasted only a few days) was physical and psychological torture, typical of her dealings with Nash, Crosby, and indeed the entire male songwriting community of California. She claimed that she and Nash had already split before she joined ship; Nash remembered that they had merely been undergoing a period of strain. Whatever the truth, Mitchell left the *Mayan* in Panama, flew home to California, and began to plan an epic adventure of her own, to a Greek island.

With its emotional crises, seafaring dramas, and sensory highs, Nash's journey proved to be creatively stimulating. ("The *Mayan* has been a deep muse," Crosby would reflect later.) He began writing "Wind on the Water" after his first sighting of a blue whale, while the aftermath of Mitchell's chaotic sojourn on the boat provoked "Man in the Mirror," a return to the self-searching imagery of the Hollies' "Clown."

Crosby had a female companion onboard, a young San Diego woman named Anita Treash, but as he gazed out at the ocean, his mind ran obsessively to Christine. As he told Ben Fong-Torres a few months later, his writing turned in an endless circle: "The words all come around to 'Why is it like this?' They're good songs. [But] I haven't sung them to anybody, and I don't think I'm gonna, 'cos they're pretty sad and they don't draw any useful conclusion. I'm waiting until I got something good to sing about, some joy." For the moment, "Where Will I Be?" and "Whole Cloth" were set aside, and nothing more positive followed them.

Such was CSNY's commercial profile, and Atlantic Records' impatience for new product, that the next few years would spark countless rumors about albums that had been recorded or were about to be begun, but that existed only in fantasy. Among them was a collaboration between Crosby and Nash, said to have been taped in three weeks of sessions in

April–May 1970. In reality, the pair did not even enter the studio until late June, and that liaison lasted only for two days—abandoned after a distracted Crosby ejected their old friend Cass Elliot from the premises and Nash followed in disgust. All that remained on tape was their attempt to cover Joni Mitchell's "Urge for Going," over which David Geffen added a (deliberately?) tuneless lead vocal.

The song was perfectly suited to their voices, but the choice may well have been symbolic. At the same Grammy Awards ceremony that CSN boycotted, Joni Mitchell was awarded the Best Folk Album prize for her second album, *Clouds*. She collected the trophy in a long purple gown and then set off for Greece. There, in the hippie commune of Matala on Crete, she struck up a relationship with a man she would celebrate in song, Cary Raditz, and then welcomed the much younger singer-songwriter, James Taylor, who became her partner for the next year. Back at Lookout Mountain Avenue, Graham Nash was acting as handyman, laying down a new kitchen floor, when a telegram arrived from Greece. It read: "If you hold sand too tightly, it will run through your fingers." It was, Nash realized, Mitchell's "Dear Graham" letter. He sadly gathered his things and left Lookout Mountain behind. The trauma was soon reflected in song. "Simple Man" sounded as if it had been written straight after he slit open the Western Union envelope ("I hear what you're saying, but you're spinning my head around"). Equally affecting was "I Used to Be a King." This sequel to "King Midas in Reverse" drew the curtain on their tempestuous relationship; but like David Crosby's "Games," composed under similar stress, it still declared "I love you."

"Joni and I loved each other deeply," Nash would reflect. "But in many ways, I never felt worthy. In certain ways, toward the end, I felt like I was holding her back." In her bitter interviews with David Yaffe, Mitchell would claim—quite inaccurately—that he, and not she, had stepped immediately into a new relationship. More truthful was her comment a few years earlier: "When Graham and I broke up, I was pretty much without friends. My whole family was CSN and all those people. I lost my whole community in the divorce, so to speak." Like Crosby, however, Nash would not banish Mitchell from his world.

I'm trying to make records that are not necessarily hits, [but] that people will dig to listen to for a long time.

—Neil Young, March 1970

"It's blowing my mind," Neil Young admitted when he was asked about his experience on the road with CSNY. "I didn't think it was gonna be as big as this. Makes a lot of money, and it's hard to relate to, after what I was doing before." Two years after leaving Buffalo Springfield, he had become . . . well, if not a superstar, just yet, then at least a celebrity in the world of rock and roll. There was even physical evidence to support his status. *Everybody Knows This Is Nowhere* had been rescued from oblivion and was heading up the album charts. Memphis pop band the Gentrys were picking up airplay with a cover of "Cinnamon Girl," which sounded strangely as if the Springfield had recorded it during one of Young's leaves of absence. Within weeks, Young's own "Cinnamon Girl" would be reissued and join the impostor in the lower half of the Hot 100. But first Young issued a new single, his enervated cover of Don Gibson's "Oh, Lonesome Me." "I like that because everybody else seems to hate it so much," Young confessed.

Young steadfastly ignored the song when he set out on a brief tour with an expanded Crazy Horse in late February. (Jack Nitzsche was added on piano.) As he admitted, the transition from CSNY to the Horse was not straightforward: "It took me two weeks to calm down enough so I could play with this band, because I was rushing all the time with my guitar, playing too many notes." He had certainly adjusted his pace for his show in Cincinnati, where he performed the acoustic set as if he were marginally more asleep than awake, abandoning songs after a verse and slowing everything to a near standstill. The electric set was equally awry—off-key, out of kilter—but still somehow thrilling, and throughout, the audience was ecstatic. By the time they reached the Fillmore East ten days later, Young and the Horse were both coherent and electrifying, ending their sets with a version of "Cowgirl in the Sand" that anticipated the next forty years of thrash metal. (Young was supported by the Steve Miller Band and, bizarrely, Miles Davis's fusion band at their least compromising. As the archive CD of Davis's set confirmed, many of Young's audience were baffled by the mercurial genius of modern jazz.)

At the end of March, a reviewer of Young's show in Santa Monica wrote: "To my mind, he's the best thing American rock and roll has going for itself at the moment." By then, Young had all but completed his much awaited third studio record—and dismissed Crazy Horse as his backing band, at least in the studio. (It would be 1975 before he joined them onstage again.) "Neil and Elliot called us in," bassist Billy Talbot recalled, "and said we weren't gonna work together for a while." The problem was Danny Whitten, who had slipped further into heroin addiction: "It was too crazy, with Danny doing his trips." The first few shows had convinced Young that Whitten was barely holding station onstage. As he would tell the press, "I just got up one morning and decided to do something new."

In May 1969, at the Cellar Door in Washington, the band's dressing room had been invaded by a seventeen-year-old guitarist, keyboardist, singer, and songwriter called Nils Lofgren, who was eager for Young to hear his songs. In mid-March 1970, Lofgren was invited to Young's Topanga Canyon house, with its studio now fully functioning in the basement. "I think he was under pressure from Warner Brothers to release another album," Lofgren considered. "He just didn't have any idea what to do." The teenager watched as Young recorded what was intended as the theme song for the *After the Gold Rush* movie (soon abandoned as too expensive to film). Young accompanied himself on piano and delivered his ambiguous environmental statement in a voice so cracked and high that it was almost painful to hear. Then the two men cut the more orthodox "Tell Me Why" on acoustic guitars. The next day, Danny Whitten (still coherent behind a vocal mike) and Ralph Molina joined them to add background harmonies, barroom regulars compared to CSN's choirboys.

Although Billy Talbot's playing on the tour had been exemplary, Young called in Greg Reeves to jam with Lofgren and Molina. "We just started playing together," Lofgren said, "and it sounded really nice and relaxed. The following day we just went into the studio and tried it out again, and this time it sounded really terrible; but the next day Neil brought all the equipment up to the house and recorded the whole album in less than a week in his home. He had all these unfinished songs, and they just started getting finished." Suddenly Young's repertoire had expanded to include several landmark songs: "Only Love Can Break Your Heart," a gift to Graham Nash as his relationship dissolved; "Don't Let It Bring You Down," an eerie response to CSNY's London visit in January; "When You Dance, I Can Really Love," for which he briefly reunited the Horse; and most enduringly, "Southern Man." This was his first political statement, widely acclaimed as an attack on the racism of America's Deep South—the same forces of bigotry and repression that had wiped out Fonda and Hopper at the end of *Easy Rider*. But the song was more subtle (or confused) than that. It switched positions and viewpoints almost from line to line, evoking the legacy of slavery, the evil of the Ku Klux Klan, the South's century-long plea for renewal after the Civil War and, in the final verse, a white man—then or now?—driven to the point of murder by seeing his woman (wife? sweetheart? daughter?) in the arms of "your black man." The music screamed rage and revenge, easy answers to hard questions, but the lyrics were infinitely more complex than the song's audience wanted to understand.

The same could be said for Neil Young's attitude to his career, as he and David Briggs pulled these songs into shape as an album, and the CSNY tour loomed. Like Stephen Stills, Young felt as if he could see the end of the road. "I don't know how much longer I can do it," he confessed in April. "I just want to do something else. After this next album I don't know how much longer it'll be before I put out another one, of any kind, with anyone." These were not the words of a man itching to be back in the studio with Crosby, Stills, and Nash.

Instead, a different kind of reunion seems to have intrigued him. Since the breakup of Buffalo Springfield, Young and Stills had prospered; likewise, Richie Furay, who formed the breezy country-rock band Poco. But the Springfield's original rhythm section had struggled. Dewey Martin had been regarded by some as the most disruptive element in a cantankerous band. But it was him who Young and Elliot Roberts contacted in the late spring of 1970, with the suggestion that the original Buffalo Springfield might reunite after the CSNY tour was over. Bruce Palmer was certainly available and willing, and Martin sounded out Richie Furay, who expressed provisional interest. Only one ex-Springfield member seems to have been left in the dark about these nebulous plans: Stephen Stills.

> Crosby, Stills and Nash—plus or minus Neil Young—will probably remain the band that asks the question, "What can we do that would be really heavy?" And then answers, "How about something by Joni Mitchell?"
>
> —Langdon Winner, *Rolling Stone*, April 1970

It was Lenny Bronstein, on WCBR at Brooklyn College, who stole the world exclusive. On March 9, 1970, he secured an advance copy of *Déjà Vu* and played it nonstop all morning. By the end of the month, it was in the stores, outselling everything on college campuses, on its way to becoming the bestselling album in the nation by early May. By then, "Woodstock" had climbed to number 11 on *Billboard*'s Hot 100, and "Teach Your Children" was being teed up in its wake.

In early April, headlines around the world proclaimed that the Beatles had broken up. There was now a void in pop culture, and CSNY seemed perfectly poised to fill it. They were, one reviewer insisted, "undoubtedly the most creative working group in the world." Another raved that *Déjà Vu* was "the most beautiful record ever produced." In the *LA Times*, Robert Hilburn acclaimed it as "easily the best rock album of the new year" and congratulated CSNY (alongside the Band) for outstripping the Beatles "in such areas as creative use of harmony, matching instrumentation with theme and in lyric sophistication." The addition of Neil Young to the already gifted CSN lineup was universally acclaimed, with many critics noting how skillfully he had managed to squeeze into their tight vocal blend. (He hadn't, of course; he did not sing a single note of harmony on the album.)

Inevitably, there were those who carped—not least Stephen Stills, who lamented that his relocation to London after the European shows in January meant that he hadn't been around to supervise the final mix. "I may have coasted a little bit on the production," he admitted. "A few things got past me that I've regretted since." Stills claimed credit for the

cover concept, portraying the six musicians in nineteenth-century cos-
tumes, and the tangible finesse of the packaging. The specifics had helped
to delay the album by several weeks, as printers struggled to reproduce
the band's demand for lettering embossed in gold leaf, and a surface that
would feel like leather. CSNY promised that *Déjà Vu* would resemble
an antiquarian book, not a standard record album.

Rolling Stone magazine was quick to pounce on the pretentiousness
of the package. As Langdon Winner complained, "The heralded leather
cover turns out to be nothing more than crimpled cardboard." It was a
metaphor, he felt, for the music inside: "It's still too sweet, too soothing,
too perfect and too good to be true." And as for CSNY themselves, they
were roundly attacked in the underground press for the banality and
naïvety of their image and their songs. David Crosby's "Almost Cut My
Hair" became the focus for their insults—it was described as overblown,
ridiculous, embarrassing. And as the *Woodstock* movie and soundtrack
were readied for release, *Déjà Vu* served as a symbol of everything that
the festival had claimed to be and failed to achieve. In the *East Village
Other*, Charlie Frick declared that "The album comes on like, 'Hey
gang, wasn't Woodstock fun!! Peace and love are too much, aren't they
kids!! Let's have a big hand for peace and love.' The Woodstock nation's
applause is deafening." The acclaim seemed certain to continue on April
30, when CSNY were due to resume their touring schedule at Winterland
Ballroom in San Francisco.

WOODSTOCK 5
THE MOVIE

One town council in Florida got out an injunction against the film because it shows people smoking pot, and extreme views about the Vietnam War. They said they didn't want the young people of their town being encouraged to take their bras off.

—Michael Wadleigh, director of *Woodstock*

The filming of *Woodstock* would have made as dramatic a documentary subject as the festival itself. The movie's director, Michael Wadleigh, was just short of his twenty-seventh birthday when he and his crew were compelled to manufacture a coherent motion picture out of what was nothing less than a disaster zone. He had inherited the assignment at short notice, when the promoters' hopes of auctioning the film rights to major studios were disappointed. Their lawyers had negotiated a deal with Ahmet Ertegun of Atlantic Records, who, for $75,000, purchased the license to record and issue albums of the music performed at the festival (subject to contractual clearance from the artists and their labels). "I knew that Crosby, Stills and Nash were going to be playing," Ertegun recalled, "and I was hopeful that Led Zeppelin might be on the bill as well, so it seemed a good risk to take." With the film rights still available, he was persuaded to stump up another $25,000—with the result that Atlantic's parent company, Warner Brothers, was able to exploit the festival's notoriety and turn three days of mud, rain, nudity, dope, and music into a twentieth-century legend.

One of the assistant directors on the project was Martin Scorsese, who recalled that the crew were terrified the festival would quickly capsize under the weight of its own success. "We shot everything we could at Woodstock the first night," he remembered. "We wanted to come away with something, at least." The crew faced almost every imaginable technical challenge, from a physical lack of film stock (extra supplies were helicoptered in throughout the festival) to the extreme weather. "A lot of equipment was destroyed by electricity problems or rain," Wadleigh explained. "Transport and communications were terrible. They had two mammoth generators up there, and we and the groups had to use them. The motors for the camera kept blowing, and they kept sending surges of power through, which played havoc with the equipment."

A fearless cameraman himself, who shot some of the most memorable *Woodstock* sequences, Wadleigh brought his own aesthetic to the project, including his pioneering use of split-screen imagery, running several images past the eye simultaneously. One of the songs that was given this treatment was the opening number by Crosby, Stills & Nash: "Suite: Judy Blue Eyes." As Wadleigh explained, "We took their first number because, like they said, they were scared. It was only their second performance together, and it was so interesting. The first part of the song was so bad. They were out of tune and mixed up. But the fun of watching them pull that song together—I mean, they were never better the whole evening. The tension behind that number was really nice." Or, as one of the musicians remembered his embarrassment, "It's all there in real-life living color—Stephen Stills trying to tune his guitar, keep it together, and make an impression at Woodstock."

That was CSN's only visual appearance in the original cut of the movie, although their songs were employed on the soundtrack as atmospheric coloring, beginning and ending the film. "Long Time Gone" and "Woodstock" itself bookended the picture, with "Woodstock" utilizing the original Stills lead vocal that Neil Young had insisted was better than the one heard on *Déjà Vu*. "One of the reasons we used so much of them was the idea that the movie was about community, a gathering, a sense of camaraderie, a Woodstock generation thing," Wadleigh reflected. "And there were three or four people singing in harmony."

It was that issue of numbers—three or four—that limited the band's participation in the movie. One of the production assistants on the project was given the task of securing written or, failing that, verbal agreement from each set of musicians, before the camera crew could capture them on film. Almost all agreed, although some subsequently refused permission for their footage to be utilized. But there was one musician at Woodstock who passed into legend for turning down the request even before he began to play: Neil Young.

"I didn't allow myself to be filmed because I didn't want them on the stage," Young said of the camera crew. "Get away, don't be in my way, I don't want to see your cameras, I don't want to see you . . . I just didn't want to do that." Young was not alone in resenting the distraction: at a particularly intense moment of the Who's set, Pete Townshend kicked Wadleigh's camera out of eyeshot and took Wadleigh with it. The director told his crew to lie low for a few songs, and then gradually reclaim their positions, without which the band's rousing performance of "We're Not Gonna Take It," from *Tommy*, would never have been captured on film.

Neil Young did not—or not yet—wield the power within CSNY that Pete Townshend commanded in the Who. But to avoid a situation where Young might veto any appearance by the band in the *Woodstock* movie, Wadleigh's crew chose to bow to his wishes and, as much as possible, keep him out of focus. Some footage survived to prove that Young really was there: in the sequence for "Long Time Gone," Young was lost in the shadows for all but a few seconds, when his face inadvertently filled the center of the screen. His duet with Stephen Stills on "Mr. Soul" was handled more cautiously, with only Young's forearm occasionally sneaking into the shot. In the movie, however, it was easier—and, according to Wadleigh, more dramatic—to show CSN wrestling with the "Suite" than to bother about trying to edit a recalcitrant guitarist out of CSNY footage.

Not that Young was thankful for the director's discretion. In a 1979 interview, he complained, "I saw the movie, and I wasn't in it, so maybe I wasn't too good there, I don't know"—as if he felt slighted not to have filled the *Woodstock* wide screen. Then he had the temerity to complain in his memoir that his name had been snipped out of the stage announcement that preceded the "Suite" in the movie, as if it was an act of revenge by CSN. Wadleigh would have argued that it made no sense to hear Young being introduced and then not see him onscreen.

The enigma of Neil Young's nonparticipation in the film was nothing compared to what happened to the audio recording of the CSNY set, however.

Three of their songs appeared on the triple-album soundtrack issued two months after the film: the "Suite," "Wooden Ships" and, to prove that Neil Young really was at Woodstock, "Sea of Madness." But the last of these songs had actually been recorded a month after the festival, at the Fillmore East in New York. Young described its inclusion as "kind of misleading" and couldn't explain how it had happened.

When "lost" performances from the festival were released on home video in the 1980s, CSN's "Marrakesh Express" was one of the fresh discoveries. This performance—one guitar, one shaker, three voices—had already been issued on the 1971 album *Woodstock 2*, alongside "Guinnevere" and "4+20." But on the film clip, the song mysteriously gained a bassist, pianist, and additional guitarist, while another high voice appeared in the mix—which didn't belong to any of CSN.

Responsibility for the music on the film, and the subsequent albums, belonged to Atlantic producer Eric Blackstead. He worked tirelessly for more than three months on the project, often putting in thirty-six-hour stints worthy of Stephen Stills at his most frenetic. So draining was his task that he suffered a collapsed lung and was forced to approve the final test pressings of the album while lying in a hospital bed. Blackstead's role was to ensure that the music released on the album reflected well on the artists—especially those signed to Atlantic. Listening pleasure was a higher priority than absolute fidelity to what had been heard at the festival, and so anonymous musicians were hired to provide surreptitious decoration to the raw live tapes.

"Sea of Madness" was not the only non-Woodstock recording to appear on the soundtrack album: Arlo Guthrie's "Coming In to Los Angeles" was also taped elsewhere, as his appearance in the film made clear. Why was the switch made? Legend has it that Stephen Stills vetoed the inclusion of the Woodstock "Sea of Madness," claiming it was substandard and offered Blackstead the Fillmore tape instead. The subterfuge would never have been noticed, if an audience tape of the Fillmore show had not begun to circulate among fans. Ironically, "Sea of Madness" was identified by several contemporary reviewers as the weakest track on the entire soundtrack album.

So, Neil Young had multiple reasons for regarding *Woodstock*, and the myth that blew up in its wake, with ironic distance. In 1973, he wrote a sardonic song about the life of the traveling musician, in which he announced: "I'm not going back to Woodstock for a while... I don't believe I'll be going back that way." When CSN agreed to take part in the twenty-fifth-anniversary festival in 1994, there was no issue this time about whether Neil Young had agreed to be filmed. He simply didn't attend.

CHAPTER 10

I wrecked my car, and it kinda woke me up, but it didn't last long.

—Stephen Stills

In London, Stephen Stills recorded the bulk of one solo album, the beginnings of a second, and several songs intended for the next CSNY album. Among them were "Johnny's Garden," about Starr's Surrey home; "The Treasure," mapping the search for eternal love; and "As I Come of Age." Reminded of that tune thirty-five years later, Stills groaned and said, "If it had only been true! That's why I find it difficult to sing that song—it's like, 'Aw, bullshit, you *pretended* that you'd come of age, you moron!'"

On the evening of April 14, 1970, the jetlagged twenty-five-year-old Stills was back on Shady Oak Road. He scoured the house for cigarettes, came up empty, jumped into his Mercedes, and headed into the city. As he wound his way down Laurel Canyon Drive, he picked up a police cruiser on his tail, was seized with paranoia—like David Crosby in "Almost Cut My Hair"—and rammed into a parked car. He emerged from the emergency room with a hairline fracture of the left wrist, and was unable to play guitar for three weeks. That forced the postponement of CSNY's longest and most lucrative tour to date.

Stills consoled himself in a beach cottage on the North Shore of Hawaii, paying for several of his friends, including Henry Diltz and Cyrus Faryar, to fly out from California. He was spotted with a camera in hand, filming the sights in Hale'iwa, but otherwise maintained such a low profile that it proved almost impossible for CSNY's management to contact him with the news that *Déjà Vu* had reached number 1.

Back in California on April 27, he hooked up almost indiscriminately with a woman he had met on Sunset Strip more than three years earlier. Harriet was a record company secretary when Stills made his boorish approach at a Springfield opening. She turned him down, insisting that she planned to remain a virgin until she got married. That was more tantalizing than another easy lay, and Stills pursued Harriet, with increasing displays of romanticism, for the next two years. "At first, he was always kind and gentle," she testified, "and sort of exciting to be with, although he never let me forget what he was after, and he was always on the make." Eventually he wore her down, and for several months she believed that she was his girlfriend. A few weeks after his return from Hawaii, she discovered that she was pregnant and swore that Stills must be the father. He disclaimed any responsibility.

Though CSNY were unable to perform while Stills's wrist healed, there was little likelihood they'd be forgotten. The ailing beer company Ballantine attempted to boost their market share among young adults by hiring session singers to impersonate the band in a TV commercial. Equally unauthorized was an album that showed up at underground stores. Its cover was made of white card stock, onto which was posted a photocopied sheet dominated by a grainy black-and-white shot of the six-piece CSNY in 1969. Alongside was the barest of information: a credit to the mysterious Canyon Records (weren't CSNY supposed to be on Atlantic?); a list of song titles, several unfamiliar; and the title: *Wooden Nickel*.

Anyone who read the underground press would already have registered the outcry that surrounded the distribution of an unauthorized Bob Dylan album, *Great White Wonder*, in 1969. It had been followed by other bootleg releases from the Beatles, the Rolling Stones, and Led Zeppelin. *Wooden Nickel* was the first in what would prove to be a steady stream of CSNY product available on the black market. Elliot Roberts issued a cease-and-desist order to Canyon Records, which was complicated by the fact that there was already a perfectly legitimate enterprise of the same name. Then Atlantic Records' head office in New York intervened, slapping lawsuits on the undercover Canyon and two record stores in New York. CSNY's attorney, Irwin O. Spiegel (who had just penned a learned article about the dispute over the ownership of Buffalo Springfield's name), explained that his clients' concerns were not just financial, but also the fact that *Wooden Nickel* was of substandard quality.

Crosby and Nash concurred. The album, recorded by a fan at the Big Sur festival in September 1969, was divided between acoustic and electric sides. The "wooden" half of *Wooden Nickel* was a fairly accurate representation of what was played, but the electric, Crosby said, was "just shit—it's a burn on everybody." Nash went a degree further: "It's bad shit they're putting out. If they were putting decent shit out, then I wouldn't worry so much. But something recorded out of one microphone, in front of one of the PA speakers, for that to have my name on, infuriated me. That's why I'm angry." True enough, the electric side managed to omit all of the guitars that drove the performance. But when Clinton Heylin came to write the definitive history of the bootleg phenomenon, Nash was rather more positive about the whole affair. "We were really pleased that it was out," he remarked.

Bootlegging was inescapable, it seemed. Unbeknownst to the nation, President Richard Nixon was assembling his own archive of illegal recordings of his friends (in the White House) and enemies (on the FBI's COINTELPRO hit list), and still felt as if he was losing control of his country.

> They ain't gonna be scared off by a bunch of kids in the street. A good rock and roll band can outdraw the president any day of the week. That *does* scare them.
>
> —Stephen Stills, April 1970

The Vietnam War was proceeding on two paths in April: one real, one an illusion. In Paris, peace negotiations had stalled, although the Nixon administration and the North Vietnamese government were discussing the possibility of further, secret talks. The illusion was Richard Nixon's policy of Vietnamization, or transferring responsibility for military matters to the South Vietnamese government. The reality was that although Nixon was ordering sporadic withdrawals of American troops, he was also intensifying bombing and widening the theater of war. On April 30, he declared that the new Cambodian government had invited the US to attack Viet Cong troops who had strayed across the border and conceded that despite what he had said in the past, the US was still mounting bombing raids in North Vietnam.

The "invasion" of Cambodia was like a set of electrodes to the chest of the protest movement. Suddenly there was a focus for those who hated the war but feared it might stagger on for years. Without any apparent master plan, a nationwide strike of students evolved, affecting more than one hundred colleges and universities. It involved sit-ins, boycotts, marches, rallies, even an occasional firebomb.

Kent State University in Ohio was among the campuses affected. Five years earlier, when the antiwar movement had been in its infancy, Kent's first tentative protestors had been harassed by students who supported the war. Now, on May 1, 1970, more than one thousand students assembled to chant the slogan of the Weather Underground collective: "Bring the war home." There were mild clashes between university police and students, which panicked the mayor of Kent into requesting a detachment of National Guard. They arrived to discover that the campus office of the ROTC, which sought to train students as officers, had been set on fire (the culprits were never identified). One student, Joe Lewis, recalled watching the ROTC building burn, while Buffalo Springfield's "For What It's Worth" played out of his radio. Firemen who responded to the blaze were pelted with rocks, and the National Guard commander called for reinforcements.

Jim Rhodes, governor of Ohio, warned the Guardsmen that they were facing "the worst type of people that we harbor in America. I think that we're up against the strongest, well-trained, militant, revolutionary group that has ever assembled in America." With that message ringing in their ears, it is perhaps unsurprising that the Guardsmen were so quick to squeeze their trigger fingers.

The key confrontation took place on the commons, hilly ground in the heart of the Kent State campus. On Monday May 4, two thousand students gathered to chant slogans against the National Guard, against Nixon, against the war, against the entire power structure. After they disobeyed orders to disperse, Guardsmen fired tear gas canisters into their midst. When some of the canisters came back, the Guardsmen retreated to the summit of a small hillock, turned as one, and fired into the crowd.

Two demonstrators were killed, alongside two students simply on their way to class; more than a dozen were injured, some severely. "I got to the site thirty seconds after it happened," recalled student and guitarist Joe Walsh. "People started to scream and cry. I even saw a National Guardsman throw down his gun and sob, 'What the fuck have we done?' The whole town went into shock. Nobody was allowed downtown, all the bars closed."

Chief of staff H. R. Haldeman had the task of telling Richard Nixon what had happened. The president was "afraid his decision set it off, and that is the ostensible cause of the demonstrations there," Haldeman confided to his diary. Nixon was "hoping rioters had provoked the shooting, but [there was] no real evidence they did, except throwing rocks at National Guard."

As news spread, so did the student protests. But among Nixon's vaunted "silent majority," opinion was weighted against those who had lost their lives. A Cincinnati phone-in found that 90 percent of callers believed the Guardsmen should have killed more students. When young people gathered on the streets of Manhattan to declare their outrage, they were attacked by construction workers. Those in authority did their best to blacken the reputation of the Kent State fallen. As the historian Tom Wells recounted, FBI boss "J. Edgar Hoover informed other officials that one of the female victims had been 'sleeping around' and was 'nothing more than a whore anyway.'"

Nixon himself met a delegation from Kent State but betrayed his contempt for his opponents: "You see these bums, you know, blowing up the campuses. Listen, the boys that are on the college campuses today are the luckiest people in the world, going to the greatest universities, and here they are burning up the books." Students were now enemies of the people, it seemed, as deserving of a rifleman's bullet as any Cong who strayed across the Cambodian border.

> The guys sing about the world of the future and write about the
> dirty capitalists. Crosby writes about how he almost cut his hair
> but finally let "his freak flag fly." Well, let him cut his prices instead.
>
> —Henry Staten, *Minnesota Daily* reporter, May 1970

Even at a moment of national crisis, some students found time to pursue less dramatic crusades. At Macalester College in St. Paul, Minnesota, Barry Knight and John Kane had been eagerly anticipating CSNY's impending tour—until they discovered how much it would cost to attend. While seats in other cities were being sold at a maximum of $6.50, tickets at the Metropolitan Sports Center in Minneapolis were being priced on a more draconian scale, from $5 to $10 apiece. (Few rock acts of the day charged more than $6.50 per ticket.) "We said, 'That is outrageous,'" Knight explained. "I called some friends and some record shops, and we had a meeting at the Electric Fetus [record store]. We decided to boycott the concert. Even a five-dollar ticket is outrageous at the Met. No one wants to see a rock concert through binoculars."

The initial response of the promoters was indifference. So, Knight and Kane stepped up a gear, and began distributing leaflets that read: "BOYCOTT!! Crosby, Stills, Nash & Young concert. 80,000 dollars will be made by those with this production. This is a rip-off of the people. Do not buy tickets until prices are lowered. We Will Win! The capitalistic pigs are very paranoid about this type of action. Power to the people! We don't have to pay these prices to see OUR music."

Now the promoters were forced to engage in a debate, and they declared that the culprits were CSNY themselves. The band and their management had not set the ticket prices, but they had made them inevitable by demanding such an exorbitant fee for their appearance.

When Knight and Kane began to attract national media coverage, Elliot Roberts declared that some of the farthest-flung $5 seats in the Sports Center should be reduced to $2. Knight and Kane regarded this as a token gesture. "We've been trying to get hold of the group themselves," Knight said sarcastically, "but Crosby's off on his yacht and, you know, the high cost of keeping yachts these days . . ." It was pointed out to him that Tom Jones was asking $15 at the same venue. Knight explained patiently that they were targeting CSNY because "their heads are close to ours, it's our music. Tom is strictly commercial, and that's all he says he is." "Hypocrisy is hypocrisy, whether it's straight or whether it wears a beard and long hair," one of his comrades added.

But promoter Mike Belkin claimed that there was an additional reason the original prices were justified: scarcity. "This is probably going to be their last tour," he said, "and it is the chance of a lifetime."

> At Denver, some kid came up to me and said, "Please don't split up, we need you." That really made me think, and I wondered if I wanted that kind of responsibility.
>
> —Graham Nash, June 1970

Everything masqueraded as normality when Stephen Stills returned from Hawaii, and CSNY gathered once again in the basement of Shady Oak Road. *Rolling Stone* magazine reported that Stills was "directing rehearsals" as before, throwing curveballs at the rest of the band. Electric arrangements would become acoustic, and vice versa. There were new songs for the band to learn, hot from his solo sessions—"Love the One You're With" and "As I Come of Age." Even the old songs could be ripped up and rewritten. CSNY had never actually played "Everybody I Love You" in the studio, as the album track was a collage of fragments from different sessions. Now they had to deal with the fact that Stills had written an entirely new section to the song, which he figured would slot seamlessly between the two existing parts. The rest of the band weren't convinced. Meanwhile, in the wake of Kent State, Neil Young kept mumbling that it wasn't safe to be out on the road right now. At the same time, he wanted the band to play "Southern Man," which would be catnip for conservatives if the band ever headed south. And through it all, rumors kept seeping out of their camp that CSNY were about to split up.

As Dallas Taylor claimed, with what was undeniably an excess of imagination, "Neil's relationship with his wife was going downhill, and he became really suspicious around her. I stayed at their place for a while, and she was flirting, and Neil threw me out. Then he was convinced that she was having an affair with Stephen." The only verifiably true element of this tale was that the Young marriage was in crisis. No reliable witness remembered seeing anything between Susan and Stephen Stills beyond playful affection. But whatever the precise source of the problems, the solid friendship between Stills and Young was beginning to splinter.

The tension had to be released somewhere, and CSNY's bassist was in the way. "I had written a couple of songs and thought they were great, and they weren't great at all," Greg Reeves told Richie Unterberger. "Crosby said, 'You're not ready yet.' Nash said I had weak songs and my music was not strong enough for him to sing." Reeves had a right to be disappointed, as Crosby had classed him as one of the band's five functioning songwriters when CSNY formed the previous year. Perhaps he pushed his case too hard; perhaps CSNY instinctively felt that a change of personnel might restore some equilibrium. Three days before the first date of the rearranged tour, at the Denver Coliseum on May 12, Greg Reeves was sacked. Later, Graham Nash would try to portray Reeves as some kind of witch doctor, because he traveled with a case of potions he claimed to have been given by Rolling Thunder (alias self-appointed "medicine man" Jack Pope). But Reeves could never have been criticized for his bass playing, which was everything that the band required—muscular, propulsive, careful, inspiring. Neil Young demonstrated as much when he promised that the bassist would still have a place in *his* band. (The vow was not kept, as Young opted to perform solo instead.)

Stephen Stills immediately volunteered a replacement: Fuzzy Samuel, his bassist of choice in England. (One can't help but wonder whether Stills had engineered this opportunity for his new friend.) While Samuel prepared for his flight to Denver, Stills chose to relax on horseback, at a ranch outside Santa Clarita. Soon he was back at the emergency room, having fallen off his mount and twisted his knee.

It was a motley crew who came together at the Mile-High City of Denver: an invalid, supporting himself on crutches; his three comrades, increasingly frustrated with him; a drummer convinced one of the quartet didn't trust him; and a terrified bass player, who was only familiar with Stills's solo tunes.

Onstage in front of ten thousand people, Graham Nash made a virtue out of a series of crises. "This is a real easy show," he claimed. "We thought really hard about it and figured that we would not rehearse too much and lose whatever it is that goes down when people just get together *ad lib*." The audience applauded the band's integrity.

None of that mattered during the acoustic set, when David Crosby delivered an exquisite version of "Everybody's Been Burned," and his three colleagues all unveiled new material—"Tell Me Why" from Young, Nash's "Man in the Mirror," and "We Are Not Helpless," for the only time in his life, from Stills. Several mainstays of previous CSNY shows were jettisoned, and the musicians' chief challenge was making themselves heard over a sound system that kept letting off deafening roars at inopportune moments.

If there was a loose cannon onstage, it was Stephen Stills—absent when first summoned by Crosby for his solo spot, fussy and overambitious on piano when supporting Young's "Helpless," and finally extravagant in his determination to play longer and louder than anyone else. But the first set ended with a race through "Love the One You're With," completing a run of twelve songs, only three of which had appeared on the two CSN(Y) albums.

The electric half was a voyage of discovery for audience and band alike, complicated by the presence of their new bassist. Whether it was lack of familiarity with the songs or blind panic, the unquestionably talented Samuel performed like an amateur, plucking away at the same solitary note through the opening "Pre-Road Downs," regardless of the chord changes. The live debut of "Carry On" was sabotaged, because it required a bass to drive the song, and Samuel was missing in action. So too was any sense of cohesion, as the band fell out of time with each other, and Stills began to wave his crutches in the air like a conductor, in a desperate bid to get the band back on track. "We've never played that before, so we were kinda scared," Crosby confessed at the end.

From there, things just got worse. "So Begins the Task" was a train wreck, with even the song's composer forgetting the words, and Neil Young unable to play in the same key as his friends. There were more missed cues on "Wooden Ships," which sounded like three separate bands all attempting different songs at the same time. Bizarrely, playing new material—the live premieres of Nash's "Chicago" and "As I Come of Age"—seemed to settle their nerves. But "Southern Man" reached fresh lows, with even the steadfast Dallas Taylor losing his cool, playing across the song's riff rather than accentuating it. In that moment, he sealed his fate.

It was not, perhaps, the ideal time for Stephen Stills to insist on performing his radical resetting of "Everybody I Love You," complete with extra verses and an entirely new chorus. (REO Speedwagon later recorded this revision under the title "Open Up.") Anyone in the coliseum who recognized the opening lines would soon have felt confused, though not as much as the band. For one of the musicians, things had gone too far. As the song rampaged out of anyone's control, Neil Young took off his guitar and walked off the stage.

Not all of his bandmates noticed his departure. In a depressed voice, David Crosby promised the crowd, "We're gonna do something old, to see if we do any better on stuff I *know*." Then he turned around and asked in a puzzled voice: "Where's Neil?" "He ran," Stills answered curtly. Like a seasoned entertainer, Crosby invented an explanation: "He's got two out-of-functioning guitars. He may be trying to fix one of them." And he led the band into "Long Time Gone," called them to a halt, complained they were playing "too slow," counted them off again, and had to endure a rendition that was not just pedestrian but full of gaping holes where Young's lead guitar should have been. Nobody wanted, or offered, an encore.

Backstage there was civil war. Crosby, Nash, and Young accused Stills of treating them like servants; Stills explained that he was only trying to signal them back into some kind of unity. Young blamed Taylor for screwing up "Southern Man," then pulled Crosby and Nash aside and suggested that they should ditch Stills and continue the tour without him. Samuel stood frozen at the side, watching it all go down.

There are so many good friends I could still have, if I hadn't lost my mind and embarrassed everyone completely.

—Stephen Stills

The scene immediately shifted to Chicago, as CSNY returned to the site of their debut gig nine months earlier. The nervous optimism of August

1969 had been replaced by resignation and despair, just as the musicians' personal relationships had been crushed by the pressures of fame and a cruel accident of fate. The wary novices who had played that first Chicago show were now grizzled veterans, their unity decayed from within. Last year's eager starlets had been coarsened and divided by their success. It was hardly a moment to hope for reconciliation or mutual forgiveness.

Inside the city's auditorium, there was another disastrous rehearsal. After a few songs, Stills vanished, and Young cornered Crosby and Nash again. This time there was no persuasion: Young demanded that if Stills wasn't fired, then Taylor had to go. Crosby and Young were soon embroiled in a furious argument. Management became involved, Taylor and Samuels were left to fester outside the dressing room, and then Elliot Roberts emerged to tell Dallas Taylor the bad news. The drummer who had been described onstage as "permanent" by David Crosby the previous evening was summarily sacked. "I felt betrayed," Taylor admitted years later. "Stephen and I had been working together for years, and I thought that I was a member of the band. Suddenly I was a hired hand, who could be replaced by anyone."

No drummer meant no show, and in the late afternoon, both the Chicago performances were canceled. Stephen Stills returned to the auditorium to find the theater empty, the amps taken down, his drummer sacked, and no band. "It's been a hassle from the beginning," he muttered to anyone who would listen. "Just one hassle after another."

The official word was that CSNY were "too ill to perform": as usual, Nash and Crosby had been nursing sore throats since rehearsing in Stills's basement. For the second time in a month, Geffen and Roberts had to postpone an entire US tour. Promoters couldn't mask their suspicion and demanded to see doctor's certificates. Fans in St. Louis were offered the chance to exchange their tickets for an upcoming Jimi Hendrix show in the same venue—which was also canceled at the last minute because of illness. Careless insiders whispered talk of "personality differences." Someone identified only as David Geffen's secretary said: "Remember: there has been dissension in every group Neil has been in."

Officially, there was no split: Atlantic Records boss Ahmet Ertegun was forced to issue a statement to that effect. "It became my job with CSNY to take them aside, one by one," he recalled, "listen to them all, and then try to get them to see the bigger picture—remind them that they were friends, and that they made great music together." Crosby and Nash were sent out to reassure the public and press that the band would soon be back together. Graham Nash reeled off the line that would become a weary refrain in the decades to come: "You can never say we are about to split, simply because we only work about once a month anyway. We are just four individuals who occasionally get together for recording or performing purposes." He conceded the obvious, that the show in Denver had been a disaster: "If our heads aren't right together, then our music's not. The music was rubbish, and we knew it. We had to cool ourselves out before we could get back again. People who saw us say, 'Yeah, they've split, I saw how he walked off in the middle of the show. That's it.' Well, it *was* it, for that time, but we had to get back together . . . we always come back." As Stephen Stills reflected the following year, "Everything—a whole lot of perspective—got lost. We had a couple of real crazies—scream-outs and stuff. You have to sit down and talk it out—really talk it out—no games, don't put on a charade. Get objective and it works. And that's the one we could always do with CSNY."

Though they seemed like grizzled veterans, the four were still young men: Crosby, the oldest, was twenty-eight; Young just twenty-four. They had no schooling in group dynamics or transactional analysis, merely instinct, ego, vulnerability, and cocaine. Decades later, having studied psychology and with time to reflect, Stephen Stills could see himself more clearly: "A lot of things that mystified me at the time have become obvious to me since—mainly because of me being shy, and trying to overcome it in a haphazard, clumsy kind of way. And not realizing that I could get really overbearing and impossible. I wouldn't have wanted to hang out around me."

Somehow, the combined influences of Ertegun, Geffen, and Roberts, the desire for ego gratification, and the lust to make music (and money) brought CSNY back into the same room. They staged a brief rehearsal with Fuzzy Samuel and the former drummer of the Turtles Johny Barbata. The music began to gel, so Geffen and Roberts swallowed their cynicism, and booked the US tour for the third time.

Before Kent State, the great coalition of last autumn had fallen apart.

—Mobe organizer, May 1970

The Kent State tragedy briefly seemed to have revitalized the antiwar movement. But the activism that had once shut down the heart of major cities was now mostly restricted to student campuses. There was widespread opposition to the war, and the shootings, but it failed to generate a cohesive political response. As one of the Chicago 8, David Dellinger, recalled, "We had faltered when history demanded decisive action. An unwarranted and unnecessary sense of powerlessness gripped the movement, contributing to the growing crisis of self-confidence."

For the first time, however, the rock community began to reflect the unrest shared by its core audience. *Rolling Stone* magazine, self-appointed bastion of the counterculture, abandoned its "music first" policy to declare: "It comes clear that the Nixon Presidency is going to be the most dangerous—the most disastrous—in the Nation's history. Either Nixon must be forced into resignation or he must be impeached."

Concert promoter Bill Graham and Elektra Records each took out ads in the industry journal *Billboard* to protest the shootings in Ohio. Graham's was factual and direct: "Vietnam: 147,708; Cambodia: 105; Kent State: 4. What Next?" When it was suggested that protests were cutting concert receipts by directing the focus of young people away from music, Graham commented: "A lot of do-nothing people now want to do something. If I'm going to lose a patron because he wants to do something else instead of freaking out to rock and roll every weekend, then as far as I'm concerned, fine." The Grateful Dead played a free show for striking students at MIT, while Jefferson Airplane dedicated a free show in Central Park to the student protestors in New Haven, with Grace Slick scolding the crowd for being at the gig rather than on the streets.

The jazz label Flying Dutchman Records released a documentary album entitled *Murder at Kent State University*. It featured New York DJ Rosko reading extracts from columns by journalist Pete Hamill, interspersed with jazz tunes by Ron Carter. Label boss Bob Thiele explained that "it shows the gap between the administration and young people today." The first protest song provoked by the tragedy soon followed. "Monday in May (The Kent State Tragedy)" by the Third Condition, a Florida garage band, was an overtly literal account of the shootings, as melodramatic as the Civil War ballads recorded by folk singers a decade earlier. But it sold well enough for the record company to be able to fund a scholarship out of the proceeds.

There had been little room for social comment amid the chaos of CSNY's Denver show on May 12, eight days after the shooting. Stephen Stills repeated his usual line about keeping out of the way "if the army guys show up"; David Crosby made "Let's stop the war" sound like a punch line rather than a slogan; and Graham Nash said vaguely that "everyone in the world is concerned about what's going down on the streets right now." (Neil Young didn't utter a single word that could have been mistaken as political.)

Roll forward another eight days: Young and Crosby were at the house of CSNY roadie Leo Makota in Pescadero, off Route 1 between San Francisco and Santa Cruz, when someone walked in with the latest issue of *Life* magazine. "Tragedy at Kent," announced the cover, and inside, across six pages, were graphic pictures of the confrontation and its violent aftermath. There were profiles of the students who had died, including Allison Krause, who had refused to join the New Left grouping, Students for a Democratic Society, because she thought they were "a bunch of finks." Another victim, Bill Schroeder, was revealed as a Rolling Stones fan, who went to the demonstration as a spectator and not a participant.

But it was the photographic coverage that left its mark. The most famous *Life* picture showed a young woman crouched, distraught and disbelieving, over the body of Jeffrey Miller. Another captured the National Guardsmen silhouetted at the top of the hill—looking like the tin soldiers that were a boyhood staple in the years before everything was made of molded plastic.

David Crosby saw Neil Young really register the photos, as if—two weeks after the fact—he was learning about the shootings for the first time. He handed Young an acoustic guitar and watched as Young found the riff and then the substance of a song, "Ohio." As Crosby recalled, Young turned to him almost sheepishly, as if apologizing for being so gauche, and said, "I don't know, I never wrote anything like this before." (He had recorded "Southern Man" two months earlier, of course.) Crosby phoned Stills and Nash, told them Neil had a song that they needed to record, and the next day the new CSNY lineup assembled at the Record Plant in Los Angeles. In a minimum of takes, they cut "Ohio" and its simple acoustic flip side, "Find the Cost of Freedom."

Something about this unexpected flourishing of unity in the band seemed to scramble their memories. Graham Nash was convinced by 1971 that CSNY had been rehearsing in Chicago when Young penned "Ohio." Stephen Stills recalled that the entire band had been attempting to channel their outrage into music, and "It became a contest, to see who could write the song the quickest." Young himself believed that he had seen Allison Krause's dead body in *Life*'s portfolio—hence his line, "What if you knew her, found her dead on the ground"—whereas the magazine's only picture of her was her class photo. But the details were irrelevant alongside the power of CSNY's performance. In objective terms, Stills may have been accurate to complain that "Ohio" was "a verse short" of being a truly coherent song. Its lyrics were brief and sometimes ambiguous but delivered with such passion, such disgust, that words were barely necessary. No protest song in rock history was ever as rousing or defiant, as Crosby howled a generation's anguish over the repeated refrain of "Four dead in Ohio."

Crosby was convinced that "Ohio" wouldn't get any airplay, but still he and the band insisted that Ahmet Ertegun should release the single at once. Ertegun reminded them that Nash's "Teach Your Children" had just been issued. (Contrary to what everyone involved came to believe, "Teach Your Children" was not on the charts when "Ohio" was recorded, let alone "going to number one," as Nash described in his autobiography.) Letting two singles loose at the same time would hamper them both, Ertegun argued. But the band insisted: "Ohio" needed to be out, immediately. "Teach Your Children" had a three-week head start, but the two singles hit the Top 20 in the same week—and then stalled, "Ohio" peaking two slots above Nash's country tune at number 14.

"Ohio" had the advantage of timeliness, attracting buyers who wouldn't normally bother with singles, but it lacked airplay. Political disquiet wasn't the issue, as Edwin Starr's "War" and the Temptations' "Ball of Confusion" both went into rotation on Top 40 stations. What held back "Ohio" was its specificity: as David Crosby noted, "This one names names," and one presidential name in particular.

As he had with *Déjà Vu*, Lenny Bronstein at Brooklyn College scooped the rest of the world with the radio premiere. "I had a habit of visiting Jerry Greenberg at Atlantic every Tuesday, and he would play new music for me," he explained. "That Tuesday I walked in and he said that if I could identify who this song was by, I could have the test pressing. He played me the first three chords and I said it was Neil Young. He said, 'Get out of my office!' and handed me the record." But beyond college radio, radio programmers were more cautious. Detroit provided a perfect microcosm. At CKLW, program director Frank Brody claimed that his station only played "the heaviest hits—hits that are proven," even as "Ohio" sat high in the charts. "We would much rather let the opposition break a song," he said, effectively making his job irrelevant. But elsewhere—such as WHLO in Akron, ten miles from the Kent State campus—"Ohio" was warmly welcomed. "We played it extensively and in mid-July it was number one," program director Johnny Andrews explained. "Our interpretation was that it was a rock group giving a message to protestors to cool it for a while or get shot."

Whatever "Ohio" was, it signaled a new CSNY: spontaneous and raw, raucous and unafraid. More than Crosby's "Long Time Gone" and "Almost Cut My Hair," or Stills's wild onstage rants about Nixon and Agnew, it proclaimed that here was a band prepared to confront the straight establishment and display its crimes to the world. It also promoted Neil Young from enigmatic outsider to the front line and exercised a profound and enduring shift in CSNY's always-precarious balance of power.

> When you're tied to people, it drives you crazy and eventually leads to crisis, which is not conducive to creativity.
>
> —Roger McGuinn

Third time around, the tour went ahead. When the rearranged dates were announced, there was a six-night run in New York, at Bill Graham's Fillmore East. Lines began to form outside the venue several days before tickets went on sale. "It's getting too much, they're getting like the Beatles," one underground journalist lamented. As Stephen Stills recalled, CSNY's managers viewed the sight of "people sleeping around all the corner" as "dollar signs, dollar signs. I think that was the first crack in our little piece of granite."

Dollar signs were causing trouble on another front, as fans continued to complain about the ticket prices. Bill Graham agreed. "The damned ticket buyers get mad at me," he complained. "I've been called a filthy capitalist pig. But then it's easier to attack me than it is to attack their damn fucking idols. The mass public is stupid. Their goddamned heroes have raised the prices, not the promoters. It's unfair to everyone. Neither the promoters nor the group should make that much money. Everyone is on the gravy train, but no one will admit it, and that's dishonest. Those damned superheroes are nothing but con artists."

In Minneapolis, scene of the boycott on the original schedule, the cost of top-priced seats was slashed from $10 to $7, to prove that the protestors had been right. Instead, disquiet was centered on St. Louis, where another boycott preceded CSNY's show at Kiel Auditorium. After the performance, Crosby and Nash were tracked down to the Tack Room at the city's plush Chase Park Plaza Hotel, where they were relaxing over hamburgers. A local journalist quizzed Crosby about the controversy and recorded his reply: "Hey, man, what do you mean? The prices are the same as other cities. Like, that's what it is, man, dig it? I don't know what you mean, man. See the booking agent and let him run it down for you, dig it?" Then he grabbed Nash and the pair fled to the safety of their rooms, followed "by a flock of admiring young groupies." As veteran critic Ralph Gleason noted, "The artists want to be cultural heroes and millionaires at the same time. They avoid the angry mob by pawning it off on a middleman, but if they could ever be made to confront the real issue, they would have to admit responsibility."

CSNY were being pressured by fans who regarded them as pop stars and by critics who saw them as bread-heads. Their management wanted them to maximize profits, while they were struggling to cope with fame and keep some sense of personal communication alive. They chose to set out on this twenty-two-date US tour with additional burdens. With their internal conflicts making it virtually impossible for the band to record anything more than a spontaneous single, they needed product to keep their profile high and the cash flowing. So, a crew led by Bill Halverson recorded their shows at the Fillmore, the LA Forum, and the Chicago Auditorium. In addition, a film crew was hired to chronicle the tour.

The latter decision made profound commercial sense in the wake of *Woodstock*. As their director of photography, they selected David Myers who, despite being in his late fifties, had proved himself to be the cinematographer of choice for concert movies. He'd helped to document Johnny Cash's visit to San Quentin Prison, had worked at Woodstock and Altamont, and most recently headed the camera crew on Joe Cocker's tempestuous Mad Dogs and Englishmen tour. Graham Nash explained that the band had been inundated with offers from major movie studios: "They've decided we have a superstar status and think we can make money. We grossed 4.5 million dollars this past year—just us four ordinary guys. So, they'll let us do whatever we want." That explained some of the wilder cinematic decisions, such as skipping the show in Philadelphia to concentrate on the band's limo driver, and likewise filming Graham Nash arguing with a security guard backstage in Detroit ("Why are you carrying a gun, man?").

When the tour was over, Gary Burden led a small team who prepared a forty-minute rough cut. They were working on the first floor of the Clear Thoughts Building on La Cienega Avenue, alongside Elliot Roberts's office, in the same suite where Jim Morrison of the Doors had edited footage of his own a few months earlier. Burden even designed a special letterhead for the project and the band, with the words "Hopefully Helping" at the top in the same design he'd used for the *Déjà Vu* album cover. But there the documentary stalled, like the *Wooden Ships* script before it.

In the week between recording "Ohio" and the opening show at the fifteen-thousand-seater Boston Garden on May 29, 1970, CSNY had occupied a Hollywood soundstage. They whipped their new rhythm section, Johny Barbata and Fuzzy Samuel, into shape, and rediscovered what it was to be a band. The difference between Boston and Denver a mere seventeen days earlier was startling, as if they'd matured from callow beginners into seasoned professionals. The perennial issues never disappeared: Neil Young's guitar was often out of tune, and the harmonies in the electric set were chaotic, sometimes painful. In Boston, the audience yelled constant demands for the sound to be turned up, as if they were staging their own avant-garde performance. But when CSNY debuted "Ohio" ("a really serious song," Nash explained helpfully), Barbata thrashed his drums as if trying to evoke a fusillade of rifle fire, Crosby screamed his heart out over the refrain, and the entire auditorium was transformed into a righteous political rally.

From the opening songs of the show, a new order was apparent. The acoustic set opened with the "Suite," as ever, but Stills's masterpiece now acted as a prelude to what seemed to be the real event of the night, the early introduction of Neil Young. All their previous shows had emphasized Stills as the leader of the band; now it was as if there had been a palace coup. Of the first ten songs in the set, only one was his. Some sense of equality was retained later in the show, where the climactic "Down by the River" was replaced by two opportunities for extended guitar heroics, Young's "Southern Man" and Stills's "Carry On." These two songs became longer and longer as the tour ran. But there was still room for moments of extreme intimacy, as when Graham Nash shyly premiered a fragile piano ballad about the demise of his relationship with Joni Mitchell, "Simple Man." (He played the song again a few days later, at the Fillmore, with Mitchell in the audience.)

As the tour progressed, the acoustic sets would offer each of the quartet the chance to lay himself bare. Nash ventured a one-off solo performance of the Hollies' "King Midas in Reverse" at the Fillmore, where Crosby offered a gorgeous rendition of "Laughing." (Crosby regularly played "Triad" in his solo spot, leading Nash to joke one night: "David Crosby is the only guy in the hotel who, every morning, orders breakfast for five.") Neil Young experimented with translating electric songs into "wooden" arrangements, and then—as if he was a Las Vegas showman—began to cram them together into medleys.

But (perhaps inevitably) it was Stephen Stills who managed to turn acoustic spontaneity into a crisis. The band's unwritten rule was that each member would be allowed two solo numbers in the first half of the show. On the second night at the Fillmore, Stills threw the rulebook away. Maybe it was because he was ill ("I am lonely, and I have a cold," he had sung during the "Suite"), maybe he wanted to seize back control of the band, or maybe he was simply responding to the audience. He opened his acoustic set with the most poignant version imaginable of "Bluebird," skipping phrases as if it filled him with anguish to sing about his passion for Judy Collins. (She was in the house a couple of nights later with her son, Clark.) Then he launched into "Black Queen," which was still changing from night to night and mood to mood. At this point he might have expected to see his colleagues shuffling back onstage for the final blast of "Love the One You're With" before the intermission. But their cue was his "For What It's Worth" rant, and they hadn't heard it yet. So, Stills offered a delicious version of "4+20," to enormous applause. By now, Crosby, Nash, and Young were beginning to realize that something unusual was happening onstage. Before they could cut him short, Stills was sitting behind the piano and throwing himself into a wild, sometimes shambolic but always impassioned howl of political rage. "This ain't a free country," he roared, and the audience sounded as if they were ready to march out of the building and overthrow Nixon there and then. When his twenty-minute set finally ended, it was to the sound of the tour's biggest ovation. How could anyone resent him for that?

Backstage, the fifteen-minute break between acoustic and electric mutated into a lengthy and violent confrontation between Nash and Stills. "I was arguing like fuck with him," Nash recalled. "Me and Stephen were fucking screaming at each other. Stephen had a Budweiser can in his hand, and he was slowly crushing it to a flat thing." This altercation has passed into CSNY legend, erroneously conflated with the final night of the Fillmore run, when Bob Dylan was in the audience. According to the myth, most often recounted by Nash, his standoff with Stills was followed by "the best electric set we had ever done," which was a subjective judgment, not necessarily borne out by aural evidence. It takes its place alongside other familiar anecdotes from the tour: Bill Graham stuffing hundred-dollar bills under the Fillmore dressing-room door to persuade CSNY to return for a second encore ("Woodstock" or "Find the Cost of Freedom"); the Persian carpet that they demanded center stage every night; the spontaneous badinage that was repeated at almost every show; the poker games where one or other of the band could drop several hundred dollars in a single hand. Much of it was true, and all of it grew in the endless retelling.

There were certainly signs at their six-night residency at the Fillmore that the Crosby-Nash team were now bonding more easily with Young than with Stills, who tended to keep his distance from the snappy dialogue. But on the fifth night, all four began to swap jokes as they attempted to tune up for "Teach Your Children," and just for an instant, they sounded like what they were supposed to be—four musicians who were together because they loved each other's work. As Stills took center stage, requests arced out of the audience. "If you get into requests with Stephen," Nash told them, "he's written so many, we're going to be here until next week." But there was no sense of bitterness, and Stills felt free to extend his set again, without fear of repercussions.

And so the tour continued, with reliably frantic response from their fans—who screamed as if they were watching teen idols in Los Angeles and made so much noise in Philadelphia that the band had to beg them to sit down and be quiet. ("But how can you be still when your ears don't believe what your eyes and mind are telling you is taking place?" one lovestruck reporter wrote.) There might be an occasional night when someone was out of sorts, like David Crosby during the first acoustic set in Chicago or Stephen Stills later the same evening. But music could eventually bring them around. As they played "Carry On," the *Chicago Tribune* reported, "Stills and Crosby seemed to have patched up the differences of the evening—the four of them improvising like crazy; Stills jumping up and down; Young hunching over his guitar, hair flying; and Crosby just dancing all over the place, smiling at Stills." That was CSNY in 1970, ecstatic and impassioned, but also a group of four willful musicians, jostling for center stage, each growing ever-more dependent on indulging his own ego.

One ego in particular required special attention. "What happened," according to David Geffen, "was that Stephen kinda thought it was his band, while all the others thought they were pretty equal. In order for a band to stay together, they've got to have a certain amount of unity—one for all and all for one. Three of them felt this way, but Stephen felt it was his thing. It was obvious it couldn't last like that."

"We started to compete with each other," Stills conceded. "And when the heat got too bad and we started falling apart, when we were hurting each other and doing really nasty things to each other, starting to work out our frustrations on each other like it was a marriage, we realized we'd have to hold up, and go do a record by ourselves or something, and come back together later."

There were symbolic endings along the way—an end-of-run party at the Fillmore, attended by Bob Dylan (who then dragged Crosby along as he collected an honorary Princeton degree and referred to him in the song he wrote about the occasion, "Day of the Locust"); an end-of-tour banquet in Minneapolis; a gathering where, as Neil Young explained, "the four of us and our handlers were kind of dividing up the loot and finding out exactly how much we'd all made." Then they parted company and waited to see whether this was the close of a chapter, or if the final credits were about to roll.

Only in hindsight was the truth obvious: that regardless when, or whether, Crosby, Stills, Nash, and Young worked together again, they would not be the same band, operating on the strictly egalitarian principles they had espoused from the start. In his first autobiography, Young mused that "The band didn't break up; it just stopped. It did not regenerate itself. It stopped functioning, like it had a lapse or a heart attack or something." But there were always people standing over the corpse, desperate to bring it back to life, refusing to believe that the dream—and the money stream—was gone.

CHAPTER 11

There are rifts sometimes, and we have differences of opinion,
but we've all got too much experience to let it come between
us permanently. Our association will probably go on for at least
another ten years.

—Graham Nash, July 1970

The band renowned for harmony was now a trademark of discord. Frank
Zappa worked up a satirical routine called "Do You Like My New
Car," joking about the hottest currency on the groupie circuit: "three
unreleased recordings of Crosby, Stills, Nash & Young fighting at the
Fillmore East."

Even when they weren't together, the four songwriters were jostling
for attention and fame. "If only we could get rid of this damn competi-
tiveness, once and for all," Stephen Stills lamented. But each man knew
that his influence within the band—if they ever reunited—would depend
on the status of his solo career.

Their voracious appetite for individual success prompted Ahmet Ertegun to issue an official statement in October 1970, aimed at reassuring
the industry. "Contrary to all of the rumors about Crosby, Stills, Nash
and Young, they are not breaking up," he announced. Indeed, they were
issuing a live album before Christmas, preparing a BBC-TV show, creating
a studio record in January, then touring America . . . and completing a
full house of solo albums. It was a remarkably similar fantasy to the one
Ertegun had spun the previous year, and it was equally fanciful.

As Rita Coolidge would explain, "It's very hard in this business to stay
peaceful. In a way, we're all competing with each other professionally.

We're all accustomed to fighting and being stubborn, because you gotta do both to make it." In summer 1970, Coolidge was a twenty-five-year-old veteran of tempestuous tours with Delaney & Bonnie and then with Joe Cocker's Mad Dogs and Englishmen ensemble. She had just escaped from a violent relationship (with drummer Jim Gordon) when she and her sister Priscilla were invited to join CSN and John Sebastian at Wally Heider's Los Angeles studio. Stills intended the chorale to overdub songs for his first solo album, foremost among them "Love the One You're With."

Taking that message to heart, Graham Nash invited the "startlingly gorgeous" Coolidge to be his guest when CSNY performed in LA. "Phone me at Stephen's house," he said, not imagining that Stills would intercept the call and tell her that Nash had changed his mind. Coolidge arrived at the Forum as Stills's date instead and couldn't understand why Nash refused to speak to her. No sooner had she ended up in Stills's bed than the incurable romantic—his passion doubled when he discovered that Coolidge and Judy Collins shared the same birthday—began to write songs about her. The first was "Cherokee," acknowledging her father's Native American ancestry. She recalled thinking: "This would probably be really cool if I cared about him as much as he does about me."

Within a few weeks, Coolidge discovered how she had been cheated out of her rendezvous with Graham Nash, and the pair began their own affair. As (in his own words) an Englishman and a gentleman, Nash felt obliged to tell Stephen Stills in person that he had just lost his girlfriend. Stills, she recalled, "just came out swinging. And Graham, of course, is not a fighter; somebody separated them and pulled Stephen off." The fallout from an overlong acoustic set at the Fillmore paled by comparison; indeed, Nash would remember (erroneously) that he and Stills did not speak for more than two years. Meanwhile, Stills was reinforced in his defensive, doomed romanticism and provoked into one of the hottest writing streaks of his life.

The crisis also provided creative stimulus for Nash and Crosby. Nash penned the bitter but still affectionate "Frozen Smiles" for Stills. (The title referenced the jocular name given to Stills and Crosby in 1968 by Mitchel Reed, who had dubbed the duo "the Frozen Noses," because of their predilection for cocaine.) "I forgot that Graham Nash is really one of my best friends ever, and Graham forgot the same thing," Stills would reflect a decade later. But something deep within the two men's relationship was fractured and never entirely healed. Ego and cocaine had already separated and hardened the members of CSN; now the crevice between Nash and Stills was widened by what Stills saw as a fundamental breach of trust.

Outwardly unaffected by these dramas, David Crosby remained suspicious of Coolidge and her motives. She alleged that Crosby regarded her as the devil incarnate, accusing her of trying to poison him. He placed Coolidge, thinly disguised as "the Indian girl," at the heart of a mythological recasting of the CSNY story. In the song "Cowboy Movie," Crosby is the only character unimpressed by "Raven," a dark-haired temptress who is revealed to be "the law." One of his friends recalled that, at his most paranoid, Crosby "actually thought that Rita must be a government agent, who'd been sent purposefully to sabotage CSNY and prevent them from representing a threat to the Nixon administration." But as David Geffen said, President Nixon "probably doesn't know who David Crosby is." (Crosby wasn't the only paranoid musician in town. In July 1970, Stephen Stills explained that, as the composer of "For What It's Worth," he would be sent to jail if the United States ever became a dictatorship. Cocaine did not always encourage rational thinking, about politics or affairs of the heart.)

The bond between Stephen Stills and each of the others was now frayed and unreliable. He had once been the most powerful of three bonded brothers; now he was the eternal outsider in a distant quartet. As if to demonstrate the point, David Crosby, Graham Nash, and Neil Young shared a recording session in Hollywood on August 23, 1970. The three men conjured up improvisational magic from an acoustic jam, emerging with the ultimate declaration of Crosby's philosophy, "Music Is Love." The track was briefly considered as a CNY single, which would have advertised Stills's isolation; but ultimately it was saved for Crosby's solo record.

On August 25, their missing compadre made his own stand—at the Municipal Court in San Diego. The previous week, he had checked into a seedy motel in La Jolla with a female companion. The manager called police and an ambulance after finding a young man crawling down the corridor, groaning and frothing at the mouth. Officer Dixon discovered Stills slumped on the bed, barely conscious. There were tablets scattered across the bedside table, and a search revealed more of the same in a suitcase, alongside a packet of white powder. When the man became more coherent, he told Dixon he had "taken a number of downers." The tablets were barbiturates; the powder two grams of cocaine. Both Stephen Arthur Stills and his friend were imprisoned overnight.

In court, Stills pleaded not guilty to felony charges of possessing narcotics and dangerous drugs. Five months later, the felony was bargained down to a misdemeanor, and he changed his plea to "guilty." Stills was fined $1,000 in April 1971 and placed on a year's probation. In her autobiography, Rita Coolidge alleged that before Stills had collapsed, he had written a message of love to her on his bathroom mirror.

The attention of the law was something CSNY could still share. Soon after Stills's arrest, Graham Nash and Neil Young were stopped as they walked down Sunset Strip. A search revealed that Nash was carrying $8,000 in cash, which the cops regarded as perfectly normal. But Young had a packet of rolling papers, which they deemed deeply suspicious. He was only allowed to walk away after revealing the name of a nearby head shop that was giving away the papers for free.

David Crosby encountered the police on June 9, 1971, at Newport Bay, where the *Mayan* was moored at Lido Shipyard. A dutiful patrolman thought he could detect a hint of marijuana in the air, emanating from the boat. Then he heard the bilge pump start, almost as if someone on board was trying to dispose of his stash. Unfortunately, the debris didn't vanish into the Pacific Ocean, but came bobbing to the surface. Police ultimately recovered twenty ounces of marijuana and four of hashish — sufficient for Crosby, as owner of the *Mayan*, to be held "on suspicion of possessing marijuana for sale." The others on board — three men of Crosby's age or older, and three women in their teens, among them his current girlfriend — were charged with possession of marijuana. The police seized the *Mayan* for lengthy inspection, after which customs officials took their turn. Crosby consoled himself at the Pioneer Inn on Maui. But when the case came to court a few weeks later, all charges were dropped, as the police were unable to prove, conclusively, that the marijuana belonged to any of those arrested. Crosby was able to resume his self-appointed task of undermining the straight world by "Swiping their kids . . . changing their value systems, which removes them from their parents' world very effectively."

We're really proud of it—we like it better than the other ones.

—Neil Young on *4 Way Street*, 1971

I thought that record was atrocious. We all did.

—Stephen Stills on *4 Way Street*, 1974

One promise on Ahmet Ertegun's list was fulfilled in October 1970. CSNY had identified the BBC as the only TV outlet that would allow them to present music without commercial interruption or compromise. But union rules made it virtually impossible for an American band to appear in Britain without weeks of negotiations, while the BBC did not have a budget for filming rock music overseas.

Instead, the British-born Graham Nash accepted an invitation to appear on the BBC's *In Concert* series featuring contemporary songwriters—on the tacit understanding that one or more of his American colleagues could appear as unexpected guests. Nash flew to London with David Crosby and met up with Stephen Stills (so much for Nash not talking to him for two years!), already immersed in another enervating set of recording sessions. The three men duly rehearsed an "impromptu" reunion. But, as Stills recalled, "I had been up the night before on a session, and I collapsed in the dressing room. I was just too ill." He was sent back to Nash's apartment in a taxi, and the remaining duo performed without him—the birth of a musical partnership that would endure for more than forty years. The twenty-five-minute show exhibited the pair's comradeship and compatibility, and the small audience was treated to exquisite versions of Crosby's "Song with No Words" and "Traction in the Rain."

Also in London on BBC business were a pair of lovers: Joni Mitchell and James Taylor. Mitchell met her two ex-partners after the show and the uneasy trio joined Donovan for a private evening in the round, as if it were still 1968. A former heroin addict who had spent time in a mental hospital, James Taylor was on the verge of being acclaimed as "the hottest composer-performer of 1971" and even "the New Rock Messiah." His publisher explained that "Taylor has been through a lot of trips and there's no put-on or phoniness in his songs." Crosby and Nash must have felt like aged roués, ushered offstage by a younger gigolo.

To fulfill Ertegun's schedule, CSNY's next task was a live album. Shows had been taped in New York, Los Angeles, and Chicago, and Graham Nash helped the tireless Bill Halverson to assemble the most acceptable recordings. It was then Halverson's unenviable task to translate those into a viable double album, weaving fragments of dialogue between songs, erasing some of the more erratic periods of jamming (while ensuring that Young's guitar was not given prominence over Stills's or vice versa), and combining performances of the same song in different cities. Nash was his key aide for the acoustic recordings, while Young and Crosby oversaw the electric mixes. Stephen Stills insisted that the band should replace some of their most wayward harmonies in the studio but was overruled. "The others wouldn't cheat," he lamented. Only later would Crosby and Nash concede that he might have been right.

The project required so much engineering that its Christmas deadline was unachievable, and 4 Way Street finally appeared in April 1971. It was then nine months since CSNY had last performed together, and the erratic electric half of the set did little to kindle enthusiasm for a swift reunion. The acoustic record was more acceptable but reinforced the idea that the four men were merely a collection of individuals who happened to be on the same stage. Nonetheless, 4 Way Street went gold in its week of release and topped the US charts.

To promote the album, Crosby and Nash joined their friend Mitchel Reed for a five-hour radio spectacular. Elliot Roberts kept the pot simmering by claiming that all four members of CSNY had been swapping songs and were planning a major tour — possibly a farewell? — in February 1972. But Ahmet Ertegun's dream of a successor to Déjà Vu was allowed to fade away, without ever officially being put to sleep.

I think we owe it to ourselves as musicians and to the whole generation that grew up with us to get together as much as possible, to help each other out, and not to compete.

—Stephen Stills, June 1971

Like the four ex-Beatles, Crosby, Stills, Nash & Young embarked on an intensive series of solo projects in the year after the group's effective demise. Unlike the Beatles, they managed to avoid legal battles over scheduling and release dates. But they still managed to compress a solo album apiece, plus 4 Way Street, into an eight-month period, by the end of which both Stills and Young were preparing new records, their creativity in full flow and impossible to suppress.

If the contest could be judged by statistics, then the ostensible victor was Stephen Stills. His self-titled solo debut reached number 3 in the US charts in the first week of 1971, and "Love the One You're With" was a worldwide hit single ("possibly the best song of the year," one paper declared). The album was the work of a multidimensional showman, equally at home with folk balladry, blues, or Latin rock. Even the least feted songs, such as the achingly beautiful "To a Flame," testified to his ambition. But critics castigated the epic arrangements of "Church" and "We Are Not Helpless," as if it was a sin to be seen to try so hard. (Despite its title, "We Are Not Helpless" was not a sequel or a riposte to Neil Young's CSNY song. Instead, it extended a statement by Henry Fonda's US president character in the final minutes of *Fail-Safe*, Sidney Lumet's 1964 movie about nuclear catastrophe.) "I remember mistakes I made on my early albums," Stills admitted thirty-five years later, "beating the songs to death, working for two days without a break, so it sounds real rushed, it's not in the pocket, *it's too fast*, like it has foam in it, frothing in the mouth."

The album was all but complete in mid-September 1970 when Stills took a Lear jet to his Colorado cabin, accompanied by his longtime friend Dan Campbell, bassist Fuzzy Samuel, and photographer Henry Diltz. Two days after the event, word filtered up to the Rockies that Jimi Hendrix had died in London. "I went up the mountain and cried," Stills recalled. "His death really tore my brains out. When Jimi died, I really thought, This is the time for me to get off the rock and roll circus." He laid plans for business ventures in Colorado and his return to Ringo Starr's house in London. But first he asked Diltz to photograph him in the snow, playing guitar outside the cabin. To Diltz's aesthetic displeasure, Stills insisted that every shot should feature a pink inflatable giraffe—a memento from his brief relationship with Rita Coolidge. One of Diltz's pictures formed the cover to the *Stephen Stills* album, which was dedicated to Hendrix.

By then, Neil Young's *After the Gold Rush* also was established in the Top 10. Lacking a hit single, it was outsold by Stills's effort, but unlike *Stephen Stills*, it became a period classic. Not that the album was any more of a critical success, complaints focusing on the anguished falsetto Young adopted on the title track and elsewhere. Many reviews found the record "disappointing," "inoffensive," "like a demo," "rarely truly profound," "really not worth the wait," or "pretty amateurish." Some, such as Robert Hilburn in the *LA Times*, acclaimed it as "a delicate, fragile jewel" and "highly rewarding," and that was the verdict echoed by the public. The album's blend of poignant romanticism, environmental concern, acoustic whimsy, and political comment proved irresistible to a teenage market searching for fresh heroes. A few months later, a readership survey in the magazine *Seventeen* found that teenage American girls most admired their fathers, followed by President Nixon and Bob Hope. But their favorite singers were James Taylor, Andy Williams, Neil Diamond—and Neil Young. (Teenage America's top band? CSNY.)

Young's success enabled him to buy a sizable ranch, which occupied one thousand acres in Northern California between Redwood City and the ocean. He moved there in September 1970, leaving his wife and stepdaughter behind. All he would say about the end of his marriage was that Susan liked to be surrounded by people, and he didn't; that he was too young and selfish for commitment; and that fame (and its associated temptations) had eroded their relationship. Soon afterward, Graham Nash was belatedly divorced from his wife, Rose Eccles—"on grounds," the wire services reported, "of her misconduct with an unnamed man." Nobody mentioned Joni Mitchell.

All this is just part of a growing trend among group members to perform sort of "super session" albums. We feel we should encourage them to break out and do their own things.

—Bill Thompson, manager of
Jefferson Airplane, August 1970

It is much better. There's more chaos and anarchy now. Nobody knows what anybody else is doing.

—Grace Slick, Jefferson Airplane, December 1970

Elsewhere in Northern California, David Crosby and his friends were sketching nirvana and reviving the bohemian spirit of Sausalito in 1963. The energy source was Jefferson Airplane's Paul Kantner, who had devised a vast conceptual extension of the "Wooden Ships" escape fantasy. He envisaged a world in which seven thousand turned-on pioneers, fueled by acid and coke, would hijack a starship at some far-flung date such as 1990, and build an alternative society in outer space. "It's about natural evolution for our species," he explained, "as the few explore the universe on behalf of the many. It's refusing to be hemmed in by this world and accepting the responsibility of making a new start in idealistic circumstances."

This scenario inspired the second side of *Blows Against the Empire*, Kantner's first adventure with the then-imaginary Jefferson Starship. But that merely hinted at the scale of his imagination. Owsley Stanley (Grateful Dead soundman and distributor of LSD) was imprisoned when the Dead were busted in February 1970. Kantner wanted to break Owsley out of jail and use the combined wealth of the Airplane, the Dead, and CSNY to purchase an island. There, he believed, Owsley could create a multidimensional starship, more like a country than an Apollo space capsule. It would include virgin earth, immaculate forests, and a glistening ocean, on which David Crosby could sail the *Mayan* into infinity. Faced with the charge of elitism once flung at "Wooden Ships," Kantner retorted: "Who said there was only one starship? There's a whole fleet of them."

Kantner was entirely open to musical collaboration, which is how Crosby and Graham Nash came to board the bridge of the Starship. "Whoever gets to the cockpit first any day is the captain for that day," Kantner explained. "Graham ended up mixing the album after I had been working on it for two weeks. He did it in two days, for hours at a stretch. He added a few little things and tied the whole thing up. David came up with a lot of the ideas." Crosby's contributions were also musically sublime. On "A Child Is Coming," a hymn of welcome to the baby that Grace Slick was carrying, the triplet voices of Kantner, Slick, and Crosby wound around each other with exquisite grace. "Have You Seen the Stars Tonite" was simpler but just as beautiful, Crosby's voice soaring above those of his friends like a comet tracing across a pitch-black sky. *Blows Against the Empire* was exhilarating and faintly ridiculous, politically naïve and conceptually far-fetched—almost universally loathed by critics but held dear by those prepared to transgress the borders of reality.

Since the end of 1969, Kantner, Slick, Crosby, and Jerry Garcia of the Grateful Dead had kicked around the idea of forming their own anti-business fraternity. At its most concrete (which was not very), the scheme involved the Airplane, the Dead, and CSNY establishing a record company—something the Airplane achieved by themselves in 1970 (Grunt Records), and the Dead would attempt several years later.

The same spirit of collectivism was carried into David Crosby's long-awaited first solo record. Some of the time he worked alone, layering his voice tirelessly over exquisitely recorded acoustic guitars (kudos to engineer Stephen Barncard). He also pulled in his friends—Nash and Young, Joni Mitchell, Kantner and Slick, and the core of the Grateful Dead. Earlier, he had dreamed aloud about working with Jerry Garcia ("I would just be so knocked out") and Phil Lesh ("I would like to make a record sometime with him playing classical music on electric bass"). Garcia threw himself into the project as Crosby's partner-in-exploration and producer in all but name, encouraging Crosby to go faster and further away from musical orthodoxy. The album would baffle any listeners expecting a collection of recognizable pop songs.

At the end of 1970, these ongoing experiments took another left turn, as Kantner invented the Planet Earth Rock and Roll Orchestra. "It's just a lot of people getting together to play music," he explained. "We have four or five songs together, but we haven't got all the songs for it written yet." The concept was boundless: an amorphous collective of like-minded souls, built around the hub of Kantner, Slick, Garcia, and Crosby, and the aesthetic principles of freedom and musical communism. There was a brief flurry of live performances billed as the Acoustic Dead or Garcia and Friends, starring Crosby, Garcia, and the Dead's rhythm section. They surprised club audiences with semi-improvised sets featuring tunes from Crosby's sessions, a pick or two from the Dead's repertoire, and blues standards. Back at Wally Heider's, Stephen Barncard captured material on tape as it was being created, before corporate commitments stole the participants' attention. Tendrils from this exotic bloom would touch various albums over the next two or three years—Kantner and Slick's *Sunfighter, Baron Von Tolbooth*, and *Manhole*; Nash's *Songs for Beginners*; Crosby and Nash's first joint venture; plus occasional cameos onstage. This explosion of creativity, which endured for almost five months in the second half of 1970, represented the West Coast rock fellowship at its most utopian and least egotistical. After that, everything would necessarily feel like a falling away.

> The first time I met Neil, I knew this was it, I'd met my guy.
>
> —Carrie Snodgress

Tina Walser was a jaded, exploited, ignored, and insecure woman caught in a dull, conventional marriage, who found that neither a lover nor a therapist could bring her life purpose. She was the key character in *Diary of a Mad Housewife*, a 1970 movie based on a novel by Sue Kaufman. The role was played by a twenty-five-year-old newcomer from Illinois named Carrie Snodgress, who invested Walser with a brittle sense of isolation. The role won her two Golden Globe Awards and an Oscar nomination as Best Actress of 1970. To the disgust of the Hollywood establishment, she chose not to attend the Academy Awards ceremony in April 1971, after her boyfriend, a musician named Neil Young, refused to accompany her. "Honey, it's a big thing for you," he told her, "but I've got nothing going on down there."

That might have ended some relationships, but Snodgress interpreted it as a sign that she too should avoid the Hollywood publicity machine. "I was doing interviews by the second," she recalled. "I was putting so much out. I had to look at my own life." It was exactly the same decision that her boyfriend had already made about his own career.

Snodgress had been living in a rented house in North Hollywood with an English springer spaniel named after Laura Nyro's song "Timer." While reviewing scripts sent by Universal Studios, who were desperate to exploit her fame, she took a theater part. One night she came offstage to find a message that Neil Young had called her. She had no idea who he was: "I was living with these two girls, and when I got home I showed them the note. They said, 'Oh my God, you have to call this guy!'" She didn't, so Young "sent a couple of friends to see the play and check me out. He was really a shy guy, and he wanted to know if I was a big Hollywood la-di-da, or if I was real." The pair finally met at a James Taylor show at the Troubadour, after which Young invited her to his ranch. "The first time we drove up to his place," she remembered, "I knew this was it, this was what I'd always wanted." As Young would write in the early days of their relationship, "I fell in love with the actress / she was playing a part I could understand." Or, as Snodgress put it: "Neil saw *Diary* and came after me."

No sooner had they met than Young was hospitalized for back surgery, having injured several discs in his spine while clearing his ranch. "I'm going to have to wear a brace for a couple of months, but it's not going to stop me from doing a tour," he explained. In almost every area of his life, he was taking stock. He was preparing a double live album as a career retrospective, sequencing the set on a cassette machine while in the hospital. But the project was canceled when he hit a rich seam of new songs. Some were sparked by his meeting with Carrie; others, such as "Old Man," by life on the ranch. A troubling visit from Crazy Horse guitarist Danny Whitten at the Cellar Door in Washington triggered one of his most enduringly popular compositions, "The Needle and the Damage Done."

His last shows before surgery were two nights at New York's Carnegie Hall. He was the first member of CSNY to discover that a side effect of fame was a restless, over-adoring, and demanding audience. Any hope that he might be able to deliver a recital rather than a rock gig was dispelled when fans kept up a barrage of requests for "Southern Man" and flew paper planes around the venue. His performances were audibly affected, and on the second night he called an intermission after only thirty minutes in response to being disturbed by a noise from the crowd. Worse was to follow.

In January 1971, he set out on a monthlong trek around North America, writing and rewriting material as he went. In Chicago, Carrie's absence inspired the delicate "Love in Mind." "A Man Needs a Maid," the song that acknowledged her movie role, started out as a lengthy medley, in which he acknowledged that he was "searching for a heart of gold" but "a man feels afraid." By the end of the tour, the two halves had taken on independent life. "I don't really want a maid," he explained apologetically to one audience, "it's just a sign that something else is happening."

His show in Minneapolis was intended to soothe anyone still upset by the furor over CSNY ticket prices. Young had promised to deliver "a long, intimate evening." So, there was fresh disappointment when a support act filled the first half, and then Young performed only twelve songs. In Boulder, several hundred fans without tickets attempted to storm through the doors of the university auditorium. In Boston, the show was less than a minute old when someone called out from the crowd, and Young screamed, "Shut up!," like a teacher driven beyond his tether. "I can't do it," he explained. "I'm not together enough tonight to put up with any shit, and I won't play if there's a lot of noise. I'll just split." Every member of CSNY would discover that fans could get impatient with acoustic music. One solution, Young learned, was to wheel out "Sugar Mountain"—not just because audiences enjoyed it, but because it could be transformed into a vehicle for crowd participation. Neil Young became the first of the quartet to employ that oldest of showbiz tricks: the audience singalong.

Young's mood improved as he returned to California, and Carrie. David Crosby joined him for an encore of "Dance Dance Dance" in Berkeley, where Young quelled constant demands for "Down by the River" by suggesting that fans could sing those lyrics to the tune of "Sugar Mountain." After a brief respite at home, he flew to London, where he was treated like a conquering hero. He ended the visit by recording "A Man Needs a Maid" and "There's a World" with the London Symphony Orchestra, under the direction of his friend Jack Nitzsche. (Nitzsche would subsequently denounce Young's lyrics during this period as "dumb and pretentious.")

When Young returned to the US in early March, Carrie Snodgress agreed to move up to the ranch. "He really needed somebody to help him," she explained, "to be with him and understand him. He was the focal point of a whole circle. I saw this vulnerable, sensitive guy with people kind of going, 'Gimme, gimme, gimme, give me a job, give me money, give me attention.' It was so intense."

Snodgress seemed content to abandon Hollywood in favor of the role of housewife. "I cook three meals a day, and I'm always prepared to feed visitors who are not expected," she said proudly. "Neil has helped me know who I am and where I am." She let Hollywood slide, turning down scripts and publicity to the point where Universal suspended her contract. This freed her to appear in a very different kind of movie: one written, edited, and directed by her lover.

Journey Through the Past began when Young licensed David Myers's footage of the 1970 CSNY tour from the rest of the band. He merged that material with a hazy fictional conceit of his own devising, involving symbolic characters and vintage cars. Meanwhile, he employed Myers to film recording sessions in his barn, plus clips of him at large in Nashville.

The singer took responsibility for editing the results into an anti-narrative, in which onstage scenes of CSNY at the Fillmore East might be intercut with anything from a junkie shooting up to the president preaching at the converted. Some scenes starred a fourteen-year-old Nashville kid, Gil Gilliam, who bore a strange facial resemblance to Young's own childhood photos; others a quasi-mysterious preacher, who wandered purposelessly through sequences that cried out for abbreviation. Into vision might come Stephen Stills, uttering dazed pronouncements about the future; David Crosby, a beatific smile across his face, rapping about America's children choosing between hippie utopia and grim-faced militarism; or Carrie and Neil, traversing the ranch in scenes devoid of drama. Throughout, the smoke of endless joints blurred the visual and psychological landscape. *Journey Through the Past* was premiered in summer 1973, slammed by the critics, withdrawn for further editing, and then reissued after the 1974 CSNY tour. By then, it was not contemporary or remotely coherent, leaving fans to lament the lost opportunity of a more orthodox portrait of the band at their youthful peak.

> Stills has always come on like the ultimate rich hippie—arrogant, self-pitying, sexist, shallow. Keep it up, SS—it'll be a pleasure to watch you fail.
>
> —Robert Christgau, *Village Voice*, 1971

> It's like I've got a giant target on me and it says, "Here's someone to pick on."
>
> —Stephen Stills, 1974

July 1971 was, according to Atlantic Records, "Crosby, Stills, Nash & Young Month." The company distributed a compilation album named *Celebration Copy* to radio stations, who were encouraged to use it as a prize for phone-in contests. They also booked extensive radio ads to promote albums by the group and its members (but not Neil Young). Rumors were carefully planted in the gossip columns that CSNY were about to announce their farewell tour.

Meanwhile, the reputations of the group, and the counterculture it had once represented, were under constant assault. More than a year after the Kent State shootings had briefly promised to unite the disparate elements of the anti-Nixon youth movement, there was no collective agenda or impetus. Energy was focused on individual campaigns, to which CSN lent occasional support. Crosby and Nash raised funds for Vietnam Veterans Against the War and for protests against the hunting of whales. With a certain amount of irony, Stephen Stills gave concert receipts to organizations in the nation's capital dedicated to fighting drug abuse. But these were leaves in the wind amid a desert of hedonistic despair.

The despair came from the sense that hippie idealism had been drained of its meaning; the hedonism from drugs offered no hint of spiritual union, with one's peers or one's planet. Cocaine was now the driving force of the music industry, isolating and distracting its stars, while the mass teenage audience—the younger brothers and sisters of those entranced by the Summer of Love and the Woodstock nation—was clouding its cultural emptiness with downers such as barbiturates and tranquilizers, reds and blues, soapers and Quaaludes, sweet wine and cheap beer. These were substances designed to anesthetize the soul, not spur it into ecstatic visions, and they required a musical soundtrack to match, a void often filled by hard rock and heavy metal, from Black Sabbath and Grand Funk Railroad to Led Zeppelin.

There was still an audience, mostly young and female, for sensitive balladeers exploring their self-doubt in song. But CSNY no longer bestrode this landscape, as the likes of James Taylor and Cat Stevens held sway. For the first time, Crosby, Stills, Nash & Young became dimly aware that they could no longer "steal" (in David Crosby's phrase) America's children. Instead, they could only act as bards for one generation: their own.

Almost as one, the global rock press began to treat yesterday's superstars with ridicule and contempt, as if ashamed of the compliments they had once paid them. It was fortunate, perhaps, for Neil Young that he did not release his *Harvest* album in summer 1971, as originally planned. While he tinkered and prevaricated, his three former colleagues discovered how abruptly the atmosphere had changed.

The first to suffer was David Crosby, whose *If I Could Only Remember My Name* album was defiantly lacking in radio-friendly songs. Neither was it filled (one chant aside) with political rallying cries. It traded instead on uncannily beautiful vocal harmonies and rich musical textures—prompting most reviewers to denounce it as lazy and empty. Robert Christgau in the *Village Voice* was invariably CSN's most outspoken critic, and he dubbed Crosby's album a "disgraceful performance." *Melody Maker* in London was equally negative ("a grotesque display of self-indulgence"), prompting reviewer Richard Williams to be swamped by abusive mail from outraged fans. It was only in the 1990s that critical opinion was finally prepared to acknowledge Crosby's unique vision.

Graham Nash's *Songs for Beginners* underwent similar abuse. *Melody Maker* opined that the record was "at times so tired and obvious I feel myself cringing with embarrassment." The *Minneapolis Star* reckoned it was the worst album of 1971. Not surprisingly, *Stephen Stills 2* was also lambasted. "Crosby can out-write him, Nash can out-sing him, Young can out-compose him," one acerbic journalist concluded.

Since his first solo album, Stills had been promising a tour that would be "a real road show—the biggest since Ray Charles hit the stage." Timed to coincide with the chart success of "Love the One You're With," it might have established him as a superstar to rival the former Beatles. Instead, it was delayed while, in Stills's words, "Elliot [Roberts] and David [Geffen] made it difficult for me to put my band together." The problems, as so often with Stills, were excess and that most forgivable of flaws, artistic ambition. Both were powered by an ego determined to prove that he was more potent and eclectic than the CSNY mothership. He set out to design a show that would encompass a variety of formats and moods, from solo acoustic confessionals and folk duets to rock anthems and big-band R&B. As he confessed early in the tour, he wound up with "a marathon where you watch the singer bleed from the throat while he tries to sing eighteen songs in a row."

Stills would remember the tour as a disaster. It began with an impromptu appearance at a June 1971 festival in Louisiana that was billed as a Celebration of Life, but made Altamont seem like a church picnic. Hells Angels dragged young women out of the crowd to be gang-raped, hundreds collapsed with heatstroke, and police charged admission for adults eager to stare at the naked hippies. "If Woodstock was the beginning, the Celebration of Life is the end of rock festivals as we have known them," the event's emcee admitted.

On the road, arenas were often barely half-filled, audiences were too restless or stoned to sit through Stills's acoustic sets, and reviewers were heartless. A roadie plummeted from the rigging onto the stage and died at Madison Square Garden, where Stills provided equipment for George Harrison's Bangladesh charity concerts on August 1 and waited in vain for an invitation to perform. A few days later, Stills fell off a motorbike and tore knee ligaments, forcing him to see out the tour in a brace. Afterward, his Colorado buddy and new acoustic partner, Steve Fromholz, admitted: "I couldn't take that lifestyle. I can't live on a diet of Jim Beam, cocaine, and cheeseburgers." But amid the chaos and overindulgence, Stills did create rousing music, especially with the Memphis Horns. The tour ended in California, where David Crosby briefly guested at a couple of shows, and Stills claimed wildly that "the revolution's over, and we won it."

He then fled to his new home in the Rocky Mountains. "A year ago, I got sick of being a rock and roll star," he explained to his audience in Cleveland. "So, I moved away from Hollywood and up to Colorado, 'cos they don't care about that kind of thing up there." He discovered a house that was ideal for a studio complex, but couldn't raise the cash in time, and so the Caribou ranch fell into the hands of James William Guercio. Supposedly Ahmet Ertegun promised to give the singer $4,000 for a cabin but received an itemized bill that included $37,000 for a snow plow. Stills's excuse? "Well, it's snowing up here, man, and I had to have the road cleared."

In time, Stills would lead a music business exodus to the Boulder region, where he founded a holding company for his publishing and investments, Gold Hill Enterprises. He purchased a thirteen-acre ranch in a national forest preserve and attracted more than a dozen employees to set up home nearby. And it was in Boulder that he renewed acquaintance with someone he'd known at school in Miami: Michael John Bowen, a former sergeant in the Green Berets, who became the head of all his Colorado operations.

Stills was lured down from the mountains by none other than David Crosby and Graham Nash, who had embarked on an entirely acoustic tour as a duo. Unlike Stills, they made no attempt to fill arenas, trading instead on the intimacy of small theaters and the stoned gaiety of their personal bond. (Their first show had been in Vancouver, after which Nash was hassled by US immigration officials and wrote a song about the incident.) This stripped-down approach freed them to experiment with new material and allowed for unrehearsed reunions with old friends.

At Carnegie Hall on September 30, 1971, there was a howl of disbelief from the audience when Stephen Stills walked on unannounced, midway through the show. "I'd sure like to thank you guys for warming the house up," he drawled. For around forty-five minutes, CSN rekindled the spirit of Laurel Canyon, venturing an attempt at the "Suite" during which fans had to act as prompts for lyrics the trio simply couldn't remember.

"In honor of our missing member," they even performed Neil Young's "Ohio," with Nash taking the Canadian's place. Young did not rush to repay the compliment by tackling *their* songs.

Three days later in Boston, the distant quartet—still friends, but not always comrades—was complete for the first time in fifteen months, and Young reclaimed "Ohio" as his own. There, and again at Carnegie Hall the following night, Crosby and Nash played an hour by themselves, before first Stills and then—to a response worthy of the Second Coming—Young appeared. In New York, CSN offered a version of "So Begins the Task" so daring and joyous that it seemed impossible to imagine the three men ever parting company. With Young, they performed "Alabama," the song's composer calling out the chord changes for the rest to follow. And while Stephen Stills flew back to Colorado, and Crosby and Nash battled what a very stoned Crosby called the "Lebanese flu," the duo was reunited with Neil Young in Berkeley. Managers and record company executives began to glimpse the dollar signs of 1970 on the horizon. But no sooner had this mirage appeared than it vanished in a haze of ambition.

It's not totally a partnership, but it's enough of a partnership that everyone is satisfied and everyone's cool behind it.

—Stephen Stills on Manassas, 1972

Defiant arrogance was Stephen Stills's stance after his first solo tour. As he used to boast, "My mediocre is better than your best." Scolded by his management and slayed by the critics, he chose to think bigger still. In late 1971 he set up camp at Criteria Studios in Miami, where brothers Ron and Howard Alpert would become his production aides for the next two decades. Despite having issued two albums in eight months, he arrived with a vast backlog of songs, some reflecting his continuing passion for Rita Coolidge, others his separation from CSNY: "I'm not the one to tell you what to do," he assured them in "What to Do," "I have no desire to run your life."

David Geffen had already persuaded him to condense *Stephen Stills 2* into a single record, and the manager was horrified by Stills's latest plan. It involved a multidimensional survey of his entire musical spectrum, allotting a vinyl side apiece to country, folk, rock, and a twenty-minute suite dedicated to "The Raven" (his lyrical image for Coolidge). He began work with Bill Wyman of the Rolling Stones and Dallas Taylor, before recruiting several members of the Flying Burrito Brothers for the country tunes. "Then Stephen proposed putting together a band," steel guitarist Al Perkins recalled, "with me and Chris Hillman."

David Crosby's former Byrds colleague became Stills's right-hand man for the project. "That band could cover everything from a very hard-core, Latino, salsa-type song to a traditional bluegrass tune," Hillman said. "Out of everybody I've ever known in rock and roll, Stephen really understood country music. He's an amazing singer, songwriter, player—but unfortunately he shoots himself in the foot quite a bit."

Initially it was a literal leg injury, not a metaphorical one, that Stills had to overcome, as Perkins explained: "He checked himself into a hospital in New York to have knee surgery, which he'd needed for some time." But first Stills arranged for the band to stage a wintry photo shoot at Manassas Junction station in Virginia, close to the site of two nineteenth-century battles. "Stephen was a big Civil War buff," Perkins said. "That's when we discovered we were going to be called Manassas. After the operation, he wanted to recuperate in his Surrey home, so he asked us to come over and rehearse. We did a TV show in February 1972, and then our first concert as an electric band in Holland." The band survived the deprivations of an English winter, as Stills's sister Tai recalled: "There were about twenty of us staying in Stephen's house. The big problem was that England was going through a coal strike, and we had blackouts. The band needed the power to rehearse, so I cooked in the kitchen with eight camp-out stoves. My assistant and I prepared every meal in candlelight."

By the time the strike was over, Stills was ready to launch Manassas the band, and *Stephen Stills Manassas* the double album. "That was a great record, as good as anything I've ever worked on," Hillman said. Its musical scope—albeit within the traditional bounds of American rock and roll and roots music—was breathtaking, and the composing, almost entirely by Stills, was equally rich and diverse. Yet the entire Manassas project had a wider meaning for its creator: it divorced him from CSNY and his old managers' expectation of a speedy reunion. "It was like cutting the final cord," Stills reflected. "I thought that if I formed a band, then they're fucked."

Manassas raced into the US Top 5, where—ironically, given Stills's motives—it shared space with the debut album by Graham Nash and David Crosby, and Neil Young's first solo album, for more than eighteen months. Of the three records, Young's *Harvest* was arguably the least ambitious, and easily the most successful. Its spin-off single, "Heart of Gold," also scaled the charts. Although many reviews were scathing, the album provided a timely blend of ramshackle rock and mellow country moods, with songs that offered political commentary, whimsical romanticism, and the patina of stoned hippie bliss. Stephen Stills's emotions, on discovering that his strongest-ever collection was being overshadowed and outsold by a record from his lifelong sparring partner, could easily be imagined.

As if to emphasize his distance from CSNY, Stills was on tour in Europe—in Paris, to be precise, where he was introduced to a young singer-songwriter named Véronique Sanson—on March 26, 1972, when Crosby, Nash, and Young staged a prison benefit at Winterland in San Francisco. The three men were given a rousing, not to mention rowdy, reception from an audience who seemed to view CNY as a tourist attraction. Whereas the brief CSN reunions the previous year had recaptured the trio's harmony blend, Young's addition to the mix demolished any chance of vocal precision. Four months later, an equally raucous set of voices was raised at a Manassas gig in Berkeley, with David Crosby the only absentee. Each gathering provided a sense of occasion, but little musical evidence that the quartet actually needed to be together.

If CSNY wouldn't oblige, then Elliot Roberts and David Geffen could take comfort (and a percentage) from the best available substitute. America (one-third English) were a songwriting trio who smoothed and simplified CSN's harmony blend. Among their number was Dewey Bunnell, whose voice was eerily similar to Neil Young's. He took the lead on "Horse with No Name," which supplanted Young's "Heart of Gold" at the top of the US chart. In 1972 David Geffen also launched his own label, Asylum Records, signing Joni Mitchell alongside a new generation of artists who acknowledged her and CSNY as their musical mentors, led by Jackson Browne and the Eagles.

Yet Geffen still fantasized about a deal that would amaze the industry and replace the unreliable CSNY in his portfolio. His plan was to pull off a legal, logistical, and psychological miracle by reuniting one of the few bands in rock history who could rival CSNY for internal conflict: the original five-man lineup of the Byrds. The band had lost its status as a major recording act after Crosby's departure in 1967 but retained their place in fans' hearts as the most creative American band of the mid-1960s. Geffen hoped to add them to his Asylum roster, prompting Clive Davis of Columbia Records to insist that *his* label still owned the rights to the Byrds' catalog and any further recordings by the group.

Davis and Geffen sparred and negotiated over the contractual niceties for several months. Meanwhile, Geffen, with the aid of ex-Byrds producer Terry Melcher, attempted to lay all the dominoes in line. The key relationship requiring repair was that of Roger McGuinn and David Crosby—the leader, founder, and sole original member of the band and the ex-colleague whom he had first jettisoned and then watched soar beyond him in wealth and acclaim. The gulf between Crosby and the rest was illustrated by Chris Hillman's onetime partner in the Flying Burrito Brothers, Rick Roberts: "Chris sees David Crosby riding around in his Mercedes, and he gets things [from Crosby] like, 'You're really going on the road again? We're just off on a yachting holiday.'"

The two labels eventually compromised on an arrangement whereby Columbia would keep both McGuinn and the Byrds, but Asylum would issue the band's reunion album. In return, Crosby and McGuinn would collaborate on a duo record for Columbia. The rapprochement between the two men seemed to clear the path for the reunion. But friction arose elsewhere: "David and I started fighting on the phone," Hillman recalled. The bassist was still recording and touring with Manassas, and Crosby became convinced that Stephen Stills would sabotage the Byrds by making it impossible for Hillman to participate. Another gentleman's agreement was forged, whereby the Byrds would record on weekdays in October and November 1972, and Manassas would perform on weekends.

Trepidation and skepticism were aired before the sessions began. "It's easy to mess up," McGuinn reflected. "You get wrapped up in something, thinking it's great. And you keep thinking it's great until it comes out, and everyone tells you it stinks." The Byrds' leader informed the current lineup that they would be disbanding, so that the originals could tour in their stead. "If they last three weeks, I'll give them a medal," one of the rejected musicians said. "They're going to kill each other."

Instead, the five originals drowned each other in compliments and good intentions. Roger McGuinn swore that the album "picks up where *The Notorious Byrd Brothers* left off" and was now his favorite Byrds record of all. "It's definitely on the fringe of what's happening today," he promised. Crosby concurred: "To me it's a fulfillment of what we could have been. It was so much fun, I'm sure we'll want to make more records."

As the sessions progressed, David Crosby—not to anyone's surprise—emerged as the dominant force. He not only claimed sole production credit, and the royalties that entailed, but insinuated his own musical family into the sessions, to the point where the Byrds were playing not only his songs, but two by Neil Young and one by Graham Nash (the unreleased "Bright Sunny Day"). Both of CSNY's drummers, Dallas Taylor and Johny Barbata, also guested anonymously on the album. For the moment, optimism prevailed, and the band began to talk excitedly about their long-term future. Then *The Byrds* was released in March 1973—and reviewers concurred with Chris Hillman's subsequent judgment that it was "the blandest album you've ever heard." There was an obvious scapegoat: the record's self-appointed producer. The tour was forgotten and so was the promise of a Crosby-McGuinn collaboration. The project's underwhelming impact demonstrated that mere nostalgia was not sufficient to sustain a Byrds reunion in an era when Led Zeppelin carried more weight than vintage folk rock. For the first time, David Geffen must have wondered whether a CSNY reunion would be met by the same derisory response.

In America, when you go to elementary school, they have a report card for "Works well with others." I'd say Stephen would have to get an F!

—David Geffen, 1972

Just as it seemed that David Geffen, Elliot Roberts, and Asylum could corral the entire California songwriter community, one of its most prominent members fled the pen. Wounded by their constant undermining of his schemes, Stephen Stills sacked Geffen-Roberts as his managers and turned to Michael John Bowen. "Stephen is a loner," Geffen reflected, and "at some point we lost the faith that was implicit and important in a relationship of that kind." Then he lacerated Stills for his selfishness, his excesses, his lack of humility, and his inability to share creative responsibility. Beyond that, Geffen said, Stills was reckless: "I'm certainly not going to be part of somebody ruining their career or doing those things that I think are tragically wrong." Instead, the manager suggested that the remaining members of CSNY would form a trio. "No doubt they will eventually get around to making an album together," Geffen concluded.

Through the summer of 1972, the only solid evidence of his conviction was "War Song," a single written by Young and co-credited to Nash. It was prompted by the latest twist in the Vietnam conflict, whereby President Nixon would once again try to bomb the North into submission, and it was intended (by a Canadian and an Englishman, no less) to influence the 1972 US presidential election. But any hope that the record might speed the antiwar Democratic candidate Senator George McGovern into the White House vanished when Nixon won an overwhelming electoral victory.

At that point, the reunion of the Byrds was still promising to be a 1973 landmark, and David Geffen was anxious to repeat the trick. Around election time, he persuaded CSN to consider an album, and possibly a tour. Sessions were booked for January 1973, and Geffen assured fans that the album would be in the shops by April. Graham Nash told his old bandmate Tony Hicks that CSN would surpass Manassas by releasing a triple album: one record of new material by the trio, one of solo tracks by each musician, and a third compiling the three men's finest pre-CSN work. Talk proved to be easier than action, as Dallas Taylor, the band's designated drummer, explained, "We started to get together, but it was a bit early. We all want to do it. It's just a matter of getting together and working things out." The album promised by Geffen never materialized.

Each member of CSN was distracted: Crosby by the Byrds, Stills and Nash by romance and its repercussions. "I had a girlfriend named Amy Gossage, a very beautiful young woman," Nash recalled. "Her father invented the international paper airplane race. Rather more importantly, he was the guy who put Beethoven on a T-shirt in the 1950s—the very first guy ever to put an image on a T-shirt. She came from this hard-living, hard-driving, hard-drinking family." Amelia Luck Gossage was just sixteen when she became involved with the thirty-year-old Nash in 1972. She played the cello, sketched constantly, and dreamed of a starring movie role as her heroine, Joan of Arc. Amy and her slightly older brother, Eben, had been raised in San Francisco in an extremely liberal environment in which nothing was forbidden. After their father, Howard, died in 1969, Eben became an alcoholic and then a heroin addict, and began forging checks from the account of his alcoholic mother, Mary. Amy's excesses were more conventional. "She had a fetish for weed," a friend remembered. "Amy just kept on getting high. She was so into having a good time." Another friend explained how, even in her mid-teens, she could exploit her sexual appeal: "She liked playing with guys, playing with their heads. It was more mind sex than body sex." Nash courted her as if she were a princess, hiring society bandleader Nick Jordan's ensemble to greet her at the San Francisco airport when she returned from a vacation in Paris.

Stephen Stills had become equally entranced with Véronique Sanson, whom he began dating after their meeting at the Olympia in Paris. But the early months of their relationship were shadowed by a previous affair. Stills's onetime lover Harriet had given birth to a son, Justin, in January 1971, insisting that the musician was still the only man she had ever slept with. Stills denied he was the father but offered to set up a trust fund for the child if Harriet withdrew her claim. She refused, determined that Justin would have a legal father. Her case passed into the hands of Marvin Mitchelson, a lawyer who would soon become famous for his involvement in celebrity divorce proceedings. (Stills was clearly impressed by Mitchelson's expertise in court, as he subsequently hired him to handle his own divorce.)

"Stills's main defense was that he had not been with Harriet or been intimate with her during the week that medical evidence had established the child was conceived," Mitchelson wrote. Dallas Taylor was among those who gave evidence on his behalf. "Stills's lawyers tried to show that it was impossible for him to be the father," Mitchelson continued, because "he was either in Hawaii, in a recording studio with the band, or in bed with another woman. His claim of being in a recording studio was undermined when we pointed out the reason for his Hawaiian trip: he had broken his hand, it was in a cast, and he couldn't play the guitar with any great facility." The jury unanimously agreed that Stills was the boy's father. "He's just won a wonderful son," Harriet declared after the proceedings were over. In time, Stephen Stills would recognize the truth of her remark, building a strong relationship with his first-born child.

On September 8, 1972, Neil Young became the first member of CSNY to *acknowledge* a child, when Carrie Snodgress gave birth to Zeke. Within two months, Young's domesticity was interrupted by rehearsals with the Stray Gators, who had helped him record *Harvest*. Young had agreed to a three-month-long North American tour, beginning in Madison, Wisconsin, on January 4, 1973. Danny Whitten was invited to participate with the understanding that he would be free from heroin at the sessions. Instead, the guitarist arrived at the ranch incoherent and incapable, having replaced junk with copious quantities of alcohol and downers. "He couldn't remember anything," Young recalled. For a couple of days, he attempted to believe that Whitten could straighten himself out. When it became obvious that the guitarist couldn't function, Young put some cash in his hand and bought him a ticket back to LA. Within hours, Whitten had ingested enough pills and booze to shut down his system; he was pronounced dead on November 18, 1972.

It was a prophetic omen for the most turbulent tour of Neil Young's career. These were his first official appearances since the chart-topping success of *Harvest*, and he was booked into vast sports arenas and amphitheaters in more than fifty cities. These venues had replaced theaters, college halls, and ballrooms on contemporary tour schedules, and many acts struggled to get their songs across in these expanded spaces. Neil Young's audiences were expecting the sensitive troubadour of "Heart of Gold," but much of his new material was abrasive and confrontational. So were many of the concerts, which highlighted the challenge of performing acoustic songs to crowds of drunken star-seekers who only wanted to hear "Southern Man."

At the second show, in Milwaukee, Young scolded the audience: "I don't know why you pay to come and talk to your friends." In Minneapolis, he sang while ushers touted soft drinks in front of the stage. When a bunch of teenage girls in Chicago begged him to "Shut up and sing," he retorted: "Do I look like a Wurlitzer?" A superb show in Toronto was followed by a disaster in Ottawa where, as drummer Kenny Buttrey said, "nothing stayed in tune." Three nights later in Baltimore, Young told fans, "I can't handle playing with people yelling at me," and brought out the band early. Then he abandoned "Out on the Weekend" and called the Gators back offstage because latecomers were still taking their seats. Meanwhile, exhaustion and depression were taking their toll. As a Baltimore reviewer noted, "By the end Mr. Young's voice was so strained that he couldn't possibly have sung an encore if he'd wanted to" (and he didn't).

And so the tour crawled on. Before his show in New Haven, rumors spread among local kids that a prominent psychic had predicted that the Coliseum would collapse during the concert and hundreds of fans would be killed. When that didn't happen, the story changed: now the same mystic had threatened that everyone who attended the show would die within a year. In Orlando, the concert ran side by side with a riot, as kids without tickets threw everything from bottles to rolls of barbed wire at police for two hours. The Shreveport show was canceled because of poor ticket sales; in Des Moines, Young came close to being electrocuted during the first number; and in Tucson, he was distracted for the rest of the night after a fan set off a camera flash in his face while he was trying to sing "Old Man."

There was no relief backstage, as the Stray Gators witnessed the sold-out arenas, did some mental arithmetic, and demanded a pay raise. Midway through the tour, Young sacked Kenny Buttrey for not playing loud enough, although the drummer already had open wounds on both hands from the effort of trying to match up to Young's demands. "Neil was constantly ill on that tour," Joel Bernstein recalled, "with one cold after another. It didn't help that they were traveling on an unheated plane in winter." And through it all, keyboardist Jack Nitzsche made it obvious that he was as miserable as Young. "The tour was torture," Nitzsche complained. "Everyone in the band was bored to death with those terrible guitar solos. He would turn and face the band with this stupid grimace while he was playing, and I would nearly roll on the stage laughing. He takes himself so seriously."

By early March, Young's voice had deteriorated so much that a handful of shows were canceled. To lighten his load when the tour resumed on March 10, Young invited Graham Nash and David Crosby to join him. Their musical contribution most nights was negligible, as they only stepped out for the final electric set and frequently sang off-key. But their friendship and visible support raised Young's morale sufficiently to drag him through the remainder of the schedule.

Inevitably, there were dramas along the way. Crosby's mother, Aliph, was dying of cancer in a Santa Barbara hospital, and he flew back to her bedside for a final meeting before resuming the tour that night. A week later in Anaheim, he threw himself around the stage with such enthusiasm that he dislocated his knee and missed the final five shows. He thereby avoided the Oakland Coliseum, where Young was singing the first chorus of "Southern Man" when a security man clubbed an overexcited fan to the ground in front of the stage. Young called the band to a halt, told the crowd, "I can't fucking sing if that happens," and left the stage. (One audience member subsequently tried to win a class-action lawsuit against Young, on the basis that he hadn't completed the show and therefore ticket holders should be compensated.) "Who needs to be a dot in the distance for twenty thousand people and give the cops another excuse to get uptight and stop kids being happy?" Young declared later. "The circus might be all right for some acts, but it's not for me anymore."

Stephen Stills would have agreed. The impetus and enthusiasm that had propelled Manassas through the making of a double album and several months of touring had dissipated a year later, after Stephen Stills had shepherded the band through lengthy and chaotic sessions for another record, Down the Road. "It became a real nightmare," Chris Hillman recalled, "the self-indulgence, the forty-eight-hours-in-the-studio stuff, all that excess. It just stopped being enjoyable." While Young and Nash were playing the final show in Salt Lake City and Crosby sat at home with his leg in a cast, digesting the reviews of the Byrds' reunion album, Stills, Hillman, and Manassas ran out of patience in front of an arena crowd in Pittsburgh on March 27, 1973. "I've seen people asleep," Stills wisecracked, "and I've seen people drunk, and I've seen people stoned, but I've never seen a bunch of people that were all of that at once, but mostly asleep." CSNY had always struggled to stay in tune with each other; now they were increasingly out of sync with their audience, too.

CHAPTER 12

I fell into a kind of hurricane . . . where drugs and alcohol were
part of everyday life.

—Véronique Sanson

The wedding had just taken place on March 14, 1973, at Artington
House in Guildford, and the bride went into the bathroom with her
sister. "She and I were standing by the window," the bride recalled, "and
she said to me, 'Vero, the car is outside. You could break the window and
get away.'" The bride hesitated for a few seconds, mulling it over. "I'll
get divorced later," she told her sister. "We're here now."

The reluctant bride was twenty-three-year-old Véronique Sanson; her
husband was Stephen Stills. "To be honest, I think I got married out of
politeness," she would confess. "I was already saying to myself, 'I'm not
sure I can live with this man.' But I didn't want to upset my parents or
his parents. That sounds very cold, but it's the truth."

Engaged to the singer Michel Berger when she met Stills in March
1972, she had abandoned her comfortable life in France. "Stephen has
fantastic charisma," she admitted. "When he sang and played, I immediately fell under his spell." But she soon realized that loving Stills meant
dealing with his excessive habits: "It was like a minefield, because of drugs
and alcohol. My body wasn't strong enough to live like that."

Sanson's courtship coincided with her elevation to stardom. Her song
"Amoureuse" became a huge hit in her homeland and was widely covered in an English translation (most famously by Kiki Dee). Stills made
sure that, wherever they were living, Sanson had a piano at her disposal;
he advised her about recording facilities and producers and would later

lend her his band for live shows and studio sessions. But whenever San-son was among Stills and his musical friends, "I never dared play 'The Artist,'" she said. "Steve wouldn't suggest it, either. I was always just his wife, not a musician who was well known in her own country. I always said to myself, 'One day . . .'"

At the end of May 1973, Stills and his new wife flew to Hawaii to meet up with David Crosby and Graham Nash. "I decided to take my boat to Lahaina on Maui for some diving," Crosby said, "and Graham decided to come along. When Stephen heard, he thought, 'Why should they have all the fun?' and so he came out to join us." Enter Neil Young, who rented a beach house at Mala Wharf. Between there and the *Mayan*, CSNY achieved an easy rapport that they had never quite found at home. "Before we knew it," Crosby remembered, "we were all hanging out on my boat, diving, getting really healthy, and having a swell time. After a while the guitars came out and we found ourselves playing and singing each other's songs. And that's where it began to take off." This idyllic vision of brotherhood was captured in a photo taken toward the end of their stay—four beatific beach bums, glazed and mellow. Nash envisaged this as the cover of a CSNY reunion album, which would take its name from a Neil Young composition: *Human Highway*. Only in retrospect would a key line from the song seem prophetic: "I got lost on the human highway."

Another reading of this tale would surface decades later, in Jimmy McDonough's originally authorized, then unauthorized, biography of Neil Young, *Shakey*. In this alternate narrative, the entire Hawaii trip was staged by Crosby and Nash to wean Stephen Stills off cocaine, and thereby would demonstrate to Young that CSN were capable of par-ticipating in a reunion. Linked to this version was the death of Young's roadie Bruce Berry, a heroin addict whose body was found in early June. McDonough suggested that Berry had arrived in Hawaii with cocaine for one of the musicians, been sent home to California, and then OD'd. In his autobiography, Nash blurred the tale by relating that straight after the group portrait of CSNY was taken, "some business, some cocaine thing, went down, and suddenly we weren't talking to each other." As he added, "I'm still not quite sure what happened—and I'm not sure if anyone exactly knows." So CSNY bonded in paradise, and cocaine shaped and capsized their reunion. With these musicians, at this point in history, both extremes were within reach at the same moment, without anyone present having a sober recollection of what had happened.

There was certainly optimism in the air when CSNY regrouped in California. David Geffen and Elliot Roberts announced an imminent stadium tour—six to ten concerts across America that summer, followed by indoor venues in the winter. Neil Young, usually the most fainthearted participant in any CSNY reunion, was sufficiently enthused in mid-July 1973 to sketch out, on the back of an envelope, his vision of how the band might structure their shows. He envisaged the band playing three sets— electric, acoustic, electric—with soloists taking their turn in the middle of the show. Each concert would be bookended by "Carry On"; "Lookout Joe," "New Mama," and "Last Dance" would be retrieved from his recent solo tour; Stills's Manassas showcase "The Treasure" would be added to the group's collective repertoire; and the band would also perform the long-lost "Curious Joe" (described as "a bad Crosby song" by one of the few who ever heard it). CSNY would also delve into the distant past by reviving the Byrds' "Eight Miles High" and Buffalo Springfield's "Rock 'n' Roll Woman."

"I'll do anything I can to make it easy," Stephen Stills pledged that month. "I don't want to be the pusher this time—I'm looking to somebody else for the energy." But CSNY had never operated in the studio or on the road without Stills being the driving force, regardless of whether or not his colleagues responded to his efforts. Young opened his ranch to the band for extended rehearsals, which resulted in a series of semipro-fessional recording sessions—documents of work in progress rather than attempts at studio masters. Each member of CSN had set aside material for this overdue reunion, and Young had earmarked "New Mama" and "Human Highway." "It would have been our best album," Nash remarked on numerous occasions.

What's apparent from this distance is that the much-vaunted *Human Highway* album never came close to being made. Recordings did even-tually surface from the ranch, thanks to an indiscreet radio station, but with a single exception, they were not ready for release. The one genuine survivor from these impromptu sessions—"It was so obviously a keeper," Joel Bernstein noted—was Stills's "See the Changes." "Stephen has always been adept at writing melodies that turn into great Crosby, Stills and Nash records," Bernstein said, and the ranch recording of the song had that elusive feel—campfire at twilight (or Canyon pool in mid-afternoon)—that was the hallmark of CSN.

"See the Changes" featured a rhythm section that seemed to have been assembled by committee: percussionist Joe Lala from Manassas; bassist Tim Drummond from Young's tour band; and drummer Russ Kunkel from sessions with Crosby and Nash. They were also heard on "Little Blind Fish," a playful piece of improvisation that afforded each member of CSNY a vocal cameo. The only other song to reach tape during these rehearsals was Nash's "Prison Song," influenced by his father's experience in the 1950s and by a letter he'd received from a kid in a Texas jail, who was facing a lengthy sentence for possessing a single marijuana joint.

No sooner had the band cohered than—as Stills recalled— "one day we stopped playing." "There was a lot of disagreement about how to go about it," Crosby noted. Nash remembered: "It wasn't as exciting as we wanted." In Tim Drummond's recollection, "We decided against it. Something wasn't right." Joel Bernstein's memory was that Young greeted CSN one day with the message: "I'm just too tired." "He had gone through this ordeal on the road earlier in the year," Bernstein explained, "and he had been ill. But it's possible that Neil had just got tired of CSN. They could never believe that Neil would want to play with anyone else, because to them, working with him was so good that nothing else could beat it. But for Neil . . . well, first of all, it wasn't his band. And then there was always the issue that before long he would be having a major head-to-head with Stephen. So, Neil wanted out—and then it seemed to CSN that no sooner had he quit than he was back in the studio with his own people. I imagine they were very pissed at him."

Young's producer David Briggs recalled an unannounced knock at his door: "I opened it and there was Neil. He said, 'Hey, I was just on my way to a CSNY session and I just don't feel like going there. Let's go make some rock and roll.' So, we packed our bags and came to LA and wound up with the *Tonight's the Night* album."

If Geffen had never mooted the possibility of a reunion, no one's reputation would have suffered. Instead, everyone was free to speculate and exaggerate. One anonymous Atlantic Records employee claimed: "The four of them could not even agree on one song to play, not one." When your own record company was spreading damaging rumors, you were in trouble.

More pertinent was Joel Bernstein's observation: "If you save your best songs for the band, but then record them with someone else, how can you still say you're a functioning band?" As Graham Nash explained, "When we first got together, the idea was that the group would be our highest means of expression." Like Crosby and Stills, he had reserved material for CSNY, only to discover that CSNY were incapable of staying together long enough to record it. "Those songs were just cramming up my head," he recalled. As Stephen Stills concluded, "We all got disgusted and made our own solo albums." As they did, it was their supposedly exhausted colleague who gained the upper hand.

> Graham doesn't like the style of my solo stuff—he thinks it's too loud and too lush. But then I think his album drags.
>
> —Stephen Stills, April 1974

After the multifaceted panache of *Stephen Stills Manassas*, *Down the Road* was a supreme disappointment. As Chris Hillman put it, with a touch of understatement, "It really wasn't very good." Manassas continued to function after the CSNY rehearsals collapsed, but the band had lost its pulse. Dallas Taylor was struggling with heroin addiction, while Fuzzy Samuel drifted in and out of the lineup. Stills was aware that his reputation was under threat: "I know I've blown my music and offended my friends because I was crazy behind coke," he admitted, "but I'm not like that anymore." To underline the point, he recorded two of the songs he'd been saving for CSNY, "First Things First" and "As I Come of Age," enlisting vocal support from Crosby and Nash. Simultaneously, Nash worked off his dissatisfaction in his basement studio, where he assembled his own solo record, *Wild Tales*. As Joel Bernstein's remarkable cover photo revealed, the mod matinee idol of Swinging London now resembled an Old Testament prophet, raging against the emptiness of modern life, and the music was every bit as stark.

At SIR in Hollywood, Young assembled a small group of musicians in late August 1973 to stage an Irish wake for lost friends. Night after night, they waited until they were perfectly pitched between inebriated freedom and total oblivion and then performed the same set of songs—brutal, passionate laments for Danny Whitten and Bruce Berry, celebrations of nihilism and despair, chronicles of drug deals and psychological violence. In its original form, always mourned by producer David Briggs, *Tonight's the Night* was a collage of musical extremism and drunken dialogue. But having exorcised his emotions and his songs, Young filed the tape away, convinced that it would be impossible to release.

No sooner had he completed the record than a rumor spread that Young was dead, victim of a drug overdose. Nobody who had heard *Tonight's the Night* would have doubted the tale for a second. Indeed, Reprise Records began work on an obituary before they thought to ask the artist himself if he was still alive.

To confirm his existence, Young headlined three nights of shows in September 1973 at the newly opened Roxy Theatre in Hollywood (then co-owned by David Geffen). Graham Nash stood in as his support act at short notice, previewing *Wild Tales*. Anyone seeking nostalgia was sadly disappointed, as Young reeled off his *Tonight's the Night* song cycle in the guise of a wasted huckster shepherding tourists to Miami Beach— musically exhilarating but deeply disorientating for those still searching for the creator of *Harvest*. "There was this deathly silence when Neil's shows emptied out," David Crosby reported. "Apparently, people were in a state of complete shock—they didn't believe what they'd just seen and heard." Similar reactions occurred when Young carried an extended version of this show into Canada, the UK, and back across the States, leaving listeners stunned or audibly frustrated by his refusal to supply comforting nostalgia. Young was becoming as willful and as driven as Miles Davis, and like his former support act, he had chosen to pursue creative satisfaction at any cost.

Before he headed north, Young had turned up at Winterland in San Francisco on October 4, 1973, for one of the final Manassas shows. Midway through the program, when fans expected a Stills solo set, they were amazed to see CSN take the stage for a slightly shambolic quartet of songs.

Predictable mayhem ensued when a shaggy Neil Young wandered out to join them. "It's been a long time since this happened," Nash crowed. "I quit!" Young shouted with a broad smile on his face.

CSNY proceeded to deliver five unreleased songs, three by Young and two by Nash, most of which Stephen Stills didn't appear to recognize. "I'm sorry I don't know the words," he mumbled after Young sang "Roll Another Number for the Road." The irony of using CSNY to perform a song that satirized the myth of Woodstock can't have escaped its composer. Stills did claim a verse of "Human Highway" but bore a look of profound confusion during "New Mama" and greeted Nash's announcement of "And So It Goes" plaintively: "By the end of the song, I might learn it." After more orderly versions of "Long Time Gone" and "Change Partners," Crosby, Nash, and Young vanished into the wings, leaving Stills and Manassas to follow the main event. "I knew then and there that Manassas was over," Chris Hillman recollected.

Two nights later, Crosby showed up in Long Beach for the next Manassas show. There were calls throughout his duo set with Stills for Neil Young to appear. "He ain't here," Stills growled. "And if you want your money back, you can have it." The following day, it was back to Winterland, where Stills announced: "I conned 'em into it again." But this was only a partial reunion: to the inevitable call of "Where's Neil?" Stills replied, "On the farm." (Crosby offered a better response to the same question: "He's standing right next to you.") CSN briefly managed to revive the spirit of their original union and delivered one of their finest-ever live performances. Though absent in body, Young was still represented in the setlist, as Stills announced "a new song that was written by the snake himself" and gave "Human Highway" a fresh melodic setting. When Manassas returned to the stage, Stills yelled out, "To me, *this* band is home"; but less than a week later, the tour ended, and—without any official announcement—Manassas slipped gently away.

Stills would always believe that Atlantic Records had deliberately underpromoted the Manassas records, in case solo success forestalled a lucrative CSNY reunion. After Nash's *Wild Tales* was released in January 1974, its creator reached the same conclusion. The album peaked at number 34 in the US and failed to yield a hit single. "I have it on very good authority that *Wild Tales* was buried," Nash said later. "No promotion." But the simple truth was that *Wild Tales* was not a commercial record. It bore a sonic resemblance to Neil Young's *Harvest*, but with a ragged, enervated air closer in spirit to Young's contemporary work. Raw, deeply personal, and often affecting (never more so than on Nash's collaboration with Joni Mitchell, "Another Sleep Song"), it was anything but easy listening and, therefore, not what a mass audience wanted from the creator of "Teach Your Children" and "Our House."

As *Wild Tales* was released, Ahmet Ertegun flew to California for one-on-one meetings with CSN. He listened politely to their latest compositions and then suggested equally politely that it might be time for them to swallow their pride and reunite. Meanwhile, Elliot Roberts went to Neil Young and—as legend has it—told him that CSNY were "all just pissing in the wind." Together the good cop–bad cop offensive from Ertegun and Roberts began to take effect.

Individually, all four of the quartet had realized that they were increasingly at odds with their audiences. Stephen Stills was talking openly about quitting the business and becoming an actor, or a novelist, or maybe a film director. As Joe Lala recalled, "Stephen was complaining about being in a rut. He was trying too hard and felt stale." David Crosby was upset to see "all those people turning out for the heavy metal and glitter stuff, the ambisexual shock rock." But perhaps the power of the CSNY name and myth could conquer the effects of age and waning careers. "I think we're all older and more mature now," Stills said cautiously. "I think we could handle it."

> My new band is a dictatorship—I like that. My experience with democracy in rock and roll is that it is a total failure.
>
> —Stephen Stills, February 1974

In January and February 1974, Bob Dylan and the Band performed to sold-out arenas across North America—Dylan's first run of concerts in almost eight years. It was also the most lucrative tour ever staged at that point, the forty concerts in forty-three days grossing more than five million dollars. It has been estimated that more than twelve million applications were received for the five hundred thousand tickets on sale.

The promoter of that tour, Bill Graham, was the obvious choice when David Geffen and Elliot Roberts mapped out a plan to reunite CSNY and surpass Dylan. He was one of the few industry professionals to whom musicians listened with respect, having proved his pedigree on the San Francisco concert scene since the mid-1960s. Graham, Geffen, and Roberts fashioned a schedule whereby CSNY could play a dozen shows in North American sports stadiums, averaging fifty thousand fans a night, and play to more people than Dylan had achieved in six weeks.

The band's experience at Balboa Stadium in December 1969 had convinced them that huge outdoor shows did not suit their music. Even large indoor arenas precluded personal communication with an audience and damaged their fragile harmony sound. But those issues had to be weighed against the mind-boggling quantities of cash that a CSNY stadium tour could generate. As Stephen Stills admitted, "There are these bagsful of money across the street, and all we have to do is go over and pick them up." In retrospect, both David Crosby and Graham Nash would blame Stills and Neil Young for taking them down the stadium route: "Stephen and Neil like to play big places for the sake of big," Crosby would claim. "And they like big bucks." But Crosby and Nash had an equal power of veto, and they chose not to employ it. "We've got to play blimp hangars," Crosby explained. "If we played the kind of places I'd like—say, a nice ten-thousand-seater—we'd have to play for days and days to take care of the ticket demand."

Whatever their motivations, by early March 1974 all four musicians had agreed to a reunion. Stephen Stills broke the news from the stage of Auditorium Theatre in Chicago, where CSNY had played their debut show less than five years earlier. Backstage, he boasted: "It's going to out-gross the Dylan tour. In fact, it already has"—although not a single ticket had gone on sale. Beyond his customary swagger, however, Stills spoke like a man who had been hurt too often to expect a happy ending: "If it doesn't happen, it'll be because everybody has grown too far apart. We'll see." Then he sighed resignedly and let his cynicism show: "Everybody will have a new 'I've been there' patch for their Levi jackets," as if CSNY were just another rite of passage for the rock generation. Nor could he ignore the human dynamics: "The hardest part is going to be for everyone to remember how to sit and take orders. And me too."

Graham Nash was no more starry-eyed. He could act like a PR man for a sentence at a time: "Something happens when the four of us get together, some special sort of chemistry." But then reality and experience intruded, as he lamented the "bullshit" he'd endured from his CSNY buddies: "Sometimes people aren't who you expect them to be. You expect people to be trustworthy and they turn out not to be." Then he tried to turn that around: "So what if friends are assholes some of the time? Aren't we all? Before, in the group, it used to get serious and we'd get real crazy about it and not communicate. We're growing up, I think. At last!" And he laid out a rationale for the reunion that was deeply idealistic but betrayed his distance from teenage culture: "I see a giant hole everywhere. I find very little of that special magic in the music. The indefinable something that was there around 'sixty-nine/'seventy, the Woodstock period. We're going to bring that feeling back. There's good music around, but I haven't, for a long time, seen people get off the way they did when CSNY really hit."

But Woodstock was almost five years in the past, and "the indefinable something" of its culture had vanished. As Paul Kantner said in March 1974, "The youth movement died at Kent State, and there's nowhere for it to go. There's just no possible way of dealing with those forces. It's like trying to play poker with a dead man. You're dealing cards and he doesn't pick them up." The "dead man" was Richard Nixon, by now mired in the Watergate scandal that was, one by one, picking off his closest aides and edging ever nearer to incriminating the man in the Oval Office. Watergate was becoming a rallying point for investigative journalists, and for political opponents keen to contrast themselves to the gray, jowly mask of the Republican president. But for teenage America, Watergate wasn't a matter of party affiliation. It suggested nihilism as the only rational response to an establishment inextricably bound up with corruption and greed. The scandal didn't bring young people together; it merely alienated them from the system and all its alternatives.

The single issue that could unite American youth in outrage had been the Vietnam War, and that had faded from the national consciousness.

Onstage in New York, on January 23, 1973, Neil Young had been handed a note that read, "The war is over." It wasn't, as the inhabitants of Southeast Asia could confirm; but on that day the Paris Peace Accord was signed, the United States slowly began to disentangle itself from its most disastrous overseas venture. Once young men were no longer threatened with the draft, most could afford to ignore geopolitics. Instead, they focused on the struggle to get a job, as a global energy crisis triggered a recession throughout the capitalist West, and cultural depression stalked the world's wealthiest nations.

That aura of despair also lingered over the members of CSNY. Graham Nash had endured emotional extremes with Amy Gossage and, by his own telling, "went through two years of total depression" after the lukewarm reception of *Wild Tales*. But his psychological pain was more deep-seated than that, as he revealed to Ben Fong-Torres that summer: "All my aware life, from age sixteen, seventeen, eighteen, I've been an object. A fucking object. That's why I try very hard to be as unrecognizable as possible." Not even a lover's embrace could lift his mood. "I don't know, I don't *feel* anything," he admitted.

Neil Young and Carrie Snodgress were still together, and their son, Zeke, was almost eighteen months old. But their suspicions about his development were confirmed when doctors diagnosed him with cerebral palsy. Their anxiety over the future of their child ate away at a relationship that was already beginning to decay from within.

Stephen Stills and Véronique Sanson had also endured a traumatic introduction to parenthood. Three days after their son, Christopher, was born in April 1974, doctors said he was suffering from cholera and toxicosis, and the parents were warned that he wasn't expected to live through the night. He recovered, but Sanson still felt unable to settle into her marriage. Her initial thrill at living in the Rocky Mountains had dissipated into boredom: "Our house was so isolated. You needed a snow plow, because you couldn't get up there by car. What I didn't know was that, at ten thousand feet, the snow season lasts for seven months. It was terrible. One day the temperature was minus forty-five, and if you opened the window, everything frosted up in three seconds. And just that snow everywhere, that incredible whiteness—it became very draining after a while."

She also felt completely isolated. "I was fed up with his world revolving around drugs and alcohol. The thing was with Steve, when he said, 'Bye, see you later,' he often wouldn't come back for three days. Mostly he'd come home in an appalling state. So, I was waiting to leave until the right moment came."

We can't go out and do "Southern Man" for eighteen minutes, or "Our House" again. We've got to go out and say something we mean now.

—Graham Nash, April 1974

Throughout 1973, a comedy troupe assembled by *National Lampoon* magazine staged a theater show entitled *Lemmings*. Act 2 was entirely devoted to the comic rock opera that gave the evening its name, as the assembled cast offered a wicked satire of the Woodstock Nation. In prime position, singing "Woodshuck" (aka "Lemmings Lament"), were none other than Freud, Marx, Engels, and Jung, a thinly disguised parody of another legendary quartet. "We are lemmings, we are crazies," the ensemble sang with strained harmonies, before a Crosby-style scat vocal and a mock–Neil Young guitar solo made the objects of their sarcasm unmistakable.

A couple of years later, the *Lampoon* team concocted another demolition of Young's image, with the double bill of "History of Neil Young" and "Southern California Brings Me Down." "Could he have been a drug abuser?" the stoned narrator asked—and *National Lampoon* had not even heard the then-unreleased *Tonight's the Night* album.

The artist almost seemed to demand an apocalyptic interpretation of his state of mind, by the studied anti-commercialism of his actions. Rather than forget his traumatic 1973 US tour, Young chose to commemorate it with a live album, *Time Fades Away*. It was comprised purely of unreleased material; or, as Nick Kent proclaimed in *NME*, "murky, sloppy attempts at rock and roll, built around tiresome chord progressions and obscure nonsense lyrics." Kent concluded: "Neil Young has now got nothing to say for himself." This wasn't an isolated verdict:

several reviewers named it as the worst album of 1973, and the *Arizona Republic* declared: "At a party, someone sounding like Young and trying to sing would be laughed at." An anonymous record executive extended the theme: "Neil's getting to be a fat cat. He doesn't have to try, so he isn't. His boredom is killing us."

These might have been career-ending reviews, but Young dauntlessly pursued his own creative agenda. In spring 1974, he recorded *On the Beach*, which would attract an equally vitriolic response when it was released during the CSNY tour. Few recognized at the time that, rather than betraying his lack of inspiration, Young was actually reinventing his aesthetic principles—the confessional spirit of his earlier songs mutating into a coruscating analysis of his psyche, the scene around him, and his adopted homeland. Both Nash and Crosby guested on the album, but neither of them seemed to comprehend the depth of Young's achievements during this period; indeed, Crosby would famously try to persuade Young not to play "your dark stuff," little realizing that darkness was where Young shone most brightly.

None of CSNY was at a commercial peak in spring 1974; but together the band still amounted to an event. Once the tour was announced, ticket sales were phenomenal, and the schedule now stretched from July into September. The one area it ignored, ironically, was Southern California, where what was proposed as the biggest single-day gathering in the state's history—a star-laden bill at the Ontario Motor Speedway, outside Los Angeles—was postponed twice before being abandoned. As the promoters claimed, there were vast logistical problems attached to the venue; but more damaging was the fact that only about 25 percent of the available tickets had been sold. Elsewhere across North America, potential receipts for the tour promised to top $10 million (thereby doubling the Dylan tour value). Spectacular support bills were arranged, with headline acts such as the Band and the Beach Boys prepared to forget their pride for a suitable share of the gate. (At the event, CSNY kept their distance from their peers on tour, never deigning to guest with them onstage or suggest any collaboration.)

All four men were adamant that the tour should not just celebrate the past, although that was what the majority of audience members might be expecting. "There's plenty of new songs too," Stills explained as rehearsals began. "We've all been writing a lot, especially Neil." But Stills and Nash had already recorded much of the material they had prepared for the abortive reunion the previous year. David Crosby had held his songs back, but they were few in number and—like much of his material—intensely personal in theme and style. Neil Young appeared to have struck an endlessly refilled seam of fresh material, even after recording three solo albums in eighteen months. But he had a very precise, and blinkered, view of what CSNY were, and what they did best. "I remember CSNY as a great acoustic thing, sitting around somewhere without the crowd," he would recall. When they worked with Neil Young, CSN relished the frenetic energy he brought to their electric sets. But in Young's eyes, electricity was always more powerful in the hands of Crazy Horse.

Young opened his ranch as a CSNY base camp in June 1974, a month ahead of the first show in Seattle. As Crosby recalled, "He built this full-size, forty-foot stage in the middle of a grove of redwoods, right across from his studios, so we could record." He and Nash drove in each day, while Stills stayed at Young's house, and "two chicks," as Crosby put it, helped Carrie Snodgress feed the band and crew. Nash admitted to being "apprehensive" about the relationship between Young and Stills until "we picked up our electric guitars and Stephen and Neil took a solo and looked each other in the eyes. If those two people get along, me and David are cool." Stills was ecstatic: "We haven't done the old tunes in years, man. It's almost like playing them for the first time."

The rehearsal stage was only a few yards from Young's home studio. In mid-June, he began to lay down a batch of demos—gentle, melodic, reflective, and light on the angst and trauma that was shaping his contemporary solo material. He cut several of them solo, or with stray members of the tour band: the lullaby "Barefoot Floors," "Homefires," "Love Art Blues," and "Love Is a Rose." With Crosby and Nash, he refined an acoustic arrangement of "New Mama." And on three tunes, including a reprise of "Love Art Blues" and the slender "Hawaiian Sunrise," he employed CSN's vocal harmonies in their natural state. All of their frail but tender humanity was apparent when Young eventually released the third CSNY collaboration from these sessions: "Sailboat Song" (aka "Through My Sails"). "When you hear how beautiful that track is," Joel Bernstein said, "you just feel so frustrated that they couldn't do that more often." Graham Nash's "Fieldworker," dedicated to the plight of migrant farmhands, was the only song written by CSN to be attempted in the studio. "They weren't trying to make an album," Bernstein recalled, "just hearing songs back to see how they sounded."

The balance of material reinforced Young's suspicion about the creative weight that he was being asked to carry. In "The Old Homestead," which he wrote in 1974 but didn't release for another six years, Young worked through the ambiguity he felt about being required to step back inside CSNY. "He still feels the pull," the song ended, half in longing, half regret. Yet in an unguarded moment with Jimmy McDonough, Young laid bare his dissatisfaction with CSN: "That tour was disappointing to me. I think CSN really blew it. Last time I played with 'em had been two or three years before that. They hadn't made an album, and they didn't have any new songs. What were they doing? How could they just stop like that?" The answer was simple: CSN had been waiting for Neil Young. It was he, after all, who had pulled out of the reunion sessions the previous year, forcing his colleagues to record without him if they ever wanted to see their songs released. But his comments revealed a gulf in understanding between the original trio and their maverick partner. Once CSN started working with Young, they assumed that CSNY was now the ultimate—the creative—priority. Young, meanwhile, took CSN at their original word: that they could work in whatever combination suited them at the time. In his mind, there was no reason CSN couldn't have made an album without him (and he was right). To which they would have countered: why make a CSN record when it could have been CSNY?

His jibe about their lack of material wasn't accurate, or fair, but it was understandable from a man for whom creativity was now as natural as eating or sleeping. Since the completion of *Déjà Vu*, Stephen Stills had issued five records, with songs still to spare; his output was the numerical equal of Young's. Graham Nash had two solo albums and a collaboration with David Crosby to his credit; Crosby, always the least prolific of the quartet, had completed one solo project of his own, plus collaborations with Paul Kantner and the Byrds. What was undeniably true, however, was that all three members of CSN had been revising or repeating their old creative moves; Young had set out on a course that they barely understood and had no way of matching. That is not to criticize the quality of CSN's individual work through the first half of the '70s; merely to note that Young changed profoundly, while they didn't. They were now four individuals, with little pretense of being a band. Once, Stephen Stills had been the unchallenged creative force within the quartet; now only Neil Young had the power to force *his* vision onto theirs.

Nothing exemplified that shift in influence better than "Pushed It Over the End" (or "Citizen Kane Junior Blues," as Young first announced the song at an unannounced cameo after a Ry Cooder gig in May 1974). It was a clumsy, raw-yet-compelling collage of musical fragments, and the same adjectives applied to the narrative, which touched on the brief terrorist career of kidnapping victim Patty Hearst, the rise of feminism, and Young's growing misgivings about his relationship with Carrie Snodgress. Translating it into a vehicle for CSNY was as much of a stretch as Stills persuading the band to tackle one of his excursions into Latin soul, or Crosby to drag Stills and Young into a wordless harmony chorale. But through willpower on his side, and willingness on theirs, Young coaxed CSN into creating arguably the most thrilling series of performances heard on the two-month tour. A full set of such experiments would have lived up to Nash's pre-tour demand for "something we mean now." Instead, CSN chose to rely on perhaps the only menu that a stadium crowd could appreciate: nostalgia.

> The first ten shows were like, "What song do you wanna do?" "I don't know. What do you wanna do?" "Who's got the list?" "What list? We don't use a list."
>
> —Stephen Stills

From the ranch, where they emerged with an estimated six hours of material at their command (approximately 20 percent of which was new), CSNY headed north to Seattle, and one of the few indoor shows on their summer schedule. At precisely 9:00 p.m. on July 9, 1974, Russ Kunkel,

Joe Lala, and Tim Drummond set up a Latin rhythm, the audience joined in, and even before Stephen Stills kicked into a superb "Love the One You're With," the evening was on fire. At 1:30 a.m. the following morning, the band were still onstage, as Graham Nash croaked his way through "Chicago" and David Crosby rasped out a harmony. "Seattle was really good," Crosby explained. "The feeling in the band is better than I've ever seen it, even better than it was when we started the first time." Across forty songs and nearly four hours of music, nobody's ego needed to be squashed, no one's excesses required toning down. Instead, CSNY indulged themselves in a feast of togetherness, tinged with self-doubt. ("How are we doing?" Stills asked nervously, three songs in. "We can't tell.")

If the initial burst of excitement died down during the hourlong opening set, the audience was roused to fresh heights of hysteria when CSN embarked on their familiar, perilous journey through the "Suite." Outdoors, the acoustic sets would often be lost in the wind; by comparison, even a basketball arena in Seattle felt like a backroom. By the time they'd each unveiled new songs and played every possible combination of three- or four-part harmony, ninety minutes had passed—virtually a show in itself. The Seattle crowd hushed themselves as Nash performed the delicate "Another Sleep Song" alone, squealed with delight as Crosby played Joni Mitchell's "For Free," and laughed along as Neil Young introduced what seemed to be a comedy number, "Long May You Run." Then there was another brief pause before the electric music resumed, and the band set out on its homeward run, stuffed with new material from Stills and Young. Crosby scorched his voice with an incoherent rant on "Long Time Gone" before Young delivered a searing double play of "Revolution Blues" and "Pushed It Over the End." As the long night neared its climax, CSNY burst into "Carry On," jamming with far more purpose and control than they had in 1970. "That was an amazing show," Nash said afterward. "We put everything into it."

That effort took its toll. Within the first twenty minutes, Nash had begun to growl and scream rather than sing, struggling to be heard over his colleagues' overamplified guitars. The louder he rasped, the more erratic his harmonies became. By the close Stills was also wailing way off-key. "They often had no floor wedges in front of them," Joel Bernstein recalled. "The monitors were all off at the side, so the band couldn't hear anything." One of the patterns for the tour was set: coke-ravaged tonsils, strained voices, erratic harmonies. Any or all of Nash, Stills, and Young might drift out of tune, leaving only Crosby reliable in front of a microphone. But not in Vancouver, second stop of the tour, where he was effectively silenced by the previous night's excesses in Seattle. His voice returned, but the longer the tour progressed, the more it lost its mellow purr, as if his throat was gradually becoming coated in steel wool.

Three shows in, CSNY arrived outdoors, facing seventy thousand fans at the Oakland Coliseum. Now the problem wasn't the voices, but the crowd—heat-baked, distracted, playful, and only vaguely in tune with the band. Even the "Suite," which could unite any audience in the world, was lost in a melee of complaints when kids at the front decided to stand up, blocking the view of the multitudes beyond. Amid the chaos, Neil Young had the courage and the nerve to sing the eight-minute "Ambulance Blues"—and the charisma to seize the audience's attention.

Almost every show had its moments of communion and bliss—a delicate "Simple Man" in Kansas City, the mass singalong of "Sugar Mountain" in Denver, a deliciously down-home "The Losing End" in Boston. All the way, Neil Young kept slipping fresh material into the set, and pulled it off; while CSN increasingly relied on the songs that they already knew their audience loved as the best way of calming the multitudes.

For anyone studying the band's precarious internal balance, perhaps the most gratifying aspect of the shows was their generosity of spirit. In 1970, when careers seemed to be at stake, every show seemed like a competition for the fans' attention. Four years later, with fifty thousand or more people every night paying ten dollars apiece to be in CSNY's company, their status was assured. If they weren't the biggest band in the world—the Rolling Stones could have outgrossed them if they'd tried, and probably Led Zeppelin, too—they were the highest paid. So, they could afford to lend each other their talents, to add an unrehearsed harmony, throw in some unexpected piano licks, or maybe bow out during someone else's solo spot to enhance their moment, rather than steal it. "The acoustic set was always spontaneous," Stills explained, "and it worked nicely with everybody slipping in little harmonies. I was the one that instigated that 'Don't light me' business. You'd go out and sing on someone's tune, and they'd bring the spotlights up. But I had them stop that." Lack of ego could be its own reward, the way they'd once imagined that ego would be.

On this tour, ego was satisfied in other ways—by the size of the crowds, the lure of the record-breaking gross, and the excess that surrounded the entire adventure. At its most mundane, the scale of CSNY's reunion could be calculated in numbers—the eighty or more crew and assistants (with varying skill sets) who accompanied them, the double-stage setup that allowed one team to be preparing the next show while the last was still in progress, the state-of-the-art amplification, even the quarter of a million dollars spent on Astroturf to protect the sports grounds from damage. Some of the budget was spent on vanity—the fifty thousand LP-sized CSNY Frisbees manufactured when the tour was announced, the bed linen branded with a CSNY logo designed by Joni Mitchell, the cooks and bartenders primed to cater to the musicians' culinary whims. There was a vast management structure to support: not just the headline promoters of the tour, but the local representatives of each venue, and the individual aides that each of the principals required—tour managers, financial managers, guitar techs, and assistants whose job was to respond instantly to every rock-star need, from a fresh supply of cocaine to a room upgrade at three in the morning. Wives and official girlfriends flitted in and out of the ensemble, replaced when necessary by the groupies who inevitably haunted the backstage area at every venue.

Cocaine, alongside various other mood enhancers and stabilizers, was written discreetly into the deal at each venue, available freely at the back of the stage for those regular moments when one or all of the band needed to be refueled. At least one of the three shows at the Landover Capital Centre, just southeast of the nation's seat of government, was marred by the installation of an onstage bar. Intended for the amusement of Stephen Stills, it was inevitably sampled by the entire band, even those who didn't usually drink to excess. The music that night was rather less coherent than usual. There was nothing strange about drink, drugs, or even groupies being available on demand at mid-1970s rock concerts;

what was different about CSNY in 1974 was the professional—indeed, industrial—method with which all these desires (and many more) were fulfilled. But sometimes, even the most hedonistic musicians wanted nothing more than to make music. A reporter backstage at one of the Oakland gigs overheard Stephen Stills being approached by a polite teenage fan: "Can I stay with you tonight—please, please?" But Stills already had a date across town, onstage at a Jerry Garcia gig. "Can I go jam first?" he asked the girl.

Onstage, CSNY bonded as never before, with a display of mutual congratulation and support often lacking in the past. First time around, Neil Young had been the mysterious outsider, an add-on to the chart-busting trio. In 1974, he was integral to almost every song, adding vocals, guitar, or piano to songs that had once been CSN territory, such as the "Suite." Offstage, however, Young separated himself from the rest of the band, traveling in a mobile home with his young son and a couple of trusted friends. This helped to maintain his sanity on the road but reinforced the impression that there were three together—and then there was one.

> There's no chance of this thing turning sour.
>
> —David Crosby, July 1974

> It seems like it's a little bit too good to be true.
>
> —David Crosby, August 1974

> We seem to have a two-month half-life, and then it blows.
>
> —David Crosby, September 1974

On what was, give or take a week, the fifth anniversary of Woodstock, CSNY performed at the Atlantic City Race Track. Like Woodstock, the event turned into an ordeal by summer storms, which drenched the three thousand or so fans who camped out to secure places in front of the stage. Their reward the following afternoon was to see Santana in an

insistent drizzle, which soon became a downpour. The audience improvised canopies to protect themselves, as the weather set in and CSNY
took the stage. Several thousand left early; several thousand more scaled
the fences and gained access for free. But the hard-core fans kept station
in front of the stage. "By the time we came on, they were soaked to the
skin," David Crosby said, "but they stayed for another four hours and
sang along on all the songs. Man, that really moved me. I almost cried."

Almost every outdoor show on the tour turned into an endurance test,
which was why many of the audience were as well fueled as the band. In
some cases, their consumption became perilous, not least in Cleveland,
where—another Woodstock throwback—announcers warned about the
"little blue pills" in circulation. That was where a twenty-three-year-old
man broke his back when he decided he could fly and threw himself
twenty-five feet off a ledge into the netting that was designed to protect
home plate. It broke under the strain, and he plummeted into the stands.
That same night, someone let off a skyrocket during the show, and a fire
broke out in the crowd. Back at Atlantic City, a navy sonar technician
died from a drug overdose (although his friends claimed that he'd been
hit by lightning). In Tempe, the mid-July Arizona heat was so intense that
the audience didn't respond to the electric sets because it required too
much energy to dance. Fans in Norfolk were kept sane and safe during
a heat wave by firemen regularly hosing them down. Throughout the
tour, as *Chicago Tribune* reviewer Lynn Van Matre complained, "After
four hours of music it's hard to think of anything much except how numb
your tail's getting. Some of the crowd fidgeted, a few started trickling out."

For the most part, the band were secluded from these inconveniences;
their biggest hassle was a set of malfunctioning monitors—or, in New
York, Neil Young's mobile home running out of gas midway across the
Fifty-Ninth Street Bridge. But there was one event that pierced their
armor. On the morning of July 29, waking up after a show at the Houston
University Stadium, they heard the news from London that their friend
and mentor Cass Elliot had died from heart failure in London, at just
thirty-two. Russ Kunkel, the tour's drummer, was married to Cass's sister,
Leah, so he booked an emergency flight home to Martha's Vineyard to
be at her side, before returning the next day for the show in Dallas. "We

were all heartbroken," Graham Nash recalled. "Without Cass, none of this would ever have happened."

Ten days later, the carnival had moved on to Jersey City, where the CSNY show coincided with the long-anticipated resignation of President Nixon. A giant TV screen was set up onstage to carry the speech, followed by a round of fireworks. Elliot Roberts interpreted the event as the culmination of a long relationship between the band and an American generation: "Now that the Nixon regime has come to a halt, and things are more or less out in the open, American youth feel like they've come to the end of a very traumatic era. All the riots, picketing, sit-ins, and student demonstrations now appear to have had some positive effect, and songs like 'Ohio' and 'Chicago'—which at the time we thought were just hollow voices on the wind—now take on even more meaning than before." CSNY opened their show in ebullient spirit, dedicating "Love the One You're With" to incoming President Gerald Ford. But their voices were rough after a two-night stand in Boston, and the famous harmonies descended into feline screeching. The celebratory audience didn't help, making so much noise that the band abandoned their acoustic set after five minutes, thereby cutting the show from three hours to two.

Midway through the tour, as the schedule reached New York, Crosby and Nash forced themselves out of bed before the second show at the Nassau Coliseum—an indoor venue that housed Crosby's favorite shows of the entire trip. They were put in front of a line of journalists at the Plaza Hotel, ostensibly to promote the new CSNY album. This was not a collection of fresh songs or even a hastily assembled souvenir of the first month's shows. *So Far* was nothing more enticing than a compilation of the band's first era, featuring four songs from the 1969 debut and five from *Déjà Vu*. The only enticements for consumers were a caricature of the band sketched by Joni Mitchell, and the inclusion of both sides of the "Ohio" single. Of the eleven tracks, Neil Young appeared on just four. In the *New York Times*, Henry Edwards noted sagely that there was no need for CSNY to extend their reunion into the studio "if their public is willing to pay for the same music every three years, as long as it is packaged with a new cover and a new album title." Apparently, they were, as *So Far* quickly became the bestselling LP in the US.

Two of the four recipients of this adulation played their part to perfection at the Plaza, Crosby proclaiming that the tour was "the most fun I've ever had on a stage in my whole life." But with fifteen years' hindsight, Elliot Roberts would recall: "It wasn't a very pleasant tour. The crew was underpaid. We were all overworked. The expenses were astronomical." None of those issues (bar the belated discovery that little of the $10 million gross would end up in their pockets) affected the principal players, for whom the crew were merely worker ants. Yet David Crosby would soon come to label the 1974 excursion "The Doom Tour." Graham Nash remembered it as "a bad experience" because "we had taken away part of our music . . . part of the atmosphere and the ambience, by not being able to make eye contact with our audience." And as early as 1975, Crosby confessed that they had been burning their audience by playing in stadiums: "You are stealing their money, frankly . . . If big is baseball stadiums, I'll pass. If that's the only way CSNY can play, CSNY will never play again." Even Neil Young, fingered by Crosby as one of the prime movers behind the stadium concept, agreed: "It's a huge money trip, which was the exact antithesis of what all those people are idealistically trying to see in their heads when they come to see us play."

There was no single event that transformed the relentlessly positive PR spokesmen of August 1974 into the fearless self-critics of the years ahead. CSNY never dipped beneath a certain standard of professionalism throughout the tour. (The vocal harmonies were another matter: when, forty years later, Graham Nash and Joel Bernstein prepared the *CSNY 1974* box set from the tapes recorded in New York, Washington, Chicago, and London, they had to apply subtle pitch correction to individual notes on almost every song.) So, what did happen, beyond the opportunity to escape the melee and apply a cold-eyed stare to two months of artificially stimulated experience? The answer wasn't so much what took place on the tour, but what came next—and what didn't.

> What's really horrible is when you think you've played a really hot gig, and then you listen to the tapes and it's just horrible.
>
> —Stephen Stills, 1975

The American tour schedule that had begun in Seattle on July 9 ended with the New York area's largest rock event of the summer, at Roosevelt Raceway on September 8. That final show took place a few hours after it was announced that the archenemy of the counterculture, Richard Nixon, had been granted a pardon by his successor for any crimes and misdemeanors he had committed in office. Nixon was gone, the boys were mostly home from Vietnam, but the Republican Party was still in power, and the war veterans had arrived in the States to find themselves a collective embarrassment—shunned by those who'd opposed the conflict and ignored by supporters of the war because it was obvious that, formal pronouncements to the contrary, the United States had lost.

That same feeling haunted the road. Elliot Roberts and David Geffen were eager to cash in on the financial potential of the CSNY reunion. The focus of this project was the long-delayed concert date in Southern California. In July 1974, fans were invited to put September 21 in their calendars—and then the date was abruptly canceled. The shocked promoters directed press inquiries to the CSNY camp, who were first silent, then enigmatic. But inevitably rumors crept out from those close to the band, claiming that CSNY would not be doing any further concerts after their solitary show in London on September 14. Gone from the schedule was not only Los Angeles, but a series of arena shows later in the year and the promise of an extensive visit to Europe, including some groundbreaking performances behind the Iron Curtain.

It would have been easy for the band's managers to plead ill health or exhaustion, obtain sick notes from friendly doctors, and slip out of CSNY's commitments that way. The fact that they didn't reflected their continued hope that the shows would take place after all. But eventually it became known (without ever being officially announced) that "internal problems" had forced the cancellation of all further dates. It was strongly hinted that one particular member of the band—the one, perhaps, who had insisted on keeping himself separate from the rest—had decided that the road had stretched far enough.

There was also, in Stephen Stills's version of the tour, an anonymous "someone" in the band who had insisted that the trip to London—the one-date European tour—should follow just six days after the last of the

American extravaganzas. "We should have had a week over there to relax and get ready," he complained. "We were dog-tired." The tension exploded on the flight over, when Stills and his wife had a heated argument. It proved to be so traumatic that it hung over the Wembley show, with the result that Stills delivered the most passionate performance imaginable of "Myth of Sisyphus," his torch ballad for a "Parisienne." Earlier, he had walked out to offer a harmony on Crosby's "Time After Time," tears in his eyes, clutching his baby son to his breast, sending out a message to one particular spectator.

That morning Stills had burst into Graham Nash's room at nine, waking him up after two hours' sleep, pulled back the curtains to reveal blue sky, and burbled like a child on Christmas morning, "Show me a cloud! Show me a cloud!" The curse of oversignificance that had surrounded their only previous London concert in 1970 had returned, and everyone felt it to some degree—none more than Graham Nash, who was rewarded with a standing ovation from seventy-two thousand fans at the end of "Our House." His three bandmates joined in. Later in the show David Crosby forced Neil Young to recognize a similar roar of approval from the crowd, after a raggedly emotional reading of "Don't Be Denied." That sense of intensity, a collective feeling that this gig really mattered, was evident from the start. But it was heightened by the peculiarly British fare available at the rear of the stage, where the cocaine was less than high-grade, throwing the band's emotional responses out of sync.

David Crosby exuded ecstasy, showing particular affection for his duet partner of 1968 and trying to provoke Stephen Stills into a sense of joy. But Stills was caught in some ghastly no-man's-land between passion and despair. There was a line in the "Suite"—"remember what we've said, and done, and felt about each other"—that almost begged for a moment of mutual affection. But at Wembley, Stills looked across at Crosby and gave a soul-stricken shrug, as if he no longer knew what he felt about anything or anyone. As he ended "Black Queen," he looked so distraught and disturbed that Crosby had to act as nursemaid to keep him onstage. There were psychodramas playing out everywhere that evening, never more poignantly than when Graham Nash laid his heart bare on a solo rendition of "Another Sleep Song," and his ex-lover Joni

Mitchell slipped onto the stage to vocalize the despair he'd felt when their relationship ended.

Mitchell's contribution to the night wasn't always so mellifluous, as she came close to sinking the "Suite" with her haphazard attempts at harmony. But her presence added to the notion that this was a troubled family gathered for one last reunion, uncertain whether this was a moment for anger, affection, or something far more ambiguous.

All this turmoil was played out in front of Stanley Dorfman's team of BBC cameramen. "There will be no live album," Elliot Roberts had pledged before the tour began. "It's not being filmed—we are not going to do any of those trips." CSNY had supposedly declined a lucrative offer from ABC-TV, because the network was unwilling to give them a "kill clause," whereby the band could pull out of the deal if their performance wasn't good enough. But eventually money spoke too loudly, and so a local crew was assigned to capture the show on film. There was only one problem: the technicians had been given no opportunity to plan their shoot—no setlist, and no clues as to where the cameras should be focused for each song. So Joel Bernstein, the official tour photographer, was positioned in the pit with a pair of headphones and a microphone link to the director. "It was my job to tell them what was likely to happen next," Bernstein recalled. "Obviously I knew the material, so I would say, 'Okay, there's a solo coming up in about ten seconds, and it's probably going to be Neil who takes it,' and Stanley Dorfman would relay that to the camera crew."

Unlike the Albert Hall show four years earlier, CSNY left the stage convinced that they had lived up to their reputation and delivered one of their finest shows ever. They were ferried to Quaglino's restaurant in central London for an end-of-tour celebration, where Stephen Stills and Neil Young took part in a cacophonous jam with Jimmy Page and John Bonham from Led Zeppelin and Rick Danko and Levon Helm from the Band. The next day they gathered one last time at a BBC screening room, where Dorfman showed them a rough mix of some of his Wembley footage. "They were sat there," remembered Joel Bernstein, "looking at the monitor, and they were really shocked at how bad they sounded—*really* shocked." "Graham Nash was almost in tears when he watched the video," Stills said. "He wanted to crawl under the carpet. He kept saying, 'What can I do now?' He was really furious. I told him, 'C'mon, man. The show's over. Forget it.'" But Stills didn't argue with Nash's perception: "We were awful . . . the harmonies were way off—really excruciating. I mean, painful. I just don't know how we got away with it." Neil Young concurred: "It is pretty obvious that we were either too high or just no good. I am saying too high." Only David Crosby was able to maintain some equilibrium in the face of the truth: "Wembley was quite a good concert in the general run of CSNY concerts. It had its faults—there were some harmonies that were horrendous, but that's bound to happen when you can't hear what you're doing." And he was right: compared to most of the earlier shows on the 1974 tour, Wembley was something of a triumph. The harmonies were wayward, but only in the final stretch; Graham Nash was, as ever, the chief culprit, but only because he couldn't hear the monitors. Otherwise, under all the stress, individual and collective, it was a remarkable performance. But reviewers didn't think so, chiding the group's mutual self-congratulation, their histrionics, their betrayal of the aging process and their hippie philosophy. And neither did the band, despite the fact that they would have been far more mortified if they had witnessed, for example, a film of their chaotic first show at Oakland Coliseum.

After the screening, the principals left in stunned silence. Joel Bernstein shared a car with Stills and Young. "They were both kind of withdrawn," he said, "not saying a word, and there was this real tension in the car. I can remember looking at them and thinking: 'Wow, these guys just broke up.'"

POSTSCRIPT

I've got a real problem. People seem to think CSNY was one of
the greatest fucking groups in the world.

—Stephen Stills, 1975

There was still work to do. "We just want to take a well-deserved rest,"
David Crosby said, "and then we'll go into the studio in November and
record an album." But they were now operating on Neil Young's calendar,
and he had other priorities. His relationship with Carrie Snodgress had
effectively collapsed during the final weeks of the tour. "There were a
lot of people in our lives," she said euphemistically, while swearing that
she had never been unfaithful to him. "I just wanted something different, and instead of spending the next five years getting real frustrated, I
left." Over a tortuous few months, the couple acted out their differences
by inadvertently causing each other pain. Amid the anguish, Carrie's
mother died.

That tragedy pulled Young away from his own recording sessions,
which he resumed in Nashville and Chicago during December 1974.
In little more than a week, he cut an entire album, *Homegrown*, that at
the time of this writing remains unreleased. It was full of songs steeped
in sadness and regret, acoustic ballads of the type that CSN could have
embellished. Instead, Young waited until this set was complete before
traveling back to San Francisco.

On December 14, CSNY gathered at Nash's home by Buena Vista Park
with Russ Kunkel and bassist Lee Sklar. They moved into the basement
studio and spent the next two days trying to revive the bonhomie with
which they'd approached their rehearsals in June. But, as Joel Bernstein

noted, "that studio was way too small a room for CSNY to work in. You could just about work in there with acoustic guitars, but with a rhythm section? Forget it. There was no baffling, no space with which to get a sound, and that was part of Neil's frustration. He told them it wasn't working and left." In his absence, CSN attempted to concoct a vocal arrangement for Stills's song "Guardian Angel," during which Stills and Nash staged a vitriolic argument. Stills lashed out with a razor at a master tape that held Nash's demo for "Wind on the Water," and Nash (with the help of his manager, Leo Makota) bodily ejected him from the house.

Somehow the quartet managed to regroup the following day at the Record Plant in Sausalito. There they cut a subdued, brooding version of David Crosby's "Homeward Through the Haze," a lyric that seemed to capture the sense of loss that divided 1970 from 1974. Young's guitar was almost inaudible, while Stills didn't add his voice to the harmonies. Over the next five days, they attempted to nail two further Crosby tunes, "Time After Time" and "Carry Me," and laid down the skeleton of Nash's angry lament for the fate of hunted sea mammals, "Wind on the Water." Only one Neil Young song was tackled during the sessions. Realizing that he might never be able to match the raw passion of his live-in-Chicago performance of "Pushed It Over the End," he brought along the multi-track from the tour tapes and set Crosby and Nash loose to decorate it with a harmony chorale.

Seized with uncharacteristic optimism, Stephen Stills put pen to paper at the Record Plant and sketched out the riches at their disposal for the elusive CSNY album. He added his own "One Way Ride," "Different Tongues," and "Soldier" to a list of songs first attempted on the tour and rounded off their collective repertoire with the mysterious "Artful Dodgers," a song that allowed each member of the band to describe the others' quirks and absurdities.

It was a final, doomed gesture of solidarity. After a week at the Record Plant, Neil Young wished his comrades good night—and never returned. "Even Neil was less than his usual nice self—Neil, Mr. Dependable," Crosby said wryly a few months later. Stephen Stills was left to reflect on the man he had nicknamed "the snake" for his ability to upset the Garden of Eden. When sessions at the Record Plant resumed after New Year

1975, there was no Young, no Crosby, no Nash—just Stills, readjusting to his increasingly familiar role as the outsider. "Looking back," Young considered a few months later, "we might have been wiser to do the album before the tour." But hindsight was no consolation for broken dreams.

Personal and professional were soon fogged in the same gloom. The most crushing blow was the murder of Amy Gossage by her brother, Eben, in February 1975. She and Nash were no longer an exclusive couple: the nineteen-year-old had recently been dating a fifty-six-year-old businessman, with whom a friend said she "played fantasy games of kings and queens and vampires and princesses." But Nash was still supportive, advising her when Eben had sought parole from his prison sentence. Her brutal, senseless death shook Nash so deeply that it overturned his sense of time: for many years he pointed to her loss to explain the air of depression that coated *Wild Tales*, which had been released a year before she died. Meanwhile, Neil Young and Carrie Snodgress finally parted company; David Crosby and Debbie Donovan had a daughter, Donovan, though Crosby had already left her for Nancy Brown; while Stephen and Véronique Stills were still playing out all the varieties of marital trauma in snow-ridden Colorado.

Yet amid this turmoil, all four men managed to create and prosper. Neil Young released *Tonight's the Night*, which was greeted by a Philadelphia newspaper as "an all-time-low" and "the worst vocal performance of the year," but was rightly acclaimed elsewhere as a masterpiece. He celebrated by reuniting with Crazy Horse in summer 1975 and releasing the more commercial *Zuma*, which included CSNY's June 1974 recording of "Through My Sails." Stephen Stills finally unveiled CSN's versions of "First Things First" and "As I Come of Age," as he launched a new career on Columbia Records with *Stills*—the unimaginative title belying the strength of the music within. "I just wanted to remind everyone that I didn't crawl into a hole and die," Stills admitted with the self-deprecation that would become his habitual stance toward the outside world.

Most surprisingly, perhaps, Crosby and Nash bloomed from a nostalgic acoustic duo into the heart of a mighty live band, the Jitters. Their 1975 album was *Wind on the Water*, every bit as powerful as *Zuma* or *Stills*. They also lent themselves out as backing vocalists for friends and ex-lovers, striking a particularly rich blend with James Taylor on his album *Gorilla*. Joni Mitchell, Elton John, Carole King, Art Garfunkel, and Jackson Browne would benefit in similar style, as Crosby-Nash became a slick LA watchword for studio sophistication. But the air of experimentation that had steered Crosby through his encounters with Paul Kantner and Jerry Garcia was not quite dead. He took part in the computerized, musique concrète soundscapes of Ned Lagin's *Seastones* project, both in the studio and onstage, while on the road he encouraged the Jitters to translate "Déjà Vu" from a West Coast jazz tune into a free-form extravaganza.

Through all of this endeavor, the media kept informing CSN (and, to a lesser extent, Y) that they were a pale shadow of the real deal. The four musicians could barely venture out in public without being asked when CSNY were getting back together. Stills provided the definitive riposte: "We're not ready to tour again, and the public isn't ready to see us so soon." His heart was set on self-fulfilment. "There's a lot of people who are gonna do a fast fade soon," he said prophetically, "and I don't want to be one of them."

Yet he continued to hanker after the danger and excitement of a creative relationship with Neil Young. The two men kicked around the idea of making an album together. "We'll terrorize the industry," Young laughed. Stills picked up that promise and kept repeating it in public, with the result that he was the one whose hubris was mocked when the industry wasn't terrorized. Like moths returning to the flame that will singe their wings, Crosby and Nash were soon sucked back into the same orbit.

What was briefly promoted as a CSNY album began as a Stills-Young project, to which Young brought only his slightest material. Stills was not flush with new songs either, having just set a dozen aside for a solo record. To spice up a collaboration that was catching fire only in their joint imagination, they invited Crosby and Nash down to Criteria in Florida to contribute vocal finesse and perhaps a couple of songs. The duo also had a record in preparation, but typically set their agenda aside in search of an ever-more-elusive treasure.

Crosby succeeded in upsetting one of the young women who looked after studio visitors, after he "yelled at Jeri for an hour because his artichokes were overcooked." But with their customary panache, he and

Nash added harmonies to the tracks Stills and Young had completed and ventured to introduce some of their own material. One song, "Taken at All" (issued on the *CSN* box set in 1991), a melancholy postscript to the 1974 tour ("we lost it on the highway") was given the authentic ranch treatment, as Young forced them to cut it live in a single take, before all four overdubbed harmonies. On Stephen Stills's "Black Coral" (premiered on his retrospective CD box, *Carry On*), Crosby's and Nash's vocals achieved an emotional resonance barely surpassed in their own work. But then, with the inevitability of a biblical prophecy, the pair were called away for the final mixes on their own album. Their sometime bandmates made the fateful decision to strip out Crosby's and Nash's harmonies and songs, and release what was left as the Stills-Young album it was always intended to be.

Reluctant even then to blame Neil Young, Graham Nash let forth a sustained barrage of criticism aimed at Stills: "I think it's his cock he keeps putting in the meat grinder. Stephen's totally stupid, man . . . I'll thump that fucker right in the nose when I see him again." He concluded more evenhandedly: "I see Stephen's career going downhill and I see Neil's career going downhill, and I don't give a shit. I WILL NOT work with them again." He trained his disappointment into a song entitled "Mutiny" and took a more practical revenge by refusing to let Young use the CSN-enhanced version of "Pushed It Over the End" on his *Decade* retrospective.

Nash's sense of schadenfreude must have been gratified when Stills and Young set out on tour together and attracted mediocre reviews (Stills being the chief target). In one of the most crushing maneuvers in rock history, Young abandoned Stills on the road in late July, pleading a throat injury. Young left his friend a pointed message — "Funny how some things that start spontaneously end that way. Eat a peach." — thereby ensuring that he would be seen as the comic hero of the piece, Stills as the buffoon. "I have no future," Stills said poignantly when approached for a comment. He attempted to keep the tour afloat on his own, then went home to Colorado to find that Véronique wanted a divorce. Young rested his voice for a couple of weeks before returning to the stage without Stills.

When their duo album, *Long May You Run*, finally emerged in

September, it was like a coffin arriving too late for a funeral. Critics almost universally panned Stills's work on the record, which was never less than professional, and lauded Young's, which rarely broke a sweat. To complete the circle of reincarnated hopes, Nash and Crosby allowed Stills to join them onstage in LA, mere weeks after Nash had declared their relationship over; and by the end of the year a Crosby-Nash recording project evolved seamlessly into a long-delayed trio album.

Though the undeniably enjoyable *CSN* (1977) turned the magical inspiration of *Crosby, Stills & Nash* (1969) into solid craftsmanship, it still outsold any of the individual CSNY projects since *Harvest*. It also allowed the trio a rare escape from their eternal obeisance to Neil Young, as they created a radio-friendly sound that owed nothing to their errant friend. "Neil is Neil, and CSN is CSN," Stills told Cameron Crowe. "Neil does what the hell he wants." "I don't know how to deal with my relationship to Neil at all," added David Crosby. For the first time in public, Young was asked to confront the balance in his life between self-expression and selfishness. "I see people really hurt by what I do, by the fact that I have to choose one person, when three want to do something," he conceded. "I say, 'You know, I'm just on my own course here. I'm likely to be gone at any time.'" As Stills admitted, "The pressure for that group [CSNY] to happen again is a destructive force on all of us." But equally destructive for Stills was the loss of confidence he had suffered at the hands of his friend. If Neil Young no longer believed in him, then what was he worth? The man who had filled the press at the start of the decade with boasts about his talent was now dismissing his solo career as "mostly garbage." He could at least cling to the remnants of his marriage, after Véronique Sanson postponed her calls for a divorce, and the couple celebrated their fifth anniversary with a belated honeymoon in Hawaii.

Though Crosby, Stills, and Nash (to varying degrees) had been hurt and even scarred by the way Young had treated them, they were far from blameless. It was they, after all, who had chosen to grant him such an elevated position in their lives—to allow him the power to hurt and harm them. In doing so, they had also undercut their own stature in the music industry, both as soloists and as a trio. As their friend Joel Bernstein reflected, "None of them understood that by making CSN into CSNY, the CSN brand would be diminished from that point on. Nobody had any grasp of the implications of that choice. With hindsight, from CSN's point of view it was just bad thinking to bring Neil into the band—despite all the great music they made together. Think back to the way people reacted when they first heard CSN in Laurel Canyon. People were completely overwhelmed by them—by their sound, their songs, their harmonies. Why would you create something so magical and then immediately change it into something different?" Nor did it help when Stephen Stills described CSNY as "a full-time job," while "when it's just CSN, we can move in and out of it like an old shoe." Comments like that simply reinforced the consensus that Young's music was vital, raw, spontaneous, and challenging, whereas CSN's was as cozy and comfortable as slippers. The truth was that CSN and Young were working on different artistic principles, to starkly contrasting ends. By the late 1970s, Stephen Stills was relieved to report, "We don't get as many 'Where's Neil?' questions on tour as we used to. I think people are finally getting the message."

But there was another message that was impossible to ignore. Throughout the late 1970s, Neil Young was constantly creative and innovative. Individually and collectively, CSN were struggling to produce anything but nostalgia. David Crosby's cocaine habit had mutated from decadent to life-threatening, while Stephen Stills's response to the final collapse of his marriage in 1978 was also excessive. "Sometimes I think I'm the only sane one in the band," Graham Nash remarked. "I think Stephen and David are mad."

Crosby stopped writing songs entirely but cobbled together a solo album from 1970s leftovers; his record company refused to release it. Stills learned the hard way that Neil Young could confound audience expectations, yet he wouldn't be allowed to. When he tried to keep pace with contemporary pop trends on his *Thoroughfare Gap* album, a canny blend of disco and R&B, he was derided or ignored. Nash pursued a more familiar route, but his intriguing *Earth and Sky* album suffered a similar fate. It was at this moment that Neil Young chose to release the superb *Rust Never Sleeps* album, in which he updated the social critique and self-criticism of *On the Beach* for the era of punk rock. It included

"Thrasher," in which he recounted his relationship to CSN in obscure imagery, before suddenly cutting through the ambiguity: "I got bored and left them there / They were just dead weight to me." Asked about a CSNY reunion, Young shrugged: "It's possible. Who cares?"

As David Crosby's autobiography *Long Time Gone* chronicled in lurid detail, his only goal in the early 1980s was to get his next hit of freebase. Personal relationships, contracts, creativity—they were all sacrificed to the pipe. For Stills and Nash, CSN was like being shackled to a corpse; but the pretense that they were still the representatives of the Woodstock Nation guaranteed them a healthy income, and Crosby the cash to maintain his crippling habit.

When the almost-Crosby-free CSN album *Daylight Again* was released in 1982, Graham Nash was asked why they hadn't invited Neil Young to take part. His reply testified to the grotesque imbalance of their relationship. "We're afraid to approach him," Nash said. "We're so afraid of rejection. We're scared of him. I swear we are. Can you believe that? We've had so much heartbreak with him. Who wants to be rejected by a mad musician?" But despite everything, Nash admitted: "Every day I expect Neil to call. It's my fantasy." It was the prayer of the jilted teenager alone in his bedroom—that one day his true love would come back. But as Nash mused: "Maybe Neil doesn't think CSN music is very good. I haven't asked him." At an Indianapolis concert the following year, Young sarcastically mentioned "my old buddies a long time ago. They couldn't be here tonight 'cos some of them can't walk too good anymore." Then he sang "Helpless."

By then, David Crosby had spiraled into the series of drug busts and weapons charges that would eventually lead him to a Texas jail. A judge in California told him, "The only good Crosby is dead," and David seemed determined to fulfill that prophecy. "He will either do the [prison] time," Graham Nash said sadly, "which I don't believe, or he will blow himself away, or he will [leave] the country."

The extent of Crosby's decline was apparent to a global audience on July 13, 1985, when Crosby, Stills & Nash were invited to perform at the Live Aid concert in Philadelphia. Also on the bill was Neil Young, and Nash persuaded him to overlook Crosby's plight and use the commercial power of the CSNY brand to raise more cash for the starving in Africa. Like other acoustic acts on the bill, they were ill served by the stadium's sound system. "It was very embarrassing," Young said later. "It was totally untogether." But as Crosby explained, "Absolutely toasted as I was, only a couple of hours before that, we had been in a dressing room and we sang together, the four of us, and we sounded good. We did 'Only Love Can Break Your Heart' and it was beautiful."

That glimmer of hope in Young's backstage trailer was enough to persuade the Canadian to make a remarkable promise: a full CSNY reunion. All it needed was "for Crosby to clean up his act, leave the cocaine connections behind. If he does, I'll join them, and it will show that no matter how bad off you are, you can pull yourself together." Later that year, Crosby emerged from prison clean of freebase, and Young came through. A brief reunion formed the emotional climax of the 1986 Bridge School Benefit, and CSNY continued to gather occasionally at charity events, their very survival a trigger for relieved nostalgia.

"People love to cling to their memories because they're scared of the future," Graham Nash said in 1987. To a certain extent, almost every act associated with the 1960s was now a vehicle for remembering the past rather than remaking it. "There's no getting around the fact that a CSNY tour would be a nostalgia tour to a great degree," Neil Young declared in 1988. "CSNY is Woodstock—it's that era, that whole generation."

The following year, Bob Dylan, Lou Reed, and Young himself would all reemerge from periods of musical torpor with albums that revitalized their creativity. But when CSNY went into the studio to cut the reunion record that Young had promised Crosby, innovation and artistry were in short supply.

American Dream had no core, no heart, no community, no soul. Whatever its minor pleasures (and there were several), it didn't sound like a record by a band, or even the work of four creative songwriters pushing themselves to break new ground. David Crosby was restricted to just two songs out of fourteen: "I decided not to argue about it," he explained. "I was just pleased to be there at all." Neil Young's material was, for the most part, inconsequential; and Stephen Stills, the one-man tornado of 1969–70, was unable to contribute anything like a significant song. "Stephen spent too much time in the bathroom," one participant in the sessions said euphemistically. Challenged about his lack of creative input on the album, Stills merely said: "Well, it was like I was there, but I wasn't *there*." That much was obvious from the record, and CSNY without a functioning Stephen Stills was not CSNY at all. "How could they let *American Dream* out as the follow-up to *Déjà Vu*?" Joel Bernstein asked. "I can't believe one of them didn't say, 'Hey, this isn't good enough for CSNY.'" The record's impact was brief and unspectacular in the US; virtually zero in Britain, where the Atlantic Records press office denied all knowledge of CSNY's existence in the week their album was due for release.

That indifference was reinforced when CSN delivered their first studio record in eight years, the abysmal *Live It Up* in 1990 (or *Live It Down*, as Stills retitled it). Its cover art betrayed the album's lack of imagination. For years, they were incapable of finding a photograph of the trio that all three of them liked. As a result, they issued a series of records bearing some of the most embarrassing artwork in pop history.

Back on the road, however, CSN found a sense of unity that enabled them to make their best album since 1977, *After the Storm*. It peaked at number 98 on the US chart in 1994, proof that their core audience, the people who continued to flock to their live shows, were no longer buying records—or, at least, not records by CSN. Ironically, their live shows during this decade were more consistent—and consistently excellent—than most of their appearances during the 1970s, thanks to the vast improvement in onstage monitors. Increasingly, though, audiences were celebrating the band's survival, and their own, more than their music.

As the decade ended, there was one final attempt to refashion CSNY as a living unit: an album overoptimistically titled *Looking Forward*. It began as a CSN record, to which Young brought several acoustic tracks he'd already recorded for his own purposes. So, the project was a compromise, at best, with Young restricting the nature of his input (none of the raucous energy he still displayed onstage) but still carrying more weight in the decision-making process than his colleagues. Individually, almost every song had its merits, but together they added up to something pleasant but inconsequential—less a manifesto for a new century than a reminder that, despite their best efforts, all four men were still alive.

In 2000, CSNY finally achieved what they hadn't for twenty-six years: a concert tour of the United States. There were no stadiums, no abrupt departures halfway through the schedules, just a collective dedication to proving that the quartet had once meant something to their generation and could still deliver on their original promise. They also took advantage of the massive hike in ticket prices for veteran acts, triggered by the Eagles' 1994 reunion tour. Highest-priced seats for CSNY in many venues topped the $150 mark. Fortunately, the music went a long way toward justifying the expense. Neil Young's presence brought a ferocious energy to the stage, spurring Stephen Stills in particular into his fieriest guitar work in years. But nobody attempted to disguise the fact that the entire operation was being run on Young's terms: he vetoed the band members, had the casting vote over what they played, and decided when it would happen again.

That was in 2002, when there was no CSNY record to promote, so instead the band became a vehicle for Young to sell arguably his least impressive album to date, *Are You Passionate*. The concerts were as passionate and splendid as before, but the joy was in seeing the past come back to life—the communion between band and audience, and among the audience themselves.

And then there was 2006. By then, Stephen Stills had been an active supporter of the Democratic Party for more than thirty years, while David Crosby and Graham Nash continued to lend their names and their voices to causes that sometimes included specific Democrat candidates. But it was Neil Young—excoriated in Europe after he provocatively made the case for supporting President Ronald Reagan in the mid-1980s—who responded to President George W. Bush's handling of the US war in Iraq with an entire album of hastily assembled, entirely unambiguous protest songs.

It was perhaps inevitable that he would call on CSN to help him carry those rather banal tunes around the United States. The 2006 Freedom of Speech tour offered exactly what Graham Nash had demanded in 1980, when he said, "If we did fifteen brand-new songs, there's no nostalgia involved." Musically, this was by far the least interesting of the band's three twenty-first-century concert outings. But, as Young's documentary film *CSNY/Déjà Vu* demonstrated, the tour proved to be a powerful piece of performance art—a method of confronting their nostalgic fans and forcing them to face up to what they, and the band, had become. Here were the archetypes of the Woodstock generation, exemplars of the counterculture, princes of late-1960s idealism, still confronting the US government and spotlighting its crimes, just as they had done with Richard Nixon. But whereas in 1970 there was scarcely a soul in a CSNY arena who would have disagreed with the sentiments of "Ohio," in 2006 the very notion that a bunch of old hippies might get up in public and sing "Let's Impeach the President" proved to be as divisive as the mention of Hillary Clinton's name a decade later. As David Crosby said, "Who are these people who come to a CSNY show and complain that we're political? We've *always* been political." But the politics of one generation did not automatically translate to another.

All of those in the audience, those who stood up and roared their approval and those who stomped out, showing the band the finger, would have imagined themselves the inheritors of the Woodstock Nation and the freedoms it promised. But what the Freedom of Speech Tour proved is that people can share a culture without sharing its values; can follow the same crusade without agreeing on its legacy; can inhabit the same nation and preach the same slogans, but mean something entirely different from their friends and neighbors. In their collective passion and inability to avoid conflict, Crosby, Stills, Nash & Young had perhaps become a more accurate reflection of their generation, their country, and their times than they could ever have imagined. There is, after all, nothing more beautiful than harmony—and nothing more fragile.

In August 2019, many of the original musicians, and many of the millions who claim to have been among the five hundred thousand who watched them, will likely make the pilgrimage to the Woodstock site, to celebrate the fiftieth anniversary of the world's most famous rock festival. There will be the usual excessive hype around the Woodstock Nation, as well as plenty of expensive trivia available to satisfy the consumerist urges of the baby-boomer generation: vast CD box sets, books, and the latest in a long succession of "definitive" extensions of the original *Woodstock* movie.

Financially and nostalgically, this would be the perfect moment for CSNY to capitalize on their indelible link to the festival by regrouping for the anniversary concert. First, however, they would have to soothe the deepest and most enduring wounds ever to afflict their tempestuous personal relationships—the gulf between the trio of Stills, Nash, and Young on one flank, and David Crosby in defiant isolation on the other.

Crosby provoked the feud in 2014 with some graceless comments about Neil Young's relationship with the actor Daryl Hannah. Although Crosby duly apologized to Young and Hannah, Young sealed the door shut on any further work with CSN. The financial implications of that decision were not lost on Stills and Nash, which helped to sour relations within CSN.

Meanwhile, Graham Nash had become the second CSNY member to abandon a lengthy (and ostensibly cloudless) marriage for a much younger woman. During CSN's late-2014 US tour, Nash could be overheard off-mike, telling his best friend David Crosby to "fuck the fuck off" as Crosby teased him once too often about his thirty-five-year-old girlfriend. A year later, when CSN played their final shows in Europe, the apparently unbreakable camaraderie between Crosby and Nash had disintegrated as publicly as Nash's marriage. One night in London, Nash prowled back and forth across the stage, his face a study in thunder, while Crosby stood in front of him, informing the crowd that at least *he* was still keeping faith with his marriage vows. By the time the tour ended, Crosby had told his colleagues that their artistic inertia was stifling his own creativity, effectively calling time on CSN. Their farewell performance on December 2015 was catastrophic: a tuneless rendition of "Silent Night" at the National Christmas Tree Lighting near the White House.

Nash responded early to Crosby's departure with a volley of savage interviews, declaring that Crosby had "ripped the heart out" of CSN and CSNY, and that he would never work with Crosby again as long as he lived. In one journalistic encounter, Nash was even quoted as suggesting that his old friend's artistic abilities were now impaired. Crosby responded with (for him) rare restraint. With fresh musical comrades (among them his son, James Raymond, unacknowledged at birth but reconnected with his father in the mid-1990s) Crosby unleashed a flurry of admirable new albums, which offered an articulate defense of his undimmed powers. His 2018 collaboration with three much younger musicians, *Here If You Listen*, proved to be his most consistently rewarding work since his solo debut, forty-seven years earlier.

Despite occasional hints at rapprochement from both sides, the Crosby-Nash impasse continued throughout 2017 and 2018. Crosby was also still estranged from both Stills and Young, though the two ex–Buffalo Springfield comrades could still occasionally be glimpsed onstage together. All four men insisted that there was no prospect of a CSNY reunion. Yet by the time this book is published, it would not be a surprise if friendship, mutual regret, the quartet's shared contempt for the forty-fifth president of the United States—and, of course, the promise of lavish financial rewards—had encouraged this most protean of musical ensembles to round up their forces for one last celebration of everything that CSNY once stood for—and will always represent in the history of American culture.

JOURNEY THROUGH THE PAST

Together or alone, CSNY have been responsible for some of the most thrilling musical moments of my life. I will never forget Stephen Stills reinventing the language of the guitar during his "Suite: Judy Blue Eyes" solo at my first CSN show; Graham Nash scaling the octaves like an acrobat in the final bars of an awe-inspiring "Guinnevere"; David Crosby roaring a defiant "Almost Cut My Hair" in the city that once sent him to jail; or Neil Young sculpting a "Tonight's the Night" so long and disturbing that it might still be echoing today through another dimension. But nothing has touched me as deeply as the glorious rush of their voices raised in harmony. If there's a more thrilling sound in creation, I haven't found it yet.

I wouldn't have considered writing this book if I didn't love these musicians, and their music. But any close observer of this unpredictable and often catastrophically self-sabotaging group of songwriters has to confront the gulf between the spirit of their songs and the way they have conducted themselves in private and in public. Their songs are anthems of love, hope, and the power of togetherness; their career is testament to humanity's frailty in the face of temptation and egotism.

In their own attempt to confront this enigma, three members of CSNY have already published memoirs. They have laid themselves bare in interviews and confessional songs. Yet despite all those words, all those explanations and excuses, I still felt as if the real story of this crusading, troubled band remained tantalizingly out of reach.

That was my quest. I wanted to find exactly who these four mercurial musicians were: where they came from, how they evolved, how they came together, and most important how they interacted with each other. Besides using my own interviews with them and their peers, I have delved deep into audio and video archives, which preserved almost sixty years of their music. I also exhumed decades of CSNY press coverage, because the media, and print journalism in particular, came to play a crucial role in the band's career. Any history of public figures is also necessarily a history of their reputation, and few acts have been raised so high and then plunged so low by critical opinion. Each of the quartet has been hurt and bewildered by the way they were handled in the press, and those often-brutal verdicts left scars on the men and their music.

If you write about the past, even the recent past, you face the challenge of who and what to believe. As David Crosby used to say onstage in the heady and high 1970s, "Memory is the first thing to go." That invariably amused fans who were probably almost as stoned as he was, and fertilized his well-tended image as the most artificially enhanced man in rock.

Even without cellular deterioration, the human memory is fallible, inaccurate, vague, in a state of constant flux, and susceptible to endless revision. We can accept that other people interpret events in vastly different ways from ourselves. What's less comfortable for our delicate egos is that our own foolproof brains are just as capable of reinvention and plain misremembering.

The truth is that once we move beyond facts that can be checked or confirmed by documentary sources, all of our glimpses of the past are fragmentary. Imagine, then, the plight of those who are condemned to live in the past—to retrieve it for our collective entertainment. Imagine being asked questions (usually the same questions) about events that grow hazier every hour, and being expected to deliver verifiable Truth about a Past that can only be a *Matrix*-style simulation.

The first time I interviewed David Crosby, he shuffled into the room with Graham Nash, twenty minutes late, grumbling under his breath, and carefully avoiding any eye contact. Nash, ever the professional, shook my hand warmly and apologized for his friend. "David is suffering from jet shock," he explained. Crosby reacted instantly to the mention of his name. "Ask me some questions if you fucking dare," he snapped, still staring at the floor.

It was a moment for humor or bust. "Sounds like it's time to ask Crosby the Woodstock question," I said to Nash. Crosby spluttered slightly, then looked at me for the first time and couldn't prevent the sparkle from creeping back into his eyes. "Yeah," he muttered, "or what about 'When are you guys getting back together?' That's the other one people always ask us, even when we're all in the same room."

Any celebrity lives under the same curse: being asked to relive solitary moments from a hectic lifetime of experience and make them new. With each retelling of what really happened at Woodstock, another sliver of genuine memory is shaved away, and replaced by the pseudo-memory of myth. That's why most celebrities rely on a selection of well-worn anecdotes: it's easier to remember those than it is to wade through decades of mist in search of an authentic reminiscence of the past. In any case, "authentic" memory has long since slipped away. Answer the same question every day for fifty years, and soon all you can remember is what you said yesterday.

With Crosby, Stills, Nash, and Young, the issue is complicated manifold by the fact that four individuals with turbulent pasts and rampant egos have often sparred over the same raw material. A classic example is the disagreement about when and where Crosby, Stills, and Nash first sang together. For anyone who has tried to locate verifiable facts amid the band's collective fog of misinformation, it's strangely gratifying to learn that as early as December 1968, CSN were unable to agree on a mutually satisfactory answer to this question, and the three men have been squabbling about it ever since.

Crosby, Stills, Nash, and Young are all notoriously uncertain about the past, but only occasionally admit it. Of the quartet, Graham Nash has often been the least reliable, not because he has a worse memory than his former partners, but because he has always been more generous in granting interviews and has offered more hostages to fortune. As an example, he has variously claimed to have written "Teach Your Children" as early as 1967 and as late as 1971. (And why should he care that it was actually 1968? What's important to him is *how* he wrote the song, not *when*.) Even close proximity to events did not always improve his recall. The day after the conclusion of CSNY's six-night run at the Fillmore

East in 1970, Nash recounted memorable moments from the shows in an interview—and got the chronology completely wrong. Does it matter? Only if you like to believe everything you are told.

The same applied to David Crosby, who at least had the grace to admit that "I'm no good with years and dates, man." I initially met him at a promotional party for his first autobiography, at the end of which he fell into a heated argument with a friend of mine about whether or not he had ever written a song called "Psychodrama City." He had, and I knew it, but I timidly kept out of the fight to avoid upsetting one of my musical heroes. What I remember more than my cowardice is Crosby's absolute conviction in his false memory and his refusal to consider backing down. My friend could have played him a tape of the song there and then, and Crosby would still have insisted that he was right.

As for Stephen Stills, he would remember that he was in Los Angeles when he heard Jimi Hendrix had died, or at his mother's house in San Francisco, but he was actually in the Rocky Mountains of Colorado. He had an authentic memory of his sense of bereavement but could no longer summon up the circumstances. Distanced by age from the more turbulent episodes of his youth, Stills came to dismiss discussion of his misdemeanors as "just *gossip*," in a tone that carried its own "Do Not Enter" sign. His interview currency was impressions, not facts; emotional shockwaves from the past, not statements about it. His dry, deadpan humor and often-combative nature could lead him to goad companions with tales of his service in Vietnam during the 1960s, which in turn would lead them, and all those who transmitted the stories, to conclude that Stills was certifiably insane. Graham Nash may once have mused that "if Stephen was not Stephen Stills, he would have been committed long ago." But the man I've met over the decades has not been crazy, merely erratic and wounded by events—many of which, located in his childhood, were utterly beyond his control.

And Neil Young? As befitted a man who built a career around ambiguity and lack of commitment, he was the first member of CSNY to admit—or plead—frailty of memory. As early as 1970, he would lazily deflect questions about Buffalo Springfield, who had split just two years earlier: "Well, I can't really remember, man. That's back so long." In

1975 he admitted to the teenage journalist Cameron Crowe, who skill-fully elicited Young's most revealing confessions: "Just keep one thing in mind—I may remember it all differently tomorrow."

Unlike his peers, Young rarely sought to offer the press variations on well-practiced tales. Perhaps the closest he came was a familiar story about sharing a pickup with Jimi Hendrix at the Woodstock festival. But when Sylvie Simmons of *Mojo* magazine urged him to repeat the yarn in 1997, Young was honest enough to refuse: "You know, to tell the truth, it's been so long since it happened . . . I don't know, I can't remember. You know, at first it was pretty clear, and then people started giving me so many different versions of how it was, I started going, 'Well, what do I know?' I'm getting so vacant." Of course, by the time he came to write his first book, fifteen years later, he trotted out the anecdote as if he had just stepped off the truck, because publishers don't like their memoirists to advertise their evasion and amnesia too blatantly.

As if CSNY weren't prey to their own erratic recall, their fame and its excesses left them open to exaggeration, invention, and worse from those who spent time in their orbit (or claimed they did). The four men have been so open about their dalliances with women, narcotics, and herbal stimulants that people will believe almost anything about them. All of them—but especially David Crosby and Stephen Stills—have become such powerful symbols of hedonism and egomania that any story about them can easily be embellished by quadrupling the quantity of drugs, doubling their unpleasantness, or simply substituting their names for those of Jimi Hendrix, Jim Morrison, or Keith Richards in rock's most jaded tales of debauchery.

All of which is an explanation of why, in writing about CSNY, sharing time with them and their peer group as a journalist and now biographer, and endlessly revisiting their lives and their music, I have chosen to mix my curiosity with a healthy dose of skepticism. In my experience, contemporary accounts of events are almost always more accurate and reliable than recollections delivered decades later. Hindsight may improve your understanding of your life, but the passage of time can also distance you from its reality.

ACKNOWLEDGMENTS

It has been my privilege to spend time with David Crosby, Stephen Stills, and Graham Nash in a variety of settings over the past thirty years, and to interview them together and alone on many occasions. Our communications have sometimes extended to phone calls and emails. As a lifelong fan of their music, I will never forget the first time I sat at a table, looked around, and counted off: "Crosby . . . Stills . . . Nash . . . and me." It was a surreal moment.

I have been fortunate enough to meet and interview many people who were vital to CSNY's career, including their original drummer, the late Dallas Taylor; the man who signed them to Atlantic Records, the late Ahmet Ertegun; their close friend (closer to some than others) Joni Mitchell; and their archivist, photographer, musical collaborator, and friend, Joel Bernstein.

My conversations over many years with other musical comrades and friends were also invaluable in my research: from the Byrds, Roger McGuinn and Chris Hillman; from the Hollies, Allan Clarke, Bobby Elliott, Tony Hicks, the late Eric Haydock, Bernie Calvert, and Terry Sylvester; plus "Heavy Lenny" Bronstein, Jackson Browne, Denny Bruce, Judy Collins, Craig Doerge, Micky Dolenz, Art Garfunkel, David Gates, Alan Gerber, Richie Havens, the late Levon Helm, Judy Henske, Tom Jones, the late Paul Kantner, Phil Kaufman, Al Kooper, Michael Lang, Bernie Leadon, Country Joe McDonald, Barry Miles, Ralph Molina, Mark Naftalin, Michael Nesmith, Andrew Loog Oldham, Van Dyke Parks, Al Perkins, the late John Phillips, Terry Reid, the late Ron Richards, Rick Rubin, Tom Rush, the late Leon Russell, Bill Siddons, Billy Talbot, the late Derek Taylor, James Taylor, Jimmy Webb, Bob Weir, the late Paul Williams, Baron Wolman, and Bill Wyman.

Thanks also to those who provided additional insight or connections down the years: Bill Allison, Stuart Batsford, Tim Chacksfield, Chris Charlesworth, Barbara Charone, John Einarson, Stefano Frollano, Mike Heatley (EMI Records), Clinton Heylin, Paul Higham (and everyone else on the Lee Shore discussion group), Sarah Hodgson, Alan Jenkins, Michael Jensen, Kathy Lafferty at Kenneth Spencer Research Library, Dave Lemieux at dead.net, Pete Long, Francesco Lucarelli, Greil Marcus, Jim Marshall, Dennis McNally, Lee Ellen Newman, Tony Nourmand, Jeff Pevar, Sally Reeves, John Robertson, Johnny Rogan, Ellen Sander, Jeff Tamarkin, John Tobler, Kieron Tyler, Lucien van Diggelen, Herman Verbeke, Carey Wallace, Richard Wootton, and Dave Zimmer.

Thanks also to Andrew Sclanders (beatbooks.com) for opening his archive to me one more time; likewise to Clinton Heylin and Scott Curran; and to the staff of the British Library, the National Sound Archive, and Senate House Library in London.

Of all those mentioned, special thanks must go to Joel Bernstein for his generosity and patience in answering hours' worth of queries about CSNY and their archives, and for his passionate regard for the musicians and their work. He was able to unpack many mysteries about the details of their career—but any mistakes I've made in interpreting those mysteries are entirely mine.

On a personal level, I'd like to thank Steve Dearne for first playing me CSNY's music and infecting me with his own teenage passion for Stephen Stills's work; and others with whom I've shared in-depth discussions about CSNY and their music down the years, whether they liked it or not: especially Debbie Cassell, Mike Grant, and Brian Hogg; plus, in memoriam, Sean Body. Apologies to those I've forgotten (or bored!). This section would not be complete unless I also acknowledged the many hundreds of hours I have spent since 1981 discussing the intricacies of CSNY's history with Johnny Rogan, one of the few writers who was prepared to champion CSN's work (and especially David Crosby's) during the years when they were routinely dismissed and ridiculed by critics around the world.

ACKNOWLEDGMENTS

Thanks to all of those who showed their enthusiasm for this project and helped guide it through to publication, especially my agents, Matthew Hamilton (Aitken Alexander) and Matthew Elblonk; my editors Jörg Hensgen and Stuart Williams at the Bodley Head, and Matthew Benjamin at Simon & Schuster; Sara Kitchen; Celeste Phillips; and Patricia Romanowski Bashe.

Finally, I would have been unable, physically or emotionally, to complete this book without the tireless and selfless love and support of my wife, Rachel Baylis. She has survived many more CSNY-related concerts and thousands more CSNY-related conversations than she could ever have imagined when we first met, but has somehow come through with her sanity intact (and with one of Stephen Stills's guitar picks). Much love as ever to her, our wonderful daughters, Catrin and Becca, and to the irrepressible Freddie.

MAJOR SOURCES

Besides the interviews I carried out myself, this book also relied upon the following sources, uncredited in the text. To avoid repetition, each source is listed only once.

CHAPTER 1

Crosby on delinquency: *Asbury Park Press* (11/21/75).
Crosby's 1967 philosophy: *Oracle of Southern California* (10/67).
Crosby on schoolgirls: *Goldmine* (7/7/95).
Crosby on politics: *KRLA Beat* (11/27/65 and 3/12/66).
Crosby on acid: Metzner: *The Ecstatic Adventure*.
Lilian Roxon on Cass: *Sydney Morning Herald* (10/30/66).
Nash on elections, Dylan, and parties: *Melody Maker* (7/3/65 and 3/19/66).
Allan Clarke on Nash: *Melody Maker* (7/23/66) and *NME* (3/18/67).
Nash on Hollies' arguments: *International Times* (3/13–26/67).

CHAPTER 2

Stills's major retrospective interviews were with *Rolling Stone* (3/4/71) and *Sounds* (6/26/71 and 7/3/71).
Stills's mother profiled: *Tampa Sunday Tribune* (5/11/58).
Buffalo Springfield profiled: *KRLA Beat* (9/10/66).
Bob Rafelson on the Monkees: *NME* (8/12/67).
Derek Taylor: *Disc* (3/4/67 and 6/3/67).
Monterey: *LA Times* (6/4/67 and 7/6/67); *Monterey Herald* (6/10/07); Crosby interview on KFWB (8/30/67).
Richie Furay: *Sounds* (2/19/72) and Sioux Falls (SD) *Argus Leader* (2/19/82).

CHAPTER 3

Crosby's *Rolling Stone* interview included his comments on leaving the Byrds (7/23/70); likewise Cameron Crowe's epic CSNY piece in *Crawdaddy* (10/74).
Nash on other planets: *Disc* (10/14/67).
Young on songwriting: *LA Times* (9/17/67).
Talitha Stills on groupies: *Santa Cruz* (CA) *Patch* (4/27/11).
Crosby on retiring: *LA Times* (5/24/66).
Roger McGuinn on Crosby: *LA Times* (4/21/68) and *NME* (5/5/73).
Gary Usher: *Cosmic American Music News* (Winter 1992–93).
Joni Mitchell on recording: *Broadside* (2/14–27/68).
Rose Nash interview: *Disc* (5/4/68).
Last Buffalo Springfield gig: *LA Times* (5/7/68).

CHAPTER 4

Mitchell on Leonard Cohen and Nash on CSN's first performance: *Ann Arbor Argus* (3/13–27/69).
Mitchell on omens: *Open City* (6/14/68).
Salli Sachse: Weller: *Girls Like Us*.
Stills on "Wooden Ships": *American Songwriter* (1/08).
Crosby on "Long Time Gone": *Record Mirror* (1/3/70).
Peter Tork: *Open City* (4/19/68).
Buzzy Linhart: *Miami News* (2/11/81) and *Burlington* (VT) *Free Press* (3/10/81).
Nash on Hollies: *NME* (5/18/68) and *Disc* (6/1/68).
Tony Hicks on Hollies: *Disc* (10/19/68).

CHAPTER 5

Young on revolution and CSN: *Ann Arbor Argus* (1/24/69–2/7/69).
John Sebastian: *LA Times* (9/30/68) and *Record Mirror* (12/7/68).
Hollies split: *NME* (11/16/68) and *Melody Maker* (11/23/68).
Judy Collins: *Detroit Free Press* (12/1/68).
CSN in London: *NME* (12/7/68 and 12/14/68); *Melody Maker* (12/7/68); *Disc* (12/7/68); *International Times* (1/1–16/69).
Robin Lane: *Q Classic* (6/05).
Young on Crazy Horse: *Rolling Stone* (4/30/70).
Mama Cass on CSN: *Record Mirror* (3/1/69).
Stills on recording CSN LP: *Rolling Stone* (4/5/69).
Paul Kantner on coke: *Dark Star* (12/78).
David Geffen: Wexler: *Rhythm and the Blues*.
Nash on Bill Halverson and LP: *Fusion* (5/12/69).

MAJOR SOURCES

CHAPTER 6

LA: Mama Cass *Disc* (7/5/69); Paul Kantner *Corpus Christi* (TX) *Caller-Times* (8/2/69); Crosby *Disc* (8/16/69).
Nash on Mitchell: *Newsweek* (8/29/69).
Fusion on CSNY: 5/26/69 and 6/14/69.
Bruce Palmer: Einarson and Furay: *For What It's Worth*.
Young on role in CSNY: *Toronto Globe & Mail* (7/26/69).
Young to Cameron Crowe: *Rolling Stone* (8/14/75).
Crosby/Stills on CSNY: *Melody Maker* and *Record Mirror* (both 8/9/69).
Crosby/Stills on side trips: *LA Times* (8/24/69).
Stills on supergroups: *Disc* (7/26/69).
Nash on Chicago gig: *NME* (8/30/69).

WOODSTOCK 2

Grace Slick: *Somebody to Love*.
Nash: *Rolling Stone* (4/13/00); *LA Times* (7/15/79).
Greil Marcus: *Rolling Stone* (9/20/69).
Stills: *Philadelphia Daily News* (8/15/84).
Crosby: *Uncut* (7/08).
Young: *Waging Heavy Peace*.
Joni Mitchell: *Life* (8/94).

CHAPTER 7

James Doolittle: *Rolling Stone* (10/4/69).
Judy Sims: *Disc* (9/6/69).
June Harris: *NME* (10/4/69).
Woodstock: *Time* (8/29/69).
Big Sur: *Berkeley Barb* and *Berkeley Tribe* (both 9/19–25/69).
Stills on changing CSNY and TV: *Disc* (10/11/69).
Nash on TV: *Melody Maker* (4/20/74) and *NME* (11/7/70).
On long hair: Crosby *Santa Cruz* (CA) *Sentinel* (6/5/80) and *KRLA Beat* (7/15/67); Mama Cass *East Village Other* (10/1–15/67); Joni Mitchell *Rolling Stone* (7/26/79).
Christine Hinton's death: fullest contemporary report is *San Rafael* (CA) *Daily Independent* (10/1/69).

WOODSTOCK 3

Stills: *NME* (6/6/70).

MAJOR SOURCES

CHAPTER 8

Crosby on grief: *Vox* (7/93).

On CSNY LP: Young, *Fusion* (11/28/69) and *Rolling Stone* (12/27/69); Stills, *Melody Maker* (2/28/70), *Philadelphia Inquirer* (6/7/70), *Rolling Stone* (7/23/70), and musicradar.com (6/28/12); Nash, *Mojo* (9/14).

Crosby on youth: *Disc* (1/10/70).

Robert Greenfield: *Fusion* (4/17/70).

Stills on piano medley: *Rolling Stone* (8/29/74).

Altamont comments: *Great Speckled Bird* (1/19/70); Reich and Wenner, *Garcia*.

Altamont reports: *Good Times* (12/11/69), *Berkeley Barb* (12/12–18/69), *Berkeley Tribe* (12/19–26/69 and 1/16–23/70), *International Times* (1/28/70–2/11/70), *Scanlan's* (3/70).

CSNY university show: *Disc* (12/20/69).

WOODSTOCK 4

Dale Bell, ed.: *Woodstock*.

Abbie Hoffman: *Woodstock Nation*.

Jon Landau in Clinton Heylin: *Penguin Book of Rock & Roll Writing*.

CHAPTER 9

Stills on Stanley Kubrick and stadium gigs: *Melody Maker* (1/10/70).

Crosby on *Wooden Ships* film: his intro to Theodore Sturgeon: *Baby Makes Three*.

Young on screenplay: *Mojo* (12/95).

Robert Hammer: *Colorado Springs Gazette-Telegraph* (4/15/71).

Joni Mitchell: *Rolling Stone* (3/4/71) and *Disc* (1/10/70).

Elliot Roberts on Mitchell: *Rolling Stone* #48 (12/13/69).

Stills on Albert Hall: *Disc* and *Melody Maker* (both 2/28/70).

Crosby on CSNY: *Record Mirror* (1/3/70) and *Disc* (1/17/70).

Robert Plant: *Friends* (2/20/70).

Stills on Ringo Starr's house: *Ottawa Journal* (4/17/70).

Stills "pooped": *Detroit Free Press* (6/12/70).

Stills on sailing: *Uncut* (4/13).

Crosby on sailing: *Wall Street Journal* (6/6/13).

Nash on sailing: *NME* (5/23/70) and *Asbury Park Press* (11/21/75).

Ronee Blakely: *Arizona Republic* (9/30/82).

Young on recording: *Fusion* (4/17/70) and *Rolling Stone* (4/30/70).

Nils Lofgren: *Melody Maker* (11/24/73) and *Sounds* (5/13/72).

MAJOR SOURCES

WOODSTOCK 5

Michael Wadleigh: *Melody Maker* (7/4/70) and *Detroit Free Press* (4/26/70).
Martin Scorsese: *Los Angeles Free Press* (8/20/71).
Young on cameras and movie: *Mojo* (7/97) and NME (12/8/79).

CHAPTER 10

Harriet testimony: Marvin Mitchelson: *Made in Heaven*.
Nash on bootlegs: NME (11/7/70) and Heylin: *Bootleg*.
Joe Walsh: *Rolling Stone* (2/27/75).
H. R. Haldeman: *The Haldeman Diaries*.
Tom Wells: *The War Within*.
CSNY boycott: *Minneapolis Star Tribune* (5/10/70).
Nash on Denver show: *Melody Maker* (6/20/70).
Greg Reeves: *Mojo* (11/11).
Impeach Nixon editorial: *Rolling Stone* (5/28/70).
Tragedy at Kent: *Life* (5/15/70).
"Ohio" airplay: *Detroit Free Press* (8/28/70).
Bill Graham on pricing: *Billboard* (11/14/70).
CSNY in St. Louis: *St. Louis Post-Dispatch* (8/2/70).
Nash on filming tour: *Chicago Tribune* (7/8/70).
Nash and Stills: Bill Graham and Robert Greenfield: *Bill Graham Presents*.
David Geffen: NME (7/29/72).

CHAPTER 11

Nash on CSNY future: *Record Mirror* (7/25/70).
Rita Coolidge: *Rolling Stone* (4/25/74) and *Delta Lady*.
Stills on Nash: *Rochester* (NY) *Democrat & Chronicle* (11/4/82).
Stills on BBC and Hendrix: *Disc* (11/28/70).
Paul Kantner: *Melody Maker* (5/15/71).
Carrie Snodgress interviews: *Newport* (VA) *News Daily Press* (9/28/71), *Chicago Tribune*, and *Appleton Post-Crescent* (both 10/3/71) and *Indianapolis News* (5/20/78).
Jack Nitzsche: *Crawdaddy* (11/74).
Stills on Geffen-Roberts: *Rolling Stone* (9/27/73).
Steve Fromholz: *Lubbock* (TX) *Avalanche-Journal* (9/15/76).
Stills on Manassas: *Disc* (3/18/72) and *Record Collector* (3/10).
Rick Roberts: *Disc* (2/5/72).
Byrds reunion: *Philadelphia Inquirer* (10/1/72), *Record World* (12/9/72), and *Rolling Stone* (1/4/73).

MAJOR SOURCES

Geffen on Stills: *Disc* (7/29/72).
Amy Gossage: Associated Press syndication (3/75).

CHAPTER 12

Véronique Sanson: *La Douceur du Danger* (my translations from French original).
1973 and 1974 CSNY reunions covered in depth in *Rolling Stone* (8/29/74) and *NME* (8/31/74).
David Briggs: James McDonough: *Shakey*.
Atlantic Records spokesman: *Shreveport* (LA) *Times* (9/24/73).
Stills on Nash and money: *Pampa* (TX) *Daily News* (4/30/74).
Nash on *Wild Tales*: *Cincinnati Enquirer* (4/13/80).
Crosby on shock rock and blimps: *Chicago Tribune* (8/25/74).
Stills on maturity: *Philadelphia Inquirer* (2/17/74).
Stills on reunion: *NME* (3/16/74).
Nash on reunion: *NME* and *Melody Maker* (both 4/20/74).
Paul Kantner on Nixon: *NME* (3/30/74).
Young as fat cat: *Cincinnati Enquirer* (1/13/74).
Young on CSNY as acoustic band: *Waging Heavy Peace*.
Crosby on Seattle: *LA Times* (7/16/74).
Young on 1974 tour: *Rolling Stone* (2/8/79).
Crosby on Wembley: *Melody Maker* (11/1/75).
Stills on Wembley: *Melody Maker* (7/12/75).

POSTSCRIPT

Stills on problem of CSNY: *Creem* (11/75).
Carrie Snodgress on split: *Detroit Free Press* (6/24/77).
Stills on avoiding a fast fade: *Sounds* (8/16/75).
Crosby yelling: *Fort Lauderdale* (FL) *News* (8/28/83).
Nash attacks Stills: *Sounds* (9/18/76).
Stills and Crosby on Young: *Rolling Stone* (6/2/77).
Young on upsetting people: *New York Times* (11/27/77).
Stills on CSNY as destructive force: *LA Times* (1/21/79).
Nash on sanity and being scared of Young: *LA Times* (11/27/82).
Nash on Crosby's drug convictions: *Chicago Tribune* (8/21/83).
Young promises reunion: *Hartford* (CT) *Courant* (1/12/86).
Young on nostalgia: *Rolling Stone* (6/2/88).

BIBLIOGRAPHY

Bego, Mark. *Joni Mitchell*. Lanham, MD: Taylor Trade, 2005.

Bell, Dale, ed. *Woodstock*. Studio City, CA: Michael Wiese, 1999.

Bennett, Andy, ed. *Remembering Woodstock*. Surrey: Ashgate Publishing, 2004.

Bingham, Clara. *Witness to the Revolution*. New York: Random House, 2016.

Booth, Stanley. *The True Adventures of the Rolling Stones*. London: Abacus, 1986.

Boyd, Glen. *Neil Young FAQ*. Milwaukee: Backbeat, 2012.

Burdick, Eugene, and Harvey Wheeler. *Fail-Safe*. London: Hutchinson, 1963.

Chong, Kevin. *Neil Young Nation*. Vancouver: Greystone Books, 2005.

Christgau, Robert. *Christgau's Guide: Rock Albums of the Seventies*. London: Vermilion, 1982.

Clark, Tom. *Neil Young*. Toronto: Coach House Press, 1971.

Cohn, Nik. *Awopbopaloobopalopbamboom*. London: Paladin, 1972.

Collins, Judy. *Sweet Judy Blue Eyes: My Life in Music*. New York: Crown Archetype, 2011.

Coolidge, Rita, with Michael Walker. *Delta Lady: A Memoir*. New York: Harper, 2016.

Crosby, David, and Carl Gottlieb. *Long Time Gone: The Autobiography of David Crosby*. New York: Doubleday, 1988.

———. *Since Then: How I Survived Everything and Lived to Tell About It*. New York: G. P. Putnam's Sons, 2006.

Dannen, Frederic. *Hit Men: Power Brokers and Fast Money Inside the Music Business*. New York: Frederic Muller, 1990.

Didion, Joan. *The White Album*. London: Weidenfeld & Nicolson, 1979.

Diltz, Henry. *California Dreaming*. Guildford: Genesis Books, 2007.

Doggett, Peter. *There's a Riot Going On: Revolutionaries, Rock Stars and the Rise and Fall of '60s Counter-Culture*. Edinburgh: Canongate, 2007.

Dylan, Bob. *Chronicles Vol. 1*. New York: Simon & Schuster, 2004.

Einarson, John. *Mr. Tambourine Man: The Life and Legacy of the Byrds' Gene Clark*. San Francisco: Backbeat, 2005.

Einarson, John, and Richie Furay. *For What It's Worth: The Story of Buffalo Springfield*. London: Rogan House, 1997.

BIBLIOGRAPHY

Eisen, Jonathan, ed. *Altamont: Death of Innocence in the Woodstock Nation.* New York: Avon, 1970.

Fenton, Craig. *Take Me to a Circus Tent: The Jefferson Airplane Flight Manual.* West Conshohocken, PA: Infinity, 2006.

Fiegel, Eddi. *Dream a Little Dream of Me: The Life of "Mama" Cass Elliot.* London: Sidgwick & Jackson, 2005.

Flanagan, Bill. *Written in My Soul: Rock's Great Songwriters Talk About Creating Their Music.* Chicago: Contemporary Books, 1986.

Fonda, Peter. *Don't Tell Dad.* New York: Hyperion, 1998.

Fong-Torres, Ben. *Hickory Wind: The Life and Times of Gram Parsons.* London: Omnibus, 1992.

Fornatale, Pete. *Back to the Garden.* New York: Touchstone, 2009.

Gleason, Ralph J. *The Jefferson Airplane and the San Francisco Sound.* New York: Ballantine Books, 1969.

Goldstein, Richard. *Another Little Piece of My Heart: My Life and Rock and Revolution in the '60s.* London: Bloomsbury Circus, 2015.

Graham, Bill, and Robert Greenfield. *Bill Graham Presents: My Life Inside Rock and Out.* New York: Doubleday, 1992.

Greenfield, Robert. *The Last Sultan: The Life and Times of Ahmet Ertegun.* New York: Simon & Schuster, 2011.

Greenwald, Matthew. *Go Where You Wanna Go: The Oral History of the Mamas & the Papas.* New York: Cooper Square Press, 2002.

Gustaitis, Rara. *Turning On.* London: Weidenfeld & Nicolson, 1969.

Haldeman, H. R. *The Haldeman Diaries.* New York: G. P. Putnam's Sons, 1994.

Hale, Dennis, and Jonathan Eisen, eds. *The California Dream.* New York: Collier, 1968.

Halliwell, Martin. *Neil Young: American Traveller.* London: Reaktion Books, 2015.

Heinlein, Robert A. *Stranger in a Strange Land.* London: NEL, 1965.

Heylin, Clinton, ed. *The Penguin Book of Rock & Roll Writing.* London: Viking, 1992.

Hinton, Brian. *Joni Mitchell: Both Sides Now—The Biography.* London: Sanctuary, 2000.

Hoffman, Abbie. *Woodstock Nation: A Talk-Rock Album.* New York: Pocket Books, 1971.

Hunt, Andrew E. *The Turning: The History of Vietnam Vets Against the War.* New York: New York University Press, 1999.

Inglis, Sam. *Harvest.* New York: Continuum, 2003.

James, Rick, and David Ritz. *Glow: The Autobiography of Rick James.* New York: Atria Books, 2014.

Jenkins, Alan, ed. *Neil Young and Broken Arrow: On a Journey Through the Past.* Bridgend, UK: Neil Young Appreciation Society, 1994.

Kaufman, Phil, and Colin White. *Road Mangler Deluxe.* Glendale, CA: White Boucke Publishing, 1993.

Kooper, Al. *Backstage Passes & Backstabbing Bastards*. New York: Backbeat, 2008.

Krantz, Steve. *Laurel Canyon*. London: Coronet, 1980.

Lang, Michael, with Holly George-Warren. *The Road to Woodstock*. New York: Ecco/Harper Collins, 2009.

Lasch, Christopher. *The Culture of Narcissism: American Life in an Age of Diminishing Expectations*. New York: W. W. Norton, 1978.

Long, Pete. *Ghosts on the Road: Neil Young in Concert*. London: Old Homestead Press, 1996.

Makower, Joel. *Woodstock: The Oral History*. London: Sidgwick & Jackson, 1989.

Marom, Malka. *Joni Mitchell: Both Sides Now — Conversations with Malka Marom*. London: Omnibus, 2014.

Marsh, Dave, with John Swenson. *The Rolling Stone Record Guide*. London: Virgin Books/Rolling Stone Press, 1980.

May, Kirse Granat. *Golden State, Golden Youth*. Chapel Hill: University of North Carolina Press, 2002.

McDermott, John, Eddie Kramer, and Billy Cox. *Ultimate Hendrix*. Milwaukee: Backbeat, 2009.

McDonough, James. *Shakey: Neil Young's Biography*. London: Jonathan Cape, 2002.

McGowan, David. *Weird Scenes Inside the Canyon*. London: Headpress, 2014.

McNally, Dennis. *A Long Strange Trip: The Inside History of the Grateful Dead*. London: Bantam Press, 2002.

Menger, Lucy. *Theodore Sturgeon*. New York: Frederic Ungar, 1981.

Mercer, Michelle. *Will You Take Me as I Am: Joni Mitchell's Blue Period*. Milwaukee: Backbeat, 2012.

Metzner, Ralph. *The Ecstatic Adventure*. New York: Macmillan, 1968.

Meyer, David N. *Twenty Thousand Roads: The Ballad of Gram Parsons and His Cosmic American Music*. London: Bloomsbury, 2009.

Mitchell, Mitch, and John Platt. *The Hendrix Experience*. London: Pyramid, 1990.

Mitchelson, Marvin M. *Made in Heaven, Settled in Court*. Los Angeles: J. P. Tarcher, 1976.

Nash, Graham. *Wild Tales: A Rock & Roll Life*. London: Viking, 2013.

O'Dell, Chris, with Katherine Ketcham. *Miss O'Dell*. New York: Touchstone, 2009.

Oldham, Andrew Loog. *2Stoned*. London: Secker & Warburg, 2002.

Perone, James E. *Woodstock: An Encyclopedia of the Music and Art Fair*. Westport, CT: Greenwood Press, 2005.

Phillips, John, with Jim Jerome. *Papa John: An Autobiography*. New York: Dolphin Books, 1986.

Phillips, Michelle. *California Dreamin': The True Story of the Mamas and the Papas*. New York: Warner Books, 1986.

Reed, Rex. *People Are Crazy Here*. New York: Delacorte Press, 1974.

Reich, Charles, and Jann Wenner. *Garcia: A Signpost to New Space*. San Francisco: Straight Arrow, 1972.

Rogan, Johnny. *Neil Young: Zero to Sixty*. London: Rogan House, 2000.

Rogan, Johnny. *Byrds: Requiem for the Timeless*, vols. 1 & 2. London: Rogan House, 2011 & 2017.

Rolling Stone editors. *The Rolling Stone Interviews*, vol. 1. New York: Warner Paperback Library, 1971.

Rosenman, Joel, John Roberts, and Robert Pilpel. *Young Men with Unlimited Capital*. New York: Harcourt Brace Jovanovich, 1974.

Sander, Ellen. *Trips: Rock Life in the Sixties*. New York: Scribner, 1973.

Sanson, Véronique, and Didier Varrod. *La Douceur du Danger*. Paris: Plon, 2005.

Sarlot, Raymond, and Fred E. Basten. *Life at the Marmont: The Inside Story of Hollywood's Legendary Hotel of the Stars—Chateau Marmont*. New York: Penguin, 2013.

Scoppa, Bud. *The Byrds*. New York: Scholastic Book Services, 1971.

Selvin, Joel. *Summer of Love: The Inside Story of LSD, Rock and Roll, Free Love and High Times in the Wild West*. London: Dutton, 1994.

———. *Altamont: The Rolling Stones, the Hells Angels, and the Inside Story of Rock's Darkest Day*. New York: Dey Street Books, 2017.

Slick, Grace, with Andrea Cagan. *Somebody to Love*. New York: Warner Books, 1998.

Spitz, Robert Stephen. *Barefoot in Babylon: The Creation of the Woodstock Festival 1969*. New York: Viking, 1979.

Stacewicz, Richard. *Winter Soldiers: An Oral History of the Vietnam Veterans Against the War*. New York: Twayne, 1997.

Sturgeon, Theodore. *Baby Makes Three: The Complete Stories of Theodore Sturgeon*, vol. 6. Berkeley: North Atlantic Books, 1999.

Tamarkin, Jeff. *Got a Revolution: The Turbulent Flight of Jefferson Airplane*. London: Helter Skelter, 2003.

Taylor, Derek. *Fifty Years Adrift*. Guildford, UK: Genesis Books, 1984.

Unterberger, Richie. *Turn! Turn! Turn! The '60s Folk-Rock Revolution*. San Francisco: Backbeat Books, 2002.

Verbeke, Herman, Francesco Lucarelli, Stefano Frollano, and Lucien van Diggelen. *Crosby, Stills, Nash and Sometimes Young*, 3 vols. Groningen: Gopher Publishers, 2002.

Weller, Sheila. *Girls Like Us: Carole King, Joni Mitchell, Carly Simon—and the Journey of a Generation*. London: Ebury Press, 2008.

Wells, Tom. *The War Within: America's Battle Over Vietnam*. Berkeley: University of California Press, 1994.

Wexler, Jerry, and David Ritz. *Rhythm and the Blues*. New York: Knopf, 1993.

Whitesell, Lloyd. *The Music of Joni Mitchell*. New York: Oxford University Press, 2008.

Whiting, Cecile. *Pop LA: Art and the City in the 1960s*. Berkeley: University of California Press, 2006.

Williams, Paul. *Pushing Upwards*. New York: Links, 1973.

———. *Neil Young: Love to Burn: Thirty Years of Speaking Out 1966–1996*. London: Omnibus, 1997.

Willis, Ellen. *The Essential Ellen Willis*. Minneapolis: University of Minnesota Press, 2014.

Wolman, Baron. *Woodstock*. London: Reel Art Press, 2014.

Yaffe, David. *Reckless Daughter: A Portrait of Joni Mitchell*. New York: Sarah Crichton Books, 2017.

Young, Astrid. *Being Young*. Toronto: Insomniac Press, 2007.

Young, Neil. *Waging Heavy Peace: A Hippie Dream*. London: Viking, 2012.

———. *Special Deluxe: A Memoir of Life & Cars*. London: Viking, 2014.

Young, Scott. *Neil and Me*. Rogan House, London, 1997.

Zimmer, Dave, ed. *Four Way Street: The Crosby, Stills, Nash & Young Reader*. New York: Da Capo Press, 2004.

———. *Crosby, Stills & Nash: The Biography*. New York: Da Capo Press, 2008.

Zollo, Paul. *Songwriters on Songwriting*. New York: Da Capo Press, 2003.

INDEX

INDEX

INDEX

ABOUT THE AUTHOR

Peter Doggett has been writing about rock music and interviewing rock stars for more than thirty years. He is the author of *You Never Give Me Your Money*, the definitive story of the Beatles' breakup and its aftermath, chosen as one of the best ten books of the year by the *Los Angeles Times*. His other books include his panoramic history of popular music, *Electric Shock*; *The Man Who Sold the World*; *There's a Riot Going On*; and *Are You Ready for the Country*.